LIFE WITH PAPA

GROWING UP WITH DR. FEELGOOD

JILL JACOBSON

JACOBSON PRESS 2026

Cover design by: Jeffrey Dingsor, Full Armor Media Group, LLC

Visit: fullarmorvideo.com

First edition 2026

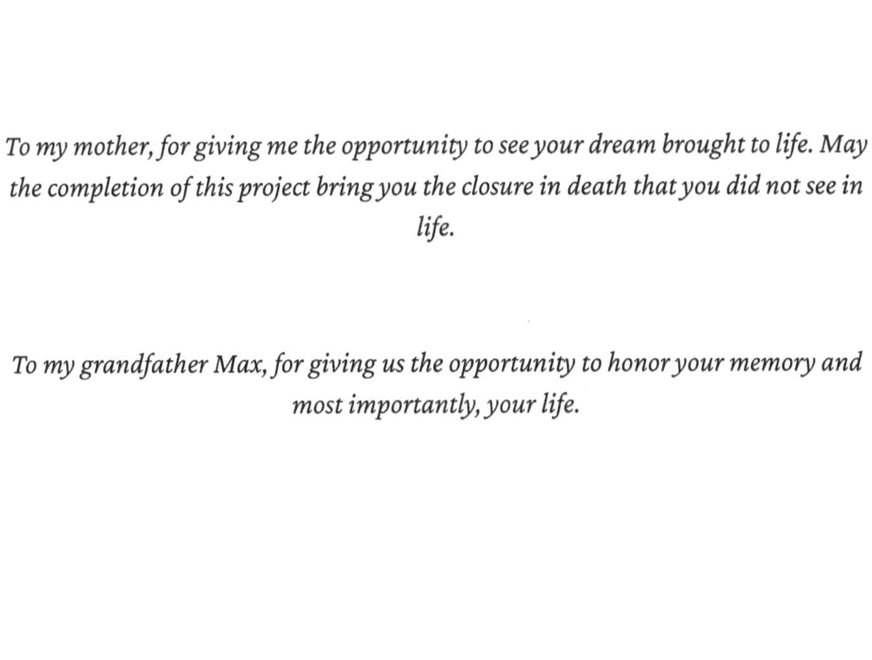

To my mother, for giving me the opportunity to see your dream brought to life. May the completion of this project bring you the closure in death that you did not see in life.

To my grandfather Max, for giving us the opportunity to honor your memory and most importantly, your life.

In Loving Memory

Nina Hagen Jacobson
June 15th, 1914 to May 28th, 1964

-Matthew

A Special Thank You

I want to extend a special thanks to Adrea Tomars for getting me started on this massive book project. Stephanie Simon was my memory. George Gruenthal, for being a friend and getting me out there. Lewis Malin, my unofficial brother-in-law and the uncle of my younger son Matthew, for making me feel less intimidated and more comfortable about writing everything that I might have otherwise not had the courage to do. I told him he was my Valium. I hope this book will bring as much pleasure, entertainment and interest to the reader as my intriguing life has brought me.

To my mother, Nina Hagen Jacobson, who died sadly when I was only 15 1/2 years old, whose spirit came forward through a psychic [during a reading I recently had] to suggest I take on this massive project. And who through her undying love for my father and me helped make me the person I am today. I never stopped missing her for one day. I will mourn her death and take the mourning to my grave when I die.

To Papa, Max, whose persistence, love and determination towards making me succeed, and always strive to be productive and constructive, might have finally paid off! And who by endless giving set the example of greatness by caring for others consistently, night and day. His insistence on helping all those in need, whether it be medically, or otherwise. I will always be in your highest esteem. You set a great example for me. On the basis of your vision, pursuing that vision and making that dream become a reality. With love and gratitude, I pursue this book.

Contents

1

IN THE BEGINNING

Papa (Dr. Max Jacobson, right) and
newborn Jill, circa 1947

In the beginning of civilization, there was Adam and Eve. For the beginning of my life, I have chosen to start with East 72nd Street, the infamous office of the notorious Dr. Max Jacobson, wherein behind whose walls the very rich, very famous were treated with incredible medicines concocted by the doctor himself, my father. They came from near and far to see him, and his efforts proved masterful, magical, and successful, beyond their greatest expectations.

Nina Jacobson (right) and newborn Jill, circa 1947

In that office at 155 East 72nd Street, behind the desk of the rather large waiting room sat a lady of European beauty of exquisite proportions, poised and with an air of distinction yet possessed about her an air of simplicity. She was noticeably discreet, charming, and polite in greeting patients. Beautiful, tall and slender, she was the doctor's wife Nina, whom the doctor had enlisted to work for him as his full-time receptionist. She had suffered permanent leg injuries so sitting down wasn't so bad. However, she had to leave their small child Juliet [me], with her parents.

Nina and the doctor worked hard at the office, morning to late night. Evenings they returned to their beautiful penthouse apartment at 152 East 94th Street where mommy, after a long stay in a Boston hospital to successfully carry the pregnancy to term, carried me, Juliet, home after birth.

The view from the apartment was as breathtaking as the doctor's wife, only different. The apartment had a terrace that went all around, so one could see all the way uptown and beyond the Triborough Bridge and have a generous view of the East River, going all the way uptown and downtown. Granny, Nina's mother, was there for my afternoon naps.

In my room was a poster of *The Red Boy* by Francisco de Goya y Lucientes; the painting of the boy dressed like Shakespeare with the animals and the bird in the cage, I loved that. On occasion, I was brought to my father's office to be watched over by my busy parents. When I did, I suppose because my grandparents had gone to the opera and couldn't watch me, I would make things, especially necklaces out of paper clips at the front desk to keep myself occupied. Then mommy and daddy would take me home.

Many celebrities came to the office to see my father for treatment. Betty Cashman, the theatrical acting coach, was one of my early favorites. She adored my father and me. She was so sweet and funny, and years later helped me recite a poem I wrote.

Besides Betty Cashman, there was a big photo on the wall above the desk where my mother sat. It was me; age 4, 5 or 6 with bangs and sort of short hair. The photo showed me puffing on a cigarette, a candy cigarette. Under the picture was the caption "No Smoking". Ronny Graham upon entering the office for the first time noticed the picture right away and reminded me of it ever since. That was his very first memory of coming to see my father. He too was very nice, a great entertainer, singer, and piano player. Sometimes he also brought his wife Ellen for treatment. I was a little girl then; all I knew were all these people were coming in, so grateful to be there and being so sweet and overly friendly to my mother. My mother was always gracious with them.

My mother kept her distance from them all. They were not her friends. They were my father's patients, although I felt she had made a connection, developed a kinship with a few of them including Roddy McDowall. I was a little girl around many celebrities, and yet my favorite people were my parents and grandparents. I loved them more than anyone could love anything, they were the best. They were a consistent and stable force in my life and very loving. Granny peeled me fresh fruit every day while we waited for Grandpi to finish playing tennis.

Granny and Grandpi took me for tennis lessons on our way to our country home in Point Lookout, Long Island during the week. We all went to Point Lookout on the weekend. One time, Grandpi took me to the opening of the Central Park Zoo. We were interviewed on T.V by some anchor man named Leonard something. That night we sat by the T.V. set and watched him talk to me; that was exciting. My grandparents took me many places while my parents worked very hard at the office all day.

Papa with baby Jill on lap, late 1940s

When I was about 3 years old, I had a little room behind the kitchen. It was the one bedroom in the penthouse apartment. I was afraid of the dark from my crib. I would wake up in the middle of the night and see people standing in my doorway, one Indian Chief with the feather headdress on his head and face paint, a cook with the big white puffy hat on, the next one I believe was a fireman with the fire chief hat on. There were two other figures, only I cannot remember who they were. They were just looking at me and that scared me. After what seemed like hours, I finally got the courage to cry out for help. I cried to daddy "Daddy, I want some soda water, daddy, bring me some soda water". My parents' bed was further away from the kitchen than my crib was. After a while he got up, turned on the light, went to the fridge and poured me a glass of soda water. Sometimes, just turning the light on in the kitchen made the figures disappear. At other times, he would bring me the soda, I would drink several sips and feel so relieved that he was there, and the figures disappeared. He would stay with me for several moments and then I'd fall back asleep. Daddy was there every night after work, and he was the only one who got up every night to comfort me when I woke up afraid of the dark. Night lights hadn't been invented yet. This happened every night from 1949 to 1952 while we lived on East 94th Street. In those days he was home every night, even if he came home late around 10pm.

We had a weathervane right outside my bedroom window. It would make a creaking noise at the slightest gust of wind and that was spooky. Especially to a little child like me who got spooked out by the slightest thing. This creaking noise frightened me, so daddy got up each night and brought me some soda water.

When I got a little older, I recall coming to the office with my parents on a Sunday afternoon. My father had to meet Marlene Dietrich at the office. She arrived in her silk light blue pajamas. While Daddy opened the office and turned on the lights, mommy and Marlene stood on the sidewalk outside the office and carried on a conversation, about what I don't know, while Marlene nervously puffed away at a cigarette. We were finally told to come in and then mommy and I waited until daddy had finished treating her. On one occasion Marlene arrived at the office carrying a Pyrex pan filled with hot homemade Hungarian Goulash which she had made especially for my father; she said she had made a big pot of it. She had saved some for her daughter and grandchildren and made a special serving for my father. She brought enough for us to have for an entire week, and it was absolutely delicious.

Baby Jill on Papa's shoulders, late 1940s

In between those times, my parents and I were fortunate enough to have fun visits from my cousins Little Nina, Karen and their younger brother Tony [Mommy's nieces and nephew from her brother K.V., short for Karl Victor]. We enjoyed playing countless hours outside in our private pebbled yard, where my other favorite cousins on my mother's side Gaby Dunn, Granny's sister's daughter, arrived with her children Jackie, John and later baby Jennifer. Gaby took us to the beach often.

Those times were the best of my childhood. Often, we'd spend weekends in Point Lookout going to the beach. Mommy bought matching sun dresses for us girls, Little Nina, Karen, and me. And then she would film us and take pictures of us standing on the long bench against the wall in the pebbled yard looking absolutely lovely.

When we met in the city, mommy would take us out to the theatre often since daddy's actor patients, Broadway stars who were appearing in shows, would present us with complimentary theatre tickets, such as Ellen Hanley and Ronny Graham.

2

A Little Family Background

Every so often, my father reminded us, but especially himself out loud, "I was the son of a kosher butcher". He was born in Fordon, Poland having two brothers and a very loving and supportive mother. They were taken to Germany in 1910 so they could get a better education.

Simon was the oldest, Heinz the middle son, and Max, my father, the youngest. All three brothers were exactly three years apart. Whenever my father spoke to me, he spoke of starving children all over the world, and how grateful I should be for everything I had and for all the food on my plate.

My father spoke Czech, English, German, and French. When he was very young, Max hurt himself trying to salvage money meant for an organ grinder playing music and his monkey. His pants had gotten stuck on a spike on a tall iron fence that he was trying to scale to get the money thrown for the organ grinder. The spike went through his pants and penetrated his skin. He tried to salvage the money because he knew the organ grinder needed it.

His parents sent for a doctor whose care and treatment of little Max impressed him with his compassionate and understanding manner, so much that he decided he wanted someday to become a doctor. Max was so impressed by the doctor's car when he arrived to treat the boy, that Max momentarily forgot about his pain from his wound. He decided he wanted to be a doctor so that he too could have a nice car.

Simon Jacobson, Papa's oldest brother, mid 1950s

Simon, nicknamed "Simm", was around constantly and Heinz lived in Australia for my entire existence. Simon was a big man who was rather off the wall, with quite a temper and seemingly quite full of himself. My father chose to pick him as his own personal chauffeur for several years. He had an ex-wife Simone, and a daughter named Eve who didn't live with him but whom we visited often on Long Island.

Simon was big and tall, maybe one hundred pounds overweight and almost bald with a very demanding, commanding walk. He wore suits all the time, never casual wear. He looked very German and was always tan. He didn't look anything like my father. And he didn't have the intelligence of my father, neither did I. Simon thought he was god's gift to women, all women. He had a hearty laugh that sounded like a smoker's laugh. I inherited that same laugh. He drove daddy in his car to the airport and wherever my father had to go, and he drove my mother and me crazy with his insanity of arguing, fighting and constant yelling.

When my father had his office on East 83rd Street and we lived upstairs, Simon guarded daddy's car, standing in the street literally blocking most of the traffic. It was funny but annoying as hell too. My father did his share of yelling and threatening, but that was to his receptionist and his nurses. The way I saw it, my father had a legitimate right to yell. He had an office to run.

Simon was perennially unemployed and insisted on being treated like a big shot. He and my father got along, how and why eludes me. Only that every time my father needed to go somewhere, and Simon was in the waiting room pacing the floor and telling tales of his many different girlfriends, my father would have his assistant call Simon in. My father would utter something under his breath, wipe his mouth, which he often did, and my uncle would leave the office and get the car ready.

When I gave birth to my oldest son Jason, he was visiting New York from Germany and gifted us with a home baked turkey. I didn't see much of Simon over the years. He drove us all rather crazy. I was friends, however, with his daughter Eve who was nice, quiet and a sweetheart.

Heinz was the most quiet, soft spoken and settled. He was nice, pleasant and sweet. No temper and he was short, not stocky like my father and Simon. Heinz had a sweet wife named Kitty, also quiet, nice and so kind. They had two children whom they adopted, Peter and Catherine, who were so sweet, and very well behaved. They all lived in Australia. Heinz was the only quiet one of the three. We went to visit him years ago, probably after my mother died. We were there one month. Otherwise, we never saw him. He came here for a visit with his wife in 1977 when Jason was about three years old.

Max related more to his brother Heinz [Henry] with whom he shared many interests, such as flying and a general fascination with airplanes. They built small model airplanes with propellers run by a rubber band. Max's determination to become a physician had not changed by the age of eleven. He received a microscope and often accompanied his father to the slaughterhouse to obtain specimens for microscopic observations. His interest was greatly stimulated by excellent physics, chemistry and zoology teachers. Then came the outbreak of the war of 1914. Many friends and relatives were killed. People had to stand in line to receive bare necessities.

In 1917, Max graduated from high school, one year ahead of time. He received his abortorium, aware that he would be drafted one year later when he turned 18. His brother Heinz, with whom he was very close had been hospitalized at the front fighting and was sent home with a severe case of dysentery. His brother Simon had been injured by shrapnel splinter but had been returned to the front lines. When Max became eligible to be drafted, his mother contacted a doctor friend of hers and arranged for Max to get employment from Dr. Adler, a surgeon, since Max wanted to become a doctor anyway. He started out his medical training by working under the guidance of Dr. Lutz and was instructed to clean surgical instruments and disinfect the operating rooms. No wonder he got into the disinfectant Lysol in later years and until very recently. He used it in his practice, sterilizing his vials by spraying them with Lysol. He also sprayed his patients between the thigh and the hip area, right before injecting them intramuscularly. He was then permitted to be present during operations and autopsies. He was promoted to joining the doctors while they were doing their rounds, taking blood pressure, pulses and later was trained to administer injections and change dressings. He received extensive medical training at the Pankow Hospital during the war. There were such shortages of doctors, nurses and surgeons due to the increased number of severely injured soldiers being brought in. While he was training, he encountered patients who had infectious conditions which often lasted for years. Gas gangrene often progressed faster than the amputations performed to arrest it. At the time neither prevention nor treatment of Tetanus infection had yet been discovered. The doctors knew there was nothing that they could do. It rendered them helpless.

I suspect that due to the frustration my father felt while he trained at the Pankow Hospital, as the result of his limitations due to the lack of proper medicines being in existence at the time, that later in his practice he compensated by forging ahead and being determined to treat all cases no matter how hard they were.

The parents of a close friend of Max's, Helmut Barnay, owned a sanitorium located in Pankow and close to the hospital where Max worked. Max often visited them. The grandfather had been a German actor and the mother a classical Soprano and Pianist. Helmut, Max's friend, was gifted in sculpting, painting, music, and as an actor. Through his family, Max was exposed to the arts and had his first lessons in etiquette, which I, his very own daughter, to this day find very amusing. It was Max's first introduction to people of the artistic milieu, and he thoroughly enjoyed them. He acquired an affection and understanding for creative personalities and attained lifelong friends from these introductions.

The time came for Max to report for induction into the army and since it was wartime and they were already amid war, he knew they needed him. Equipped with a box of Liederkranz cheese which the Sargeant had a passion for and prepared to inform the Sargeant of his present duties at Pankow Hospital and his pending enrollment in Medical School, he managed to talk his way out of duty and instead enrolled himself in Friedrich Wilhelm University in Berlin in the Pre-Med Curriculum, where for starters he took a course in Introduction to Anatomy.

"I'm Max Jacobson," he replied. "I was instructed to report here today for induction". "Very commendable" replied the Sergeant. He got to his feet [the Sargeant] his eyes never leaving the box of cheese. He walked around the desk towards me. The Kaiser needs everyman he can get at the Polish front". "So, I understand", he replied. I told him about my family conditions, and about my two brothers in the army. I spoke of my present duties at Pankow Hospital, and of my pending enrollment in medical school. I placed the cheese on his desk. The weight of the evidence supported by the smell of the cheese achieved the desired result. The head of the selective service stared at the package then said "Well, what's one man more or less at the Polish front?".

Max enrolled himself in Friedrich Wilhelm University in Berlin in the pre-med curriculum. The first class he attended was the introductory lecture of his anatomy course. And it went from there. He passed the course and went on to continue his studies at the Albert Ludwigs –Universität located in Freiberg, one of the oldest universities in Germany. Although not part of the curriculum, he attended lectures by Professor Wilhelm C. Roentgen.

During his work at the hospital in Pankow, Germany, X-Rays were already being used for diagnostic purposes. Doctor Jacobson became fascinated while watching on a fluorescent screen the Barium paste going down the esophagus through the stomach and into the intestinal tract.

The doctors watched with amazement the rising and falling of the diaphragm during respiration, the mechanism of joints in use, and the simultaneous peristalsis of the intestines. While he attended lectures at Freiberg, he acquired an understanding of the nature of X-rays.

Much later he became fascinated with fluorescent lights. Another path he took later to earn pocket money; Max worked as an extra in the Opera and in the theatre. Long before he ever got involved in the theatre and with Broadway stars, Max got involved in the theatre in Germany with Director Max Reinhart and producer Richard Hauptman. Reinhardt's changed concepts captured Max's attention. Max was very athletic, agile and always eager to entertain. At parties he occasionally entertained his friends with demonstrations of Jui jitsu techniques, he also entertained by doing acrobatic tricks, pantomiming jugglers, and weightlifters.

Berlin was not peaceful. There was constant conflict between the loyal forces of the new government and the extreme rightist Black Army, Leftist contingent of the Army and Navy as well as by the spread of anti-war propaganda by the liberals, social Democrats, and communists. These confrontations led to open fighting in the streets. During one of those fights, Max took cover in the entrance way of one of the buildings and met Albert Einstein.

While still in Germany, Max was called in on a consultation to assist a young lady whose family he knew, who had fallen from a horse and had been told by another doctor that she'd never walk again. He studied her X-ray and told her that it was nonsense. He told her she would walk again. As I've heard, he saved her life. Her name was Nina Hagen.

3

LOUIS AND VICTORIA (VICKY) HAGEN

Jill with Granny (Victoria Hagen, center), Grandpi (Louis Hagen, left), and Nina in Point Lookout, circa 1951

Granny and Grandpi, as we always called them, raised me from when I was about three years old. They resided on East 89th Street, right across the street from Dalton Elementary School, between Park and Madison Avenue. When I was still young, about six years old, they took over our penthouse apartment on East 94th Street. We moved to 225 East 73rd Street so my parents could be closer to the office.

Grandpi was very strict with all of us, me and all my cousins. Granny was the kind, forgiving and understanding one. In our family, the Hagen's, my cousins from K.V. (Karl Victor) were so sweet, so nice. They were Little Nina, named after my mother, Karen, and then little mischievous Tony. Then there were the Dunn's, Gaby 's children who were Jackie, John and then Jennifer. They were really nice too.

There were seven all together between us and then I had friends who also came out to Point Lookout. Every time my mother went shopping for dresses for me, she always bought matching dresses for Little Nina and Karen also. We didn't see Jackie or John as often, but they did come out to see us in Point lookout. And I spent several Thanksgiving dinners with Gaby, Jackie, John, Jennifer, and their father Jack. That was a big to do. I watched Gaby sewing up the turkey. And then they invited us out for Christmas although that was in later years. Jack was an Irish Catholic. None of my cousins were Jewish. All their mothers were Christian or non-Jews. The brother of Yvonne, Little Nina, Karen and Tony's mother, was a minister all his life. The only actual Jew was my father and of course our little family.

Granny and Grandpi never discussed their life in Germany with any of us. The discussions were always and only with regards to family, all of us children, their grandchildren. They left Germany in 1941. Louie wrote a philosophy book. They were secularized protestants. They didn't believe in anything, they were Atheists, nudists and vegetarians. They believed in free body culture.

In 1923, Louis Hagen bought a large quantity of film stock as an investment to fight the spiraling inflation of the period, but the gamble had failed. And the film had become worthless. He decided to give it to Lotte Reiniger to make a feature film. The result of this gift was a pilot that is a compilation of stories from the "Thousand and One Night's". The film was a critical and popular success.

4

MY MOTHER

Jill and Nina, early 1950s

How can I describe her best? Everything you would consider to be a perfect mother, including a beautiful appearance like Queen Nefertiti. She was born in Potsdam, Germany and later moved to Munich, also spending time in Paris, France. She spoke English, German, and French. She was a very distinguished woman, tall in stature and always above it all. She had a deep voice, a beautiful British accent, and appeared serious most of the time. She was almost 5' 10" inches tall and quite slim. She stood upright and tall with perfect posture, was somewhat reserved and appeared rather distant, firm, and disciplined. And a disciplinarian. Yet she was the kindest, gentle, and most nurturing soul in the world. She dressed exquisitely, very elegantly, yet simple, unless she was painting in her studio. Then she wore a wraparound denim skirt and a silk blouse, or cotton button down shirts.

She had her own studio where she spent days painting. She wore a silk taffeta, a fancy long sleeve shirt, and a blue jean wrap around skirt. Her blouses, always fancy, never reflected her activity for that day. When she painted that was precisely what she wore. She wore pants only on Long Island. When she was painting, she seldom brushed her hair. I'd see her with her hair in snarls, long hair, uncombed wearing her blue jean, wrap around skirt either going to her studio to paint or returning from her studio after painting.

When I was a little older, my mom always made it her business to come home at least half an hour before I returned home from elementary school so she could be refreshed and wide awake to deal with me. That was my mommy. When she had to work at the office for my dad, she'd send one of the nurses that she knew I liked to be there when I woke up. Mommy always made plans for me to have friends, playmates on hand when I had free time and definitely on weekends. She arranged play dates and arranged with my father to get theatre tickets so she could take my friends and me to the theatre. She took us to the movies and to Serendipity for a sundae with a sugar cube on top, on fire. She bought us these notebooks called Mad Libs, where you made a sentence by adding an adverb or an adjective. It was such fun and we always laughed a lot. That was a mountain of fun. At home and alone Mommy had this game she played with me where she tickled me to death, nearly. When I started screaming "stop", finally she did because I was ready to pass out.

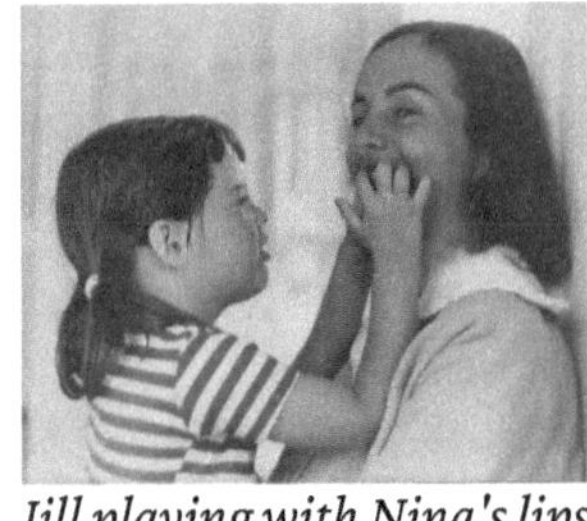

Jill playing with Nina's lips

Mommy had her hands full with me. I was learning disabled. I didn't know it, she and my father and my grandparents knew. It was their secret. She tutored me like crazy, in math especially. When I was younger, maybe 11 or 12, I got a part in my junior high school play. It was called "The Boyfriend". I still remember all the songs. I was the one who got married. Richard Bijon, daddy's assistant, hand stitched the most beautiful wedding dress I've ever seen with the border of the veil lined with lilies of the valley stitched by Richard personally. It fit me perfectly. My one request to the people in the school in charge of the production was to promise me to do the lighting in a way so that when I walked down the aisle, there would be a white cloud over the whole audience, I wouldn't see anyone but my mother. They did it, it worked, Thank God. She was always there for me. Between my mother and my father, they arranged to have live entertainment. Music, piano players, singers came to our Maison, home, and performed so I would hear music and learn the piano and sing. First it was Ronny Graham then Eddie Fisher, but mostly it was Ronny Graham. Then my parents tried to hook me up with their darling son, Ron Jr. That didn't work. That was really my stupidity.

When we went out to Point Lookout, it was just me, mommy and then daddy. Sometimes daddy came out late that night or the next day on Saturday. When I had a part in a play, she read to me after I'd fallen asleep so that hopefully the next day, I would retain my lines. I don't know whether that worked or not. I do know she was consistently there for me. And she was so nice to my friends and my cousins. She took us out all the time to restaurants, movies, and the theatre. As I've said, I was a handful. She was always sweet to me and so sweet to all the children all around me. She did my hair and took me with her when she went for her weekly massage. She made sure I learned to love animals. We had a cat named Amahl and went to visit Maya Deren who had a litter of cats and promised me one whom we named Amahl after Van Cliburn, who always came over during the night to visit and get some sleep.

My mother had a temper. She only lost her temper with me when I didn't listen to what I was told to do. There was only one occasion where she gave me a beating, and it was my fault for not listening to her. We had a parakeet. One day she had to take it out of its cage so she could clean out the cage. Then she had a hard time getting it back in. We had arranged to go shopping at Bloomingdales, a rare occasion. Well, mommy asked me to wait in the next room until she got the parakeet back into its cage and then we could leave. We needed to buy turtleneck sweaters for school.

Well, I grew impatient waiting for her to come out. I couldn't wait another minute; I finally pushed open the door. At just that moment she had almost gotten the bird into the cage but because I opened the door, the bird freaked out and flew away. My mother flew into a rage with me, all over me. I got smacked about 8 or 9 times. Boy was that traumatic. I hate to say it, but I deserved it. I couldn't blame her considering the circumstances. That was the first and last time she ever did that. Thank God. I think we finally went shopping. Somehow it seems every time I got a beating in my life, afterwards I no longer trusted the beater. First it was my grandfather, my mothers' father, Grandpi to me, Louie to everybody else. Afterwards, after that one beating, I never trusted him again. Now it was my mother.

There was one thing about my mother. She was so beautiful, like Michelle Pfeiffer. So naturally, breathtakingly beautiful, and yet she didn't comb her hair half the time. That didn't lessen her beauty. She didn't need to do anything; she looked simply stunning. I knew that. And even though her features were exquisite, she went to the beauty salon weekly, where she had her hair and nails done. And she wore beautiful jewelry. She wore makeup but really didn't need to. Her smile was so complete to her full picture.

She was totally devoted to my father and seemingly very much in love with him. It was really mommy's devotion to my father that I noticed. There were times she didn't want to deal with all the fanfare of my father and his celebrity patients but did it graciously.

Driving out to the country, daddy would drive, mommy would read, either to him, correspondence letters or drill me on my studies. I had problems with my memory. She taught me how to remember things by association, it worked. I still use that method today. She was a wonderful mother in every way imaginable. She must have been for me to love her as much as I did and then upon her death miss her as much as I have. She was special in every way. She protected me from the insanity of my father's office and always arranged to have children brought over for play dates, as it is now called, so I would have company since mommy couldn't have any more children. She always arranged afternoon festivities to ensure me and my friends had a good time. She sent Grandpi skating with me at Wollman Rink in Central Park.

Funny thing I must mention, not that it belongs here but worried that I'd forget. When we drove out to Point Lookout, we'd stop just upon entering Point Lookout so daddy could run into the grocery store and get a couple of bags of groceries. While he was in the store, mommy and I entertained ourselves in the car. For some reason I went into a tirade every time. I would start barking like a puppy and jump up to mommy and try to lick her ear. She'd laugh and tell me to "Get down silly". I guess there must have been a car driving by with a dog in it. Or maybe I wanted a dog so much I played doggie. I did this a lot. By the time daddy reappeared they got so busy juggling the bags into the car that I had to quiet down. Once we arrived at Point Lookout, both my parents, but mostly daddy, brought all the groceries into the house, and we got ready to go to the beach.

5

MY BROTHER TOMMY

Tommy Jacobson carrying Jill in
Point Lookout, early 1950s

Tommy, who is now a cardiologist for more than 40 years and 75 years old, is 15 years my senior and was the product of my father's first marriage to Alice Loewner Jacobson, we called her Litzi. Everyone said Tommy looked just like Max, I never saw it. I saw a resemblance to his mother, and maybe a physical resemblance to our father. By the time my mother and father were together, and I was old enough to recognize relationships, and the ones between my parents and my brother Tommy, I was about three or four years old already. My father and Tommy got along well for the most part. Heck, they were both doctors. My brother was studying medicine early on. He knew when he was young that he wanted to be a doctor. He was studying to be a cardiologist and became one. I wasn't informed until very recently that my sister-in-law financed my brother through medical school. He first set up his practice in Long Island, then joined the Airforce and was stationed in Wichita, Kansas. My father was consumed with my mother and my family. He made time for

Tommy, his ex-wife and ex mother-in-law, but not much.

Even though my father divorced Litzi she never remarried, she and her mother Bobbi loved my father and came to the office every month to see my father for treatment, brought him a homemade pie, and got Litzi's monthly alimony check. When Litzi and Bobbi went traveling, they stopped by the office for treatment and a visit.

Tommy and my mother got along very well. Why? I don't know. My mother didn't particularly like his mother, that was all. But my mother was so kind, nice and caring. It was hard not to like her, and she loved my father. When Tommy got his first office on Long Island, my mother bought him a big-name plaque for his desk. We delivered it to him. My mother and Bebe, his first wife, also got along well, and my mother bought things for their first child Gail when she was born. They all really got along very well.

Tommy acknowledged me, but I was only his half-sister and a very little girl. He was nice to me, like a big brother which he was. His own mother and grandmother were very kind to me. There was no trouble there. He changed my name from Julie to Jill when I was five years old, and I've always loved him for that. He had his life with his new wife. When he came to America he came with his grandmother and his mother. My mother was already with my father. Because my father and my brother were doctors and I was a little girl I didn't get to see them interact much, mostly on the beach. Tommy and Bebe used to come out to Point Lookout Long Island, where we had our summer home.

My parents and I flew to Wichita Kansas where Tommy was assigned in the Airforce to visit him and Bebe. We went to visit on two occasions and never stayed longer than a week. One night Bebe left. They had their second child, a very tiny baby girl, Lauren. I had to take care of her for that night. Bebe didn't return until the next day. I changed Gails diapers and took care of Lauren. I was about 12 years old. The next day Bebe baked me a chocolate cake as a thank you for changing diapers. The whole event is not clear to me. I don't see how I was able to care for two- or three-month-old Lauren, but I did take care of Gail. But then who took care of Lauren?

Tommy carrying Jill on his shoulders in Point Lookout, mid 1950s

Tommy visited occasionally and mostly came to Point Lookout on weekends. Almost as soon as they arrived Tommy and daddy would throw on their bathing suits and walk to the beach, my father carrying me on his shoulder as we headed to the beach. The funny thing was at times my father would forget I was on his shoulder, and he and Tommy would walk to the beach and walk right into the water and swim. The times he'd forget he had me on his shoulder I would go into the water with a scream. You know, my father and Tommy would take me far out into the water and throw me around like a ball back and forth. Sometimes they'd get deeply engrossed in a conversation and miss, and I'd go underwater. My brother had a great sense of humor and was always poking fun of our father's patients, they'd have a good laugh over it. They would scoop me up fast and I guess at that point I was screaming or crying. Tommy would laugh and they'd throw me up in the air.

Papa teaching Jill to swim in Point Lookout, mid 1950s

I think at some point they realized I was somewhat lazy or a slow swimmer. I guess I didn't swim fast enough to satisfy my brother, he came up with an idea. While Tommy was trying to teach me how to swim, he would tell me there was a shark in the water, I'd swim ferociously like a maniac. Sometimes he'd say there was a big fish coming and I'd panic and swim faster and faster. Years later I figured he told me this to get me to swim and swim faster.

Recently I told all this to my first sister-in-law, Bebe. She said it was very mean of Tommy to do that. I told her I felt the reasoning behind him saying that wasn't mean spirited. I explained to her he did it to get me to swim. He doesn't have a mean bone in his body. A problem that happened because of that was since that time, I have hallucinated sharks and big fish swimming near me in the ocean. I even feel the stillness, scary calmness and silence before the attack. I never know when it is real or not, but I deal with it. It seems my imagination has really been playing tricks on me. It still happens. However now I don't swim alone. I always swim around people.

Tommy and I had our rough spots. When Bebe was 8 1/2 months pregnant, for some crazy reason Tommy decided to race some boy down Glenwood Avenue where we lived in Point Lookout and both my brother, and the boy were on bikes. Well, they had their race. I watched in sheer horror as the two raced down the block. Tommy was racing fast and somehow crashed right into a tree. There was blood everywhere. The terrifying thing was I had to go and break the news to my father without Bebe hearing about it. I was afraid she was going to go into labor. I didn't do a very good job of it. Daddy went out with only a black bathing suit on, walked down the street and scooped Tommy up.

They returned with daddy holding up a bleeding Tommy with blood everywhere. There was blood all over Tommy and all over the street. I don't think I'd ever seen so much blood in my life. Bebe got upset, naturally. My father took Tommy into his bedroom and closed the door. About half an hour to forty minutes later they reappeared, Tommy all bandaged and cleaned up. What an episode that was. Since that day, anytime I hear or see anyone suggesting racing on bikes, I go into a rage. I lecture them and tell them what happened to my brother.

Papa, Tommy, Bebe (top right) Jill, and baby Gail (bottom right), late 1950s

A few weeks later, Gail was born. That night, Saturday night I remember, there were no doctors in the hospital. Tommy had to deliver his own baby, that was shocking to hear. Once Gail was born, she was the love of the family and a little baby for me to play with. This was daddy's first grandchild by his only son. There was a girl named Maria, the daughter of a childhood friend of Tommy's mother, about two years older than me. We had a tug of war with each other over who would hold and babysit for Gail. We fought hard over her! Sometimes she would win, sometimes I would, but we shared her. Tommy had two daughters, Gail and Lauren, and a son, Randall. I never had sisters or brothers to live with, so I enjoyed playing with Gail.

Papa, Tommy, Jill, and baby Lauren (center right), late 1950s

When Gail was about two, Tommy, Bebe and Gail were visiting us at our apartment one Sunday afternoon on East 73rd Street, on the 14th floor. I was ten when Gail was born so I had to be about twelve. For some reason Gail was restless, very restless and started fussing and crying. They happened to be in my bedroom probably visiting me and Gail was fussing, having a mild tantrum. Tommy picked her up, held her dangling from his arm with her one arm also dangling and with his other hand gave her a spanking on her behind. Well, I thought, she was the family darling, how dare he? Not my niece Gail, no way. I totally freaked out. I went running to both my parents, told them what had happened and ordered my poor father to order Tommy to leave the apartment immediately. I was so upset. Tommy and Bebe left and went down to their car and sat in the car. Daddy went downstairs to visit them while I went through my meltdown. I cannot tell you how freaked out and upset I was by this whole thing happening.

There is a moral to this true story which is, years later when I had my first-born son Jason, one day I got terribly upset at my little boy, who was maybe two years old, for spilling his Biosil oily yellow liquid vitamins all over his brand-new white undershirt. And in turn I went berserk and gave him a real spanking, much worse than what Tommy did to Gail. And my son cried and cried.

The moral is, don't be so quick to judge another person's actions until you are placed in a similar situation. Then see how well you are able to deal with it. It took that long, until I had my children to realize just how easily tempers can flare up. And yes, I feel so bad for my dear brother. Tommy and I have kept in touch. I attended the wedding of his daughter Lauren. He has been there for me if and when I needed him. After our father died, he sent me money when I needed it for clothing, and we've kept in touch.

I suppose Tommy could have harbored resentment towards me. After all, my mother took his father away from his mother, supposedly. Besides that, I had an easier life than he did. My brother was raised to become very self-sufficient, he always worked hard. I think it is better to raise a child to be very self-sufficient, it makes it easier later on. Now I can only wish the best for him and happiness. I am sure he doesn't need me, but if he did. I'd be there in a heartbeat.

6

HELGA (LUTTE) HAGEN

Helga (Lutte) came to the United States from Germany sponsored by my father. That is what she told me countless times. I was still a very little girl when I met her. She arrived at our penthouse apartment at 152 East 94th Street. My crib was still in my bedroom. Lutte was so small; she climbed into my crib to impress me when she came for the first time. She went out to Point Lookout with us on several occasions for which I have photos. I don't remember this but there is a picture of her helping me out of my bathing suit.

She was a Hagen; mommy's cousin but she adored, worshipped and idolized my father and reminisced constantly about how my father sponsored her to this country and was the love of her life. Lutte had a son whom she brought to this country after some time and arranged for him to stay with a nice foster family on a farm out on Long Island. Lutte worked all the time she was here in this country. She worked for Timex Watch for many years. She lived all her years here in a nice apartment on West 86th Street. A 5th floor walkup. We visited each other at our home many times.

 In later years, my father called upon Lutte to mediate a touchy situation between me and my boyfriend, Bill. He wasn't well, needed help, wasn't willing to get it and needed coaxing. My father enlisted Lutte to come over to my apartment and talk to him. She tried but it didn't help.

She turned to me and offered her support when I had to appear in court to fight Bill on a legality. Afterwards she invited me to dinner which I thought was nice. Once in the restaurant she asked me if I would like a drink while I awaited my dinner. I thought, how nice, of course after such a hard day, so I ordered and had a drink. Soon after I returned to my apartment my phone rang. It was my father, furious that he found out that I had a drink. He threatened me never to have a drink again, or else. Apparently, Lutte went back home to her apartment and called my father immediately to tell on me and told him I had a drink. Of course he was furious. My father was really against booze, and she really knew it. I was always oblivious to that fact, always. I don't know why.

Lutte, although she was nice, was also the family snitch. She reveled in doing it. It was like an itch with her. She simply had to do it, and it hurt, at times it really hurt. She snitched on everybody in the entire family, and they didn't know it. I did. She said damaging things, damaging gossip about all our family members. It was so sad.

Lutte did extend herself to keep the family in touch after my Aunt Carla died. I just resented and felt personally hurt by her meddling, mischief making within our family. She seemed to achieve great happiness by spreading rumors and malicious gossip within our family. Yes, Lutte meant well, had her good moments. I guess one could say she enjoyed playing games with the family's shortcomings. It was sad because people's feelings got hurt, especially mine.

7

BERNARD LEWIN

Bernard Lewin was a cousin from my father's side of the family that was never really made apparent to me. I always thought of him as a patient, although he was known to me pretty much as "the salami man". He came to our home on Sunday's delivering an entire long salami or bologna. I met his daughter Bunny and his wife. I was told many years later that it was him and his wife who introduced Ruth, my stepmother, to my father.

8

EARLY CHILDHOOD

— • —

*Jill with Papa and Nina riding wag-
on in the snow, early 1950s*

Daddy would be working hard in the office all day, all week, so he spent the weekend swimming, walking, and enjoying a fancy home cooked early dinner Sunday of roast beef and potatoes before we headed back to the city and home. On the way out or on the way back, we'd stop by Lilo and Herb's to play tennis. My father played against both of them. I also got lessons. Mommy had bad legs, so she just sat and watched, and she took long walks with me on the grounds around the tennis court in Roslyn, Long Island until my father finished playing. We saw a large windmill, which when it was functional, used to produce paper and wind. It had been shut down for years when we were there. There were mint leaves growing wild all around the exterior grounds of the tennis court. There was a girl who sold lemonade in the spring and summer, so when she was there, we purchased lemonade from her and picked the mint leaves to put in the lemonade. Then it would be my turn for a lesson which lasted half an hour to an hour, after which time we either went to Lilo and Herb's home for a visit or drove back home to New York. I liked Lilo and Herb a lot. They were nice.

If it wasn't tennis, then my mother took me for piano lessons. Granny took me weekdays to the Y on 92nd Street to get swimming lessons although my father and brother kind of taught me how to swim.

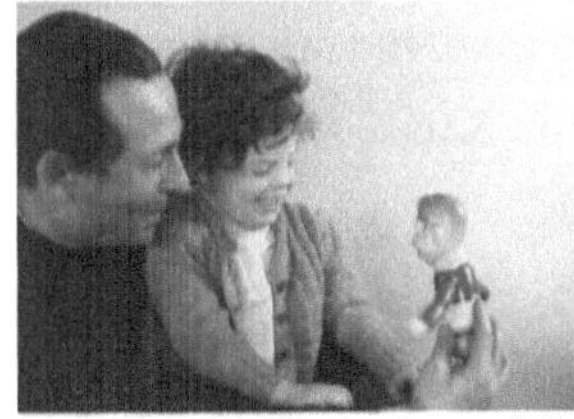

Papa and Jill playing with a doll, early 1950s

My father provided us with an array of entertainment. He would have Ronny Graham at our apartment who would play the piano and sing. Van Cliburn was invited to stay at our apartment before his performance at Carnegie Hall and practiced on our piano. And when I got a little older, Alice Ghostley and her husband, Felice Orlandi, took me out driving and sightseeing. They babysat me. It was wonderful and so much fun. My father was in the office a lot during the week, and unless he had to see someone in an emergency at the office, we had him all weekend. One Sunday, he opened his office to accommodate Marlene Dietrich. My mother and I waited outside the office with Marlene while he got the office ready for her.

My parents made sure I had a full schedule. My mother made me take afternoon naps until I was about 11 years old. I fought hard to stop that, but she wouldn't give in. When we went to Point Lookout, I fell asleep in the car, both going and coming back from the country.

Every time I visited my father in the office, he doted on me. All the patients swooned all over me. He was so proud of me; I was his darling daughter. I loved him, naturally. To me he was the best father in the world. He was always entertaining, either putting on a show with his medicines, or making jokes. He had so many creative, colorful people around him that I guess it rubbed off. He got together with Betty Cashman, the acting coach to the stars in the 50's through the mid 80's. She had a wild sense of humor and got a kick out of my father demanding that his patients cooperate with him. She cracked up when he tossed the syringe, which he did after giving each patient their treatment and right after administering an injection would demand a response, "Well, how was it?". To which he expected an immediate response. If it didn't come right away, he snarled and that made Betty laugh.

As far as mommy was concerned, she was quiet, reserved, and very shy. She was always kind and polite but very distant. She was distant in that she kept her distance from everyone since her world of art, artists, and paintings were far apart from the world of entertainment which my father was becoming increasingly involved with. She was intellectually charged and into the arts, and she seemed to be in her own world, and rather involved with her own inner thoughts. She was a painter and a great teacher. She took on teaching and tutoring me full time at home in the evening, and on weekends tutoring me in math while driving to the country when I would rather have rested or simply enjoyed the scenic view.

She was persistent, that she was. She was always consistent, told silly jokes and laughed a lot, especially around children. She was very motherly with me, yet she was constantly tutoring me. And unfortunately, I needed it. She also tried to help me learn how to play the piano. She did alright. She really interacted well with my father. I'm not saying that she forgot I was there. She just had a rapport and communication with my father that went over my head literally. But they were both so terribly devoted to me that one could hardly tell when or even if they momentarily forgot my presence. When he took us along to see a patient, I was momentarily alone with her. She was so gentle and caring. If someone had pets, she would go to pet them immediately. She always liked children. It was so cute, so endearing. My mother would explode with charm and melt with warm glee as soon as children entered the room, whether it be my cousins, friends or the children of patients who had become friends, she would be so delighted to be around all the children. She had a beautiful full smile which would come out whenever children were there.

She took my friends and me out all the time to the theatre, movies, lunch and dinner. She didn't have that pretentious air about her that most people did. She was so natural and low key. And if she learned that someone didn't have money for clothes or toys for their children, she arranged to get them whatever they needed. She didn't drive, so the only way for her to get around, since walking was not an option, she took cabs, or my father drove us. When we went to Point Lookout, my father always drove. At home mommy cooked occasionally. Mostly our cook prepared our meals. Granny did a lot of work for mommy, like clothes shopping for me. She had to assign Granny to do my clothes shopping because she had trouble with her legs from her horseback riding accident that happened when she was in her teens in Germany that left her permanently crippled, partially for life. It wasn't until years later that she routinely suffered from migraines.

At the office, she only had to sit in a chair and answer phones. That she did very well. She never really got into celebrities, she only befriended some. Mostly people who needed help, for instance a blind patient got assistance from her. She socialized with artists like Buffie Johnston and Olive Gavert. Beatrice Moore, who years before was a ballerina whom my mother had already known from Germany and who was now in America, had become her best friend, unfortunately. I never liked Beatrice. I even felt sorry for her children whom I feared were mistreated by her mean bitchy demeanor.

Karen (left), Nina (center), and Jill, mid 1950s

On weekends, when we went out to Point Lookout and my cousins paid a visit, mommy was so happy. She would be seen laughing and entertaining all my cousins. She wanted my cousins around to play with me. She especially enjoyed my cousins from K.V [Karl Victor]. He was her favorite brother who had been killed in the Berlin Airlift. She doted on them; they deserved it. My father had a patient whose family emigrated from Israel; his name was Mr. Auerhan. They arrived here in this country, and my parents were told that the children never had dolls, that they were too poor and that they couldn't afford to buy dolls, so my mother went out and bought a nice doll for each little girl, Ora and Mazal. At first the girls didn't know what to do with the dolls. Then we were later told they had slowly become acclimated to America and to the dolls. My parents later became friends with the family. Their father later taught me how to ride a bicycle, or at least he tried. I never really learned how to ride that bike. It was two sizes too big. If they had only figured it out and purchased one my size, it would have made life much easier.

When we first went to Point Lookout, we had an old house there that my parents rented or bought. It burned down in the middle of the night when I was about three years old.

*Re-building of Point Look-
out house, around 1951*

My parents had a brand-new house built out of scratch. We had to go out and check on the contractors during the winter and summer months. When I was about four years old the house must have been built because there are pictures of me outside with my cousins. Next to our house in Point Lookout, my father had another house built. He called it "Dr. Jacobson's Bedside Manor". It was a one-story house with an A-frame roof, small inside but large outside. Around the corner there were two levels. In it, he housed my bicycle and in the very next room he had a treatment room. It was rather small, but it had the patient's bed in it, and he used it from time to time to treat patients. We went to Point Lookout until I was 14 years old.

*Jill looking out from the
Point Lookout house deck,
early 1950s*

There were times, mostly in the late afternoon, when mommy was busy inside and I was happily alone. I enjoyed his treatment house because I found a path behind the house that only I knew about. I would run like hell around the building. I used to climb up to get on the roof, straining my arms and legs and climbing around the entangled vines as quickly and as quietly as I could until I got to the roof. I had to climb quite a bit, almost stumbling. But once I got up there, I was all by myself and enjoyed hiding out. It had quite a deep slide to it so mostly I sat still. I felt like I was really high up. It was such fun. Oh yes, I also slid down the roof.

I could see other people's alleys and the backyard of their houses. Every time

I was up there, there was nothing happening in anybody's backyard. Only once in a great while would I invite any playmate to join me. Usually, I went up there by myself. I would sit quietly, all alone feeling slightly sneaky knowing no one really knew I was hiding there. I was high enough so I could see the world. At 6 or 7, that was great. I never spied on anybody. Just climbing up there was such fun. Sometimes it seemed like I was there forever, and at other times it felt like I was there just for a few moments. Either way, that was my hideout. I don't think my parents ever knew that I was up there. But then I was a little girl, what did I know. Daddy was never treating patients inside when I was up there. It was very uneventful up there. Nothing was ever happening on the ground besides the barking dogs and parents calling their kids. And I always came back down by myself. There was a time when the roof felt as if it was wearing down. I had to place my shoe in a certain position so I wouldn't slide down accidentally. Otherwise, I was alright.

Our yard was filled with pebbles, and we had chairs laid out so that guests of my parents could sunbathe. When my cousins and I went swimming and returned from the beach sopping wet and full of sand, Grandpi would line us up on the bench against the wall in the pebble stone yard to make us change from our wet bathing suits. We had an outside shower where we rinsed off. Sometimes I'd come back from the beach with a pail full of starfish that I would put down in the yard.

Going to the beach with my father, riding on his neck was such fun. And my parents would hold me between them and swing me. That was when I was only three years old.

Happy New Year from the Jacobson's, Point Lookout, early 1950s

*Papa during winter plunge
in Point Lookout, early
1950s*

Papa tried to convince mommy to come for a swim in the cold ocean because it would do her a world of good. She answered, "I know Max, only I hate the walk". "Your legs need the exercise without having to carry your body's weight", he explained.

I want to try to describe my father's reaction when I entered the room, his office room mostly. I was his baby girl, the pride and joy of his life. There was a glow on his face when I came into the room. It's hard to describe from a daughter's perspective but I guess he was so busy working at the office, and mommy was so busy manning the phone, that to see me come bounding into the room, sort of unannounced and to know that I loved him just because he was my daddy, that was a relationship like no other. He always pointed his fingers, two fingers to his cheek, and said, "Put it here" in an almost demanding, comical manner, and then I would know to give him a big kiss. Sometimes I would miss and get his lips by mistake, he would roar with laughter. He would always say to whatever people were around at the time, "There's my daughter". Everyone was kind to me because I was the doctor's daughter. There were no exceptions, except for Grandpi, mommy's father, who was rather strict and unwaveringly stern. If he put his foot down with me, well, my father couldn't really yell at him. He would just chuckle and try to laugh it off or try to cheer my grandfather up. Grandpi loved me though and was usually very endearing to me, more so than to any of his other grandchildren. Daddy wasn't just wonderful to me because I was his daughter. He didn't really get to see me during the week until late at night, and yes also in the middle of the night, but that was when I was very little, from maybe when I was two to five years old. After that time, and the middle of the night, he didn't really get to spend quality time with me. But it was on weekends when he really got to be with me, my friends and cousins. My cousins joined us in Point Lookout during the spring and summer. My parents and I went to Point Lookout in the winter alone mostly, unless Landshoff or some other patients joined us.

One summer my uncle Peter came to America from Germany. He had gotten a job with General Electric and came over with his wife and child. My father allowed him to stay at our cottage in Point Lookout for the duration of the time even though it was only for a few months. Sometimes my big brother Tommy would come to Point Lookout and visit with his wife Bebe. My father always went with him to the beach for a swim. And then I got to ride on Daddy's shoulders, and they would take me into the water and toss me around like a ball. Fun, not exactly. A few times they missed, and I went under. That was awful. Then they scooped me up. I think at that point I was probably screaming.

Daddy would also sit at the piano on weekends in Point Lookout with me, mostly in the winter and try to teach me how to play. The first piece was Fur Elise which I still love, daddy sang too. He could sight read and magically hit the right notes and sing along. He did very well. He insisted I join him and sing and play the piano. Between my father and Ronny Graham, I had quite a musical appreciation training. Mommy also sat at the piano and tried to teach me to play, she sang too. Between my mother, father and Ronny Graham, I got in a lot of practice.

When I got a little older, old enough to have play dates as it is called, I would be invited to friends' apartments for the afternoon. Because mommy couldn't get around too easily and was physically limited, she would take a cab and pick me up. When friends would visit us and leave, they would go blocks away and we'd wave to each other. Granny, or mommy and me would be on our L shaped terrace. The view was magnificent.

My father would stand on his head against any wall. Really amazing to me. I wanted to learn how to do cartwheels. I never learned, I was too scared of landing on my hands and getting hurt.

When I was a little girl, he had his office on East 72nd Street. He was very fit, slim and had a wonderfully perfect physique. He ate lunch at a regular time, sometimes came home for lunch although rarely. He went to sleep at a reasonable hour, slept every night and left his office each night around 7 pm. He was full of vim and vigor and not only had tons of energy; he had so much love and enthusiasm for helping people and love of life. I guess after surviving the war that left him being very grateful just to be alive and well. It was this enthusiasm, and I guess delight at having become a successful physician, and at having people so grateful for his help and the knowledge that he could make a difference in people's lives by making them feel well, that made him feel on top of the world. He had this over exuberant love of life and embraced all those around him with optimism and the desire and determination to do the best that they could, and the desire and the will to be happy, healthy, and to exercise, be fit, and help and please others. All this made him a magnetic soul who drew everyone to him. I in turn inherited this love of life, intense wonderful happiness and knowledge that I was abundantly loved by all. My parents and grandparents, but especially my father, were the most outgoing, sociable, and full of life people in the world. He enveloped me into this maze of splendor as soon as my arrival was announced by the nurse at his office or by my mother. As soon as he got wind of my arrival, he made his patients get decent, opened his door, called me in, I came running in and kissed and hugged him. Nothing ever came between us, no patients, nothing. And if I was at home and had become sick, he immediately left the office, came home and treated me. Like the time when I touched a cactus plant and had poison oak all over me. He had to come home and treat me. Boy I was a lucky little girl. When my father had to go out of town on business, which happened only rarely and then he always went with my mother, they left me with my grandmother. I got sick several times so he arranged with his answering service to awaken granny and me in the middle of the night so that I could take my medicine. So that I wouldn't resist taking it, granny gave me the medicine with either chocolate or vanilla ice cream which I enjoyed very much. When I got older my father taught me how to take my pills with a tablespoonful of apple sauce. That was very good too.

Daddy always seemed to be naturally energized. It was his spirit. It was him long before the amphetamines.

He attracted his patients like magnets, Eddie Fisher, Alan J. Lerner, Van Cliburn, Mark Shaw with constancy. Congressman Claude Pepper. Ronny Graham, Leonard Sillman, Carol Channing, Marlene Dietrich, Alice Ghostley and Felice Orlandi. The Everly Brothers. Dona Felisa Rincon De Gautier, the Mayoress of El San Juan, Puerto Rico. Betty Cashman. Yul Brynner, Cecil

B. DeMille, Carroll Baker and Jack Garfein, even before they were married. Bob Richardson, Maya Deren, Katherine Dunham, Cecily Tyson, Roddy Mc Dowall, Patrick O'Neal, and the real estate tycoon of the early 60's, Stanley Broff. Then Leonard Holzer. Sir Davis York from Europe. Franco Zeffirelli from Rome. The list goes on and on.

I was such a happy girl in a world of my own who happened to have the most loving, wonderful, devoted parents by my side, always. I was also a lonely child, not having my brother with me or a sister to share my life with. My parents tried to compensate for that by taking me places, doing so many things with me, and arranging for my cousins and friends to come visit as often as possible. The father of one of my friends said my mother was always so nice to take in his two daughters all the time. I told him it wasn't that. It was that I got along so well with the two sisters that my mother was so delighted to have them come and keep me company, which they did very well. I was told that my mother offered to take the girls so that their parents could work. She took them for me. That was the reason. The only companionship I had besides that was when I was younger, my two dolls.

Jill walking Johnny and Pammy in the city, mid 1950s

They were big, like two-year-old kids. One was a girl; the other was a boy. They were called Johnny and Pammy, and I dragged them around everywhere. But this was when I was two and a half to about 5 years old, maybe 6. And my doll had its own stroller. It was a real stroller for a real child.

Jill riding her pedal car in Point Lookout, early 1950s

And for me, I had a real miniature car with a seat in it. It was a pedal car. It had wheels but you had to pedal it like a bike to get it to move. I don't recall driving it too much.

Mommy would help me get dressed in the morning on weekends. She would read books to me every night. And when we got a cat, one night she left the cat in the room with me just to keep me company. When the lights went out, the cat's big eyes lit up and I screamed. That was so funny. Mommy came rushing into the room and had to take the cat out, I think. Mommy took me to all my afternoon activities, both mommy and granny. She accompanied me to my piano lessons, and always to see my psychiatrist who lived on 96th Street between Madison and Fifth. Mommy told me funny stories; we giggled together a lot, and she tickled me. Sometimes she would tickle me so hard that I would nearly pass out, and then I would scream, "Stop!", but then she would continue tickling me again. She took me with her once a week when she went for a massage. I never went with her when she got her hair done. I didn't like the smell of the place. She always had nice long nails and had them painted either red or coral. She wore makeup when she went out. Foundation, powder, lipstick, mascara and dark brown eye liner. She never wore rouge. She was so pretty that she didn't need makeup, she wore her hair in a French twist.

9

THE HURRICANE IN POINT LOOKOUT

It was during the summer in Point Lookout when I was five years old, Granny and I happened to be alone when there was a bad hurricane approaching. Everyone was told to stay inside their houses and close their shutters. Point Lookout was a small village on the other side of Long Beach. They had this alarm that went off, it was long and loud, and they had it for fires, hurricanes, and in case there was a war going on. The hurricane came very early in the morning and lasted most of the day.

After the hurricane was over Granny opened the shutters and I climbed out of the window. She didn't know I climbed out of the window. I went running down the block to the beach to assess the damage from the hurricane. Nobody knew I went there. I've done this all my life, I just took off and ran, I don't even realize I'm doing it.

The boardwalk on the beach was not well built and got damaged by the hurricane, there were pieces of wood protruding. I was running on the board-walk, and a piece of wood went right through my foot. I don't remember any pain; I remember being there and there was a netted fence running all along the beach. I must have been gone from the house for a while. There was a boy who came to ask me what I was doing there, how I was and what happened. I told him what happened and that I got hurt. He went running to my house to get my grandmother. The next thing I remember, my father came out to Point Lookout. This must have been so traumatic because I remember it in pieces.

My father took me to Long Beach Hospital in an ambulance. We got stuck in a traffic jam. I'm just realizing now the reason why there was a traffic jam, because it was right after a hurricane. There was so much blood coming from my foot, he was trying to stitch me up and he couldn't stitch me up fast enough. The next thing I remember is waking up in the living room on the couch with all my relatives, neighbors, and friends standing around and watching me. I guess to see when I would wake up from the anesthesia. I don't ever remember being in Long Beach in the hospital. All I remember was being on the sofa. I had bandages on my toe and my foot, I was laying down and everybody wanted to find out if I was alright. I don't ever remember having any pain at all, I just remember screaming in the ambulance. After that happened, my mother was taking me from doctor to doctor, taking x-rays, to see how she would have my toe and foot corrected after the surgery. The doctors said they couldn't do anything. My toe and foot were permanently disfigured.

10

KIDNAP AND CAPTURE

— • —

It was summertime in Point Lookout, around 1955. About six children were involved. Donna, Betty, Susan, Dotty, Peggy, and two others, I cannot remember exactly who, and me. Dotty and Susan Pulitz were on their own but together, and close as sisters. They were each other's best friends. Peggy joined the group when she felt like it. I remember Betty's name, but not the face.

Dotty, it seemed, had a flair for mischief. You could see that look come onto her face. Her big blue playful eyes got even bigger than usual. She'd get this great big smile like she'd been drinking. Susan just went along for the ride. I guess at least four of the girls were bored and concocted a rather dangerous and hurtful scheme to lock me in Donna Kullen's parents' house. Donna's parents had their own life and Donna, being very sociable and popular on her own, did her own thing. Her parents were out for the entire day, and she knew it well.

The children brought me to this house and persuaded me to go to the basement, they claimed to look for food for us to cook or fix and eat. Once I was down there, they locked me up. They locked me in there for what seemed to be hours. We were all practically the same age, around eight. I thought maybe they were playing a game. Surely someone would come and rescue me. No one did, no one came to check on me. No one outside of the kids knew I was there. All the things that went through my mind. Will someone come by and rescue me? Every few minutes which passed, I still couldn't believe it.

What a nightmare to happen to such a young child! Thank God it was daytime and light outside. Every so often I would look out the back window and spot someone going into their backyard to do something. I'd wave like mad, but they didn't notice me at all.

All along I never believed my so-called friends would do this to me. The room I was locked in was facing the back of the house, no one went there. I called for help, even though I didn't want the kids to hear me and think I was scared. I started banging on the windows, but no one came, there was no way out. Time went on, it seemed like forever. Finally, after hours, probably shortly before their parents came home (I was a scared little girl and hadn't figured that part out yet), they came and released me.

By that time, I was out of breath, crying and fiercely mad, mad at them, mad at the world, mad at any living breathing thing. I ran straight home and went flying through the front door. I screamed to Granny and raced into her arms crying and screaming and told her what happened. Why hadn't she gone looking for me? She was just about to but hadn't yet. All the children were punished. I never forgave them. I had been hungry from the start and because of everything that happened, I forgot all about eating and food. After all, I was held captive and upset that no one came looking for me. It never occurred to me that I may never have been missed.

11

MY TENTH BIRTHDAY PARTY

*Intro to Jill's 10th birthday
party, circa 1957*

My parents threw me a big birthday party when I turned ten years old. My father arranged for a patient to drive all the way out to Point Lookout and bring my friends into the city for the party and then to return them to their homes out on Long Island. Then there were some of my friends in the city who were invited. There were my friends, the children of mommy and daddy's friends and some cousins. Doc Marcus, the magician, was the guest entertainer. I don't remember any of the presents I got, if any.

*Jill shuffling cards with Doc
Marcus*

Papa entertaining children

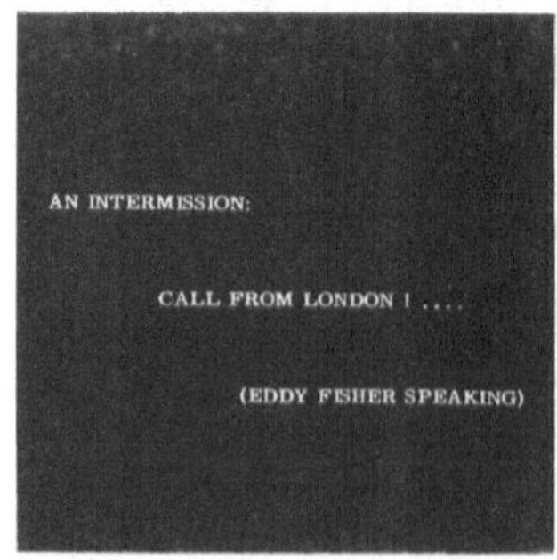

*Jill and Papa on phone with
Eddie Fisher*

*Jill and friends blowing out
birthday cake*

*Doc Marcus says goodbye to
Jill during party*

12

A Daisy with a Broom

— • —

I was raised as a very privileged child since I was very little. Both of my parents worked full-time, my father was a very well-known and popular physician, and my mother was his dutiful wife and receptionist at his office all week from 9 am to 7pm.

Max and Nina hired servants, cooks, housekeepers, and maids' fulltime to run the household. Nina's mommy Vicky volunteered to do clothes shopping for me when I was a very little girl. They had their bases covered. The housekeeper Celeste was given a shopping list, did the shopping, laundry, and ironing with such a sweet smile on her face, and did French style gourmet cooking.

She was darling; sweet, wonderful, and kind. I stayed with my grandparents Monday through Friday from 9 to 6 while my parents worked in the office, from the early 50's through the late 50's. They had me in the daytime for what seemed to be 10 years. It was great. Celeste, our maid, taught me how to knit. She was with us for at least four years, from when I was six until at least ten years old. Then in the early 60's, I 've forgotten why, Celeste left, and my parents sadly had to find another housekeeper. My mother and I visited Celeste from time to time where she resided nearby.

The replacement, which we always called her respectfully, was Madam Dupont. She arrived with references and an attitude. She made fresh soup DuJour daily and threatened all who ventured into the kitchen to "Get out of my keetchin" as she screamed, yelling hysterically, in a neurotically fueled momentary rage. She was a nervous wreck and seemed a bit old to be holding such a demanding job.

My parents were always working in the office, and I was being cared for by my mother's parents. I had my own full schedule of afternoon activities which included swimming, dancing, piano, and tennis lessons.

When I was in elementary school, 1st through 5th grade, mornings before leaving for school my father would get up early to make coffee for himself and prepare breakfast for us. Every day he prepared the eggs differently. Some days he made me soft boiled eggs, other days hardboiled eggs with a little butter or margarine, and a touch of salt on it. He made it so delicious. He made me two eggs, one he put in an egg warmer, the other with a cover on top. My mother would give me a snack after school and then she would heat up dinner. But it was always my father who made breakfast. When I got a little older, he gave me Grape Nuts cereal, which I loved.

My parents always had help around. If it wasn't a maid, housekeeper or cook, it was a patient enlisted for that day, mostly weekends to do the cooking. Sometimes on weekends in Point Lookout, my father enlisted the assistance of some of his eager patients, one being Albert Dekker, who loved to indulge the Jacobsons and their guests with his fancy cooking and loved showing off his unique preparations. Also, a man who was the architect for the house in Point Lookout, Nepo, would cook and prepare snacks for the crowd on weekends.

In later years Max had an assistant at the office, Richard Bijon, who was so efficient at the office that my father decided to request his presence at our home to help with me. Richard literally took over; he did impressive interior decorating. Whenever I went away traveling or on vacation, he would surprise me by completely redecorating my room from top to bottom and I would return pleasantly surprised. It never occurred to me how much money was spent on these endeavors.

Prior to an evening at Lincoln Center, my father and I were invited to an opening of Cleopatra directed by Franco Zeffirelli and starring friend and patient Leontyne Price. The doctor sent his patient, hairdresser to the elite, Marc Sinclair, over to groom me and coordinate a formal outfit for me to wear and loaned me a wig for the occasion. Marc Sinclair was brilliant in how easily he coordinated simple articles of clothing into a masterpiece of formal wear;

he did this in a matter of minutes with ease.

I was no Jewish American Princess, not by a long shot, I was a hippie at heart. And I was not spoiled. The one thing I wanted as a child and was refused was a Christmas tree. My father yelled at me and told me I had so many things that other children didn't have and that I should be thankful for what I had and not harp on it. Although he was accused of spoiling me, I wasn't spoiled. I got a lot of love from everyone.

I always opted to wear black Levi's and black turtleneck sweaters. I had one nice skirt, my choice. I never dressed up; I just wasn't into it. Some patients tried to gift me fur coats. Just the mere thought of it angered and insulted me. I was an animal lover and resented the very sight of fur. I was constantly accused of being a hippie.

Whenever Richard redecorated my room, I was surprised and happy. It never occurred to me to do it for myself. I was a very privileged girl who ultimately realized I had no training whatsoever to prepare me for life, a career, or any basic skills, even though my father arranged for me to receive training in the theatre. The funny thing was, because everything was always done for me by my father's grateful patients who aimed to please, I never learned how to do anything for myself. In my silly little head, all I thought about, which was instilled in me since childhood by my father and my Jewish upbringing, was to get married, have children, and live in a house with a white picket fence and have kittens and puppies all around. That was it. Well, most of that didn't happen, not even close.

13

THE MASTER MAGICIAN

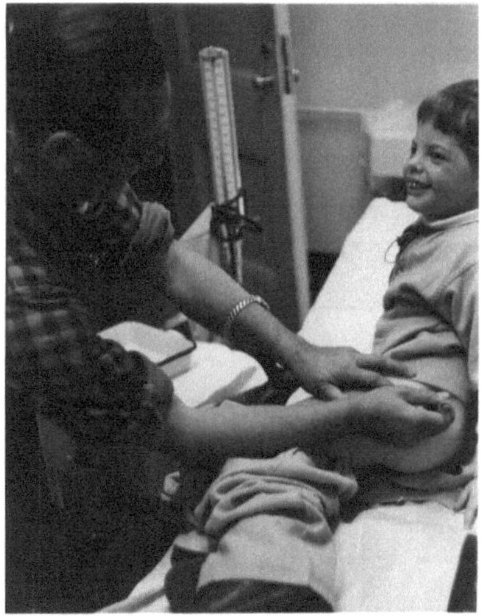

Papa giving Jill a treatment, mid 1950s

He was one of the most controversial figures of our time, and my time. He had a vision well beyond any of our years, and he possessed a brilliant mind. He was a genius, and crazy in many ways. He was crazy in that he acted on intuition rather than based on educated facts. He would rather quickly get to the root of the patient's problems and symptoms. To begin with, he would come up with a question or statement for them, what had they previously eaten, etc., the kinds of questions a layman would never even think of. Something that he picked up on clear out of the blue, that baffled and amazed them. When he asked them a simple question, he often got a vague response. He would intuitively know in which direction to proceed. His wisdom guided him.

I called him from school one afternoon. I was away at boarding school in
the Berkshires, some two and a half hours away from my father. I called him
because my stomach was really bothering me for hours. I didn't know what
to make of it. After talking to him for five minutes on the phone, he asked me
questions and realized that I had ingested something with spoiled milk in it
and just didn't realize it. He told me what to do. Within an hour I was fine.
That was just a little experience. I had others later in my life. He always bailed
me out successfully.

*Medical vials (B6, C, ri-
boflavin and others) on
shelf in Papa's lab*

The doctor, with his just cleaned and pressed ster-
ile white shirt, starched collar, fancy new tie and
pants (patients always gifted him with fancy new
ties out of gratitude so he felt obligated to wear
them), seated on his swivel chair in his treatment room wearing his heavy wide rimmed glasses [ready to fall at any moment down the steep hill
of his nose – skiers' paradise] prepared one of his
mixtures for his next victim, patient. A little bit of
this, and a little bit of that.

Papa filling syringe with solution

One cc of vitamin B-2, B-6, B-12, riboflavin, an ampule of calcium, which came separately (in a glass ampule which my father abruptly broke off), and gave a warm feeling all over when injected, amino acids, and some unadulterated human placenta (donated by patients), about 7 or 8 milligrams.

By this time his newly pressed white shirt displayed the hues of some of the vitamins that he was mixing. Lutte acknowledged, as does Eddie Fisher, that the front of Papa's shirt was dirty and spotted with brown and yellow dots. There were some rich reds, resembling cranberry juice, some oily yellows, which as my father put it resembled tiger piss, the riboflavin was brownish, and maybe a little blood from the vein of the patient he was treating. It was obvious that his vanity was not directed at his exterior, that he only cared for the cure of his patients.

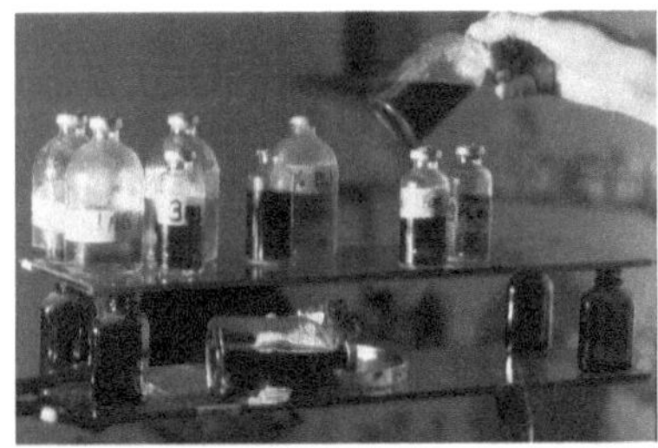

Jill holding a vial from Papa's shelf, mid 1960s

I remember only the rich reds and oily yellows, and the stones primarily displayed in most of the vials. All the elements of his scientific experiments and research, his vials, vats of solutions for both oral drops and the ones which he used for intravenous injectables. He had a pressure cooker and a sterilizer early in his practice and he used glass syringes.

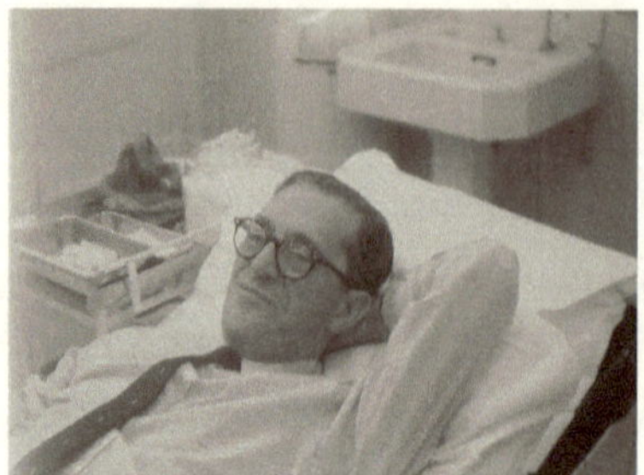

Patient receiving treatment, late 1950s

Each patient got a vial that was appropriate for them. There was no set rule, and all the cocktails were different. I suppose the genius in him was how he chose to apply it. It worked and the patient was very gratified with the result. The so-called cocktails varied in their contents. It depended on the needs of the patient at that time as to what was in it. For example, if a patient was really sick with fever, rundown and needed to work, I suspect they were given antibiotics and massive vitamins, antibiotics to help the patient fight the infection and the vitamins to give the person the strength to get back on his or her feet. Some patients suffered from food allergies and were treated accordingly.

He also treated me, especially where allergic reactions to food (M.S.G.) were concerned. We would be in the middle of eating at an upscale Chinese restaurant. Suddenly, my face would turn rose red, and I'd have trouble breathing. I didn't know what hit me. My father reached into his pocket and pulled out a bottle of pills, handed me a round pink pill, and told me to take it at once. It was Celestone, an anti-corticosteroid used for severe allergic reactions. Within minutes the symptoms disappeared.

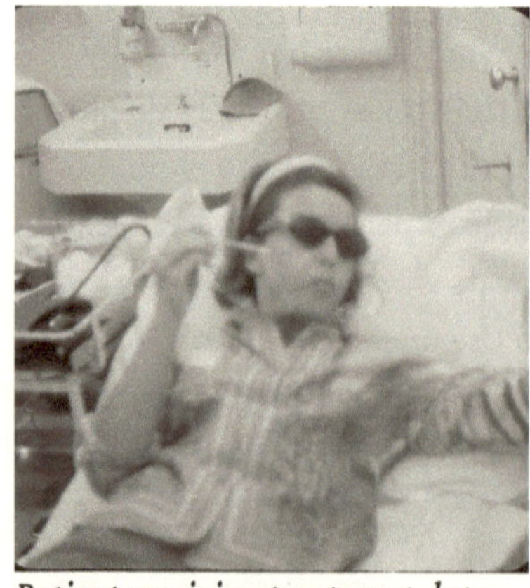

Patient receiving treatment, late 1950s

There were patients who were overworked and rundown, or simply rundown from being overworked. He treated them with vitamins, and I suppose amphetamine. However, in the early days, the 40's to early 50's, he wasn't using amphetamine yet, not until the late 50's, maybe 1957. He was also a believer in administering Gamma and Immune Globulin. I wasn't born yet.

He was the only physician who, as busy as he was, took out the time to instruct his receptionist to telephone his patients, whoever it was who had forgotten to call him with their progress report. He would always instruct his patient prior to their departure from his office after their treatment to call him the following day to let him know how they were doing. If they failed to do so, which happened from time to time, he made it a point to phone them. Never, ever have I known another doctor to do that.

After a few years of his clientele escalating from a group of celebrities to quite an impressive collection (mosaic) of celebrities and statesmen, his practice took on a change of flight. His hours of work became more hectic. The celebrities and dignitaries demanding schedules, changing performance and production schedules made them become more frequent visitors to his office. Since most of them were on the same ego level as my father, very driven and self-assured, they had begun spending more time with my father.

Many of his patients had grueling schedules, which required them to work ridiculously long hours with impossible demands being made on them. To my knowledge, they were given mostly vitamins. For all their symptoms he prescribed different medicines. And there were some patients who had drinking problems for which the doctor had an ongoing experimental treatment, which I believe consisted of loads of vitamins, calcium, and possibly amphetamine although I would not dare be so presumptuous as to assume that it was automatically included in the patients' treatment. I do know that his patients were grateful for their successful treatment and relieved that it worked.

My father had in his so called "tribe" among other people, this mad and brilliant research scientist named Maxwell Vos helping him at his office on East 72nd Street. Maxwell was one of his so-called "friend assistants", who experimented with my father's Bunsen burner and had the genius and mathematical, scientific knowledge to get some of the experiments successfully completed, naturally however under my father's guidance. Maxwell also possessed the three-dimensional vision that my father had. My father and Maxwell were both eager to take the experiment to whatever level it would take them.

Maxwell was very weird, brilliant and at times wickedly funny, wearing specs and looking like the "nutty professor" in the Jerry Lewis movies. My father was off the wall in other ways, so they made quite an interesting team.

Maxwell and several other characters aided him in his laboratory research. They were all scientifically inclined in one way or another and were very driven and inspired by my father's experiments and willing to listen, learn and experiment. Apparently, my father was an inspirational teacher. It was quite a sight.

Both my father and Maxwell had strong accents. Maxwell had a strange British Canadian accent, and my father had a very strong German accent. There were many times when I could barely understand my father because of his strong accent and of course his occasional mumbling. My father's brilliance exceeded my intelligence by far. He had many, many years of education and knowledge ahead of me naturally besides the fact that he was so much smarter. There were times, besides my not being able to understand him, where I couldn't understand what he meant because it was way over my head scientifically, and otherwise.

He invented so many things as he went along, ongoing experiments. He invented a brush, which he attached a tightly taped set of magnets with silver electric tape, one positive and one negative to the brush, and had his athletic patients pass this device over and around their knees to cause a reaction to occur as the direct result of these cross current magnets. Besides the magnet invention, long before that, he made a salve during his stay at his East 72nd street office. He made the salve with vitamins, and I believe amphetamine plus cold cream for the patient to rub on their face and neck to refresh themselves. It smelled strongly of vitamins. He pressured everyone, all his patients, to try it. I really thought he was full of bologna. He requested me to try it, silly me I had little faith in it. Well, today we have mineral ice and pain patches, all sorts of patches. Mineral Ice works best for me. He was doing this when I was 7 or 8 years old, in 1952-3. Yes, he was way ahead of his time. Boy, do I wish I had more faith in him. And his migraine treatment, cure, that was to me the best of all. My stepmother said that among other elements it contained Gynergen (for migraines) as a component.

My father was a workaholic to excessive degrees. His office was located at 155

East 72nd Street, New York City (1945-1965) with the nameplate on the office door reading "Dr. Max Jacobson". In his medical practice my father treated his patients in his office and often at home. He also treated his relatives at the office and at home as well. It was only at the pool and at the ocean he didn't treat his patients with injections, but instead with the healthy physical exercise of swim therapy.

Jill and Papa in treatment room, May 1966

He was the most intense yet comical being on Earth and luckily, he was my father. I always had an open invitation to enter daddy's treatment room before, during and after he was treating a patient unless he instructed his secretary otherwise, which he did from time to time. He always relished my visits when I was little. At times he would invite me into his treatment room if somebody famous happened to be there. Then daddy chuckled with pride beaming from ear to ear to his patients and said, "That's my daughter, Jill" and then to me he'd say, "Say hello to" so and so, whoever it was. I was shy at first. It took a while for me to come out of my shell. Daddy was so proud of me.

When I was a young girl, I entered daddy's treatment room happily skipping about, with as much upbeat energy and joyous enthusiasm as any little girl could happily display, as I knew full well that greeting me from behind those thick-rimmed glasses and strong healthy physique was a beaming, smiling and chuckling father who absolutely adored me.

 My father found it particularly enjoyable to have me come bounding into the room just like an eager happy puppy just to say "Hello". Daddy would say to me, pointing his fingers to his cheek, "Put it here", meaning give me a kiss. I was so shy, but I would kiss him on his cheek. Sometimes I'd miss and kiss him on his lips by mistake. He would laugh uproariously with all his heart. I would kiss him and hug him adoringly.

What was so wonderful back then in the early 50's was watching my father seriously concentrating on his vials. Dozens of them, squinting and concentrating on what medicines to put into the syringe then suddenly turning in his chair to greet me. It was such an immense pleasure for him to be momentarily distracted by me, his bouncy little daughter, Jill. Little did I understand what was happening all around me.

Jill holding vial in Papa's lab, May 1966

I watched in awe and amazement as celebrities, people from all walks of life and all over the world, politicians, actors, actresses, senators, congressmen, and ambassadors. They all flocked to see the great doctor, get treatment, and see him in action at his office on East 72nd Street (The Inner Sanctum, also known as his treatment room). He had become quite a phenomenon, almost surreal.

I always had access to him even when some stuck-up big shot non-celebrity was present, unless they requested confidentiality. Once years later during a vicious thunderstorm, I raced into papa's room to seek refuge from the thunder, which always terrified me. On one occasion, my father was in the middle of giving an intravenous injection. He slowly and discreetly calmed his patient and reassured him that everything was all right. He kind of chuckled at the idea that I could come rushing in out of fear of a thunderstorm. He explained politely to his patient that I was running for cover because I was afraid of the thunderstorm. He told me to feel free to take shelter until the storm was over. He managed to successfully give the intravenous injection. In my raging hysteria I forgot who the patient was, I can only recall that it was a middle-aged man. I felt so embarrassed when I realized I had interrupted a treatment in progress and was confronted with the patient's presence in my father's office.

In the early days, he worked hard until late at night. Seven days a week was not unusual. And yes, I saw him whenever I wanted to, or at least I thought so. During the week my grandparents took care of me, Monday through Friday, all day. My father insisted my mother work full time as a receptionist for him at his office. She obliged but did it reluctantly. Although she said she wanted to be at home with me, raising me, I personally don't think she had the patience because I was a handful.

I had also been afflicted with ADHD since early childhood and had enough trouble simply surviving school and college. I was hyperactive, which the family realized, and which naturally I knew nothing about. The amazing thing about all this was that no one talked about it. No one ever mentioned it. My mother constantly tutored me, plus she and my father hired tutors for me just to help me with my day-to-day homework.

I was fortunate that my parents could afford tutors, I never took anything for granted, ever, thank God! My father would always say to me. "Do you know there are starving children in the world?". And he was very strict about the wasting of any, and I mean any food. He would say, "Do you know how fortunate you are that you have everything you need?". He always took great pride and pleasure in licking his plate clean after each meal. Then he would show it to everyone at the table and would expect them all to finish their plates.

We had our private time, especially if he wanted to discuss something with me, whether I had been naughty or someone else had. Even if it was just to talk, he called me into the bedroom or into his office, chased everyone out and we had a nice quiet conversation. This happened quite frequently. I enjoyed it because he was so understanding. He wanted me to be equally understanding as well. Since I had ADHD, my father, having the patience of a saint as the expression goes, spoke to me about life, explained things to me like no other human being could or would. He would explain how certain families had to struggle because some members were not well. And he told me how proud he was that certain individuals were dealt a lousy hand in life and fought against all odds to succeed. He also lectured me about how wonderful it was to be a happy, successful human being.

He told me how important it was to have a good education for everyone, no exceptions. Yet knowing that I had ADHD, my poor father had to repeat these stories to me over and over again. I had so much trouble retaining anything, but he did explain everything to me. Regardless of what anyone thinks, I feel sad that I must even make a point of this. My father was the most doting dad in the world to me. No, I didn't get all the dresses in the world. I wasn't even into dresses. I was into black Levis and black T-shirts. I was all black for quite some time, and I felt so badly for so long after my mother died that my father was overworking himself so much that I couldn't bear to approach him for money at all. My Aunt Carla had to ask him for me and that went on for quite some time.

Papa treating bed bound patient during in home visit, mid 1960s

Last, but certainly not least, my father treated a lot of patients who had no money, free of charge. If they really suffered from something debilitating and needed treatment he saw them. There were a lot of patients whom he asked to see and treat that had diseases for which he was searching for a cure in his own laboratory. If a patient knew of someone who suffered from a disease such as Multiple Sclerosis or cancer, my father sent for them and treated them, even making available a friend or patient to pick up the person from their home and bring them to his office and then arrange for their safe return home. Never do I want to hear from anybody, anywhere, that he was after money, ever! Even his detractors have stated that it was not the money he was after. A cousin of mine wrote a book that was unfortunately never published. In this book, Lutte stated that after my parents emigrated here from Germany, years before I was born, my father was busy rescuing Jewish refugees after they arrived here from Nazi Germany helping them get settled here in America, financially, and making sure that they received treatment if they were sick which they inevitably needed. Each of these refugees had different needs. He had a patient in the clothing business and knew of a family that really needed clothes, he coordinated the two. If someone needed lodgings, he had one real estate man, maybe more who he approached to help. He did this often with positive results. He saw all the suffering during the war in Germany and was determined to improve the lives of all the refugees he could after arriving in New York.

He wouldn't allow my mother to buy furnishings for their own apartment until all the refugees were settled and standing on their own financially and otherwise. Then and only then did he allow my mother to start buying furnishings for their apartment. By the time I was born, we had everything we needed. I even had a baby nursemaid before my grandparents took over caring for me since both my parents were working full time. My nursemaid's name was Mrs. Hediger. She took care of me until I was three years old. They sent for her all the way from Switzerland. We also had a cook and a housekeeper. My mother made fish on Fridays regularly and made liver once every two weeks. She wanted me to get accustomed to them since they had already become very unpopular in many households by then and yet they were very healthy to eat. I did get accustomed to them. To this day I love both fish and liver.

The only thing I didn't have was my father at home. He was mostly around late at night, and on weekends. Except if I had a play date, a visit with a friend, I got to choose which parent I wanted to have pick me up afterwards. My mother offered to come at, let's say 8:00 pm and my father offered to come and pick me up after work, around 9:00 pm. So naturally, when I was able to get away with it, I'd choose my father so that I could have an extra hour to play with my friends.

On weekends for years, I had both my parents, and visits from many of my cousins. We would go out to Point Lookout. Some of my father's patients would come out to visit or to get treatment or both. But that wasn't often. While in Point Lookout we got to swim in the ocean where, when my brother Tommy was visiting, Daddy and Tommy would walk to the beach talking together while I sat perched joyously on Daddy's shoulders. Once at the beach and in the water, they would toss me around like a ball. They were great in the water. I wasn't a great swimmer, but that's another story.

When my cousins visited, we would play on the beach and go in the water. The grownups would have picnics for us to eat after our swim. Afterwards, before returning to the city, we enjoyed a home cooked brunch of roast beef, which I then called "roast beast", and mashed potatoes cooked by my father and sliced by him professionally too. He took great pride in attending to his ritual of knife sharpening before and during his roast beef slicing which hurt my teeth, so I screamed loud to kill the noise of his sharpening and pressed my ears as hard as I could.

In the winter we would even go to Point Lookout, taking nice long invigo-rating walks on the beach, though mostly at night. On these rare occasions, mommy, even though she had difficulty walking, walked on the beach in the sand. There would be hardly anyone there except a few people walking their dogs. My father took his brief dip in the frigid water while onlookers watched. Afterwards we returned to our cottage to a warmly lit fireplace where we all gathered to warm up after our chilly brisk walk and waited while Daddy put on warm dry clothes, had a bite to eat, and afterwards, I went to bed.

All week he would be working hard in his office. So sometimes on weekends when we didn't go to Point Lookout, which was rare even in winter, he would drive mommy and me to parts unknown and admire the view and just drive and discover all sorts of scenic places. It seems as if we drove endlessly around the outskirts of town and then beyond. We must have driven through Yonkers towards Westchester County, covering that area and points in-between.

I recall there were times when my father had a very short temper, got very impatient and angry. Those times at the office my mother would usher every-one into another room and offer to assist him, or she would suffer because then he would yell at her. He did that from time to time. She would get sad and quiet. When we were preparing for a weekend in the country, packing, and getting ready, Daddy was busy at the office and came home at the last minute, we weren't ready. He got mad. What I'm saying is not that he was a beast. I am implying that he was normal and had good and bad times.

My parents also took me to classical music concerts often and to patients' homes upstate New York where we were serenaded by Broadway stars singing and playing piano. One lady, whose name escapes me sang, "I Hear Music When There's No One There", her husband was her manager and stood guard. They had a beautiful massive estate with paths full of tall stem flowers and a huge outdoor pool.

My father attracted his patients like magnets. It seemed that everyone in high social circles, elitists, were among his many patients. Peggy Guggen-heim, I was told, was a patient although I never saw her. It seemed as if everybody who was anybody came to see the great doctor. He was such an inspiration to everyone because he was healthy, physically fit, athletic, and charming.

 He was determined to make everyone around him feel well and happily entertained his patients with magic shows which he did impromptu. He
would take a quarter, put it in his hand, make a fist then pretend to put the
quarter in his mouth, put his tongue in his cheek, pretend to eat it, then take
it out of his mouth without anyone being aware, then magically produce
it from behind his amazed patient's ear, thereby surprising and fascinating
them. Sometimes he would produce the quarter in his hand, then put his
hands behind his back, then place them closed fist in front of the patient,
and ask them to guess which hand the coin was in. They never guessed. He
would place a quarter behind his patient's ear and make it disappear. They
had a good laugh over that. Then my father, thrilled at having successfully
entertained his patient, burst out laughing. He did this mostly for his younger
patients.

He was constantly telling jokes. I was told by a former patient that he com-
mented "If you keep looking backwards, you're facing your future with your
rear end". There were so many I can only remember a few. If a patient came
into the office and stated that they were afraid they were losing their hair, my
father would respond with a puzzled look on his face and say very seriously,
"Whom else's hair did you expect to lose?". A patient would visit him and
state that they had a cough coming out of their throat. He looked at them
puzzled and asked them with a smirk on his face, "Out of whom else's throat
should your cough have come?". His patient in turn would laugh or smirk
in response. One time an elderly patient came to see him for a check-up.
My father asked his patient to remove his shoes for him to be examined
thoroughly, to which he complied. Then my father asked him to remove his
socks to which he replied, "Oh doctor, I am sorry I washed only one foot",
to which my father replied, "Next time". My father roared with laughter at
that one. He entertained his comrades with jokes and would put on shows for
them. There's a picture of him at the beach with a cooking pot on his head. He
would take a soda bottle and blow into it as if it were a flute and make a hollow
sound with it. He did all sorts of ridiculous things. He would stand on his
head against any wall, just like that, effortlessly. He inspired all his patients to
take long walks, swim, and do everything healthy, and he managed to bring

celebrities out of their shells.

His popularity soared long before the amphetamine entered the arena. He also offered treatment, or shall I say, insisted on also treating his and my mother's relatives, and their spouses. "Don't be silly", he would say, "Come on, come in here, I'll fix you up". Sometimes he'd order his patient, "Pull your pants down, hurry up, I don't have all day". Usually, he'd be totally cordial, inviting and so sweet, no one would ever turn him down. And if someone feared injections, he would tell them, "Look over here", or warn them that "You'll feel a little stick". And afterwards he would say, "Now was that so bad?" Or "Now that wasn't so bad, was it?". My father endeared all my mother's relatives to him with his migraine treatment. My mother's side of the family considered my father a crazy, mad, hysterically funny genius, and very generous with everything, including his hard-earned money, his treatments, and his good advice. Some of his patients were so grateful for his treatment that they would bestow gifts on him such as sturgeon, Steak tartar from the famed Madison Avenue Deli, and Orchids from Val Sarra, who owned his own greenhouse in midtown Manhattan behind his townhouse. Each orchid was in a glass vase filled with water.

My father also received complimentary theatre tickets from patients who were appearing on Broadway, such as Carol Channing in "Hello Dolly", Ronny Graham, Zero Mostel in "A Funny Thing Happened", and Yul Brynner in "The King And I" etc. My father received homemade beef stroganoff from Marlene Dietrich. And from Ruth Rodriguez, who was a patient and my Uncle Simons girlfriend, my father received a delicious lemon cream pudding. I wish I had gotten the recipe for it. I would have loved to make it at home myself.

My father had a patient from Puerto Rico, Antonio Betancourt, who when he came would bring him cartons of cigarettes, guava paste and cheese, which was a delicacy from Puerto Rico. My father got lots of nice gifts from many patients.

Also, we had an excellent maid and cook at home who cooked fabulous French cuisine, which was a great treat for us. My mother had to heat and reheat food for my father who would often get home unexpectedly late from having one emergency call after another on the same day.

My father was generous with his advice, thankfully he also had the gift of being able to diagnose over the phone even on long-distance calls. If a patient of his was traveling in Europe on business and needed to speak to him to get his advice, or to get emergency medical care, he was able to accommodate the patient who otherwise might have had to seek the help of a strange doctor in a strange country. In an emergency this was a blessing. A patient could call from all parts of Europe and the Middle East and consult with my father over the phone and have him tell them what the problem was by diagnosing their ailments by phone and then prescribe the necessary medications for them to take. He was also able to call foreign pharmacies close to where they were staying and instruct them to give medication to his patients. I would rather devote a chapter to "The Great Diagnostician".

Even Eddie Fisher in his book accurately stated that he consulted with my father long distance from London to New York when Elizabeth Taylor was so acutely ill and semi-comatose. Eddie had given my father a description of her condition, symptoms, vitals and so on. My father told Eddie to have the doctors check her gamma globulin. Just then the doctor at the hospital came to Eddie and said that they had made a terrible mistake. Apparently, they had forgotten to check her gamma globulin. Eddie Fisher found the coincidence "chilling". That's baloney too. Eddie knew very well that my father was very intuitive and could easily diagnose over the phone. I will get to that in a separate chapter as well.

Now to get to some important internal stuff, I must comment on my father's ability to cure migraines. One of the reasons, besides my father's magnetic personality, that the family adored him so much, was because he invented a treatment, an amazing treatment for migraines from which my mother's side of the family suffered. He would inject you in the stomach and within five minutes the migraine would go away. The fact was that even though it sounded scary to be injected in the stomach, once the patient had the migraine, they were so ill, so sick, they were incapacitated, and in too much pain to be able to think straight. All they could think of was getting relief, any way they could. At those times specifically, receiving an injection in the stomach was not so farfetched. I was really the only chicken around. Everyone else had absolute faith in my father and accepted the injection without any hesitation. In later years, before it became very popular, he experimented with acupuncture. I saw him do it once in his office. I observed uninvited from one room away. The trouble was that every time he stuck the needle into the patient, I got totally squeamish. At that moment he proceeded to throw me out, naturally, accusing me of being hysterical. I suppose he felt I was bad for business, and yes, totally hysterical.

My father had many years of medical training in Germany at Heidelberg University and seemed to know everything there was to know about medicine.

Rocks and Crystals

*Rocks and crystals used in Papa's
medical solutions*

My father had this fascination with rocks, crystals, and ultraviolet rays. I can't make a distinction between them, however that does not mean there wasn't anything to it. My father seemed to have become obsessed by the stones in conjunction with his ultraviolet and fluorescent lights.

Vial and stone used in Papa's solution

He positioned them in such a way as to make the lights reflect upon the stones to make them look their brightest and to cause the vitamin mineral value to increase directly onto the stones. I thought it was their mineral possession which he extracted from the stones by pouring his oily vitamin solution onto them repeatedly and then heating them up. Somehow, I made the connection there just by watching him do that. Others thought he put the little stones, crushed into pieces, in his vials so that when he shook them, the liquid in the vials would mix properly. The rocks he worked with had to be melted down or crushed into powder. They possessed mineral qualities. My father put them into some of his vials which contained injectables. My father didn't have the ability to test metabolism.

Vial mixture with stone on lighted shelf

I seemed to think based upon what I saw that my father got these rocks for their vitamin and especially their mineral qualities, so that he could give his patients their injections with not only vitamins but minerals also. They were magnesium sulfate, quartz, and amethyst. Or that he would direct and position the lights at certain angles to make a rock glow and to enhance the color of the rock or stone in a vial. Suggesting that the light, after a period of time, would cause a reaction to occur to the minerals, rocks, and stones. Sometimes if his patient happened to be there while he was experimenting, he would allow them to participate in his experiment, and they would be amazed by the whole process even if they didn't fully understand it. They would say, "Isn't he brilliant?". They would even question me, "Aren't you amazed by all this?" to which my response, rather silently would have been, "I don't know, I don't understand any of this". I was always my father's greatest skeptic. Boy did he prove me wrong.

14

THE AMPHETAMINE ERA

— · —

Daddy changed as soon as he got involved with amphetamine. I was about ten years old and remember this clearly. My mother and I were invited, along with my father of course, to a patient's country estate somewhere upstate New York or Connecticut, it was at least a three-hour drive and very woodsy. It was a nice country home where we spent a nice weekend. At some point, my father excused himself to go into the guest house. This was a little remote house on their property. He ended up there for maybe 45 minutes. My mother said something, exactly what I don't remember; only that he was injecting himself with something. Well, he reappeared about 45 minutes later, something was different in his mood. He looked all flustered and grumpy. He couldn't find his vein and couldn't do the injection.

Soon after, maybe an hour later, we returned home. That's all I remember. It just wasn't a happy ending. I remember the whole amphetamine era beginning then. Perhaps it started earlier, but I didn't notice, and my father had not begun injecting himself until then. It was in those days that amphetamines were unknown and mostly unavailable in this country. He didn't have a steady supply. He got them sent from Germany.

For me, it began in ways which were correct, at least for me. Papas' assistant, Richard Bijon, gave me a shot after finding me stumbling about aimlessly in a stupor, the result of a strong allergy shot of antihistamines which weren't agreeing with me. I was about ten years old. After giving me the shot, I was almost instantaneously able to think clearly, thank God. Permeating from every sweat gland, duct known and otherwise unknown from one's body and every nerve ending. Simply being aware of its very existence in every inch of my body. That was what went through my mind after receiving an injection. I wouldn't venture to say that it was so much a momentary "rush" I was experiencing. However, if it was, so be it. It passed, and then it was on to business, whatever my activities were for that day, I was able to do them.

 If you want to ask me if I took drugs or if my father gave me any of his medicines, I would answer the following. He never trusted other doctors to treat me. He felt he was the only one capable of healing me properly, he was very strict and firm about that. Also, I was learning disabled. There was little known about ADHD. My mind would drift away, quite out of control constantly and return just as quickly. Having missed everything that was happening during that time, caused me to miss out on everything that was happening in my immediate surroundings. He gave me pills so that I could retain information. The pills he gave me enabled my concentration to increase from 15 minutes, if even that long, to three hours. I still have ADHD, however, aside from this writing I never venture to take on any great tasks since I know I probably can't tackle them.

 Last, but not least, it was amphetamine, which was the only treatment for the disorder that I had. My father knew it. He did not irresponsibly administer amphetamine to me. He gave it to me, not to get high, but to help me function normally and to be able to take exams in school. It stabilized me. Tasks, which most students found stressful and rather difficult, I couldn't attend to at all even if my life depended on it. My mind would just go blank altogether.

My father also gave me immune and gamma globulin monthly so I wouldn't get sick with every little bug that was going around. It helped, but I still got sick. He administered this intramuscularly. Also speaking of monthly, I would get great discomfort when my period was approaching. Sometimes I would suffer for one to two weeks, and it would be delayed. The times that I would have great discomfort, and my period would also be delayed in its arrival, my father would play the magician. He would give me an injection intramuscularly in his office. By the time I was ready to leave the office, five rooms later, I would already experience cramping, and my period would arrive within a day. God Bless him for that. The only problem was that I would get Dysmenorrhea, which means unbearable pain with the menstrual period. He gave me shots although they didn't take away any of the pain. He made Anna Tschausoff come over to stay with me while I tossed and turned writhing in pain. He didn't believe in giving me pain medicine.

And my father, being a "father", wouldn't allow me to take the appropriate (what I considered to be the appropriate) medicine for it which was Percocet. He feared it would be addictive and strictly forbid it, so I had to suffer as a result. That is until I took it upon myself to see another doctor who was willing to help me out of my misery and agreed to give me Percocet. My father found out and had his stoolie get into my apartment and confiscated the bottle of pills from my place. And no, I didn't appreciate that one damn bit!

Of course I didn't agree with him on these philosophies. My father had female patients who would get crazy before their menses. He developed a potion for them, put it in a vial, gave them syringes to take home so they could administer it themselves before the period, and on the first day to lessen the pain, and lessen the P.M.I. (premenstrual insanity). It worked for his patients. It didn't work for me.

Papa always had a steady supply of calcium ampoules, vitamin bottles and injectables, that sort of thing. I remember my father getting professional samples of medicines through the mail. Sometimes my mother and I would come to the office with him to open and we'd find the mail man had left professional samples, on one occasion a box of healthy cereal had arrived in the mail, Post Grape Nuts. I took it home and tried it. It turned out to be the best, most delicious healthy stuff I'd ever had in my life, it was phenomenal. I had it with cold milk.

Getting back to my father's medicine, which he created in his laboratory on East 72nd street and made for his patients and for me. His vitamins, oral drops, tasted so delicious, so good, I took them maybe when I was six years old until I was at least eighteen and then I stopped for a year because I went away to Europe. When I returned, I started taking them again. I doubt there was any amphetamine in them from the time I was in high school because I ate like a pig. The food was great, and the country air gave me quite an appetite. I was very active physically and I was always very hyper. Since I always ate a lot and took the oral drops each day, I really doubt there was any amphetamine in them.

My father treated many patients with a multitude of problems. That remains a fact! A lady once came to see him after having suffered a severe rash on her back after she'd been forced to put some lotion on herself for a TV commercial. He had to give her cortisone injections and a salve. He treated her for several months to get rid of her rash.

I made some observations of patients who seemed different on the medicines. In one case a non-celebrity invited us, my parents and I over to their house. They were very hospitable, they wanted us to spend a few days and cook for us; really show us a good time. When we arrived, they kind of gave us the impression (not on amphetamine) unwittingly as though we were an imposition on them. And that their offer was insincere. For a young naïve girl which I was, to digest all that, being very shy as I was, was a bit much to handle. My father fluffed it off offering excuses for them. "Oh, that poor couple, they are working so hard to make ends meet, and her father just died, so now she has to work twice as hard". All sympathy stories, I was given those by my father. Perhaps they were true. Perhaps they and the amphetamine were both the truth. Either way, I was thrown off by this. I mean, it was the amphetamine which encouraged them to be extra hospitable with us in the first place and to invite us. It was the lack of it, days later, which caused them to relent.

Bewildered by all the comings and goings at home, at the apartment, and the constant commotion at the office, being a little girl, I was seemingly quite beside myself often. I wasn't one to ask questions, but when I did, my father gave me rather abrupt or sympathetic responses, that were mostly sympathetic to the patients. There were some instances of bazaar behavior on the part of some of the patients that had me wondering what on Earth was going on. It wasn't the amphetamine or the effects of the treatment that were so odd. It was seemingly odd behavior, the neurosis, the before the treatment insanities which the patients exhibited that were really off the wall. This happened rarely. However, when it did, I was puzzled, mystified.

Some patient's years later blamed my father for their psychosis. I wonder whether they might have been experimenting with cocaine on their own, having figured they could hide it well and get away with it and then blame my father for their rude, strange, and lewd behavior. They didn't fool me. Some of these patients, some of the well-known clientele, although not celebrities, hairdressers, some entertainers were dabbling with cocaine before seeing my father and after seeing him. I knew a few of them were, but this was many years later. Certainly, it can be said they were dabbling with cocaine around the same time that they were seeing or being treated by my father. The amazing thing was, if a patient came in, kind of spaced out and off the wall so to speak, he would give them a shot with amphetamine and massive doses of vitamins and whatever else to bring them back down to Earth; stabilize them. I was personally aware of this. He would also warn them that if they went somewhere else to be treated and it didn't coincide with his treatment, he wouldn't medicate them. I was not present for these confidential confrontations.

15

KATHERINE DUNHAM

Both patient and dear friend from the mid 1940's until my father's death in 1979. She was mostly known for being a dancer, she was also a choreographer, composer, and song writer. She taught all the black dancers how to dance. She made movies all over the world and toured the country teaching dance until shortly before her death in 2006. She invited her daughter and me to attend one of her dance classes. It was African style. I knew her as a dancer in movies because I saw her on a movie set preparing to film and as mother to Marie Christine Dunham Pratt. Katherine, Ms. Dunham as I called her, worshipped and adored my father. She felt she accomplished her greatest work with my father's injections. She trusted him to give her whatever he felt she needed. This she told me herself. I have also an in-depth fascinating interview with her, about her and mostly about my father.

During the time my father treated Katherine Dunham, things were so hurried, rushed. I never quite understood why. Although I knew that she was a very famous and important person and a very strict dance teacher, I didn't quite understand just what her accomplishments were. My father not only treated her so she could keep up her monumentally busy schedule. He treated her for her knee and joint pain so she could keep up with and continue her demanding dance schedule. She was working on big movie sets creating dance scenes magnificently. She had a lovely daughter my age whom she sent to us so I would have a playmate. We got along well together.

Katherine Dunham benefited from my father's arthritis treatments. He also treated Multiple Sclerosis patients. Ms. Dunham developed a lasting friendship with my father. In later years, the early 70's, Ms. Dunham brought gems to my father wrapped in a cloth. They possessed spiritual powers, energies.

My father was really into that. He really appreciated her bringing them to him. They were all given to him to protect him and to give him spiritual guidance. She wanted to share good things with him.

16

RONNY GRAHAM

—·—

*(Left to right) Papa, Nina, and Jill
visiting Ronny Graham in Cape Cod,
early 1960s*

I had this incredible advantage when I was growing up. I had all these celebrities with their talents all around me. Most of them were very musical. It went from Vaudeville to Broadway, sometimes on the same day.

Ronny Graham would come over to see my dad. He called my father "my dad", not doctor or Max, just my dad because he'd be speaking to me. He'd visit my dad, come out, and say, "Hi Jill" and not another word. He'd sit down at the piano and start playing and singing, hammer out a few tunes, abruptly stop, spin around, crack a sick joke, then he'd counter with more chords and crack jokes one right after the other, and all at the same time in unison. I loved it when he sang a song and in the middle of it break into a joke whose lyrics were part of the song. His timing, rhythm, and style, it all jived. He wrote comedy skits and accompanied them with upbeat, jazzy music making for a great sound. Some were tunes he was doing for a current Broadway show, naturally back in the late 50's, some he just remembered and liked and decided to play at that moment and we were just lucky enough to be his audience. Some of them he had written himself and was trying them out so he could hear them on us as an audience. Ronny had such an extraordinary personality, what a character, and he was a professional singer, pianist, and actor as well. He was a one man show.

His wife, Ellen Hanley, would come over with him occasionally. He would coax her to do a duet with him. Sometimes she did. She was also a Broadway star, actress, and singer in her own right. Ronnie was so much fun. He'd make you feel like singing and jumping and happy, just like that. He had this nervous, hyper energy, and he used it to create, and entertain. In my opinion, he was one of the most giving, sharing entertainers around. He just loved to put on an impromptu show. He was one of the best entertainers around.

Ronnie seemed to be very absorbed by his own creations. Through all his personal trials and tribulations, he was an entertainer. He performed and entertained through thick and thin. No matter how difficult his life and personal life became, he always managed to entertain everyone with his song and dance routine effortlessly. He wrote a piece, and it went like this: "I went swimming in the river on the Island of Ceylon. I lost my upper plate. I don't know why. So won't you please drop me a line, if you should happen to find my Bridge on the River Kwai, oh my! My Bridge on The River Kwai". That was Ronnie Graham.

I found out after a while that the more talented a person was, the more complicated they were and their lives as well. It was like a spec of genius he had in him and the problems that accompanied it, the neuroses etc. But with Ronnie, the music man one hardly noticed the problems because his assets, his music, his comic genius shone through every time and all the time it never failed.

Ellen was more of a devoted wife when I was around, and they were working on adding children to their repertoire as well. She didn't perform nearly as often as Ronnie did. She saved her energy for rehearsals and her shows. She was always doing a show on Broadway. She really had an incredible voice when she sang ("The Boyfriend" on Broadway) and she had the prettiest sweetest smile ever. And an enchanting personality as well. She had a stepson, Ronnie

Jr., whom she doted on so lovingly. She was very maternal. I found Ellen and Ronnie to be a very interesting show business couple. Early on though I could not understand how they could fit children in with their very busy schedules, working nights, sleeping days, or vice versa. Apparently, they managed.

17

ELLEN HANLEY

— • —

*(Left to right) Jill and Nina visiting
Ellen Hanley at their summer home
in Cape Cod, early 1960s*

My parents and I were invited to see a Broadway show one evening because a patient and friend, Ellen Hanley, wife of Ronnie Graham was performing in "First Impressions". She may have been an understudy that night. I noticed as she sang, although she sang and performed beautifully, she kept pumping one fist, then the other, unconsciously aware that she was doing it. I was personally rather surprised and disturbed by it. I thought maybe she had had a treatment from papa and was given too much in her shot. Papa may have been showing his gratitude in having been invited to see the show and out of that gratitude felt the need to give her a special shot.

It wasn't always Papa's fault. Sometimes the patient overreacted, exaggerated their ailments, or claimed they needed a treatment of specific properties. Often, he took their word for it. Ellen was a very sensitive and emotional person anyway and a good actress and excellent singer, but she was very excitable and very nervous. That night as she moved around on stage and sang, her hands kept opening and closing. I don't think that was part of the script. I sort of thought it was papa's fault.

18

HERB AND LILO RAYMOND

— • —

Herb Raymond was the most charismatic, handsome, and physically buff young man I'd ever seen. He was svelte, slim, and well-toned. Running around on the tennis court, playing, giving lessons to me and my family, and to many of his clients. He made me run for those balls. No laziness was tolerated on Herbs tennis court. He was strict, although nice, and a gentleman. Lilo was German like my family, very sweet, and had the cutest way of saying hello, half cooing and half in a laugh and smile, very affectionate. She could be a little strict, but mostly gentle and sweet, and she was very cute and pretty. Lilo and Herb were such a great couple both on and off the court.

My father went weekly for lessons. My grandparents took me twice weekly during the summer, fall and spring seasons. My grandparents played on their own and with me. We always went together and took turns on the court. Often while my father had his lesson, my mother would take me for a grand walk in the park below the court. They had a lovely park with a lake, a duck pond, a picnic area, and a promenade. It also had a windmill and papermill that had been closed for years.

I noticed both my parents bonded with Lilo and Herb, they were very friendly with them and Lilo's mother. Papa was an avid swimmer and tennis player, like Lilo and Herb. They had a lot in common. My father worked so hard that sometimes he went out to them to play tennis in the seasonable weather. Mostly spring, summer and fall. Often, I was out in Point Lookout with my grandparents, so they would take me on their way back to the city, during the week and on weekends. You see, I had a pretty normal life.

My father treated Herb, gave him vitamins and energy. After a while, Lilo received treatment so she could bear a child. He had helped other women in that specific area successfully. However, with Lilo he was not successful. After a while they split up. The treatments were secondary, very few and far between. After they retired and gave up the courts, my parents continued their friendship with them. My father remained friends with Herb until he (my father) passed away. Lilo had died from cancer years earlier.

Lilos accent (kind of German) and manner of speaking will always stand out in my memory as the most darling, affectionate European purring speaking voice ever. She was a very artsy, practical, realistic, and sophisticated individual, but her character always broke through and made her charming with such a heartwarming and gentle smile. I'll always miss her. Herb is still alive today, I believe. Although sorry to say, we've been out of touch for years. There were times when I could honestly say I was surrounded by normalcy. Being in the presence of Lilo and Herb was one of them. The only real semblance of normalcy.

19

ELLI MARCUS

Jill visiting Elli Marcus, mid 1950s

Elli was a photographer and a graphologist. She analyzed handwriting and was able to determine if a person was trustworthy. She was my mother's dearest friend and like a godmother to me. She had the greatest sense of humor and the funniest laugh. Before she passed away, she instructed her daughter-in-law to buy me a beautiful gold chain for my birthday. It was a heavy gold chain with big links. I was presented with it at her funeral. I broke down in tears at her thoughtfulness.

She adored my father. She thought everything he said and did was hysterical. She was very close and friendly with mommy. She would defend my father to my mother, constantly. She made great lunches for me the few times I accepted her invitations.

20

MABEL MERCER

Mabel Mercer was my dear mother's favorite singer. This is my beginning statement. She was a "Durable Underground Doyenne". Ms. Mercer performed for years at the Downstairs at the Upstairs. Then she moved one flight up to the Upstairs at The Downstairs, same place just one flight up.

Mabel had her own style of singing. I can't quite explain it. She had a deep crackly voice. She crackled when she sang and when she spoke, that is she was a "Basso Profundo" who put words to her own style of singing and melody. She had a Cockney-British accent, and nightclubs were her forte. Life in the country on her farm in Connecticut was the other part of her life. I remember of course her homemade blueberry muffins, never too sweet, and she used real blueberries which she picked from her garden on her estate. She made the muffins herself when she was home in the country.

I went to see her perform once for my mother. My mother simply adored her. Her singing was a kind of jazz like style. She was a darling person, absolutely quaint and charming. She was naturally very witty and absolutely adored my father.

I must especially mention Mabel because I couldn't digest her style, sound of music. It was a style I simply couldn't learn to appreciate. I think I had difficulty distinguishing the words she was singing due to her style; she trembled her voice somewhat differently from that of other singers. But I felt that was one of the qualities which made her sound so unique and so well liked (berümht). Mabel always sat when she sang. She had a sort of Katherine Hepburn sound to her voice, and that was how she sang. Her head didn't shake, her voice did. My mother, whose tastes I valued and treasured, and whose styles I admired, to my mother Mabel Mercer was her favorite. In that case I fully respected her feelings about Mabel.

Her accompanist was Bobby Short. He just recently died in 2005. She always spoke of him fondly. I have an article about Mabel, a collage of newspaper clippings about her at various times which she gave my father and which I now have. Someone wrote, "Mabel has a poet's appreciation of words and a Shakespearean actor's flair for enunciating them."

I wrote the above in memory of my dear mother who really adored Mabel. Her openings were the only ones my mother went out of her way to attend.

– God bless you, Mabel

21

ELEMENTARY SCHOOL

My parents had me enrolled in Hebrew school when I was about six years old. I couldn't handle it. After a while of being bewildered and overwhelmed, and the letters looking Chinese to me, I presented my parents with an ultimatum. It was either Hebrew School or regular school. I didn't know that the law stated that I had to attend regular school. They promptly took me out of Hebrew school so that I could concentrate on my regular studies. Besides, I resented having my weekends interrupted by Saturday classes.

Nina (back center) and Dr. Thelma Williams (front center, white necklace), mid 1950s

I was sent to private schools in the city until I was 14. First, it was early October when my parents and I had returned from a rather lengthy trip to France when I was six years old. Since we returned late in the first semester, Papa telephoned a friend named Thelma Williams who was working for the Board of Education and the Children's Center uptown in Manhattan. She was glad to be of assistance. Luckily, she got me into the private Hebrew school, Beth Hayelet. It was already in session.

My parents took me for the first time. I had a wonderfully nice teacher named Minna Shapiro. She immediately walked me over to a table and sat me with my classmates to get me acquainted. She was great to welcome me and make me feel at home and comfortable. She got me busy with the activities that the children were working on at the table. I forgot all about mom and dad.

Since I was so shy, the girls began giggling as little girls did in those days. Then it became contagious, and I started giggling also. It went back and forth. I think at some point we forgot whatever we were doing and just kept giggling. We must have almost peed in our pants because I remember running to the bathroom to pee.

Another thing happened, I had a valued photo of my parents in Paris with palm leaves in the background outside a restaurant, one of my favorite photos at the time. I remember having it in my hand and carrying it with me to the bathroom where I put it near the ledge of the window for safekeeping until I came out. Somehow it mysteriously vanished. I stopped and looked everywhere, I found it nowhere. I was baffled and confused. I thought someone had sneaked into the bathroom and taken it. Why? I don't know. I never found it again.

Back in the classroom, I enjoyed the company of my classmates and Minna Shapiro. I believe we began to learn numbers in first grade. I didn't care much about the academics. I liked my friends and giggling. I also met two dear lifetime friends, well one anyway, who would soon become my best friends for life. They were Anita and Lola Frankel, sisters. We had many wonderful times together spanning seven years, so that was a long time. Then I went away to boarding school, we kept in touch, sort of. I was not so nice to one of them, regretfully, however this book is not about me, it is about my father. I was a rebellious child. I still am now.

I also went to another private school in New York which was horrible, Bentley. Their east side school I went to during 2nd grade. I don't remember and don't want to. Their school on the west side was on 86th street, I went there maybe 4th through 7th grade. It was like a scene out of a psych ward in Belleview Hospital except it was a school on the upper west side in Manhattan. Some of the students were acting out gross impulses. They must have needed attention. Other students had no behavioral skills. I won't go on. The teachers were out of work actors. My father was so nice to the school. If his patients showered him with flowers such as orchids, he gave them to me to present to the students in my class. I hated doing that because I really felt all the students were awful and undeserving of anything, especially gifts. We took a bus trip with Shirley McLaine and her daughter, who was a student, to the taping of

Peter Pan with Mary Martin, our school was the audience. The students were gifted orchids for attending. Then happily on to Windsor Mountain for 8th through 12th grade. Happiness is a soft pillow.

My mother tutored me early on as we drove to Point Lookout. She knew I was not doing well academically, so she elected to tutor me every opportunity she had, such as driving out to our country home. She would drill me on the multiplication tables which I finally ventured to memorize, especially the 9's, so I could remember them for sure. And if I had to learn a small part for a play we had in school, or if I was having a particularly difficult time with some aspects of my studies, which we were to be tested on the very next day in school, she would softly whisper the information to me in my sleep the night before my play or exam. I don't know if that system worked though, I have no proof either way. I certainly don't recall my results the next day. I do know mommy had to hire quite a few tutors for me while I was in school in New York, meaning from 2nd to 6th grade, somewhere in there. That was all I remembered. Now back to my father. He seemed to enchant everyone he encountered, not with drugs but with his charisma. Including his knowledge of life, enthusiasm to take on all the challenges life has to offer. He always told me he wanted me to act constructively and productively. He said I owed that to myself.

22

BRACES

— • —

I must devote an entire segment to the saga of my braces. I wore those bloody contraptions for at least seven years. I had the helmet at night, the hooks in my mouth upper to lower being connected by rubber band attachments. I had no idea how much these braces cost. My parents never mentioned a word of that to me.

They took me to a dentist (butcher) named Dr. Pearlman in downtown Manhattan. He pulled my baby teeth out, five of them without anesthetics and when I began turning green from the pain, my mother demanded he stop. Coming home from the dentist in a yellow cab, all I could think of, in my state of utter shock and pain, was the trauma of what he had put me through. It was unfortunate that he had to pull my baby teeth out since they wouldn't come out on their own. My teeth were a mess.

After all my baby teeth were removed, my parents took me to an orthodontist on Central Park West to have braces put in. A year or so later in 1958, we took a trip to Hollywood to see Eddie Fisher, Van Cliburn, and of course my favorite, Debbie Reynolds.

We were invited to attend a big function and concert at the Hollywood Bowl one night for Van Cliburn's performance. I told my parents I could not attend the concert with braces on my teeth. Suddenly my parents made an appointment with an orthodontist in Los Angeles and had my braces removed. At the time, I had no idea how expensive it was. When we returned to New York, my poor dear mother had to take me to our orthodontist to have new ones put in. That was the one and only time that happened.

23

BEATRICE MOORE

Beatrice, who happened to be my mother's best friend, was a big pain in the ass. Having known my parents from when they were in Europe, she established herself here as my mother's "best friend". She came for a visit to see my mother at least once a week. She was a former ballerina who dangled and displayed her fancy schmancy charm bracelet making it chime in the air. I would come home from school and find her lying on my mother's bed, taking over my mother's life, and in my opinion her breathing space.

Her husband Carroll was low key, definitely the nicer of the two. He was charming, friendly, and rather quiet. She was definitely the vocal one, very snobby and very opinionated. She was "a bitch on wheels". I think that's where the saying came from. Amazingly, her children were darling. How that happened must have been due to the tender loving presence of her dear husband.

Years later, after Carroll died, my mother asked my father to give her a job at his office as a receptionist, which he did. Several years following that my mother died. I was told a while later Beatrice became infatuated with my father. Years later she told me when the AMA came to remove his license from the wall of his office, she felt so bad, she almost cried.

Beatrice and I did not get along. We never got along. In later years when I was about 18, she accused me of being so high that I was "hanging from chandeliers". The funny thing was, I was accused of being spaced out and off the wall by my own friends when I wasn't on medication. It was when I was on medication that I was told I became stabilized, that I had stopped bouncing off the walls. But that's another story, now back to Beatrice.

Unfortunately, I must admit that appearance wise she was pretty, very chic, and high class in her dress, makeup, and fur coat. She was also well-bred, well-educated with European charm and had a very sweet smile. But mostly she was a bitch. I hate that word, but I do use it for very worthy individuals, very few, however, Thank God for that. But there were a few associated with and around my father. He seemed to attract them like magnets.

Beatrice behaved in such a way as to seemingly convince all those around her that she was "It", the best. How my mother tolerated her was always baffling to me. Many years later when my mother needed a shoulder to lean on, Beatrice, it appeared, was not forthcoming. Either my mother had realized how infatuated Beatrice had become with my father, or my mother had chosen not to entrust Beatrice with her most guarded secrets.

24

Harvey Mann

Harvey came into our lives with much drama and flair. He was a nice, simple, decent looking man who helped in my father's office from when I was about eight years old. There are pictures of us at the Bronx Zoo. Harvey liked being photographed. He was very entertaining. Somehow, he was connected with show business. He had a friend, a lover, Bob Shane, who was bisexual. I know because I knew some women whom he dated. Harvey spent a lot of time with my mother while my father was working at the office. I would see him at home with my mother, lying on her bed with her socializing. Harvey wore thick rimmed glasses but managed to be handsome. He was a showoff too. We took a trip to Puerto Rico. Harvey, Valerie Jordan and I, we had a great time. We drove through El Yunque and spotted a man walking down the road appearing to be eating a tree branch. I thought the man had gone mad. I learned that he was eating pure sugar cane. What a lesson I learned that day. Anyway, the trip was fun, and Harvey had everyone dangling their legs and feet out the convertible window. Harvey was fun, fun, and more fun.

He took me to his mother's apartment one day for a visit. She was very poor, simple, and Italian. She was nice. Harvey was loud and, well, a blistering homosexual. He tried to pick up just about everyone. Yet it was apparent that he and Bob Shane were an item. Years later, after my father's license was revoked, my father phoned me to tell me that some news reporters contacted Harvey to speak about my father and Harvey told them he had a homosexual affair with my father while my mother was at home alone awaiting my father's return from the office. My father called to let me know what Harvey had accused him of and wanted me to know it wasn't true. I was told by a friend years ago of an article in JAMA Magazine which stated that men who indulge in amphetamine can have libidinal tendencies, meaning can resort to homosexual impulses during and after having taken the amphetamine. So, my point is if it was true, so what. Actually, Harvey wasn't that bad at all. But I side with my father. If he said it wasn't true, then it wasn't.

Harvey helped out at the office for a while also. He became a male nurse. He loved that job. He also enjoyed traveling with me. I lost touch with him when I entered my teens.

25

Van Cliburn

Jill and Van Cliburn mid-flight, mid 1950s

A classical pianist, Van first came to New York at age 20 in 1954 with his mother to appear at Carnegie Hall playing Rachmaninoff concerto #2 in a competition. His mother taught him how to play piano when he was a small child; I believe he was 3 years old. He was a patient of my father and became friends. His manager Royal Marks was a friend of my parents. On occasion he came over to sleep at our home.

Jill (front left, pattern dress), Nina (back, black dress), Van (back right seated, white shirt, dark tie) visiting the Jacobson's in NYC, mid 1950s

Vân played and practiced all the time, except when he slept. While he was in New York, he had an open invitation to practice at Steinway Hall. He played the most beautiful classical music. I used to sit and watch him play with such intensity. Playing the piano came naturally to him. At first it seemed he played like a robot, which is an awful thing to say, but once he really got into it, his mind and body really took over the piece that he was playing, and his emotion and the music became one. He was so focused on his music and on playing, that once he got the feel of it, he was in fantasy land.

There were times when an almost sad expression would come over his face and then the most tender melody would come from beyond his fingers. He was so sensitive that he played what he felt so when he played it, it sounded that much more beautiful. One could tell how much feeling he put into playing. Every time his fingers touched the keys one could feel his emotion pouring onto the keyboard. And that sound was beautiful. If one could put words into his feelings, thoughts, and music, it would have played as deeply as poetry.

Jill and Van Cliburn while visiting the Jacobson's in NYC, August 1958

We got a cat and named him Amahl, from "Amahl and the Night Visitors" Opera after Van because Van came so often late at night. He slept mostly in my room in the middle of the night, after he returned from a rigorous night of practicing at Steinway Hall. That was when he came to our apartment to sleep. There was a spare bed in my room where he slept. He got treatment from my father, especially when practicing Rachmaninoff for his Carnegie Hall recital which made his schedule so hectic that he wouldn't sleep adequately at night. He was terribly driven. He stayed with us for several nights from April to June at our apartment on East 73rd street. Mostly he stayed at a local hotel with his mother. He practiced playing on our piano in our living room. It was at his recital at Carnegie Hall, on May 19th, 1958, that my parents and I sat in front of the television set, and I had my very first glass of Champagne. I was 11 years old.

Once I walked into a room at my father's office on East 72nd Street, and there was Van lying on the patient table. His chest was bare. My father was in the process of removing a pimple from his chest. I almost got sick. I could never handle that sort of stuff. The whole time he was in New York he was treated by my father, and it did not affect his piano playing. I know he came for treatment when he had personal family tragedies. He didn't need treatment from my father to play piano. He was a very sensitive and emotional person so when something personal upset him, he really became unraveled. One could also tell he was brought up very disciplined and strict. As a person, Van was very kind and polite, always the southern gentleman.

26

MAYA DEREN AND TEIJI ITO

She was beautiful, with fluffy wild frizzy red hair and the cutest face, strongly resembling Jocelyn Wildenstein but "au natural". Like the actress Melina Mercouri in the movie "Never on Sunday", a sexy French summer blouse, X-rated sexy. She always wore a leotard and a full or tight long skirt and gypsy hoop earrings, a lit cigarette, and backless high heels. She had wild wide cat's eyes with luscious red lips. When she walked down the street looking as risqué as she did, no one ever said a word. She was quiet, had sort of a strange voice, and she spoke with a deep rattly whisp. She was an artist, musician, a cat lady, and a good witch. That was Maya. She was so gentle and very maternal and sweet to me, and with everyone.

She gave us our first kitten. We named him "Amahl" from "Amahl and The Night Visitors" the Opera. We named him that because of a joke my mother made at the time. He was black and Van Cliburn used to show up in the middle of the night for a decent night's sleep. So, we named the kitten Amahl after him. My parents and I visited her often in her apartment. Teiji Ito was always there. She would come over occasionally and take me for a lovely afternoon walk; I was about seven years old. Maya was Jewish, I learned that her father was a psychiatrist who was employed in Russia. No wonder she bonded so well with my father.

Maya held spiritual gatherings at her Greenwich Village apartment often and filmed them. They were like witchcraft séances. She was into Voodoo and Witchcraft. She was on this eerie wavelength. It all had to do with the beating of drums. It put her into a hypnotic state. She moved and swayed, tranced, and entranced by it all. Drums captivated her, the sounds, the vibration. It put her in a trance-like state. Teiji Ito played the drums. She got involved with Voodoo and dance movement. She was an experimenter, as much as my father was in his scientific medical practice and attempted to get grants so she could afford the supplies that she needed to experiment with methods of filmmaking. She applied to the J.S. Guggenheim Foundation in 1946 for financial assistance to make an experimental motion picture. She was granted the Guggenheim award but no money towards her costly filmmaking project. She was quoted as saying "People didn't realize how much work and money went into the making of a film".

 She would hold dances, not as we know them today. Dances where she would have non-restrictive movement. Where people were in a trance state, moving about within space, getting acquainted with their own beings and their own surroundings. There would be a simplicity about it all, a natural quality about it, yet they were all obviously in a trance just wandering about aimlessly. She would sit on a platform truck stand with a camera and capture every angle of this movement. This was one of her experiments.

Recently in January 2003, I was well into writing this book and my memory wasn't serving me well. I read the newspapers, although at times I feel it takes away from my work. However, one day I was going through the prior week's paper. During the process I found a Post newspaper cover ad (Pulse section) displaying a generous photo of Maya. I suddenly became very excited and energized. I read the article carefully and learned that the Anthology Archives in the East Village were showing movies written, narrated by and starring Maya Deren. I went enthusiastically to see "In the Mirror". It did more for my memory than I could have ever imagined.

 One of the rituals where she filmed people in motion, which was shown in "In the Mirror", included Buffie Johnson. Originally, I recall my mother was also in the scene, although this time I didn't see her. I believe Katherine Dunham introduced Maya to my father. I was about seven years old when we flew to the movie set she was working on and met Katherine's daughter, Marie Christine. Maya was traveling and working with Katherine at that time. I figured she introduced Maya to my father.

What concerned me at first was the man being interviewed in "In the Mirror" stated that Maya didn't know she was getting amphetamine. It was also stated that she drank a lot of coffee. At first, I was upset and momentarily shocked to hear the man say that Maya felt betrayed by my father whom she claims told her she was being given vitamins, that the amphetamine was not acknowledged. Was she on my father's treatment? Yes, she was, she loved them. They made her feel wonderful. Between the constant coffee she drank and my father's injections, especially considering her very hectic schedule, it was not extreme. It balanced itself out. I suspect because she was drinking so much coffee that she knew she was getting amphetamine, which I believe indirectly drove her to Haiti and Voodoo. Even though she denied willfully or knowingly using amphetamine, I believe she was fully aware of what she was doing. I believe there was a connection between her amphetamine use, cocaine use, which she indulged in on her own, and her obsession with witchcraft. It was a vicious cycle. Cocaine and amphetamine have been known to cause desires in people to go into seances, witchcraft and voodoo.

I also suspect, hopefully I'm wrong, that she had serious money issues and went for days without food, all in the name of amphetamine. Filmmaking is also expensive; we all know that. She was busy making films, that takes a lot of energy and money. Since it was thrice mentioned that Maya was heavily into coffee, she even stored her film in Madaglia Doro coffee tins. She was spiraling out of control due to her dependence on amphetamine. Whether my father was exclusively supplying it to her, or she had other suppliers, only she and Teiji Ito would know that. I don't know whether my father was responsible for her initial addiction, or whether she was ultimately responsible for her own undoing.

Years ago, the Ku Klux Klan was accused of taking cocaine during and after their cult rituals. What Maya Deren was doing had nothing to do with the KKK; however, she was involved with rituals, dance movement, and drumbeats. I don't think she would have gotten so obsessed with Voodoo had she not been indulging in amphetamine. I believe she knew exactly what was happening and agreed with it fully. She noticed how much she could accomplish while on it. She wouldn't have acknowledged it to anyone. This was her work that was affected by this, to her in a positive way.

Teiji Ito

I am writing so little about him, yet he was big as life. Besides being a very talented musician who played drums and guitar, he was also Maya Deren's boyfriend before becoming her husband. He was always present and playing the drums or guitar when we came to visit. He was much younger than she was. She made films and he made music. He composed most of the background music for Mayas films and played Jazz and Blues. He was so sweet to my parents and me.

27

PAUL GAVERT

Paul was first a longtime friend, then he became a patient. He was by profession "The singing coach to the Broadway stars", such as Betty Buckley who won her Tony Award for "Cats", the long running musical and for her song "Memory", and numerous others.

In my earliest recollection, I was maybe nine years old, Paul was married to the mother of his daughter Gail. Busy working, he would come and go. Then they got a divorce. Apparently, he was the patient, not his wife who was a hopeless alcoholic. After the divorce, my mother and I didn't see Paul for quite some time.

My mother had been attending an art class in the city. She had established a bonding friendship with one of the students. Periodically they went out for coffee during their break from class. After a while, my mother invited her over to our house for tea. Her name was Olive Lyford, they began getting together weekly.

One day Olive mentioned to my mother that she had met this dashing beau and was considering marrying him. Being cordial as she was and anxious to meet this beau, my mother spoke to my father, and they decided to invite Olive and her beau over for tea to welcome them into our inner circle.

Olive and her beau arrived and walked through our lobby, at which moment he turned to her and said, "You know, I have some friends who live in this building", to which she asked where they lived. He told her but she hadn't yet been to our apartment. Well, the next question from Olive was "What is their name?". To which he replied, Max and Nina Jacobson, from attending art gallery openings. Well Olive was astonished to hear it. By the time they arrived at our door, Paul and Olive were both hysterically laughing. She was so surprised and amused by it all.

They arrived at our apartment, and everyone being very surprised, had a good happy laugh. "Small world" someone said. As it turned out, Paul was Olive's beau, and they did get married. She was a bit older than he was, fifteen years older, but they got along smashingly. And Olive became the stepmother to Gail.

We all sort of became one happy family. And my mother became much better friends with Olive. I kind of liked them as a couple. He was so young looking, he had a very distinguished baby face, and he was so handsome. And Olive, being fifteen years his senior, which was very unusual in those days, had a very artsy intellectual look about her. She was a very nice-looking lady, a Quaker, and very much appeared as such.

They made a very interesting, lovely pair. When they first got engaged, because their age difference was so unusual in those days, I took an interest in them as a pair. I guess it was slightly out of curiosity. It was nice to observe how they complemented each other.

Through the years he gradually became involved in her appreciation of art and her life of attending art gallery openings. I once went to Paul for voice lessons because I was told that I could sing and had a nice voice. I went to see him for voice appraisal and for voice lessons and asked him to advise me as to what I should do with my singing voice. I wanted to know from him if I had a decent singing voice. His response was "yes". He gave me one lesson and told me that I had a good voice and that I sang on key. He offered to train me for singing in bars while sitting on a piano, but I turned him down only because singing in bars would only make me lose respect for men. God forbid!

While I was in his studio for the lesson, he offered to teach me something that my father had taught him. He really idolized my father. A process by which the pupil pulls his or her tongue out of their mouth with a handkerchief and takes the index finger and the thumb and holds the tongue out and massages the back of the tongue gently with the index finger, avoiding choking. He told me it relaxes the vocal cords. My father and Paul tried it with a patient who stuttered, and it helped with the stuttering.

Paul remained a steadfast supporter and friend till the end. His wife, Olive, adopted his daughter Gail when he and Olive first got married. Years later when she became sick with Alzheimer's, Paul put her in a nursing home. He and my father remained in touch. He and his daughter attended my father's annual Passover seders together over the years.

My last story, a true story, is the last I had heard of Paul. We had always teased him about his baby face and how young he always looked. He never seemed to age at all. Anyway, we constantly teased him about his youthful look. After he died, I asked my stepmother what happened. She told me he went to have a facelift and afterwards he came home and suffered a major heart attack from the surgery and died. The fact that he even felt the need for a facelift with his baby face was hysterical to me. That baffled me. I must say however, he was quite a high society gentleman.

28

MARLENE DIETRICH

— • —

German singer and actress Marlene Dietrich entertained American troops in North Africa and Europe from 1944 to 1945. In 1950 she was awarded an honor by the French. In 1953 and 1954 she made appearances as a show performer at the Sahara Hotel in Las Vegas and at Café de Paris in London. In 1960 she published a book, "Dietrich's ABC's".

In between she did many shows and movies and was a patient and also a friend. She was always smoking and talked very seriously, had a strong European accent, and spoke in a deep voice. Her mouth was in a frowning position just like on pictures with tons of lipstick on. Apparently, the doctor threw her out in 1969 when she started drinking, something the doctor forbid from his patients. She was working with Burt Bacharach on "Raindrops" and to calm her down, Burt suggested she have a drink. This is what terminated the long-lasting rapport between Marlene and the doctor. She came to the office on East 72nd street from 1954 through at least the mid 60's.

Marlene arrived for her treatment at my father's office at 155 East 72nd Street, usually on Sunday afternoons wearing light blue silk pajamas so that no one would recognize her. That was her brilliant disguise. I mean who would think in those days that such a famous star would dare to be seen in their pajamas. It was very clever. On the sidewalk on a weekend afternoon around 4:30 p.m., not a soul in sight – everyone gone for the weekend, I was skipping happily outside 114 East 72nd Street while Marlene Dietrich and my mother waited outside for my father to open the office. I was about eight years old. Marlene would pace back and forth smoking a cigarette while she waited for my father to prepare his treatment room for her. I don't know why my father had to see her on Sundays. It wasn't often but when he did, it interrupted my weekend because it meant my parents and I had to leave the country earlier to get to the office on time. That was one of the few times I remember being present when my father actually unlocked and opened his office. Once inside the office Marlene had to wait in the reception area for Papa to get the treatment room ready for her. To me it seemed to take at least 45 minutes. Usually, he was already there when I arrived.

She baked Beef Stroganoff for her family, her children and grandchildren and made extra which she brought us, it was enough for a week. It was absolutely delicious. My aunt told me she came to the office one day and saw Marlene scrubbing the office floor clean.

29

Jack Garfein and Carroll Baker

Jack Garfein was a flourishing director and worked briefly with his wife, Carroll Baker, whom he met at The Actor's Studio. Baby Doll had just happened around the time I met them. He had taken credit for his brilliant idea to put an enormous poster of her in baby doll pajamas in Times Square. As far as I knew, he directed several plays in New York in the early 70's and went on to teach acting in more recent years.

Carroll was a patient, mostly because Jack was a good friend and patient of my father. She had just completed "Baby Doll". At that time, she was considered to be very "Risqué". She was very pretty, and didn't have a sexy whispery voice, but a deeper more intelligent sounding clear voice, a southern country type, New England accent with a French twist style, which seemed rather unusual for a sexy blonde, but refreshingly nice and interesting. Don't ask me what that's all about, but that's how I would describe her manner of speaking and style. Personally, I found her to be nice.

The first time I met her was in 1955 during a house call my father was making. She was sitting in a chair at a table hand stitching her wedding gown which to me was very impressive. Around that time, my mother and I paid her another visit and watched her stitching lace to her white silk wedding gown. The details she was attending to looked so extensive. And she stitched so happily, she did it like it was just a hobby. My mother and I had never seen anyone personally stitching their own wedding gown, ever. So, we were very impressed.

Then, a month or so later they were married at a Jewish ceremony, where I remember Jack's foot slipping at first over the glass which was covered in a white handkerchief. After the third try he got it. Everyone laughed. The wedding cake was beautiful. It was a lovely wedding. Carroll Baker was not Jewish. I don't think she converted, but I'm not sure.

I didn't see them for a while after that. They were both working hard career wise, and they had two children, Blanche and Herschel. A few years later, my parents and I went for an evening to the theatre, what we saw I don't remember, but afterwards we were walking in the theatre district and ran into them together. They were sneaking around quietly trying to avoid someone with whom they had a misunderstanding. We stood together with them in front of the theatre talking softly. Then we went our separate ways.

I went away to school sometime after that. Time passed and papa, who has always been a very religious Jew had in the meantime bonded with Jack. At some point Jack and Carroll divorced. Carroll moved with her daughter, Blanche, to Los Angeles. Jack stayed here with his son Herschel. Jack and my father attended high holiday services together at my father's synagogue, Stephen Wise Free. He often came to visit my father and pick him up to go, and they returned together.

I hadn't seen him for many years then suddenly when I was in my early 30's and had my young son Jason, Jack reappeared with his son Herschel as guests at my father's Seder. After the Seder ended Jack gave my young son Jason and me a lift home in a cab and entertained us by singing and telling jokes and had us hysterically laughing all the way home. He was a funny character. We saw him there for several years.

I am not insinuating that the Garfein's were on amphetamine. They were patients so early on, so I would assume they were not receiving any. I am quite sure Jack wasn't taking amphetamine. He was just a very good friend of my father's. He was a very religious Jew and a devoted father to Herschel, very nice to me and to my son Jason.

30

ROBERT FISHER

A charismatic and kind soul, full of empathy towards the human race, sympathetic to all and very understanding, wise, and a Virgo like me. He and I really got along well. But then one could say the same for everyone, he got along well with everyone. We spent so much time talking together about writing and comedy. He was a comedian, and I was a writer with a strong desire to direct theatre. He wanted to help me and introduce me to people who could help me. He was as much a patient as a friend. As a matter of fact, he was much more a friend of my father and my family than a patient. He was a patient and got shots and I am sure he was given amphetamine and enjoyed it. He was getting older, pushing 50's and the amphetamine made him feel youthful, made him happy and in great good spirits.

Before he was introduced to me and before he became a patient, he co-wrote a television show with Arthur Marx called "A Life in Revue". He wrote all this while receiving treatments from my father. Arthur Marx was the son of Groucho.

He introduced me to David Alexander who was a very popular director in Los Angeles and a drama teacher at a college in Los Angeles. David had a problem with amphetamine, but that is another story. Now back to Bob Fisher. Bob was a professional writer who collaborated on work with Arthur Marx.

Both Bob and Arthur Marx worked together on the popular T.V. Show, "Alice", "All in the Family", and 'The Impossible Years" on Broadway starring Alan King. He was the series writer for The Paul Lynde Show and Bob Hope Presents The Chrysler Theatre, etc.

Bob Fisher always had a kind word to say to everyone and always had some kind thoughts to offer to anyone who crossed his path to make their day special. Wow, what a guy! He visited often for treatments and to visit us as our guest.

The last time I saw him was when he was a guest at one of my father's seders. He brought a very young lady as his date and expressed his desire to get tickets for her to "Saturday Night Live". He was so happy and enjoyed her company. I think he was in his 50's already at the time, but mentally very youthful.

31

RELIGION

— • —

The religious aspect of my entire life is so "conjumbled". Don't bother looking up that word in the dictionary, I just made it up. It means pretty much discombobulated. In my family, where my father and I were concerned, religion was a constant upheaval for all it was worth. It was so constant, yet constantly and thoroughly disrupted. I must state with the utmost sincerity, my father lived his life with deep faith and religious convictions. For years, until maybe very recently, my father to me was a very religious Jew. I used to accuse him of being an Orthodox Jew. I thought it was the intensity to which you carried your religious faith and beliefs which determined whether you were Orthodox.

 No explanations were given by anybody concerned within my close-knit family circle. Everything was so "hush hush-mum" about religion and the serious atmosphere created by my father, his embittered feelings from his past in Germany, and the tyranny with Hitler. His ambivalence, he philosophized and gave impromptu speeches, more like sermons about having to leave Germany-evacuate, and under what hostile conditions. He had such a negative, sensitive response to the entire era. He carried this on his shoulders as a burden throughout his life.

His feelings caused me to have mixed feelings towards the Jews and towards the Jewish religion. The Orthodox Jews to me were a bit stuffy. Their hairstyles, their outlook on life, and how they appeared in my eyes. Those feelings, I had trouble digesting their most primitive lifestyle. It's not sad and I'm not puzzled. It's just how I saw them. It wasn't simply the need in me to rebel. I just loathed it for some basic personal reasons, such as their refusal to allow their women to be educated. My father brought me up to be independent and to strive to become someone, to make something out of my life. And when I saw how the Jewish people had to abide by certain constricting rules, it was suffocating to me.

My grandparents took care of me during the week while my parents worked, and they took me for tennis lessons at least twice a week. We did healthy, basic, and normal things like going for walks, swimming, and plenty of tennis lessons, first on Randall's Island and later with Lilo and Herb Raymond in Roslyn, Long Island. It was never part of our schedule to stop suddenly on Fridays to observe a Sabbath. They had philosophies on life, none of which they imposed on me. I was so young, Granny died when I was 11 years old and she was more known for being a great mother, grandmother, and tending to my upkeep since Mommy couldn't walk well. She loved being a mother and grandmother. She loved taking care of me and when she had the opportunity, she also cared for her other grandchildren, although that didn't happen often.

Grandpi was the disciplinarian, the whip cracker, he was also the one in charge of lining us up outside of the house by the long white bench to make sure we took off our bathing suits, showered and dressed again. There were usually four or five of us and sometimes more. He had his limits, yet he adored me and contrary to the suspicions of my cousins, I didn't get away with anything as far as Grandpi was concerned, nor did I ever try. I wasn't like that. That was one reason they loved me as much as they did, because I didn't try to get away with anything. My cousin Tony told me in later years that he did. I still don't believe that he did, especially with granny. Granny was the sweetest person in the entire world, ever. They both doted on me. Grandpi didn't believe in giving gifts for Christmas, Easter, holidays, or birthdays. He believed in giving only if someone really needed something, such as clothing or money in an emergency. And even that he gave sparingly. That was it, which made perfect sense to me although they never imposed their philosophies on me. I suppose because they didn't want to confuse me and wanted to keep my father happy, knowing he wanted me raised as a Jew. They never imposed religion on me. They scheduled basic activities, not harsh rules that didn't make sense. And there was plenty of love all around. They were aristocrats, not orthodox Jews. Grandpi felt the catholic church was the biggest theatre. He was a cynic when it came to that.

The Passover Seder

I suppose I must climb out of the doldrums of Hanukkah's past – opposed to Christmas past, and recall the very upbeat, sociable and pleasant gatherings for Passover which my parents, while my mother was still alive, and family and friends collaborated since I was a little girl. My father routinely did not wear a yarmulke, nor did he ever wear any of the other garb. The only occasion for which he really wore a yarmulke was for the Passover Seder. And for that, he put one on right before he went to the seder table. And for as long as I can remember, Passover Eve was the only time he wore one, and religiously and meticulously resided over the whole Seder. Papa was the head Rabbi for those special times. We had the seder mostly on the first night, never on the following night. There were such extensive preparations involved that one night was enough.

Prior to the Seder, he reviewed the Haggadah with several invited guests to decide how to proceed on certain pages. My father always included non-Jews among his guests. He would ask that all in attendance participate in the ceremony and were enlisted to read a section from the Haggadah. On this night, which differs from all other nights, my non - Jewish cousins, my favorite ones were in attendance for the entire evening. He also invited a preacher friend from Long Island, Reverand Al Jeand'Heur, and some Christian doctors and patients from his practice to celebrate the Jews having been freed out of Egypt. He wanted everyone to participate in this happy night. As a Jew, this accomplishment made him feel good. I have never seen anyone do as thorough a job on a Seder before my father or since. And we had plenty of great home cooked food to eat. He was always so elated by simply having the seder that I truly believe he did the entire seder "au naturelle" as the French saying goes.

During the seder he took no phone calls, made sure he received no phone calls and treated no patients. He referred his patients to his answering service, and all emergency calls to another doctor, Dr. Ressler. My father was very serious about sticking to the seder. The seders lasted at least five hours, from 7 to 11pm. To think back and remember all the guests assembled in our apartment being ushered (called) to the table for the seder. The table was so nicely set with place mats and place cards at each plate so that each one of us knew where we were to be seated. Beautifully designed napkins adorned each place setting. I don't know who chose the place cards, I only know it was cleverly done for a good sociable mixture. The center Matzoh plate was adorned with plenty of parsley and a lamb chin bone.

Papa instructed his guests, "Please be seated". Once seated, all the guests were in anticipation, awaiting word from the head of the seder, the Rabbi (my father) to begin with the instructions on how to proceed. Papa first welcomed all the guests and began with "Look at all which you have before you. So you will become well acquainted with all these things. Let's quickly go over everything here". He continued, "Of course you have your matzoh right before you on the three shelves of this plate. The leader, being me of course", said papa, "Must distinguish the matzoh, each one individually from the other. In order that I make it perfectly clear to you, my guests, what distinguishes one from the others. On this fancy three-layer plate, as you can see, we have one sheet of matzoh. One on each shelf. We take from the middle shelf the one piece and break it. Half we take and hide for later. That one is the afikomen. The other half we use here during the service. Don't worry, you will get to eat later. I won't keep you here too long (laughs), o.k., open your Haggadah".

Everyone in attendance was called on to participate. Papa didn't drink the wine, although he should have for the service. He gestured instead. He went out of his way to make the evening active, so as not to bore or tire the younger generation assembled at the seder table.

There weren't any presents to speak of. This was a holiday of feast; food, celebration and all different Matzoh dishes. Including chocolate matzos. The food was specially prepared and catered by Celeste, Anne Montgomery, our cook Agnes, and Herb Gehagen. We only had one bottle of Manischewitz wine for the service. No one ever drank the wine. My father was against it. Besides, it was too sweet and yucky. There were tall glass pitchers with a pink drink every three feet. That was comprised of part cranberry juice, part grapefruit juice and part water. It was served instead of wine. It was pretty and very tasty, a great substitute. Papa invented it himself.

When it came time to break the matzoh, everyone got picky and fussy, not wanting to drop crumbs. My father had to take over and break the matzoh as quickly and as neatly as possible. Naturally silly as papa always was, he broke it comically, spritzing those around him with minuscule crumbs, and promptly sent the broken pieces circulating around the table.

The nicest part of the Seder to me was the exchange of jokes and conversation between my father and the invited guests, which usually consisted of his guest's reactions to his elaborate story of the Jews being led out of Egypt. Papa had this incredible way of telling the story. Each year he said something new and different as he justly described the Jews leaving Egypt and how they had to leave with unbaked (unleavened) bread, Matzoh, on their backs, and he told what the bitter herbs signified. The Jews having to leave Egypt in such a short time with only the clothes on their backs. He explained how they had to travel for seven days and seven nights to freedom. I liked how diligently my father toiled to get everything, every aspect of the seder done just right. Down to personally instructing the help as to what dishes to put on the table, which matzoh to bring, and where to put the matzoh and the bitter herbs. An hour and a half before the seder began, even before the guests arrived, my father met privately in his room with his Rabbi to decide just how the evening's service would be led, what pages would be covered, and what stories they would tell.

My father allowed his guests to give their take on it. He also asked them from time to time to be patient, that food would be forthcoming. Then shortly thereafter came the endless supply of delectable food. First, we received Matzoh Ball soup. Some were sweet, some salty. Some had cinnamon. Then we got to sample the bitter herbs together with the haroset. Papa would tell us how the bitter herbs reminded us how bitter the Egyptians made the lives of our forefathers in Egypt. My father promised if anyone had a sinus condition, the horseradish would clear it up and make their hair stand up. We all laughed and had a very good time. And lest I dare forget, I loved the haroset, which was comprised of grated apples, crushed walnuts, honey, and a touch of wine. That was it. When it was time to hide the Matzoh, the grownups made a game out of it.

One adult hid the afikomen (the hidden Matzoh) and hid it well. We were given three hints. It was only hinted how close or far we were from the afikomen by the adults hinting close - hot, very close, very hot, not so close

- cool, or very cold for very far away. Sometimes we ran around the room looking and everyone laughed because we got very anxious and excited to find the afikomen, it was the favorite game of the children. The child who found it received money and chocolate. Then there's the youngest child who is always called upon to recite the four questions which were, "Where fore is this night different from all other nights?", "Manishtano halay lah hasseh michol ha lalot". The answer, on this night we eat Matzoh, not bread. One is supposed to abstain from eating bread for one week. Luckily, we loved Matzoh. My father always abided by it. He loved the matzoh with haroset, kosher salami or butter and honey. I liked the matzoh so much that I didn't mind. I had all sorts of recipes for preparing Matzoh. Having the egg Matzoh with sweet, whipped butter got me in trouble. It was too tasty and made me gain weight. The chocolate macaroons were way too good.

Herb Gehagen visiting the treatment room, mid 1950s

Herb Gehagen, patient and friend, prepared the fish delicacy instead of us having the traditional gefilte fish, which I thought was great. One he made with a green pistachio sauce; he got a round of applause for that. For dessert we had prize winning princess pudding made by Celeste, which was comprised of pound cake engulfed by strawberry Jello which was at the bottom of the dish and was its foundation. In the middle was the strawberry Jello mixed with cool whip, which became pink. Then there was just a layer of cool whip from the upper middle to the top. On top were fresh strawberries as garnish and decoration. I never knew whether the pound cake was kosher. I figured if they prepared it the day before Passover then it didn't have to be kosher. I think no one thought of the fact that when we got to eat it, Passover would already be in session. Oh well, no one is perfect. Besides the dessert being delicious, it looked very pretty. Our maid Celeste had to stay late, very late for these grand occasions to help make the matzoh balls, and to help serve, she was the best.

When we ate the bitter herbs as part of the ritual, we mixed a small portion, or a little speck, depending on how courageous or adventurous an individual you were, to having the horseradish explode, traveling up your nose and making your eyes tear and was guaranteed to clear your sinuses up. It was the haroset that was mixed into the bitter herb that made it tolerable. It sounds awful but it was quite tasty. During the ceremony one puts a little bitter herb on the matzoh to signify the bitter times the Jews went through and covers that with the haroset. It was made to look like a mortar. We got to indulge in salt water and hard-boiled eggs which I personally loved.

The evening wasn't boring at all. My father organized it in such a way that broke it up into parts. I think it was a seven-course meal altogether. And the "Dai Dai Yehnu" came almost last, it was a sit down until that section came. I loved singing that. We all joined in a chorus of singing for that. I don't know what it meant. It was just fun singing it. Then we were allowed to get up and stretch our limbs. We each got to stretch in between servings. Thank Goodness for that.

I guess I liked a lot about the seder. I wonder how many fathers of children, being non rabbis and instead full-time physicians, would take time out of their schedules to become head rabbi for a night. To reside over a Passover seder of twenty guests or more. Well, that seems like quite an accomplishment. I never saw it that way. I suppose I grew to expect it. I cannot imagine my father having had a shot of speed prior to the seder, especially since he did eat quite substantially. However, he may have given himself a combination injection. I really am skeptical about that though.

At the end of the evening, everyone was full and enlightened, and my father retired to his bedroom for the night. That must have been a religious rule also. He never went back to the office after the seder, nor did he return to treat patients. He would only call his service to find out if there were any emergency calls. The evening ended soon after.

Hannukah

When I observed Hanukkah with my parents, it was always lonely, dark, somber, and quiet. It would be just my mother, my father and I standing beside a long dining room table, the lights out, only candles lit, and my father singing prayers. My father would slowly light the Hanukkah candles and make me, not mommy, repeat each prayer after him in Hebrew. He would insist on teaching me how to recite the prayers. He would sing them too. He would try to make me sing along, "Mah ozur ye shu ahzte. She ma ha zoh leh sha behya" etc. I never got that down pat. I didn't want to get into that. I liked the Christmas songs better. Then I would get presents. My parents had each other, but I was always alone at these times, no one to share these moments with. And because the lights were out, only the candles lit, for me being a young girl at the time, it was lonely and dark.

Then my father would faithfully and religiously attend Stephen Wise Free Synagogue. When my mother and I went with him, we always sat alone in the balcony section. Across from us on the other side sat Jerry Stiller and Anne Meara, the famous comedy team husband and wife. They never communicated with us; they never even noticed us. They sat together but apart from everybody else in their own world.

The only incredible memories I have of those times were of Stephen Wise. We would attend a sermon by Rabbi Edward E. Klein and sit in the orchestra. This I remember happened three or four times in my childhood days starting when I was eight. The amazing thing was I was a child with A.D.H.D., so normally when anyone would give a speech, my mind would wander uncontrollably, and I'd miss out on a lot. And when I returned (my mind that is) I would immediately realize I had missed something. However, and this is a big momentous however, at these sermons when Rabbi Klein spoke my mind never drifted, never. And it was kind of eerie, almost scary, but he was so saintly that I was never scared. His voice would change and at that moment one would swear that it was God speaking through him. In Rabbi Klein I had absolute faith. It was the way in which he spoke, the sound of his voice, its trembling, and the sudden increase in the volume. It was so dramatic, so reactive to one's soul and to the very core of one's being, of my being. He spoke, and as he spoke, he drew you to him in unwavering faith and belief. He could have led the Jews out of Egypt with his every word.

Purim (Jewish Halloween) was also celebrated by Stephen Wise. They made elaborate Sukkot decorations years back with tree branches, corn stalks, and real fruit. It was a splendor to see, that was on their roof space. They went all out for the children. There was a man named Herb Greenhut. He had been there for years. He was the one who set up the booths in the auditorium and the one booth where children got to throw wet sponges on the teacher's head. All the kids loved that. Herb was the guy behind that. The older children made papier mâché masks and paraded around the auditorium as Queen Esther and King Herrod. There was a booth where one could purchase tickets for all the booths.

 Over to the side they had a table set up with hamantaschen, I loved that. I especially enjoyed the Purim festivities because I was allowed to bring friends along and celebrate with a whole bunch of children. There were prizes too. Someone got a baseball glove, and others got a ping pong ball and racket set.

 When I grew up, I returned to Stephen Wise with my older son Jason who also attended Hebrew school there. He and his friends made elaborate signs for the festival and enjoyed themselves immensely.

Christmas and Easter

It also happened (and at that time it was never explained to me why) that my mother's parents threw lavish Christmas parties for the family, unforgettable ones. For the party on Christmas eve, the tree was decorated with colored balls and edible chocolate decorations, large chocolate rings decorated with nonpareils, a German delicacy. They were the best and Granny knew we loved them. I just loved to pull them off and eat them. At those Christmas parties, all the cousins would come from all over, wherever they lived. I can't remember gifts being exchanged. I only remember the sweets and the half-moon cookies. I enjoyed playing with my cousins. They were also all my first cousins from mommy's side of the family. They were Nina, Karen, Tony and Jackie, John, and Jennifer Dunn. And then Aunt Carla came by and sometimes Tiny Freeman, Cousin Tiny. I also had cousins from my grandmother Vicky's sister Margot. She had a daughter, Gaby, who had three children. They weren't Jewish either. Their father was Irish Catholic.

While I'm reminiscing about holiday's past, for Easter, we would all gather in Point Lookout outside on the front lawn where my grandmother would hold Easter egg hunts. My parents and I would meet Granny where earlier she'd hidden dozens of colored Easter eggs in the grass. The grass was high, the eggs well hidden, and my cousins and I went wild looking for them. I loved getting together with my cousins; we had such a great time. Everyone got so excited every time one of us found a hidden egg. Granny and I once learned how to color and decorate eggs. She would spend hours coloring Easter eggs. She made everything so nice. For me, those were always happy joyous occasions, wonderful memories where I got to spend happy times with those whom I loved, with all my cousins.

We had such wonderful times. They were the best of times, with all my favorite cousins and granny and grandpi there. Mommy always came later after finishing her work at daddy's office. We would all exchange gifts. I remember one gift I got which was underwear, I just loved Fruit of The Loom underwear. And when it came time to leave, mommy would call daddy and tell him that we were getting ready to leave and he could come pick us up.

He arrived at the apartment on East 94th Street, where we used to live, and waited for us to come out. He wouldn't dare set foot inside the apartment because there was a Christmas tree inside and we were celebrating Christmas. Then we'd go home together. There were years when Hanukkah and Christmas arrived at about the same time. Then we'd go home, and daddy would light the Hanukkah candles on the Menorah and sing the prayers in Hebrew. My cousins never came for that. It was just my parents and me.

Faith

When it came to my father, who had the unfortunate experience of being forced out of Germany by Hitler, never a day went by where he didn't make some statement to that effect. He spoke of the Holocaust and how he had to help some Jews escape and how in awe he was that some people, in particular Holocaust survivors such as Michael Simon's parents, escaped Hitler and the concentration camp. He had faith in a way I could not relate to. He spoke of it with undertones of bitterness attached to it, like a drink with a twist of lemon or lime. It was that bitterness which I could not digest, accept, or relate to on any level. I had not been through it, the exodus from Germany. I wasn't there so I couldn't begin to relate. That's what it was all about.

My father's parents died before I could have ever known them. Papa's father died a year before I was born. His mother died when I was a year old. I was raised by my mother's parents. They also had to survive in Germany during Hitler's terror. They raised their children Christian and Lutheran. My uncles didn't learn they were Jewish until they were in their teens. When my mother's family emigrated to The United States, they celebrated the Christian holidays, both Christmas and Easter. I always wanted a Christmas tree in my house and apartment. He adamantly refused. He was neurotically stern about this stuff because he was forced to leave Germany by Hitler and since he was a very religious Jew, it made him have a disdain for Christmas trees and everything it stood for, as well as Christmas itself. He was very opposed to even the thought of Christmas trees, anything Christian. He felt so grateful for everything he had since being in America, even though he worked hard to achieve everything. And then he thought back to his horrid times in Nazi Germany.

When I was about ten years old, Jewish actress Molly Picon came on television and appealed to the public very affectionately asking parents to please understand their children's wishes. She explained that the Jewish children wanted to have Christmas trees like their Christian friends. She expressed concern that the Jewish children felt deprived, left out because in their religion they didn't have Christmas trees. She said she knew of children who had asked their parents if they could please have one. I was one of these children. She suggested parents reconsider and perhaps buy a small tree or maybe a little Chanukah Bush. I ran to tell my mother; I was so excited. I pleaded with her. She said it was up to my father. I told him about Molly Picon. He got angry with me. He said, "Absolutely not, you have so many things, you are so fortunate you have so many things other children don't have, don't harp about a tree, you know how I feel about it". Mommy would have agreed to let me have a tree.

At Christmas time, I particularly enjoyed Christmas with my grandparents at 152 East 94th Street, Apt. PHA. The only unpleasant moment was when my father came to pick us up. He would have the doorman buzz up to say that he was on his way up. He waited outside the door. I reiterate, he would not dare set foot inside the house. So, we had to put on our coats and meet him in the hallway. That's how it was, very cold and crisp. This happened year after year. With me harboring plenty of resentment.

Lutte always alluded to being thankful to be here and how she observed the Jewish holidays. I found out only recently in 1999, right before she passed away in a Bronx hospice that she was only half Jewish. She had such admiration for my father for sponsoring her to this country, that she kept up the Jewish faith deceptive front out of love, respect, and admiration for him, that she too was a religious Jew. She used to tell me that my father sponsored her to come to the U.S. and that once she had arrived, he welcomed her with open arms. He welcomed her into the family right away. And when she got sick, he treated her and cured her migraines. He would crack jokes while he was filling syringes. She thought that was amazing as well as amusing. She was very close to him and enamored of his work and accomplishments.

When she laid in the hospital dying, there was a catholic cross on the wall opposite her bed. At her apartment on her living room table, she had a menorah prominently sitting. Somehow through all this she gave the appearance of being a Jew. The rest of my family on my mother's side, were not Jewish. My mother's brothers, there were three, Karl Victor, Budi, and Peter. They weren't raised in the Jewish faith, and they all married non-Jewish women. Their children weren't brought up in the Jewish faith.

How can a young girl caught in between two varying families come out unscathed and have a level head about religion? All my life this religion phenomenon, rite, has followed me almost like a shadow, as if it were expected of me. I know I can sing Hava Nagila very well, alto key, I also know I'd love to be able to sing "Oh Holy Night" soprano which I don't think I can do. For some reason, for many reasons, I don't think I have it in me to be a good Jew. That is to do the motions of the serious religious laws. Sorry to say, the beauty and bright lights of the Christmas tree and its festivities enlightened me more. And the singing, the beautiful singing of the Christmas songs. It was like Homer's The Iliad and The Odyssey. It was so beautiful that I felt I was driven to it.

I've often managed to fast on Yom Kippur only to learn that I have in fact fasted on the wrong day, silly me. When Hanukkah comes around, I feel with Christmas and the festivities all around, I cannot buckle down, get serious and somber and be the Jew that every Jew around me becomes. I feel like roaring with laughter, it's ludicrous. It really is. Why be so serious? Why not just be attentive and interested and obedient to our elders who are lighting the Hanukkah candles? I loved the jelly donuts, although I never partook of even one at any gathering. The potato pancakes were great.

 To finish the religious aspect of my life, I can't really finish it because when I was about six years old my parents took me on a trip to Paris, France to visit my cousins, Aunt Yvonne, Little Nina, Karen and Tony was still in Yvonne's stomach. They lived in a little town there. My parents and I returned in October. School had already started, and my parents were in a panic. They couldn't find a school for me. Enter Thelma M. Williams, she turned out to be our rescue minister. She was like a godmother to me. She found me a school, Beth Hayelet, a private Hebrew school. I don't remember how long I went there. I met the two best friends in my life there, sisters Anita and Lola Frankel. They were the best part of that school. Them and the Ish Kabibble's. We knew what that meant, and the giggles, we got those too. Then in high school, I just seemed naturally drawn to non-Jewish boys, the ones I dated except for one, weren't Jewish, no surprise. For some reason, I don't know why, I very seldom dated Jewish boys. Somehow the relationship didn't fare very well. And I didn't do it deliberately, it just happened that way. I just had very mixed feelings about religion.

Later in high school, I joined the choir. I really got into it. My Uncle Peter was an opera singer. I had always been around singers, both relatives and patients, professional singers. I got into singing, it just happened. I discovered Christmas Carols. Christmas songs I couldn't resist. That was a new beginning for me. Ever since then, since I was about twenty, every Christmas I go caroling. I once told Papa about it. He cackled a kind of low-key laugh and gave me his sigh of approval. Years later, I would adopt a song I had heard and would really practice singing it well. My father was tickled pink by that. He would always squint his face, wrinkle his nose, and make a face looking up at me, acknowledging his approval. It was a squint and a smile. As he smiled his nose wrinkled and his glasses slid up his nose. He said that at least I was doing something (zomezing) constructive and productive. He was happy that I was singing so he knew and approved. Even if he personally was going out on a limb giving a nod of approval to me under such circumstances.

 Shortly before he died, I took on "You Light up My Life". Ronny Graham happened to be around. He sang and played the piano like no other person. He had his own style. Bless his heart. He accompanied me on the piano for that number. He did a lot of comedy skits, lyrics and piano all at once for my father and would laugh after every line. That made it almost slapstick. It was darling, just darling. The last time I sang for my father before he died was that late afternoon on 86th Street with Ronny. What a memory.

My father was insistent with all my mother's relatives, the elders, the older members of my family, my aunt Carla, my cousin Lutte, all hush hush (I never did know about it then, only very recently) about keeping the religious faith and honoring the Jewish laws and the religion and fully participate when called upon to celebrate the Jewish holidays. He never imposed his faith upon my young cousins, none of them were Jewish.

 My mother tried to keep the Jewish faith, to abide by the rules and regulations. Mostly she accompanied my father to the temple for the evening before service, before the big fast, and she accompanied him at other times as well. They weren't orthodox even though I thought at times they were. My father was a conservative Jew, except at the seder table, then he became a Rabbi, besides being a totally devout health and fitness buff, he had his religion. He was a Jew in so many ways.

 For Yom Kippur, the highest holiday for the Jews, he went to temple, never failed, before the fast, the night before he went to Stephen Wise Free Synagogue. The next day he went again to the synagogue during the day. That was a long sermon. Then after dinner that night after the fast was over, I believe we went again. My father always fasted, and during the holiday he never worked either. He prayed and came home and rested in-between. He allowed me to skip fasting because for as long as I can remember, I had a problem with migraines, I got them rather frequently. So, my father excused me from fasting. Sometimes knowing that I was supposed to fast made me even more hungry. Papa was good about sticking to it.

 My brother Tommy was always a stricter Jew, his family was also. My mother didn't share in his Jewish faith. She had a totally different upbringing and simply abided by my father's wishes and commands. She was more into participating with her parents and her cousins at their Christmas and Easter holiday parties. But she put up a good front even to me. She was a distinguished European and an artist, as well as an aristocrat.

32

MY PARENTS TRIP TO EGYPT

My parents visit to Egypt was fascinating. My mother brought her own movie camera and regular camera. They both took camel and horseback rides with Yul Brynner, patient and friend. My father was sent to Egypt to be the personal physician to Cecil B. DeMille and was there also treating some of the other staff members, including Yul Brynner. My parents saw Charleston Heston on the set, to my knowledge he was not a patient. My parents were both so attractive that the photos of them with Yul Brynner were stunning. And the background with the pyramids, the views were spectacular.

My father mentioned the heat. They had huge fans, but everyone on the set got overheated and apparently Cecil B. DeMille got cranky quite often. The end result, The Ten Commandments seemed well worth all the sweating they had to endure. My mother had the opportunity to visit the villages. She was very skinny and was seeking some grains that would add a little bulk to her body. She filmed the Egyptians offering her samples of grains and the films showed children and village people carrying groceries on their heads.

My parents were on the set much of the time and were enthralled by the chariot race. Yul Brynner apparently had his hands full. It seems Cecil B. DeMille was relentless in his pursuit of perfection in the sweltering heat, and the entire cast and crew suffered as a result. When the director yelled "break" for lunch, everyone was so relieved. My father said, "You can't imagine!".

Yul Brynner was also a patient. As soon as he entered the room, it felt as if a great king had entered the room, the way he spoke and moved, I can hardly describe it. It was all strangely natural and yet I saw it in his mere presence in "The King And I". It was the deep baritone voice, the resonance, the way the words echoed and sounded as they came forth from his diaphragm as professional voice coaches would say. I guess he was putting on a performance. It certainly impressed me.

It was upon a visit with Yul Brynner here in the states that I first encountered an aura. I witnessed this massive aura appear over and around his head. This was the first time in my life, and the last, that I saw an aura when meeting someone. I will never forget it.

33

BABYSITTER FROM HELL

My parents' trip was a major experience. They loved it. It seemed to me as though they had been gone for at least six months. I think it was only three. My parents traveled together to Egypt for the entire filming of The Ten Commandments.

Unfortunately, before they left, my mother had arranged with some patients and friends to watch me while they were away. "So called friends". My mother and I had made an agreement in which we devised a code, word or sentence we would use when they called me in New York from Egypt to find out "If all was well". My mother would ask me about a cat, or I would ask about a cat. The response about the condition of the cat would determine if I was doing fine, or if anything was amiss.

 The only problem with that was the major time difference which had not been taken into consideration beforehand. It turned out that was a major problem, indeed! What happened was my parents would call their friends, The Heynemann's (the parents) who were sweethearts, at 2: 00 am. I was sound asleep. They had a daughter, Maria. Except for in the movie West Side Story, "Maria and Tony", I hate that name because of her. I've hated it ever since that time. Maria was a devil. She never had a sister or brother, Thank God for that.

 Her parents worked full time. We were home alone a lot. She tortured me. Parents, Beware!! I will include this so that parents nationwide, worldwide, should learn from this. Maria was called a Jewish American Princess, the daughter of a beauty salon hair stylist. Maria was a horror.

We would be alone. She would threaten me, tie me up. When she would let me out of her apartment to go for a walk, she would take her hand around my wrist like a handcuff. She would grab me and threaten me constantly not to tell her parents anything. If I wanted to do anything normal, she would say I should be grateful that her hard-working parents were agreeable to taking me in while my parents were far away in Egypt, on location on the set of "Ten Commandments", and we had to make the best of it.

At nighttime, she tried to lure me into lesbian sex by first telling me how to excite myself. Nothing happened! I was young with no sexual feelings yet. I didn't have the foggiest idea what she was talking about or doing. I felt absolutely nothing, except prisoner of her and her home.

Her parents were so nice. They never knew because she continually threatened me not to tell them and she never let me out of her sight. She would order me to sit on a mattress on the floor while she sat on a comfortable bed with a fancy bed cover. She would tutor me in my studies in a slave-like manner, boy she was evil and harsh. She took me for a walk one day just a few yards down the block and gripped my hand so that I could not free myself from her grip. We headed to the nearby bank. She never let go.

The only great memory I have of staying there were the delicious salads her mother made with a sweet salad dressing. I just loved the salads. Her mother always made them.

Upon my parents return from Egypt, my mother got an earful from me about Maria and all the horrors and torture. Maria never had children. Thank God for that! My mother was in shock upon hearing about my disastrous experience at Maria's hands. She apologized for miscalculating the time difference that had been a major problem for me, which had caused the failed plan of putting into effect our secret coded messages to one another. The secret coded message was, if I said I missed the cat and worried that the cat might be sick, that meant I was not having a good time at all. As it turned out, the time difference prevented us from reaching one another.

When my parents returned to New York, they took me to the Plaza Hotel to a fancy restaurant where they treated me to a strawberry short cake at 11:00 am. That was a real treat. I'll never forget that! It was delicious.

Then my mother informed me that Maria's birthday was coming up and that we had to go and make an appearance, that we had been invited to the party. I told my mother that I was not going. She said we'd go, give her the gift, a London fog coat, stay a few minutes and then leave. We did just that.

I never set foot in that apartment again except once to see a man named Michael Leizer, who happened to marry a model, a very pretty and sweet model. And that was one time for half an hour with my mother holding my hand.

I never saw that evil girl again. I'll say it again. Parents, beware!! Know who your children's caretakers are. I was traumatized by all this. And I wasn't even sexually mature then. All those things had been forced upon me. Thank God I have been normal and unscathed ever since. Although I have never left either of my children with babysitters as the result of this one experience. Except for my older son who was unfortunately mistreated once, but not since then. And I never went on trips without my children.

Only when my parents left me with my grandparents, my cousin Lutte and Thelma Williams, was I in good hands. And at times my father would send an assistant or nurse from his office to be there with me when I awakened from a nap, age six to eleven, and that would only be for an hour of one day! Hilda Alsberg was his nurse. She was sweet and gentle, and she was always laughing. So there, here's a happy ending!

34

DOÑA FELISA RINCÓN DE GAUTIER

*Jill (center left, dark dress) visiting
Dona Felisa (seated) during a pig
roast in Puerto Rico, early 1960s*

I will devote a whole chapter to Dona Felisa to cover her life, her generosity, and all that encompassed because she wholly and truly deserves it. Dona Felisa Rincon De Gautier was the former Mayoress of El San Juan, Puerto Rico for as long as I can remember (23 years), from 1946 through 1969, even before I was born. She was the oldest democrat at our last Democratic National Convention at 95 years old and was interviewed. She died in 1994 at the age of 97.

I mention this, since if she was on my father's amphetamine she certainly didn't need it. She had tons of her own natural energy. However, if she did partake of amphetamine, she trusted and adored my father. If he gave her an injection, she accepted it without questioning him. Years ago, I told her I was contemplating writing a book about my father. I asked her if she would give me permission to mention her in it. She told me she would be honored and delighted to be mentioned by me in this book.

"The great doctor" is what she called him. She had the utmost faith in my father's treatment. She trusted him and in him completely. They had so much in common. They were both generous, caring and gave to the poor. They also gave aid in clothing, food, medicine, and sometimes much needed guidance to the poor and indigent. She was politically active and knowledgeable; my father was too. She spoke English and Spanish, and spoke very fast, and when she spoke English, she spoke it with a heavy Spanish accent. My father spoke German and spoke English with a very heavy German accent. They both had a wonderful sense of humor. They would throw jokes back and forth at each other. It was hard to understand what they were saying. Between her heavy Spanish accent and laughing so hard, and my father's heavy German accent. No sooner would he say something to her than she would turn right around and translate the joke to her assistant. So, I cannot enumerate the joke.

We made many trips to Puerto Rico, both for vacation and several visits with her during our stay. She loaned us her guest house one summer for a week vacation. It was called "Little Bay" in Spanish. It was a nice little house over a brook far away from everything, nice and quiet. She was always so hospitable with my family and me.

She was one of the most colorful people I have ever met in my life in more ways than one! That is the truth. Visually she was beautiful, beautifully dressed every day like a fancy doll with a beautiful hair style. Her long hair was wrapped continuously around her head. She wore beautiful lavish party dresses all the time. She carried lovely fans to cool herself, but it was her dresses and her personality which stood out. She also wrapped scarves and flowers around her hair. She was such a vibrant person. She would grab your hand, my hand, hold it tightly and look at me seriously and tell me how important it was for her to help people in her country, how poor they were, and how pleased she was that my father was also determined to help the population as she did. She could be very sincere and extremely serious, and she could be swaying her head singing in Spanish and laughing and telling jokes. She was so alive and full of energy-so much fun, and full of promise. And she did deliver on her promises. She delivered on every front. She delivered hope to those in despair, and a promising vision for the future, which they needed to have the will to survive. She promised medicine and treatment centers for the sick and poor people in Old San Juan. A treatment center was built and dedicated to her and named after her.

She personally delivered food to the needy right outside town hall in Old San Juan. She told funny stories, true stories of past times to those of us in need of uplifting, true tales of past years (trying to cheer me and others up). She was a Good Will Ambassador. Greeting towns people outside town hall in Old San Juan. People were lined up by the hundreds to greet her and to voice their grievances. She had a big bag of food to give to each one. This was in the summer of 1955. Besides the food she offered advice to the people and had an assistant nearby so that if someone had a request, she would have her assistant take notes. They all spoke Spanish. One of her aids translated for us so that we could understand what was going on. I was about eight years old, and this experience left an indelible mark in my heart and memory. She was one of the few people who could criticize you and yet not cause any wounds because she was so deeply concerned and genuinely cared and then would say something funny to cheer you up right away after the criticism.

She told me once that years ago a terrible storm had come to Puerto Rico and that she had this big house. She invited so many people to come and stay at her house for shelter until the storm was over. She had extra blankets and had people bring extra blankets. She camped out with the people whom she gave shelter (which were quite a few I was told), and told them that once the storm was over, she would run for Mayor so that she could help all of them and more, and that was what she did.

Dona Felisa had a sister named Fini for short. Fini had a drinking problem and because of my father's admiration for Dona Felisa, he took her on as a patient. The mayoress was very grateful that my father took the exception. Papa had a rule in his practice. He would take on an alcoholic as a patient, however, if they slipped off the wagon twice, or shall I say more than once, he threw them out! With Fini he made the exception, since he was so friendly with Dona Fela as she was nicknamed (the Mayoress that is), he treated her sister whenever the occasion arose or whenever we were in Puerto Rico. He also treated Fini if Dona Fela needed her treated for some important family reason. The funny thing was you could never notice Fini had been drinking. She was always so sweet and shy at the same time. For some reason, the mayoress wanted her sister well.

She invited us to her house years ago where she was throwing an enormous anniversary party for herself and her husband. I was always afraid of him. He looked old and mean, had a scary looking face, long nose and jaw which came to a point. I was always told that he was a lawyer and harmless, I never spoke to him. I always socialized with Dona Felisa and Fini. Outside at the anniversary party, they were roasting a huge pig. I almost got sick. It petrified me to see an actual animal whole, being turned around on a skewer and roasted. I was horrified and I got upset, I refused to eat it. I couldn't wait to get out of there. I was about eight or nine years old at the time. I never again saw a full pig roasted. Thank heaven for that.

Dona Felisa saw the humor in everything around her, even if we didn't. She would call our attention to it. She would observe a sick person in tears coming to my father for treatment and watch with sheer delight as the person sat astonished and surprised after they received their treatment at how much better they were feeling. She would say "Look, he is brilliant. He is so wonderful; you see what he did?". She was one of the first to approach me and suggest I write this book, and last that I mention her name. I'll always remember, warmly, how she had the ability to laugh at anything and everything genuinely with no malice, yet she could very easily address the sensitive concerns for the needy.

35

EDDIE FISHER

— · —

Every time I saw Eddie Fisher, I got such a charge. He was everything and so much more than most celebrities. Eddie was like an uncle to me, like a big brother. He treated me like his little niece, always sweet and engaging. I was very shy like my mother. But I adored him as the person he was. He was so adorable, cute and cuddly, charming, sweet and absolutely the picture of health. He entered our lives with much fanfare, I met him when I was about eight years old. He had just been signed to represent the Coca Cola Company making commercials, which required him to make appearances all over the country in places like Disney Land in Hollywood, the site of the World's Fair in Flushing, New York, and other places. He was their spokesman. He was on a tight busy schedule. One hour press here and then on to another place. The appearances didn't even include singing engagements. Bunny, Eddie's younger brother, joined Eddie at several locations as did Eddies mother. I liked Eddie's brother Bunny; he was so cute and very approachable. Eddie was also about to marry the adorable, darling Debbie Reynolds. Even I fell in love with her. Who didn't? Everyone did, even Eddie, except that he was so busy managing his career, of course with the help of Milton Blackstone, that he didn't have much time to attend to her, unfortunately.

Eddie seemed to have little time for anything else except for his career. And managing his very neurotic manager, Milton Blackstone. I don't remember Milton being present or presenting himself in a managerial capacity, and to the best of my recollection he was oft times a loose cannon, ready to erupt into a crazy monologue at a moment's notice. I mention him twice because he was into everything, every phase of Eddie's career and his life. I only remember Eddie, my parents and I flying all over the United States to accompany him.

It was a family affair. We traveled all over the country so that my father could treat Eddie. He came to my boarding school often to perform as a favor to my dad. He and my mother were on very friendly terms. I don't remember my father treating Eddie when he went to work for Coca Cola although I wouldn't have been exposed to anything at that time. Back at home in New York, I was about 8 years old, Eddie started coming to my father's office at 155 East 72nd street for treatment. There was always a big commotion. "Eddie Fisher is coming", they would say. And he would come and make his grand entrance, like in the Copa Cabana. Eddie started coming more often for treatment.

The Eddie Fisher I knew was the Eddie Fisher we all knew. He had this air about him, this naturally great complexion, dimples, the most contagious charm, an adorable smile and an enchanting outgoing personality which he used to entertain and aimed to please the old Jewish ladies. This man was so charming, so appealing, handsome and sweet. He was always such a gentleman, you'd almost want to pinch his cheeks, he was so cute. He was clean cut and hot, and perfectly charming, which I can't help repeating, very popular and becoming even more popular as the day grew long. He always had the healthy glow of a sunbather and looked perfectly healthy even before his treatment. He never cursed, despite what he claimed in his book, at least not in my presence.

Eddie scheduled shows where he knew Jewish people were staying. He always had a Rabbi in his dressing room before he performed. He was a very religious Jew in every way. He surrounded himself with Jews, my father included. And he performed in places such as Grossinger's in The Adirondacks, which catered to Jews. He wore a yarmulke on most occasions indoors. He sang Jewish songs. He performed in Jewish nightclubs and visited Grossinger's in the Catskills often. He became a close friend of Jenny Grossinger. He worked up there a lot. His dedicated personal manager, Milton Blackstone, also Jewish, was always around whether you liked it or not. I suppose it was Milton who planned and scheduled shows in resorts where he knew Jewish people were staying.

He had it all right before he married Debbie Reynolds. I heard from him somewhere that this was to be an arranged marriage designed to bolster their careers. Someone had begged Eddie not to go through with it at the last moment. But he did anyway. I sort of didn't believe the marriage for convenience story, but I was a little girl at the time and barely 10 years old when Carrie was born, so I was too young to really know anything that was going on.

When he married Debbie Reynolds, he went up to Grossinger's to get married and perform. He shortly introduced my father to Jenny Grossinger. She and my father became fast friends. My parents and I were invited up to Grossinger's often where on one occasion we also met Doc Marcus, a magician. His wife became friends with my mother, and I was introduced to his son Donny, I think a Dodgers fan. Doc Marcus was a good magician who was hired to perform at my big 10th birthday party.

Eddie thought the world of my father because he took him under his wing. He gave him sound advice about his career, his life, and yes, he gave him treatment and some needed energy. I was present at the office on East 72nd Street while he was giving Eddie treatment, at which time he gave Eddie exactly, and not more than what he needed. Eddie would get up after his treatment, which he usually received lying down, would smile and then immediately start singing. What's wrong with that? He always behaved like a perfect gentleman and right after treatment he was able to hit those high notes. Everyone within earshot could hear him too. Usually he sang "Oh My Papa", or "Swanee" to my father, so we had vaudeville too.

Somehow and for some reason, I can't remember his manager Milton being front, center and ever present. It was my father who always appeared, front, center and present to stand by Eddie's side as a friend, doctor and possibly father figure. Hey, my father was a religious Jew and so was Eddie, except he insisted on denying it in his own book. But I was there and saw it. I remember Milton coming around occasionally. He seemed more interested in getting treatment for himself and hanging around my father than in taking care of Eddie. It appeared to me as if Eddie was looking after Milton opposed to Milton managing Eddie. Milton was old enough to be Eddie's father. Eddie was in his early 30's and Milton was in his 60's. Milton, even though he was supposedly Eddie's manager, gave Eddie double duty, forcing Eddie to manage his own career and in addition watch over Milton. Milton was consistently distracting everyone with or without amphetamines, which he insisted on getting and for which he was turned down plenty of times by my father for his own good. Eddie didn't have much time to tend to his new wife, Debbie, which was unfortunate.

Eddie was so charming, but it was his singing in nightclubs where I was present along with my parents that made me worried and nervous. I was always fearful that he wouldn't be able to hit the high notes. I remember clearly sitting at a table with my parents, next to my mother at The Copa Cabana in New York where Eddie was performing. I must have been about 10 years old. He started singing, and somehow, I heard and felt hesitation and restraint in his voice. I was scared for him. I would sit at the table, put both my hands under the table, and take my right hand; I would squeeze my left index and middle fingers until it hurt by making a fist. It just happened that way. It was because I was so worried that Eddie wouldn't be able to hit the high notes.

I really shouldn't put it here but since I discovered singer Marc Anthony, I realized how a singer who naturally has the gift in his blood can just naturally and effortlessly sing, beautifully. It was then, after hearing Marc Anthony perform, that I realized how good Marc Anthony really is and how he was just so into it. I never felt the same about Eddie. Yes, he had a great voice naturally, but it wasn't coming up from the depths of his soul. It seemed more as if he felt obligated to perform and please. I only learned many years later that amphetamine can make the throat tense and close, which is not good for a singer. A glass of wine or liquor unfortunately can help. It lubricates and warms the throat and relaxes the vocal cords, that is why many drinkers sitting at bars start singing well.

I was always in the background, and I saw a lot. Milton couldn't handle the speed at all. He became a gibbering idiot as soon as he had his injection. He always wanted treatment from my father, claiming he needed them to handle Eddie and his needs. Eddie seemed to handle the injections just fine. It was his wives which he didn't seem to handle very well. Eddie was such a nice friendly sociable gent, all the time, that I could understand him being pursued by women.

And then there was Mike Todd. Eddie Fisher and Mike Todd took trips to Vegas and Eddie took up gambling, my father had nothing to do with that, absolutely nothing. Eddie started gambling seriously. Before we knew about gambling, Eddie had invited my mother and I to meet him with Debbie, Mike Todd, and Elizabeth in the middle of Disneyland in Hollywood. It was summertime, about 4pm and Elizabeth had a dark fur stole on her shoulders. Why she wore it, I don't know. They just stood there conversing. Eddie, Debbie, Elizabeth, and Mike Todd. There were no paparazzi, no photographers. Someone, however, took a photo of us. No one paid any attention to me on that occasion. I was only a little girl, and they were grownups.

 Once when I was about 10 years old my parents accompanied Eddie to the Saratoga racetrack. Some important horse was running, and Eddie persuaded my parents to meet him there. We all went. Eddie was gung-ho about this one horse. My father suggested I offer to bet with him. I did 50/50. The horse won. He got $100.00 and split it with me. I think I was more shocked than anything. Here somebody was handing me $50.00. To me that was a lot of money. That was the last time me or my parents bet, and that was because of the gambling problem Eddie had that taught us a lesson. Every time I saw Eddie after that I was older and welcome to enter my father's large treatment room on East 72nd Street where he treated Eddie. Eddie was so proud to be treated by Doctor Max. He called my father "Wonderful", "The greatest". Whatever Eddie was getting he was very pleased with.

 When Eddie bought his first house in Beverly Hills, a gift for Debbie since they already had Carrie and Debbie had just had Todd, Eddie was so proud. He invited my parents and me over to see the house. In we walked and were guided into the lavish living room where Eddie appeared in a dark blue velveteen terrycloth robe with a pipe in his mouth wearing dark slippers. He immediately informed us that he paid $10,000 for the two-story house with its long spiral-carpeted staircase and a fancy S-shaped outdoor swimming pool. My mother and I went upstairs to see the bedrooms and to see baby Todd, who was sleeping in his crib in his little room with its fancy white window shades. The next time we saw the house was long after the divorce. My mother and I visited Debbie alone and were told she had an appointment to do a photo shoot for some magazine outside by her pool in a bathing suit. We waited inside to stay out of the way and visited with Carrie who was being fed by the nursemaid, cooked peas straight from the pot.

We saw a lot of Eddie. We went to Philadelphia once but mostly flew to Los Angeles or saw him in New York, or up at Grossinger's. At one point while in Los Angeles, my mother and I were visiting Debbie, Eddie was in Las Vegas. My mother and I were in a limousine with Debbie, where we were headed, I don't remember. Debbie was telling my mother that in the middle of the night that past night Eddie had called her, awakened her from a deep sleep and told her he had won $10,000 gambling in Vegas. And in the next breath he told her, but I lost it. Debbie was baffled, she gave my mother a look of disgust and frustration but laughed it off. I couldn't believe that on that very day Debbie didn't file for a divorce from Eddie for just that. She didn't! A short time later, months, maybe a year, time is relative, and I can't grasp it, Mike Todd was dead, killed in a plane crash. And Eddie rushed to Elizabeth's side. Everybody was so concerned for Elizabeth after the plane crash, everyone. She had a little baby, Liza who was only a few months old, and everyone was so concerned that she'd fall apart and not be able to handle it all. Eddie rushed to be by her and never strayed. That was the end. Then Elizabeth Eddie, Eddie Elizabeth, well, that whole saga happened. And then Elizabeth got the part in Cleopatra in Egypt. Eddie followed soon after. I wasn't there. I was in school in New York. I only heard bits and pieces from my parents making passing comments while working at the office.

Then one day I was hanging around the waiting room at daddy's office. His secretary announced that Eddie Fisher was coming and bringing the two sons of Elizabeth Taylor, Christopher and Michael Wilding, and I was warned that they were wild, to ignore them and that they'd probably tear the office apart. They arrived with their babysitter, Eddie himself dressed in a trench coat. Within minutes I began losing respect for him, who in my opinion had deduced himself into a mindless babysitter servant for Elizabeth Taylor. Those boys were wild and unruly. They came dressed in cowboy outfits and had rifles with them. They were "bang banging" everything in sight and running wild in the waiting room while Eddie socialized with the staff, nurses and I guess my father in his treatment room.

What saddened me was that Eddie, famous and talented and obviously busy with his own career, the celebrity star and center of attention, was now a babysitter who couldn't control kids, her kids. And I couldn't handle the thought of that. He was deducing himself to becoming a mere babysitter and a failed one at that. Thereafter, back to Elizabeth and eventually on to Egypt.

Then came Richard Burton. I always felt from the very beginning that Richard and Elizabeth were meant for each other, soulmates. I think they felt that way too. Eddie, amid a thrush of reporters, press, and God knows what else felt lost and helpless. I was no part of this.

My father was called upon to take Eddie in. He even arranged for a private luxurious townhouse on the Upper East Side for Eddie to retreat to upon his arrival in New York. It was a lavish townhouse owned by good friends and patients of my father's, C. Geist Ely, and his beautiful wife, top model Johanna Ely. At some point Eddie was introduced to Johanna who upon his arrival personally saw to it that he had food and personal care. She was after all the lady of the house. Johanna was this gorgeous Goddess, stunningly beautiful and extremely sexy who gave you the impression in her voice and body language of being a seductress, only that was her personality, not who or what she was.

Eddie mistook her as having come on to him and was so surprised because he hadn't bathed or slept for days and couldn't imagine why she found him so appealing at that time. She didn't. Well, this was Johanna, this was the way she was, beautiful and sexy, but not a seductress. I read about this in Eddie's book rather recently and had a good laugh since I knew her well and knew that Eddie misunderstood her body language and her intentions; it was easy to. Johanna was without a doubt the most sensuous being on the planet. It was her personality, her long silky shiny straight soft beautiful blonde hair, and the way she spoke, almost like a whisper, like Marilyn Monroe. And to Eddie Fisher, she was coming on to him. He didn't know she was that way with everyone except her own kids. She took one's breath away with her every glance every time she smiled. Her high cheek bones and her beautiful full smile showed her teeth and gums because her smile was so full. She was so naturally beautiful, like a nymph coming out of the water natural without any makeup. She wasn't really into Eddie. He misread her. Or did he?

Eddie had a total meltdown thereafter once Elizabeth officially took up with

Burton. Around that time Eddie came around to the office with Milton to see my father. Milton was in bad shape. By that time Eddie was taking care of Milton, his so-called manager, instead of Milton taking care of Eddie.

The next time I saw Eddie, he was secretly dating Pamela Turnure whom I presume he met when he accompanied my father to the White House to see The President. Pamela was the secretary to Jacqueline Kennedy. My father took Eddie along to keep his eye on him. He didn't want to leave him alone. They came up to my school in Lenox to visit me, Heinz and especially Gertrud often. It had a very calming and soothing effect on him. Eddie almost married Pamela right around that time. At one point while he was secretly dating Pamela Turnure, a friend of mine, wife of a teacher and former student at Windsor Mountain, Sheri O'Connor, begged me to get her a date with him. She was in the process of separating from her husband. The funny part of the whole thing was that coincidentally Sheri looked just like Elizabeth Taylor, so I didn't know what to do. Besides, there was talk that Eddie was considering marrying Pam, so I didn't pursue it beyond casually mentioning it to my parents.

One of the last times I got to see him on the east coast was when he came to Windsor Mountain School. He agreed to perform for a benefit to raise money for the Nina Jacobson Memorial Theatre. He made a special appearance to visit my dorm to see me and all my dorm mates. He came in, sat down in the gathering room and talked to some of the girls. When he left, he turned to say goodbye to me, I gathered up all the courage and strength I could muster just to walk over to him and give him a kiss on his cheek. I walked up to him and said, Eddie, wait a minute. Then I approached him. He was as surprised as I was. He was blown away by my courage. I was as shy as my mother, always.

The next time I saw him was in Los Angeles. Recently, I recalled meeting up with him in 1967 when I was studying theatre and apprenticing at the Oxford Playhouse in Hollywood. A job which my father had arranged for me in advance. He often came to see my brother Tommy and my sister-in-law for short visits. I thought he was dating my sister-in-law whom my brother had divorced. It turns out my brother was treating Eddie. My brother did not use amphetamine, or so I thought. Apparently, he made Eddie Fisher his one exception. That lasted for a short while.

Eddie had his baby Jolie Fisher, his favorite daughter in my opinion, by Connie Stevens. The last time I spoke to Eddie he was home with Jolie who was a year old then in a highchair. He was giving her breakfast; she was the apple of his eye. That was the last time I saw him. I do remember Eddie telling my brother Tommy that he kept getting lost every time he came over to Tommy's house. I lived in L.A. for a while. I got my driver's license there. When I knew that I was going to have to drive, I memorized every tree, every bush, every landscape I would see so that I wouldn't get lost. Then I got my driver's license and the first time I ventured to my brother's house, I found it immediately. My brother told that to Eddie. It became sort of an inside joke.

I must add something here, a rebuttal if you will. My father had taken Eddie under his wing in more ways than can be measured by friendship alone. It wasn't only about drugs, amphetamine. It was about true friendship, taking on someone else's problems and taking care of them in a time of need. My father didn't advise Eddie to take up with Elizabeth, but my father made himself available unconditionally for Eddie when Elizabeth threw him out over Richard Burton. The time when he was messed up, hadn't washed or slept, was not due to my father's treatment, or the possible side effects from the amphetamine. It was only because Eddie was in shock and grief stricken over the fact that Elizabeth had dumped him. That was it. My mother and I were initially shocked that he left Debbie in the first place. My mother liked Debbie. I absolutely adored Debbie. I never fully forgave Eddie for leaving her.

Yes, my father gave Eddie and Milton shots. My father didn't order Eddie to roll up his sleeve. Eddie called him long distance and pleaded for treatment. He had a full schedule. He was doing very well from the mid 50's through mid-60's, pretty much until the Elizabeth saga. When Eddie returned to New York, it was my father who arranged lodgings for him and helped him get back on his feet. Eddies relationship with Pamela Turnure was going strong. Everything my father did for Eddie Fisher was beneficial and for his own good.

As far as Eddie receiving injections from my father and going into a bath-room stall in the Waldorf Astoria Hotel to inject himself, all I can say is I cannot imagine my father even considering giving Eddie an injection to take by himself while he was in the state of mind that he was in right after the saga with Elizabeth. However, if my father deemed it necessary for that to take place, then he had a damn good reason to do so, and Eddie simply took the whole situation out of proportion. I suppose soothing his own hurt ego rather than thanking my father for helping him out at a very bad time. Eddie in later years, as was discussed in his own book, went elsewhere to get high and with other stuff. That had nothing to do with my father. Eddies voice was not always up to snuff. I believe that had nothing to do with my father. Both Eddie and my father were very religious Jews, very charismatic, immensely popular and very in demand but for different reasons.

Maybe Eddie felt lost in the world because my father kept picking him up emotionally and in friendship. I know the two were very close. Eddie had his problems with women, made many wrong choices that had nothing whatsoever to do with my father. And he had a manager who was crazy, out of it, rambling about blindly when he should have been there for Eddie. Eddie was a gambler in more ways than one. He made a lot of money but gambled it away. Amphetamine or no amphetamine, he was a seriously addicted gambler.

What's sad is that after all these years, as wonderful as times were, when they were that great, and all those people who supported Eddie in so many ways, it apparently alluded him, the memory of it all. And to me that is very sad, for those who helped him, for those he burned and for him personally [persohnlich], somehow making him appear shallow, callous and ungrateful, not to mention forgetful. I read his book. I suppose I could go on and on. For those who can recall the truth and honestly state, yes, that person helped me, he thought I was worth helping and I am so grateful for that. I am sorry that Eddie stooped so low and left reality and the truth for all the wrong reasons.

Then as far as business and friendships were concerned, just how far they both grew apart on many fronts. I guess the amphetamine drifted them apart. In the end that was what made him look bad. It saddens me to think just where my father and Eddie were in their respective lives when their paths crossed and then where they ended up many years later, so far from where they began.

36

DEBBIE REYNOLDS

She entered our lives as a lark and became my favorite celebrity. She was about to marry Eddie Fisher; I seldom saw the two together. I made my parents take me wherever she appeared. Since my father was always working, mommy had to take me. Carrie's grandmother, Debbie's mother, babysat her granddaughter a lot. Sometimes when I went to see Debbie, I had to wait until she came back from an engagement, I would sit with her mother and Carrie.

For Van Cliburn's performance engagement at the Hollywood Bowl in July 1958, I asked my parents if I could invite Debbie as my date for the event. Debbie obliged; it was all set. As soon as I knew that Debbie agreed to accompany us, I insisted my parents take me to a local orthodontist in Los Angeles to have the braces on my teeth removed for the occasion. I dared not be seen on a date with Debbie Reynolds with braces on my teeth. My parents happily obliged. My father arranged with Eddie Fisher to have a limousine for me, my mother and Debbie for the evening. Boy was I beside myself with excitement. The limousine pulled up in front of Eddie and Debbie's house and I got out. I walked up to the house, my heart pounding with anticipation, I rang the bell. Debbie came to the door, all dressed in heels and a mink stole, and greeted me, enchanting as she was. I escorted her to the limo. After we were settled inside and everyone greeted each other, apparently, I had previously bugged mommy to request that Debbie sing "Tammy" for me. It was an unforgettable moment in my life, one highlight.

Debbie was always so sweet and obliging to me and my mother, and she was always working. Either on her way to a shoot or just returning, and always very upbeat and friendly. Now knowing all the changes she went through with Eddie during their marriage, it's amazing how accommodating Debbie was with us. She really was a sweetheart.

37

ELIZABETH TAYLOR

Eddie Fisher called my father from London in emergency to rescue Elizabeth from near death, pneumonia and something with her throat. My father first conferred by phone, then flew to London and treated her. This was an isolated incident. She was not a regular patient. One time my mother and I had requested of my father to meet her while she was in New York. Because she was married to Eddie Fisher at the time, she complied. We went to meet her at a fancy hotel.

Elizabeth greeted us wearing a white fluffy shaggy Moomoo gown. It was so pretty. She talked about all her animals. She had accumulated quite a collection. She had birds, dogs, cats and more. I met her two sons, Michael and Christopher Wilding at my father's office. Eddie was babysitting them for Elizabeth. They were full of energy, very naughty and wild.

One time at Sardi's restaurant in Times Square, I ran into her alone in the ladies- room. I was about twelve years old. I was with my parents celebrating the success of one of Eddie Fisher's opening shows. I remember feeling shocked that such a famous woman with such a reputation could be wearing such a standard cocktail dress, it was certainly not in the greatest taste. It was a black sleeveless bouffant dress with a low bust line. I guess I expected Elizabeth to have more flair. That was the last time I saw Elizabeth. Funny thing, Debbie Reynolds was at Sardi's the same night and wore the same dress. However, it didn't look so bad on her.

38

MARK SHAW

—•—

He was Jacqueline Bouvier Kennedys personal photographer who was sent on assignment for "Life Magazine" to photograph her personal life as well as public. I must say he did a great job. The pictures were magnificent. It's amazing to me that he could have been capable of such greatness. You never know! They bonded together instantly; she used him ever since. I never knew what a big shot he was, he certainly didn't act like one. Mark was not a handsome man; he only had a nice smile and laugh. He had lousy posture which made him look older and less attractive. He was as short as Alan J. Lerner. Pat Suzuki, Marks widow, was so sweet and pretty. I never understood the attraction.

As far as Mark Shaw was concerned, I made no bones about it. He was one of the few people around my father that I couldn't stand and my least favorite of my father's group of so-called friends. He would show up at the darndest times, always appearing unannounced, especially when my father wasn't around. He'd just come storming through the door. I didn't even hear the doorbell ring. Once the maid or I answered it, he would say he had an emergency. It was always the same story, "Where's your father? I need to see him right away!!". I would then ask why. Marks reply "I'm having a heart attack. It's an emergency, where is he?". And when he didn't get a reaction from me, he just ordered me to "Tell him I was here". I took one look at him and easily determined he was fine, faking it. Papa did not get angry when I much later confessed to having withheld the message. It turned out Mr. Shaw wasn't having a heart attack. He was filled with anxiety, had girlfriend trouble, needed my father's advice and wanted a shot.

Papa and I were in a limousine one day on our way to the airport to catch a plane. Papa, without giving any explanation, gave Mark an intravenous injection in the car while it was in motion. There was a lot of traffic, and we were in a hurry. Suffice it to say it was a bumpy wild ride. Nevertheless, with a steady hand, my father administered the injection to Mr. Shaw. Mark accepted it without any hesitation. I never asked my father why he gave Mark the shot. The whole thing spooked me out. Mark pursued my father for shots. My father never pursued him. What happened in the car must have had a simple explanation; I simply didn't know it. That is all.

Once I was traveling with my father, Don Thayer had dropped us off somewhere, I don't recall where, and Mark Shaw was to meet us at some motel out of town. Papa and I arrived. Mark was standing outside the cabin, and on the bench under the window outside the cabin stood his little baby boy, barely a year old, David. I thought immediately, who in their right mind would leave a child in his care, even if it was his own son. I was baffled.

I found a phone conversation with an unnamed source. He told me that Mark Shaw told him President Kennedy didn't trust the people around him, including his brother Robert, so he enlisted Mark Shaw, the Kennedy photographer, to fly his plane at night over Cuba to identify missile silos and their locations. Mark flew overnight and took pictures from his plane.

I always resented him appearing unannounced at our apartment on East 83rd Street, ringing our doorbell, pounding on the door and claiming he was having a heart attack. I thought that Mark was faking it just to get treatment. Not until this phone call from this unnamed source did I put the pieces together to realize that heart attack was code for "I need a treatment, I have to work tonight".

Al "Tiny" Freeman, a cousin of mine on my mother's side who worked in my father's office as an assistant on East 83rd Street during the time my father treated the President, informed me years later that Mark Shaw would come to the office on Sundays and take meth vials from my father's cupboard. In those days one of the cupboards was never locked. Mark had a bad amphetamine habit and often hunted down my father's whereabouts for treatment. When he died, his entire system was devoured by amphetamine. That was by his own doing. I wish I could have better memories of him. I don't.

Do I think my father had any inkling that that sort of thing was going on behind his back, so to speak? Yes I do. And maybe being as kind and compassionate and understanding as he was, put up and shut up. Maybe he did confront Mark about it. I wouldn't know, I never knew about that because my father knew that I didn't like Mark in the first place. Mark Shaw later became the famous personal photographer for Jacqueline Kennedy and wrote the book with the infamous photo of the Kennedy's on the beach. I personally never saw him photographing at work, ever.

39

PAT SUZUKI

— · —

We met her in 1958 through Mark Shaw, the famous Kennedy photographer with whom she later married and had a son. Mark was a member of our inner circle; Pat soon became a member of our inner circle. To me, Pat was the greatest. She had this natural energy that just blew you away. If she said "Hi" to you, it set you on your toes. She had such a dramatic air about her. Everything she said, she said with such excitement, exploding enthusiasm. Whatever she said it didn't matter. It was how she expressed it which made it so colorfully expressive. What an exciting person to cross paths with. Her eyes would get big, they'd open super wide when she spoke. When she smiled, she had this effervescent smile. Her cheeks displayed a natural blush.

When she sang "I Enjoy Being a Girl", it was an explosion of feminine pride. She performed on Broadway in the "Flower Drum Song", "I Enjoy Being a Girl" was her song. I only wished she'd continued in the play.

One afternoon I was in my father's office on East 72nd Street. There was a big room with a desk in it behind the waiting room. I was told to go there and wait for my parents to finish working so we could go somewhere. While I waited in walked Pat Suzuki. She went to the desk at the other end of this large room, took the phone and made a call. I am sorry I heard the conversation. She told the person nonchalantly that she was leaving the show and that it was no big deal. That after all the things she had been through she had just found out she was pregnant, of all things, so she was leaving the show. It seemed as if she was looking for an excuse to bow out of the show. I almost suspected that she made up the pregnancy bit to get out of doing the show. Not the case, she was pregnant. The rest of the conversation I don't remember. I just remember how shocked I was at how emotionless she was in discussing the two big deals.

The first of course was her leaving the show. She was so good in the show, and yet in person she didn't express great pride in it. Nor did she feel obligated to please her fans at all. Second, she was having a baby. I remember the timing was all wrong. She was upset. She didn't really want to get pregnant, but she had to make changes in her life. I was shocked because the call was personal and yet she seemed so cool and business like on the phone. Where in person, when in the company of me and my mom, she was always so full of joy, happiness, enthusiasm and pride, beaming at anything and everything except now her job and her pregnancy.

I couldn't comprehend any of this, I had nothing against her before or since. She's always been a great singer. Her son turned out pretty darn well despite it all. Pat Suzuki and Mark Shaw were not your run of the mill parents. I saw Mark with his son David once, my father and I had flown somewhere and when we arrived there was Mark Shaw standing outside a cottage with little David. I was surprised that Mark Shaw even had his son visit. I never in my wildest dreams thought of him, Mark Shaw as father material, not by a long shot.

Oh, talent and ode to talent, let me get back to Pat Suzuki for an instant. Mother or not, she was a terrific singer and entertainer. She made many great albums. One of her greatest songs was, "I Enjoy Being a Girl". In my opinion it was her very best. She became a single mom after a short time and did secretarial work to make ends meet. She was a patient of my fathers for a long time.

On two rare occasions she came out to our house in Point Lookout for a visit and treatment, I was about 12 years old at the time. When the word got out that she was coming out there, our property became swamped with fans who wanted to see her and get an autograph. She finally had to come out of our house for a few minutes and give a few autographs. It was a little disturbing. Pat was Japanese and Mark was American. The weird thing is I don't remember fans showing up in droves like that ever for anyone else. Pat came over for treatment quite often without Mark.

Pat was always so nice to me and my parents. She just had this vibrant personality. Years later, after my mother died, Pat came to our apartment with a pianist to tune up her vocal cords and sing to prepare herself for doing another album, she made several. One album was titled, "The Many Sides of Pat Suzuki". She spent several hours singing and jamming. To my knowledge, she came to work, not for treatment, that was in the early 70's when she was still a patient. She never aged, not one year. She had this amazing young skin. If you ask, was she on speed? Being around Mark Shaw, I suppose. Never did my father's treatment affect her adversely. She thrived on them. In my opinion she didn't really need them. But in her case, I would say, none of your damn business, she didn't appear to be on anything ever, but sweetness.

40

ALICE GHOSTLEY AND FELICE ORLANDI

— • —

Real life husband and wife, Alice Ghostley and Felice Orlandi. She was the actress comedienne; he was the most devoted comedienne- husband to her, although not well known. They made the perfect couple and complemented each other. Together they were Laurel and Hardy, salt and pepper. They were the greatest comedy team ever in private and especially in public. They first came to see my father as patients, then became very good friends of ours. With me, they were so accommodating. They took me sightseeing and babysat me, sometimes with my friends. I was about 10 or 12 years old at the time. It was at those times that I had the best times in the world.

Felice had this Italian energy, this endless ability to joke around. He was loud and clowned around a lot. He was this handsome looking Italian stallion although he could have easily been mistaken for a mobster simply by the virtue of his looks, especially his nose. She was always her funny and sarcastic self. They were so funny. She'd start a joke, and he would finish it to which she would have the last word, or vice versa. Always entertaining. We were driving and stopped at a red light. Felice would yell something outrageous to a lady standing at the corner waiting to cross the street like, "Hey lady, your wig is coming off your head." or "Oh my God, your pants are falling down". The person would momentarily panic and look down. At which point we'd roar with laughter. Felice was a riot.

Alice was working in Manhattan and staying with her sister. She and Felice came occasionally to visit my father. I never saw them getting treatment. Afterwards, however, they were all vamped up. During the time that she was receiving treatment from my father, either with amphetamines or without, she was always very productive, making movies, doing television. And she was consistently her comedic sarcastic self.

 Some notable works she did during the time she was being treated by my father were as follows, "The Show-Off" on "The Best of Broadway" series for CBS in 1955, "Twelfth Night" for Hallmark Hall of Fame for NBC in 1957, etc. She also did theatre. In 1955, she appeared in "Trouble in Tahiti", in the Playhouse Theatre in New York. She appeared in Leonard Sillman's "New Faces" of 1956. In 1957, she was "Miss Brinklow" in Shangri-La at the Winter Garden Theatre and played "Aunt Polly" in "Livin' the Life". She played "Agnes", on" The Jackie Gleason Show" for CBS television from 1962 through 1965. She received a Tony nomination for Lorraine Hansberry's "The Sign in Sidney Brustein's Window" in 1964. She also appeared in "Car 54, Where Are You" in 1961. All these shows she appeared in while being a patient of my dad. I consider this to be quite substantial proof that she produced really good work consistently while being under the influence of my father's treatment.

As much as I enjoyed being entertained by Ms. Ghostley, I feel it is important to state that my father treated her very responsibly with his injections, whatever the content, it worked well for her, which is a testament to him. Whether she was under his influence or on her own steam, the fact is she was a patient from the late 50's through the late 60's.

Years ago, I observed Felice entering my father's main treatment room. This was in the early 60's. I thought things had gotten completely out of hand, because what would Felice have known about sterilization of medical equipment in a doctor's office? I was thinking to myself, here is Alice Ghostley's husband, also a part time actor and driver who is chauffeuring us around town, and working as an aid, assistant to my father? It all seemed so out of place. It certainly didn't sit well with me, though I never asked questions.

 It wasn't until recently in July 2007 that I learned that Alice herself was so grateful that my father had hired Felice to help at the office on East 83rd Street. Apparently at the time Alice was temporarily out of work and Felice was also not working and they would have had trouble making ends meet if my father hadn't hired him to assist at the office. I must add, I heard many similar stories in my lifetime of my father taking in patients who were having rough times and helping them out, giving them or getting them jobs. That was just something my father did.

41

RICHARD BIJON

Whenever I went out of town to Europe or Puerto Rico, wherever I went, if we moved, which was quite frequently, my room was decorated, redecorated and refurnished much to my surprise and pleasure by Richard Bijon. Richard and I got along really well. He brought his designer friends over to meet me, both hairdressers and clothing designers. Hair was by Ben Murphy, clothing for special events or occasions by Marc Sinclair. Marc was very well known in society circles. Both Ben and Marc were also patients of my fathers. Richard was papa's assistant at the office from 1956 through 1970, first on East 72nd Street and then on East 83rd Street, but I first met him when daddy was on East 72nd Street. I was about 11 years old then, he helped papa and me. And he gave me speed.

I had allergies and had been given medicine by an allergy doctor that made me horribly dopey to the point that on several occasions I nearly fell over. So, I would go home. Within minutes after I 'd arrived Richard would arrive to come check on me. Since I was so out of it, he'd pull me into the bathroom and give me an injection which immediately straightened me out. So, I'd say that Richard bailed me out. At least that was how I saw it. I would say that out of kindness and devotion to me and my family, he decided to give me speed simply to straighten me out, which was exactly what it did. He was also a friend who had a sarcastic and snappy sense of humor with a tinge of nastiness to it, typical gay banter but he was amusing, very amusing. I never once considered what he said about me behind my back. Mommy had been dead for several years by that time. Had she been alive, she wouldn't have allowed any of that, I guess. Richard became a friend in need to me and babysitter although by that time I was already in my early teens.

Inadvertently years later, when I was about 20, he introduced me to a man with whom I developed a very special lasting relationship. A man whom after several years of trial and error and experiencing growing pains together, then apart, strangely enough we became soul mates. A man whom I wanted to melt my entire being into, but he froze me out in ways that were totally oblivious to me, naïve little me. Well, this young man and I became inseparable with the exception of minor occasions where he'd disappear to be in the company of Richard or some other pal. The person I am referring to, the young man whom Richard had introduced me to who later became my boyfriend and whom I chose to become the father of my first child, was Bill.

I am still writing about Richard here so let me finish. This was stormy as hell. Richard didn't intend for us to be together, only to meet that one time. I learned much later that Richard himself wanted this young man. But so did I. Richard apparently didn't want to share him and didn't want to utter a word of it to me. Silly stupid and naïve as I was, I never had a clue. When I finally did figure out what was going on, all the destruction and neurosis right under my feet, the damage had already been done.

Richard had been in my opinion a very loyal and efficient assistant to my father who amazingly managed to slither into friendships with anyone and everyone. He knew just what to say and what to do, and how to do it. He was absolutely amazing, as I already mentioned in the beginning. Every time I went out of town, which I did quite often, he completely redecorated my room, new furniture, new drapes, and a Jefferson airplane hanging from the ceiling. He was very talented at redecorating. He also took me places, to appointments. I guess he was a gal Friday except he was a man. And he was gay although he didn't flagrantly acknowledge it around me, and I didn't know about any of that stuff. He was like a caretaker to me. We would get together and gossip about people, my stepmother included, and he'd say funny things about these people. He was really funny. What he said I remember, it's just that it wasn't nice. He could be stinging but so funny and sarcastic that one would hardly feel the sting. Richard was nice looking and attracted many, well, gay and good-looking men who were both gifted and talented. I remember mostly his jokes and his nose would wrinkle when he'd say something he knew was super funny.

He was really into speed and everyone around him was also. And let me make it perfectly clear, Richard had his speed connections, several, some I knew, others I didn't. He got speed from my father, injections, once in a while. He got speed mostly from his other connections.

My father got blamed often when his friends, assistants or patients were doing speed when in fact they had their own connections. My father was selective about who, why and when he gave speed, and to whom he gave it.

Richard was also free as a bird. He would appear at my fathers' office, disappear into a room, and give Anna Tschausoff an injection because he knew she needed one, assist my father, and then just like that take off and go somewhere else. He never went out with us to dinner or to Passover seders. He only came in to assist and help, which he did well and efficiently, that was Richard. I guess he'd become such a speed freak, so to speak, that the thought of sitting at a seder table to him was overwhelming. He just wasn't into it. His "thing" was coming and helping us do things, being active.

It really pissed me off. I was three months pregnant with my second child, ordered to bed rest by my doctor. A mutual close friend died, overdosed, I called Richard, we spoke back and forth. I really wanted to see him because we hadn't seen each other in years. He wasn't well, hadn't really seen anyone in a great while and didn't necessarily want me coming to see him at his home, domicile. But he was willing to meet me at the funeral. In order for me to attend the funeral I would have had to defy my doctors' orders to stay in bed and rest. I was pregnant with my second child. I had just suffered a miscarriage and had to rest this one out. In order for me to be able to attend the funeral, I would have had to get up, leave my apartment, take a train to another train, get out to Long Island and then take a taxi to the funeral and then walk up three flights of stairs to the Memorial Chapel.

I knew I couldn't go. Richard begged me. He told me that if I didn't go, he wouldn't go and then I wouldn't see him, I tried to explain. He didn't understand that kind of stuff, maternal and baby stuff. It was all beyond his realm of understanding, it just was. I couldn't go and didn't. I never got to see him again. A few years later he died. I didn't even know it. I was really sorry I didn't go to the funeral just because I wanted to see him again. My pregnancy went without further complications thank God, and my beautiful son was born. So at least that part turned out alright.

I realized I missed out on seeing Richard and other friends by not attending that funeral. More times than I could count Richard had been there for me. I had so many fond memories of times spent with him, running through a train station, running to get out because I whacked someone in the shoulder because they nudged me and then Richard grabbed me running furiously out of the train station and onto the street then ducking into a bar then jokingly asking for a drink. I was about 11 or 12 then.

I've heard through the years how rich lonely society women have become so dependent upon homosexuals as their most loyal companions. Well, I was neither rich nor high society, and if I was lonely, it was for perhaps one day only and to my knowledge Richard was not gay. I never really knew about that. He was a gal Friday even though he was a man; he was a multitalented fellow who was gifted, talented, smart, willing to please, and worked hard, very hard. He also knew when someone he knew needed something, what they needed, whatever it happened to be. Without ever having to be told, he just stepped in and assisted. That was Richard.

42

MOMMY'S ART EXHIBITION

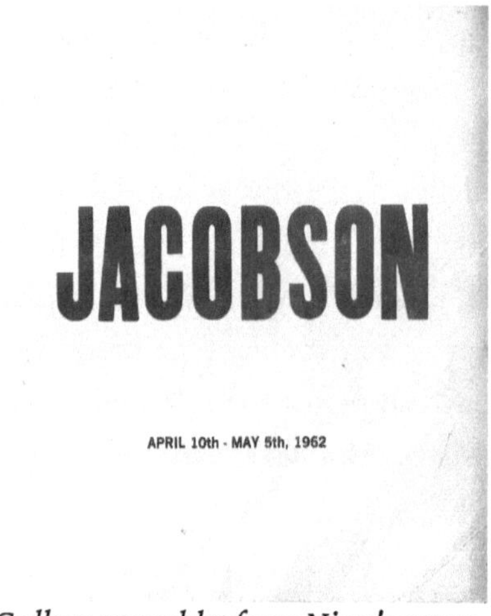

Gallery pamphlet from Nina's art ex-
hibit, April 1962

My mother painted for many years. My father rented her a studio down the hall from our apartment on East 73rd Street so she could paint. My father and I were allergic to the paint, so it was good that she had the studio down the hall, and it was perfect for her painting. She would dream at night, and the next day would go to her studio and paint those dreams pretty much all day. She was a very gifted artist, mostly abstract art in oil paint. She painted some beautiful works of art.

List of Nina's paintings

After years of painting and having completed a sizable collection of work, she discussed the possibility of having a showing of her artwork with Royal Marks, the manager of Van Cliburn, in his gallery. Royal Marks had an art gallery on East 71st Street and Madison Avenue. He was delighted to oblige.

Gallery exhibition (partial view)

Her opening was a big affair of which I have an album of photos. It ran from April 10th to May 5th, 1962. The who's who of my father's office, nurses, mommy's friends, artist Buffie Johnson were in attendance, Gertrud Bondy, our dear friend and founder of my school accompanied my mother as her guest. My cousin Nina Hagen attended.

Papa and Michael Samek (full uniform and cap, center right) attending gallery expo

There were friends, members of the inner circle such as Mike Samek, Mrs. Hediger, my baby nurse, Harvey Mann and Bob Shane. Lots of people came and viewed her paintings. She did sell quite a few paintings afterwards.

43

MICHAEL SAMEK

Michael was tall, blond and very handsome, especially when he wore his uniform. His wife invited me to their apartment on one occasion. He came soon after from a long time away, still wearing his uniform. He greeted us briefly. I was maybe 11 years old at the time.

Every time he entered my father's office on East 72nd or East 83rd Street, he looked dashing and debonair, very Cary Grant and very distinguished. He attended my mother's art opening and literally stole the show. He arrived wearing his uniform. Just the way he looked, the way he walked, and the way he carried himself was so distinguished.

He was also invited to attend our Seders once we moved to 86th Street. That was the first time he made an appearance at our apartment opposed to seeing him at my father's office. At our seders he wore either a gray or a dark blue suit, and a white yarmulke which suited him nicely. He usually took on the job of serving drinks, my father's famous pink drink or refreshing our glasses like a waiter.

When I read recently in one of the Kennedy biographies that it was Mike Samek who approached my father and came up with the idea of building a special compartment in his medical bag for his medicines, I suddenly envisioned him as underhanded and devious since he had the where with all to devise this idea. I suddenly felt crushed because I always envisioned him as being very straight and very square.

Very recently I spoke with him on the phone and asked him about it. I wanted to know why he thought up the idea of doing it. He explained to me that he approached my father and told him politely and discreetly that he couldn't enter the White House with his bag in disarray, and that he had to have an orderly and organized medical bag. So, Mike built a compartment into my father's medical bag to hold his bottles and make them not easily visible. His explanation to me made what was written and my perception of him now quite palatable. Mike was a gentleman; he was always very nice to me.

44

MAYNARD FERGUSON

He was a major band leader and trumpet player. He recorded the soundtrack for "The Ten Commandments". He and Flo, his wife forever, were very good friends and patients of my father. They came to visit my father from when I was about 10 years old until my father's license was revoked. Maynard adored my father. They went swimming together in my father's pool on East 86th street. When we were still living on East 83rd street upstairs form the office, Maynard came by one Sunday morning with his daughter, and it was the funniest sight I'd ever seen. His daughter showed up wearing a fancy dotted Swiss party dress, wearing converse all-star sneakers. The combination was the funniest thing I'd ever seen, and her hair was wild, dark and curly. She looked just like her father.

I woke up early one morning, my father's assistant must have heard me making noise, he came in and warned me to be quiet, because Maynard and Flo had arrived from the airport in the middle of the night and were fast asleep on the living room floor. Recently I saw him and asked him why they were sleeping on the living room floor and not the couch? He laughed and told me he was traveling so much and had been in so many places that he just learned to "plop down" wherever he could. He just loved my dad. Also, his wife Flo was sweet and beautiful. Yes, he was taking amphetamine with vitamins in his injections and thought it was great. At the time it was legal, and no one knew about any side effects. Later on, Maynard moved to England and produced 60's style music. Maynard and my father were very friendly. He thought my father was great and just loved to be invited for a swim. He was just as much a friend as patient.

45

Prince Stanislaus Radziwill

— · —

"Stash", as my father called him, was not only a real legitimate prince, he was also the in-law of Jacqueline Kennedy and the husband of Lee Radziwill, as well as the father of Anthony and Christina Radziwill. My father and I took a trip to England around the time that Lee was out of town preparing for her acting debut. We were invited to visit Stash at his sprawling estate just outside of London. My father and I traveled extensively all over the world after my mother's death. One of our stops was his home outside London. It was situated on several acres of land, and due to my father's influence, he had an indoor swimming pool built on the property where my father and I joined him for an afternoon swim. Stash shocked me at the time when he offered me a vodka straight. I had no idea what it was. I took it and had a sip. It was bitter and I thought it was awful and had no idea how I would get through drinking it. I had two sips and quit. My father was there busy swimming, so he was unaware. Aside from that he was a nice handsome man.

When I first met him at his townhouse across the street from Buckingham Palace, he was there with his two children since his wife was off in Philadelphia trying to become an actress. She was also gallivanting around England and the world rather openly with her amour, Rudolph Nureyev. She had a mad crush on him and went everywhere with him. Stash was very kind to us. He also invited me alone to supper at a restaurant near his country estate on the outskirts of London. We went there and I must say I had the best lasagna I have ever had in my life; it was delicious. We returned shortly to his estate and had another swim with my father. My father and Stash had lots in common besides their thin black curly wavy hair. Stash's hair was longer than my father's and they got along very well. They were two very athletic men, both from Poland, and Stash was very impressed with my father's knowledge of medicine. They really had a rapport. I met Lee at one point upon her return to England when she briefly appeared at their home in London, presumably to greet us and be cordial. She spoke mostly of Robert Kennedy. She was dressed like a thousand dollars, very simple yet smart and high class. She barely noticed me. I didn't get the impression she was interested in me [a child]. That was fine with me. It was Stash who was friendly with Papa.

When they had the famous 50-mile walk, it consisted of Stash Radziwill, my father, who went along for moral support and joined in the walk, Chuck Spaulding, the Presidents school buddy, and The President came to visit and give moral support. Stash removed his shoes after a while due to blistered feet, Stash and my father walked together.

In the late 50's, Stash visited my father at his office at 155 East 72nd Street. That was the first office that I can remember. I have a picture of Stash in pants and an undershirt observing my father in his treatment room. I was under the impression that they knew each other for many years and not through the Kennedy's. Supposedly during visits to the White House and then the town house in England, across from Buckingham Palace where Stash lived with his wife, Lee Radziwill. My father, invited to treat the president and his close family happened to meet [although I remember it differently] Stash Radziwill. I was aware of a genuine friendship that grew between these two Polish men, Stash and my father. The friendship evolved between the two with my father joining Stash on an African safari for several weeks, three I believe. Stash had invited him and managed to lure him away from the office and home. My father bought an entire wardrobe and equipment to hunt wild animals in the jungle. They both went hunting as a sport. Although it upset me, I think Papa killed a wild animal. He had the skin made into a rug and had it delivered to our apartment. It was big; long, wide and beautiful. I guess it was his souvenir. I found it unforgivable, but he was so proud of it. Well, what could I say?

Stash and my father had the same physique, both had dark curly hair, and both were very athletic and loved to swim. And they both possessed big egos. They were also kind and wonderful people. Stash had a heavy foreign accent as did my father. They got together frequently, went on trips and visited each other in their respective countries. Stash at my father's office in New York on East 72nd Street, and my father in London across the street from Buckingham Palace, and in the countryside outside of London where Stash had his estate. They were friends for years, from the 50's through early 70's. Yes, he received treatment and never complained. I don't know what these authors speak of, he met my father long before the Kennedy's.

46

GEIST AND JOHANNA ELY

Geist and Johanna were two high class models. He was a distinguished, handsome gentleman and a high-class stockbroker, who happened to be married to the most beautiful lady on Earth. Johanna and Geist were not just members of the "In" crowd, they were the "In" crowd. They were the "In couple". They were so dashing and beautiful. They dressed so elegantly all the time, and they were invited everywhere. They owned a townhouse; I don't remember maids though. They were on the cover of Bazaar, Vogue Magazine and Town and Country. There was a whole article done on them. It was a husband-and-wife model with one of their kids named Van Horn. What an incredible name. Geist bought a night club and named it after his little daughter. Their daughter was named Mariella Melinda Ondine Ely. Their nightclub was called "Ondine". They led very rich, colorful lives.

When she entered a room, any room, her alluring voice and beautiful face seduced you with her engaging smile and greeting of a simple "Hi" with every part of her being. She couldn't help it. That's just the way she was. She was gorgeous with the best placed cheek bones in the world. She had such a gentle, delicate and beautiful face, a very blonde Scandinavian look to which he appeared sort of Dutch. She also had long straight blonde hair, and the softest sexiest voice you could ever imagine. All put together she was breathtaking and naturally a top model of the 60's, besides of course Verushka who was number one.

She was the one referred to by Eddie Fisher in his book. She was the married woman who owned her own townhouse. Eddie couldn't understand how she could try to seduce him, being married and all, and him being unkempt at that time, unwashed for several days. "How could she?" said Eddie. My reply is, she didn't. He completely misunderstood her. It was very easy to. She was that way with everyone, always speaking in a seductive voice and very sensual. That was just the way she was, sorry Eddie. It was only when she was with her children that she became harsh. It was then that the sensual quality we had come to know and love had momentarily departed.

The very first time I saw her was on a set. She was preparing to model a gorgeous white silk top, with a beautiful necklace attached to it which went all around her neck all the way to her bust line. She looked just beautiful, and her outfit looked beautiful. She kept the top and wore it to my father's office the next day. Geist and Johanna were mostly together when they went out, they always came together to visit my father at his office. And yes, they got treatment from my father. Johanna, Geist and my parents and I became buddies. Johanna went up to my boarding school for a visit. I liked her and invited her to come up and see my school. She came up to Lenox, saw the school and decided right away to send her sister Bonnie and brother Eddie up there as well. The following fall they attended school with me.

A great while after that their marriage fell apart. At one point, Johanna, 7 1/2 months pregnant, took off. She apparently disappeared to Puerto Rico while here in New York Geist and my father had to track her down through friends and associates and numerous phone calls. Then Geist had to fly down to Puerto Rico to bring her back. It was a very dramatic adventure. I didn't understand any of it. When they finally split up about ten years later, Geist took the children and left town. Apparently, he married a Philadelphia socialite and was never heard from or seen again. I am sure he and the children are fine, though their mother Johanna had been longing to be in touch with her kids for years, and until recently without success.

During my friendship with Geist and Johanna I was also introduced to this 100% real genuine psychic named Bob Rhodes. He was a friend of theirs who soon became a patient of my father's. He also came for treatment. One could clearly tell when he was on speed. He was very eerie.

I have tried keeping in touch with Johanna after all these years. She moved back to Gloucester, Massachusetts with her family, got married again and had another daughter who is married now. I have pretty much kept in touch with her sister Bonnie Akerley. We all went to Windsor Mountain School together.

Johanna was like a sea urchin whom you'd imagine coming out of the water, like a mermaid with sequins all over her shiny, silky body who came out of the water and formed a human skin approaching the shore, dripping wet with her beautiful long and full hair blowing in the breeze. That was Johanna.

47

Bob Rhodes

Both eyes bulging and frighteningly amazing is what comes to mind. This man had "The Gift", the psychic gift. He would get a treatment from my father and his eyes would roll. Suddenly if you asked, he'd give you an in-depth reading on the spot. He was introduced to my father by Geist and Johanna Ely who was the top model in New York and absolutely gorgeous. He came to my apartment for a visit and offered to give my cousin Eve a reading since she was going on vacation. After she returned, surprisingly she told me he properly described the bathing suit she was wearing on the beach and the one the guy she met on the beach was wearing one month before she met him. It goes on and on. This man was an amazing psychic.

He only gave me three readings, and I don't remember what he said, only that he was very accurate and amazing. He liked to gossip about people and when he did, he whispered under his breath and had this quirky smile when he spoke. When he did his psychic readings, he took deep breaths and worked his eyeballs and fingers. He would say something and look at you in a comical way. When he accurately picked up on anything it was like a fun-filled adventure to him. Yes, he was on my father's treatments and amphetamine, and it helped him be even more psychic, he had a wicked sense of humor and almost talked under his breath. He enjoyed poking fun at his friends. I never said he was sensitive in that way. He was extremely sensitive in picking up on things.

48

ANTHONY QUINN

Anthony met my father shortly after he served as on set physician in Egypt during the filming of "The Ten Commandments". I believe my father met Anthony through Mr. DeMille, whom my father knew long before he met Mr. Quinn. "Tony" as my father called him, met and married Catherine Quinn, daughter of Cecil B. DeMille. They had several children together. One of them, Duncan, became friends with my father and later also a patient.

My mother and I traveled with Catherine to Long Island and once to Mackinaw Island. We visited their home in New York as well. One time we learned that Debbie Reynolds was going out on a date with a wealthy Texan who happened to be meeting her at Anthony Quinn's townhouse in New York near Hunter College, between Park Avenue and Madison Avenue. Naturally my mother and I arranged to go over and see her, even if only for a few moments. Anthony showed us his gun and rifle collection prominently displayed on a wall. Then we proceeded to a lavish living room and were seated with Hord 'oeuvres on a table, which I quickly devoured while I eagerly awaited Debbie's imminent arrival.

When she arrived, she appeared at the door in a breathtakingly beautiful "Snow White" like gown, it was the most gorgeous gown in the world. It was either yellow or light blue. I was so excited I couldn't even remember. We saw Anthony several times after that. My mother and I had visits with Catherine often without him being present. She was into collecting art and my mother was an artist. We also saw Duncan Quinn who looked like his mother, Catherine. Years later, Duncan and I attended The American Conservatory Theatre in San Francisco. I was about twenty and he was about twenty-three.

Tony made many memorable movies in the 50's and 60's, performed on Broadway, and worked harder and more than almost any actor. In 1952 he was in "Viva Zapata" and won a best supporting actor nomination for it. In 1956 he won an award for playing Paul Gaugain in "Guns of Navarone" and he was nominated for best actor in 1964 for "Zorba the Greek" and then "Lawrence of Arabia". He made so many movies during that time he was seeing my father and being treated with injections. Then he went on to pursue painting and sculpting. How could he have worked so well and so consistently if the treatment hadn't agreed with him?

I was told recently by Katherine Dunham that Anthony became very close with my father while I was away at boarding school. He started painting at home. He would come to see my father late at night. He seemed rather anxious for my father to acknowledge and praise his work. He even moved to be closer to my father's office so he could come over more often.

MONTI ROCK III

Monti Rock III (right, standing) and
Jill in Las Vegas, mid 2000s

In the early 60's Monty Rock was "It". "They say the neon lights are bright...on Broadway. They say there's always magic in the air...", so on and so forth. That was his signature song. When I was in high school, word traveled that there was this flamboyant man wearing nothing but a bathing suit with many necklaces on singing, and some students knew him. It so happened that a girl who attended my boarding school knew him personally. Her name was Victoria Webber.

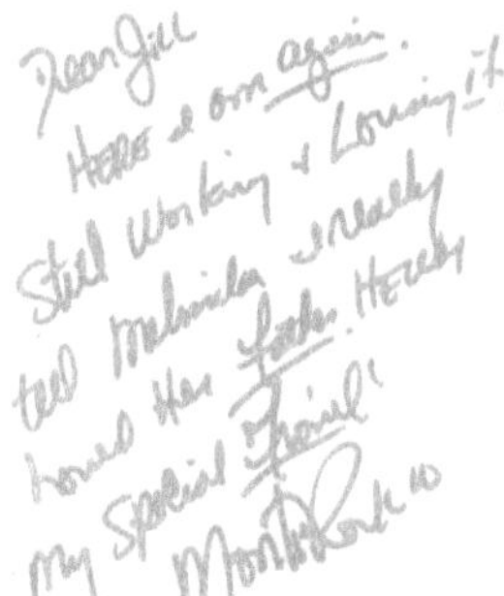

Autographed letter from Monti Rock III to Jill, "Dear Jill, Here I am again. Still working and loving it. Tell Melinda I really loved her father. He was my special friend! Monti Rock III"

Her sister, Melinda Rogers, was close to Monty.

He started off as a very flamboyant hairdresser to the very Avant Guarde and high society crowd. He went on to become a very popular singer and performer, Las Vegas style. There were 8 by 10's of him posing on stage with a bathing suit and many necklaces with Catholic crosses on them. His hair was long and tied low in the back, in a ponytail. He was so like Liberace; except he sang opposed to playing the piano. He out did Liberace with his lavish clothes and jewels. In my opinion, Monty could sing and entertain better than Frank Sinatra. He recorded the song "On Broadway". He recorded albums and later was the DJ on "Saturday Night Fever" with John Travolta.

Somehow, I found out that he became a patient of my father. I went quietly wild, I wanted to meet him. He was a patient from the early 60's. He was on my father's treatment and told me personally my father saved his life and straightened him out. Whether he was getting amphetamine, I'm sure he was. He was wild and loud as part of his act. He could handle it. My father knew I liked him so when he learned that Monty was coming to the office for treatment, he called me and told me. I camped out like the paparazzi on the sidewalk waiting for him to arrive. I was never like that with my father's patients except for Debbie Reynolds, who was not a patient but the wife of one. Anyway, I wanted to see him. I hadn't contemplated meeting him, I wanted to see him first. He arrived wearing an open thick fur coat and walked right into the office. I froze, I couldn't utter a word. He said "Hi" and walked, sashayed, into my father's office. The whole thing lasted maybe four minutes, if even that long. Within about ten minutes my father called me in to meet this great amazing man.

He was very nice, and we became friends. I must admit I was after one of the lovely chains and catholic crosses on his neck. He wore lots of them and all at one time. Far out! I told my father I wanted to borrow one specific cross. My father, being the very religious Jew that he always was, had a fit at the mere mention that his daughter even considered wearing a cross. I guess that was the end of that. During my friendship with Monty, he invited me to a Disco night club, the opening of Trudy Heller's "Tricks". I was one of his guests at the party. There was plenty of disco dancing. No, I didn't get to dance with Monty. Trudy had the honor. I got to visit Monty after that. I would visit him at his hotel suite. We'd hang out and party a little. Nothing worth talking about. We were friends. We've been friends ever since. He was and still is amazing.

50

CECILY TYSON

Cecily routinely biked to my father's office to see him. There were no limousines, no taxicabs, she never walked, she biked everywhere. I thought that was so healthy, natural and great physical exercise. She biked through Central Park or wherever she needed to go. She was such a normal and down-to-Earth person. After a short period of time, we struck up a friendship. She had such a gentle, soft-spoken voice. She would talk to me in a whisper while she waited to see my father. I would sometimes complain that I couldn't get through to my father on certain issues. She would listen intently and tell me that he would eventually come around. She wanted me to realize that he was concerned about me because he loved me. She always wanted to be our ambassador of peace. When she came for treatment and went into my father's treatment room, I never followed her and saw her get treatment, nor did she act differently afterwards, which indicated to me that she was not getting amphetamine. I cannot imagine her getting amphetamine, ever.

She invited me to go biking with her in Central Park one morning. I gladly went. We biked quite a distance while we rode in the park, which was something I would never have done on my own since I was so afraid of cars coming up behind me. I realized how much I missed just getting out and biking in the park, on this occasion viewing trees, nature, and experiencing total freedom. And since I was on a bike, I was moving rather fast with wind blowing all around me. It was exhilarating, refreshing and relaxing, especially since there was no traffic on that day. We managed to ride our bikes undisturbed. And even though I was soon feeling muscle strain, Cecily, who was in excellent form, kept going unfettered. I seemed to be the only one having trouble keeping up. This was my first time though. We didn't speak much while we rode in

Central Park. We simply enjoyed the ride, the sun and the breeze. Afterwards I got a charley horse from overexerting myself, but it was so worth it.

It was in my father's office on East 83rd Street in his waiting room that we had our major conversations. She spoke very softly with me, even though I don't remember specifics, such as particular topics she discussed with me, besides my father's relationship with me and our rapport. That was even before treatment. I noticed she had quite a brain, she was very well educated and intelligent. And she exhibited a lot of patience with me. She took the time to explain things to me. She was very soulful and compassionate, and seeing that I needed someone to dote on me, she leant a motherly sisterly hand. She was very kind. I think she was trying to come between my father and I and sew up any wedge that had been driven by the nasty females who hovered around him. This was especially after my mother died.

I never had a clue that someday she would become famous because she was so quiet, shy and soft-spoken. She wasn't egotistical and she never dressed up. She once brought her fiancée over to our apartment on East 73rd street to meet my father. Her fiancée happened to be Miles Davis. Everyone was whispering before they arrived. They were surprised and aghast that he was "Miles Davis". I met him only that one time and only for a moment. She was so courteous and shy about introducing him, she appeared to be overly polite and uneasy about it. She invited my father to their wedding, he didn't go. I really wish he had gone.

When she recently won her Oscar for her portrayal of Ms. Jean Pittman from "The Biography of Miss Jean Pittman", she thanked M.J., and I jumped up proud with delight that she felt compelled to remember and acknowledge my father upon winning. I was told she had done it before, but this was the first time I had heard it. I was touched and proud! Besides being an incredibly great dramatic actress, she is and always has been a great lady.

51

MILES DAVIS

He arrived at our apartment on East 73rd Street for an introduction to my father by his fiancée, Cecily Tyson. He sat on our simple living room couch and spoke briefly with a scratchy wispy voice, almost whispering. I was briefly introduced to him. He was pleasant. Then I left.

52

ROSCOE LEE BROWNE

Roscoe tutoring Jill in poetry in her apartment, early 1960s

Roscoe, the quintessential distinguished orator, actor, speaker, poet, and friend. I don't know where I'm going with this or exactly how. I don't even know whether I should delve into this, considering that it's a confidential matter where I'm being forced by my conscience to delve into uncharted waters, so to speak. I do know, however, that I must write something about dear Roscoe Lee Browne. He has been one of the kindest, most beautifully poetic and thoughtful souls in the world by far, and of course a very talented actor, comedienne. He has been one whose distinctive voice has gotten him very far. Since I was a young girl, it's been a great privilege for me to have known him all these years.

Roscoe reading eulogy at Nina's funeral, summer 1964

He was asked by my father back in 1964 to speak at my mother's funeral. As grief stricken as I was, I can remember a kind heartfelt eulogy that he gave in memory of my mother, Nina. Roscoe was one of a kind. He introduced my family and I to Norma Millay, sister of Edna St. Vincent Millay years ago. He arranged for us to be invited up to Norma and her husband Ellis's house, upstate New York in Austerlitz, not far from my school. Normas husband Ellis was an artist and painter who did beautifully colorful mosaics. I saw one such beautiful mosaic when I visited their home and had such a great time. Roscoe realized how much I enjoyed Edna St. Vincent Millay's poetry and presented me with a book of her poetry as a gift.

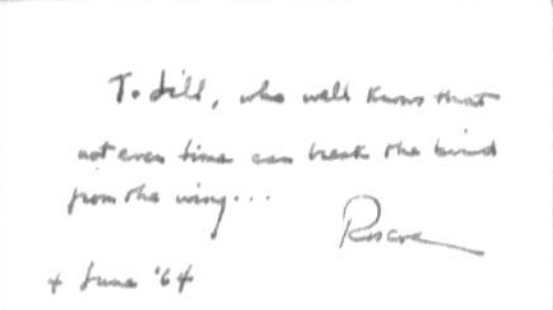

Roscoe's signed message to Jill in Edna St. Vincent Millay's poetry book

It was a hard cover dark green book titled, "The Collected Poems of Edna St. Vincent Millay", because he knew that I really loved poetry and would appreciate it. I will cherish it always. He even put an inscription in the book, "To Jill who well knows that not even time can break the bird from the wing... June 1964".

I had written poetry for years. I felt that I was a talented poet, some great poems, some good and some ridiculously lousy. It was Roscoe who encouraged me every step of the way. At my request, Papa would send Roscoe to our apartment on East 82nd Street after he visited Papa for treatment on the main floor at his office. Roscoe would come up and say, "Hello Dear", followed immediately by the most endearing sincere and glorious smile. He visited for several hours and gave me his opinion on my writings. We chatted endlessly.

Papa preparing treatment for Roscoe in home

He was truly remarkable in the ways in which he breathed creative energy, motivation, and life into all poetry and certainly into my poetry. It was like magic. And somehow the magic was sounding from the depths of his resonating voice. He inspired me through the soothing meditative quality in his voice. He commanded a dramatic Shakespearean voice, yet he would break into a devilish smile, which caused the most mischievous smile to take over his face. He created a sense of enlightenment in his voice which flowed effortlessly from drama to comedy and was theatrically charged, and especially for me creatively thought provoking. He magically infused creative juices into the core of my being. Like the sun in full orange glow at sunset. Roscoe helped me appreciate my own creativity and helped me recognize what a gift I had of writing poetry and inspired me to write. He applauded my ability to spout out my emotions, thoughts and feelings and encouraged me to continue writing. His British accent was like perfect seasoning on an otherwise ordinary dish making it rather spectacular.

For some reason, I think that Papa did something horribly wrong to Roscoe who was such a kind and dear fellow. I am not certain what Papa did to him, nor have I any idea why, but somehow things went terribly wrong, awry. Roscoe began behaving rather strangely, and he knew he wasn't right, wasn't feeling right, and just wasn't himself. He simply wasn't reacting the way he usually did, and it wasn't his fault or any wrongdoing on his part that made him become this way. I think perhaps my father got a little overzealous where Roscoe was concerned and gave him too much amphetamine. During that time, my father kept him with us. And if we traveled, my father took Roscoe along. I really don't know why, because he wasn't even helping him by doing that.

Roscoe looked to me for moral support, for some sort of assurance, an honest response that I as a naïve young girl was very forthcoming in giving him. I was very young at the time and realized that something was amiss. And I let him know that he didn't look right. Sometimes it was a look that I gave him without even knowing it that let him know that things were not right. It appeared as if my face was a mirror for him to see his reflection. He seemed to be feeling out of place, uncomfortable and questioning everyone and everything around him. It was awful.

Roscoe during a treatment

I always adored Papa, however this time I felt he was wrong. Roscoe had been so close with my family. We went many places together. We were most proud to have him in our midst. He always spoke and presented himself in a most distinguished manner, more so than all my father's other patients.

He regularly made trips up to my boarding school in Lenox, Massachusetts to lecture on the beauties of life and to recite poetry to the students and faculty there. We always looked forward to his visits. I wish not to discuss specifically whether he received amphetamine treatments from my father or not. We could have all used vitamins from time to time. In his case, Roscoe didn't need speed, and he knew it. Roscoe was all about giving and entertaining, giving of his love of poetry and of his generous kind nature.

53

MICHAEL SIMON

When I was about 7 years old, and my father made a big deal out of it, he had this close friend, actually a couple, husband and wife Fritz and Minnie Simon. There were stories about them, true stories. My father told them proudly many times. Fritz and Minni escaped from a concentration camp in Germany during Hitler's reign. Fritz was blinded in the concentration camp. Mini was pregnant from him and gave birth in the camp. Once they escaped, they came to America. My father took on the responsibility of putting their darling son Michael through school. It was my father's utmost pleasure to do so.

Minnie, medium tall and skinny, long jaw, wide teeth with a great big full smile which radiated the most wonderful grateful to be alive upbeat, enthusiasm I have ever seen. She greeted us, my mother and I with the most upbeat energetic, "So happy to see you" smile with her great big eyes which all at once opened even wider. She always boasted and beamed about her adoration for my father, what he had achieved in his life and how he had helped her, her husband and her son.

They lived in Mount Vernon, New York, in a big old house. We went to visit them frequently. They had a son, Michael, whom I didn't see very often when he was younger. I would see Michael at birthdays, my birthday parties and at some seders.

So now it happened, years later, Michael was attending a boarding school in Lenox, Massachusetts. It was a school whose founders, Max and Gertrud Bondy were long-time close friends with my mother and her family when they were in Germany. It came highly recommended. It was called Windsor Mountain School in the Berkshires.

My father was keeping in touch with Michael and learned that he had received a scholarship to college, a sports scholarship and was very happy about it. Michael apparently excelled in sports and was a good looking, charming, and flirtatious young man with a nice and polite manner. Michael looked the picture of health, with freckles and medium chubby cheeks. He looked like a soccer coach, he really did. He called my father at one point and told him that there were girls on campus who were volunteering to do his laundry for him. My father grew concerned and decided to take a trip up to the school to see how Michael was doing.

My father took my mother and I along for the trip. Once we arrived, it took me maybe an hour or two to get hooked on the school, it's beautiful scenic campus grounds. I decided I really wanted to go there, up in the Berkshires. So I asked my father if he would send me there to school. Michael graduated that June. So in the fall I began attending glorious Windsor Mountain School in the beautiful Berkshires as a freshman. It was Michael who had gotten us up there. For that I am truly grateful.

After school, after I graduated, he got married and moved out of town, so I seldom heard from him or saw him. When I graduated from Windsor Mountain my father bought me a motorcycle, a Honda 50. I couldn't ride it in New York City, and I couldn't handle wearing a helmet. So we had to park it in the basement garage in our building on East 86th Street in New York.

At some point I left town, maybe to go out to Los Angeles to pursue work in the theatre. Upon my return I found out that my father had instructed Michael to take my motorcycle, my graduation present, and sell it. I didn't even get the right to consent to the sale. I was more angry at Michael than my father.

Since that time, I seldom saw him. Besides in my early 20's Michael became very friendly with my stepmother. That was reason enough for me to keep my distance.

54

KEN MCKNIGHT

— · —

I learned from reading Ken McKnight's book "My Footprints on The Sands of Time" that Ken McKnight met my father through the Peppers, Congressman Pepper and his wife Mildred right before the inauguration of President John F. Kennedy in Washinton D.C.

Ken entered my life with his two children, Bill and Missy. We quickly became friends. Missy and I went everywhere together, to the theatre, out to Point Lookout and even boarding school. Bill, Kens son was a year or two older than I was, and we became friends too. Missy, his daughter, was my age. Since their father was around a lot, I got to see them often.

Because Missy and I expressed the desire to see Richard Burton in "Hamlet" we were given theatre tickets from Elizabeth Taylor to see the show with Richard Burton. I was crazy about Richard Burton and of course so was Missy.

We went to see "Hamlet" and were invited backstage after the show to meet Richard Burton. I will never forget that. He offered us a drink, an alcoholic drink, but we refused. We went back and told our fathers that Richard Burton offered us a drink. My father was so against alcohol. I was livid. Now I can laugh about it. Bill, Missy and I, because we were so friendly and got along so well together, we all went to Windsor Mountain School. I went from the fall of '61 to the summer of '66. They went from '64 to '66.

One summer I spent time at Point Lookout with Ken, his fiancée Anne and his two children. We were there a while. My father was busy working in the city, and my mother had already died. We spent hours at the beach, and Bill and I took evening walks on the beach with his dog Gweneviere. It was so nice, peaceful and quiet then.

I also learned from reading Kens book that he was enlisted by my father to travel with him to the White House and at one point to keep an eye on Eddie Fisher which Ken did obligingly. The more Ken traveled with my father the more I got to visit his two children Bill and Missy. He was divorced from their mother and apparently had custody of them. He was very nice to me and a great dad to his kids.

WINDSOR MOUNTAIN SCHOOL

Jill and Franny Hall (right) at the 1996 Windsor Mountain School re-union in Lenox, MA

The only school that I ever liked and loved was Windsor Mountain School in Massachusetts. Set in the countryside between Lenox and Pittsfield in the Berkshires, it was the most wonderful exclusive private boarding school ever to be born to this world. In this school were the lucky hundreds of children from very wealthy, privileged backgrounds who were fortunate enough to be able to attend this 150-acre school just up the road from the Boston Symphony Orchestras home, Tanglewood. The landscape consisted of acres of grass, hills and blue skies, green pastures and forests of trees, and a few houses, few and far between. Occasionally someone would be riding on horseback. There were just acres of free land, land to roam on, land to run on, land to walk freely on. It was all so inspirational.

My father did as much there for me as Billy Joel did for his daughter Alexa's school. I am sure other parents did the same, but my father went out of his way for me and everybody. He would come up to see me at school, fly or drive, whatever means at his disposal, unannounced and unexpected, and would naturally surprise me. I had no idea he had been visiting The President of The United States at the time.

Heinz Bondy was our headmaster, his mother Gertrude was our brilliant founder and psychologist. She had studied under Freud and founded the school along with her husband Max. They knew Max many years ago from Germany and had formed a kinship. I had the pleasure of meeting with her once a week.

I loved chorus and singing. In my junior and senior year, I elected to take German and Drama and to excel at both instead of drowning myself in biology and intermediate math. I did very well in Drama and German. I took all the German courses, I through V or VI and went to Germany alone, since Papa wouldn't volunteer to go back to that country. I went to Germany during all my summer vacations, mostly, so that I could get even more experience with the German language. Drama was great, Franny Hall was great. I didn't act in a play because I was shy. There were other students just as willing to get out there on stage and perform. I did other things instead.

There were times I just simply couldn't keep my eyes open. Gourie Mukhergee was my tutor. After a very short while, she noticed my eyeball move up and she could see the white of my eye. My eyes would drift. She would poke a pencil on the desk to get my attention, and I would immediately return my attention to what we were doing. I recall when we had city and statewide tests, separately, papa had to come up to school to give me pills or an injection so I could focus and apply myself. Without the treatment, I would sit in the gymnasium, have the test sheet put in front of me and suddenly my mind would go blank, and then naturally I would panic, which wouldn't help at all.

I don't know for sure if my father realized what it was that I was suffering from, however he treated me for ADHD which I had very badly. I was also falling asleep from the lack of ventilation in the chorus studio during choir practice at school. It was very annoying to be falling asleep out of control. At that time, I was given Preludin for several years. Then he gave me oral drops with vitamins. I wasn't always on speed or medicine.

The school nurse got a kick out of me. Whenever I felt sick, I would go to her and say, "I have such and such symptoms, please give me the appropriate pill, I'll be on my way to class", and off I went. She was accustomed to students coming to her with excuses for a sick note so that they could be excused from class. Not me. Except for the time I got German measles. Then I got quarantined with guards to make sure I didn't leave my room. I remember my mother staying with me making sure I stayed in my room, especially since it happened to be parents' weekend at school. One time my parents were visiting Gertrud and Heinz at school. I was at Gertrud's visiting them. Someone had told Gertrud that Franny was hoarse and wasn't feeling well, that she was losing her voice. I was sent up to Gertrud's room to fetch her. I went to Franny who was in the middle of rehearsal for a play. I told her Gertrud wanted to see her up at the Main House, in her room. So, Franny got someone to take over, went up to Gertrud's and there was my father who offered to treat her throat. No injections, no shots. He simply asked Gertrud if she had a bottle, a small perfume bottle he could have. She found one, gave it to him, he poured some basic stuff into it. What it was, Franny didn't know, she didn't ask. Then he had her inhale the stuff every day for two weeks. She told me it worked almost right away and cured her throat completely, and that the stuff he gave her smelled like perfume. She told me my father brought some acting group up to school that performed "Beyond the Fringe". She also said he brought Aldier Hess up to the school.

I had a chat with Liz Smollens from Windsor Mountain School. David Beller got us together because she had met my father and had taken his oral drops. She told me Gertrud must have suggested that she take them. She was Gertrud's secretary and made all her appointments with students throughout the year. She was my age. She lacked self-confidence and was sent to Mrs. Larsen's office, the school nurse, where she got a bottle of oral drops which helped her with her studies. She took the drops once, but said my father was nice and because of my father Eddie Fisher came to the school. She told me there was no amphetamine in the oral drops, no side effects.

My father was also instrumental in influencing former students at Windsor Mountain towards fulfilling their vocational dreams. He would invite them to his office and his laboratory and take them on a tour. They were innately influenced by his teachings. They were into biology, science – etc. He also assisted them in choosing their colleges and gave them very helpful advice, suggestions on which colleges to choose, apply to, and gave them priceless hours of laboratory training – hands on instruction in their experiments.

Steven Vedro was one such student who approached me at the 1996 reunion with all sorts of kudos about all the wonderful guidance, lectures, and teachings my father so generously gave to him. Stephen was the valedictorian of our graduating class in 1966. He got into Columbia University on a scholarship. Heinz asked my father to help get Stephen a job. Papa got him a job as a projectionist through John Francovilla, who was the head of the projectionist union.

Jill Jacobson in Henri Bendel at her 1966 Windsor Moutain School graduation ceremony

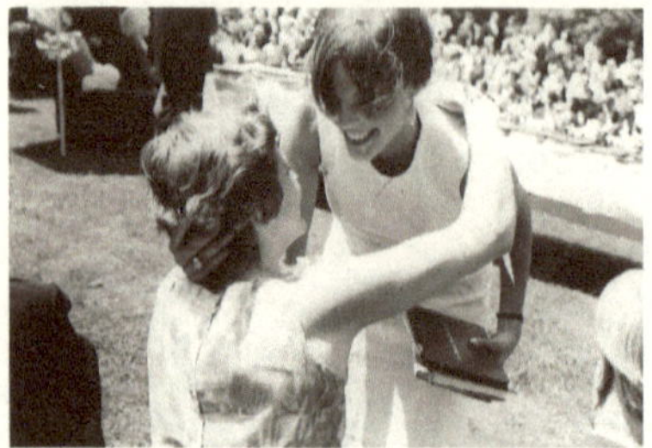

Jill receiving diploma during graduation

For my graduation, Lucretia Simmons helped me pick out a gorgeous outfit from Henri Bendel. It was all white and sleeveless with layers of lace, tastefully tight and lovely. My father made a speech at the graduation ceremony for our class.

Windsor Mountain school diploma emblem

Bob McCormick was very involved with Windsor Mountain and founded his own boarding school.

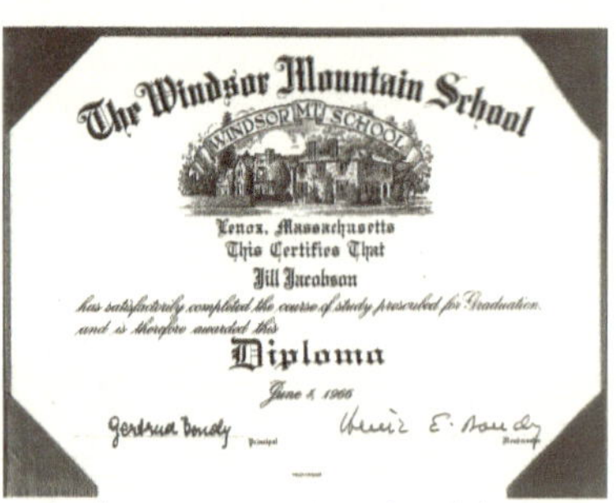

Windsor Mountain School diploma

Bob was married to another alumni, Barbara Barushka, Christine's sister. Christine married a former student as well. It was funny but true.

Group photo from reunion at Windsor Mountain School, Lenox, MA, June 15th, 1996

56

HOWARD SPAETH

"Howie" to everyone, was the assistant principal and vice president of Windsor Mountain under Heinz. I first met Howie in the main house in Gertrude's private quarters at the top of the stairs to the right. They were having group psychiatry sessions which were also run by Joel Lloyd and Howie was one of the people conducting the groups. Howie was extremely popular among the fun-loving students. He had massive energy without speed. Heinz was middle aged and mellow. Howie was 30 going on 22, very fun loving, playful and very efficient, and kind of wild. He attracted all the students with a happy-go-lucky attitude. Everyone loved him. He was an excellent pilot who had an airplane and flew places a lot.

Howie lived off campus in an A frame house with his wife Pat and their three kids, two girls, then finally one boy. Howie would take a bunch of students bowling or down to the class house on a short trip, me included, and take a pickup truck or a station wagon and play a game with us. He told us he'd score points for each innocent victim we ran off the road. There were people walking down the heavily wooded country road. So, we'd pretend to almost run them over, but he'd swerve out of harm's way at the last minute. We'd be screaming and laughing all at the same time. No one ever got hurt. Well, that was Howie, tons of fun. Howie was a big guy, about 6'2" and big, not chubby though. I guess somewhere along the way he got mixed up with the amphetamine, I think. He hooked up with Claire, our student government vice president. I have withheld her last name for obvious reasons. Well, they took off together and flew all over the country, stayed at numerous hotels and motels, ran up big bills and maxed out credit cards. The whole school knew what was going on. Claire missed her school government meetings, etc. He ended up getting into trouble and having to leave school because he owed a ton of money from maxing out the credit cards and finally ended up in jail.

After a short while my father pulled some strings and got him out citing, "How else can he support his family unless he is out of prison?". Once he got out, he turned his life around and ended up owning a fleet of airplanes. I was very fortunate that Howie became fast friends with my father and was appointed by him to fly me in his airplane to a college interview at Green Mountain College. Howie was a wild car driver, but when it came to flying, he was very focused and calm. He flew me to my college interview.

I have recently spoken to Howie regarding my writing of this book and writing of this chapter about his situation. He corrected me in certain situations to the point that I wish to correct my error of opinion and reporting of facts as I had told them, which happened to be inaccurate. I also wish to correct a story that my father told me which, although a great story with a happy ending, was unfortunately not true.

The truth was that Heinz had apparently spent part of the money earmarked for the Nina Jacobson Theatre, instead, spending it on the school to keep it running. When Heinz was threatened with exposure and needed to get more money fast, he called my father, who called on Alan J. Lerner to come up with much needed cash. Heinz instructed Howie to fly around the country to get funding for the school to keep it afloat.

Since Howie was doing a great part of the fundraising effort, Heinz made an agreement with him that gave Howie 5% of whatever he raked in. Howie was in jail in Cleveland, Ohio. It was not made clear until Heinz was called upon by Howie's lawyer exactly what the problem was and who was to blame. Heinz didn't substantiate so Howie ended up in jail until they worked it all out. After Howie got out of jail, my father called him, gave him moral support and got him work flying people around and introduced him to people in Washington whom he would fly places. And helped him get back on his feet and stood by him.

He told me my father called him often and asked him to run errands for him, like flying to Massachusetts to deliver a check from Alan J. Lerner to Heinz for $25,000 to help rescue Heinz financially and help the school. Howie was concerned because Heinz, in his opinion, abandoned Eleanor Bondy early on and that upset him. He claimed Heinz wouldn't support Eleanor or help her out and shouldn't have adopted the children to save his marriage. He felt Heinz had no right bringing children into an environment like that, with an alcoholic mother. He felt Heinz didn't treat Eleanor appropriately. Or stand by her while she was dealing with alcoholism. He also claimed that Heinz was having a relationship with Carolyn Louks while Eleanor was in rehab.

During our conversation, Howie asked me if I knew Mark Shaw of all people. I told him, unfortunately yes, I did. He went on to tell me what admiration and respect he had for Mark Shaw as a photographer and airplane pilot. I was shocked to hear him, Howard Spaeth in five minutes giving me newfound admiration and respect for Mark Shaw. It was almost unbelievable. He told me that John F. Kennedy, our beloved President didn't trust his own administration, so he had Mark Shaw fly an airplane from Andrews Air Force Base on a U2 type airplane to take pictures of Cuban Missile silos for President Kennedy. The silos had to be placed on stands and the President wanted proof of their existence and wanted them photographed. He sent Mark Shaw on the secret mission to do this for him. Mark Shaw was there to fly to Cuba and back. I was only 14 years old at the time. I was *really* in the dark about all this. Howie also told me what an incredibly great photographer Mark Shaw was for Jacqueline Kennedy and the President. He stated that Mark was a person of interest to the President.

57

DONALD THAYER

— ◦ —

Introduced to me as an airplane pilot, Don Thayer was hired by my father to redo the new office on East 78th Street, from floor to ceiling. Why he hired him I don't know. Don was an airplane pilot who owned his own small piper plane. He flew me and his son up to my school and back to New York several times. He came over often to visit. He and Mark Shaw did lots of frequent flying for my father.

58

MOMMY'S DEATH

*Nina and Jill in last years before her
mother's death*

My mother's death hit me like a ton of bricks. The last time I ever saw her she had come with my father to visit me at Windsor Mountain School on a Sunday afternoon and they were leaving. It is a lasting memory engraved indelibly on my conscience and in my brain, and I can never shake it from my memory bank. We were standing on the cobble stone driveway outside the front of the Main House, maybe three feet from the front door. She wanted me to kiss her goodbye. I hesitated, as always, shy and resisting yet trying to comply. There was always resistance, why I never knew, but there was always resistance. With Daddy it was different, always. He demanded a kiss in a very inviting and comical way. It was always a fun thing to do with him. With mommy it was different, more strained. I asked her for $5.00. She agreed, reached in her pocket for it and asked me for a kiss goodbye. That was the last time I ever spoke to her or saw her.

I tried to call her to wish her Happy Mother's Day. My father's nurse, Anna Tschausoff was with her. She wouldn't let me talk to my mother. My mother was sick. I didn't know it. Ich hatte kein ahnung (I had no idea). I then sent her a telegram from the east dorm where I lived. I don't know if she ever got it. Within a few days I was called up to the main house by Gertrud. The rest is almost a blank from here. Gertrud had to inform me that my mother had become very ill and was possibly dying, she was taken to the hospital. I started crying. Gertrud immediately gave me a few pills. They didn't work. I now firmly believe natural grieving has a way of working itself out. One mustn't take pills, antidepressants or otherwise. The grieving process is so natural, normal and vital in so many ways.

Gertrud accompanied me to New York to meet up with my father who was at the hospital. I went back to the dorm to pack, I was really upset and shaken. I returned, Gertrud had since received another call from Papa that the situation was grave, mommy had taken a turn for the worst. I started going to pieces, and as I am writing this, tears are flowing again, 35 years later. We ended up driving to our apartment to wait for my father. I was pleading with Gertrud and my father to let me see my mother, even if for the last time. But my father wouldn't allow it. Then Papa called from somewhere, he was on his way home to meet with me, Dr. Halstead also came.

 By the time my father finally arrived at the apartment my mother had already died, that was it. It was more than I could bear. I kept crying and crying, I went crazy. I remember looking at myself in the bathroom mirror and wondering how much more crying I could handle before my face exploded. I had two nervous breakdowns in a row, I was told. I couldn't think. I hit rock bottom and lost loads of weight. I couldn't handle anything anymore. Even Heinz Bondy came to visit me. Mommy died on May 28th, 1964, just two weeks shy of her 50th birthday. I don't even remember returning to school. It is hard to write this because I have never been able to get over this. Tears are streaming down my face right now. I can hardly see. I grieve for her every day. I still go to the cemetery to plant flowers.

I remember in a spur of the moment, Daddy closing his office and traveling with me far away to get me away from there. He took me to Brussels but even that I don't remember. We went away for a week or so. I didn't even realize until years later that that same summer I spent one free spirited month with Bill and Missy McKnight in Point Lookout. I knew I was out there. I just didn't realize that it was the summer after my mother died. I was out in Point Lookout in mid-July.

Not a day goes by where I don't mourn her loss. My poor mother had no one to turn to with her problems. I spent years thinking, worrying from time to time that she may have just left me, abandoned me and my father. He had been giving her a rough time, and actually so was I. I was never really supportive of her. She was devastated over Granny's passing in 1961. My father was too busy working to pay attention to her grief. I couldn't comprehend the scope of Granny's loss to her or the family. Everyone, including me, was so enthralled by my father no one ever paid any attention to her. I never knew what she was going through. She never said a word to me about anything. I guess I could look at myself in the mirror, freak out and say maybe I took her a little for granted.

The memory is still so painful. It never goes away and there is no resolve. There are times I've wondered how things would have been had she lived, alive to protect me from all the insanity that was to come and to protect my father from all the insane patients, who wandered into our lives after her death. Then I should also wonder where the happiness and peace of mind would have come from for her. And to there I only look now, not then.

For years when I was much younger, I suspected my father had something to do with my mothers' death. I actually thought he killed her. I knew she was going to divorce him. She didn't discuss it with me. It was discussed behind closed doors. While I was at Windsor Mountain, about a month before Mother's Day, I remember telling Momma Milan and some students that my parents were getting a divorce, and that I had decided I wanted to live with my mother and have unlimited access to my father. He was always at the office, always working. I had already decided I wanted to live with her and visit my father whenever I wanted. She died right before the divorce proceedings were to take place. I figured Daddy being on the ego trip he probably was, didn't want his reputation tarnished by a divorce, so he probably killed her. Mommy hated shots and he was always giving them to her. Thoughts ran through my mind like crazy.

That was until I read, "I Danced All Night" by Doris Shapiro. It was in her book that I suddenly came to the realization that it was a combination of my mother's frail health, mostly due to her hectic schedule of travel with my father and hours of keeping up with him that caused her to become so run down.

She became quite ill, and being the loving husband and doctor was insisting on treating her and making her feel better in any way that he could. My mother suffered from migraines. My father insisted that she call him at the office whenever she got one. She hated getting injections from him. Sometimes he couldn't find her vein and when he did it would leave a nasty mark on her arm for weeks. There were times she'd stay in bed and suffer so as not to call him and be subjected to an injection. Then if he found out about it later, he would be furious. They would fight. I guess she couldn't win. It seems that his treatment and her being rundown caused her to become even more ill. This indicated to me that it was my mother who chose to withhold information from my father thereby increasing her chances of becoming more ill. Yes, she did this by withholding facts and just suffering. She died of double pneumonia and a nervous breakdown. That was what I was told by Dr. Halstead and Dr. Mintz and what I believed.

59

My Cousin Tony Hagen

As a young girl I watched him laughingly cuddling up to my mother when she'd take us out to get us treats. He'd cuddle up to her, all for a pack of bubble gum and a comic book. That's all he wanted, and he was willing to swoon my mother for it. She gladly got it for him, gladly and happily.

Tony was my rock of Gibraltar right after my mother died, and he was the rowdiest comedienne. I was totally torn apart in every way imaginable, a wreck emotionally and mentally. Tony was always a comedienne. He had this awful habit of being funny at the most awkward times, embarrassing to say the least. He even had me cracking up laughing at my mother's funeral, totally impossible, but he said something at the graveside. Neither of us can remember what he said that was so funny, but that was Tony. He was also a big flirt; it was funny to watch him come on to the girls in the silliest way. He was also there to entertain me. I accepted the entertainment. I loved the shows he put on for me. He was a real jokester, very funny and entertaining. He was constantly telling jokes, for instance, he would go up to a nice, cute girl, put his arms around her and say "Marry wanna?" meaning of course "Marijuana".

When my mother died, he was by my side. We were both at Windsor Mountain school one grade apart. He said to me one day. "Jill, if you need me to comfort you and don't want to be alone and are feeling sad, you can come get me. I promise no matter who I am with or what I *am* doing, I will drop whatever I am doing and come to help you". It took months for me to come around. He was there for me the whole time. We would go to The Log Cabin or The Lenox House for dinner. I had an account there so we could just go and charge it. Mostly we went on Friday nights. He had this girlfriend, Ruthie; he would explain to her that his cousin needed him, and she'd understand. He came to me and offered me moral support.

My next year at Windsor Mountain School I met this nice young man, well boy. We really got together, went steady. We really hit it off. Well, on Sunday in school the boys were obligated to wear shirts and ties to the dining room for Sunday lunch, which was usually a special lunch. Tony was absolutely not into it. He refused to dress for the occasion and then wasn't allowed to enter the dining room. My boyfriend, J.R., took it upon himself to discipline Tony and made him put on a decent shirt and tie. J.R. even taught Tony how to put the tie on. He did it but it was so funny.

Sometime after boarding school, Tony went to Germany and met this darling girl who worked for Uncle Budi. We were close for many years, at least until he went to Europe. Then we literally lost touch. I didn't hear from him for a long time. By the time I did he was married and had a baby on the way. We visited each other in Germany. I arrived with my son, and he had his daughter. After some years he moved back to America, and we got in touch again. But very rarely.

 Several years later I got attached to his sister Karen who became a mother figure to me when I was about 19 years old. She was so comforting to me. I got into trouble once and she was right there to console me as a mother would. She was gentle, caring, kind, and so sweet. Only many years later I became friendly with my cousin Little Nina who was named after my mother Nina. Little Nina was so pretty. She was and is the prettiest member of our big family, and she is also very sweet. And if I didn't say that about her, she would be furious, absolutely! But Karen was the gentlest, caring, and kind, always ready to laugh at my jokes.

60

PAT LAMBERT

Pat Lambert (pronounced Lambear) was our reason for traveling to Brussels, Belgium shortly after my mother passed away. Pat was married to a wealthy Swiss banker named Phillipe who owned a chalet in Belgium. This was her second marriage. The walls were of such extravagant grandeur. They had a huge chandelier over their indoor swimming pool in a separate building on their estate, I wondered if it could possibly tumble and crash into the pool. It didn't. They had a masseur making home visits. The walls of the rooms were covered with lavish fancy tile which was something I've never seen before. My father and I stayed for three days then we flew back to New York.

Pat had two sons from a previous marriage to a teacher on Long Island and one daughter from this marriage. Both her new husband, Phillipe, and Pat were friends and patients of my father. I suppose one could say my father made a house call to these patients traveling all those miles from New York to Brussels just to treat them. They also had a chalet in Switzerland that we visited on another occasion.

Years later I heard that Phillipe left Pat for a neighbor that was Pat's girlfriend. After a rather nasty divorce, Pat returned to the United States with her two sons from her previous marriage and paid frequent visits to my father, both at home and the office. It's not their marriage that was impossible, it was the lavish lifestyle of this couple, the extravagant and exquisite taste of this lady and her husband. Both her homes were very scenic, the one in Brussels and her home in Warwick, NY that she shared with her two young sons after the divorce. I later became very friendly with Pat; she was quite an educated classy lady.

61

AIRPORT FIASCO

I was around sixteen years old at the time when Papa and I had just returned from a visit to Brussels, Belgium. We had originally departed from New York in our usual, last-minute rush. It seemed as if we were always rushing to the airport, and this time was no exception. This time it was for our flight to Belgium and Papa was always leaving town at the last minute and then having to rush to the airport almost missing his flight. Well, apparently, when we returned to New York, we somehow managed to return minus proper inoculation documentation and we were informed that I was amiss a Smallpox vaccination.

We were immediately whisked into a small private room by a security guard. I was carrying a knife I had purchased on a visit to Puerto Rico. It was a maroon knife, with a cross prominently displayed on the front. I liked to flick it. I was kind of wild in those days and carrying a knife so that no one would mess with me was par for the course. I also enjoyed just carrying it and having it in my possession.

 Upon our return to New York, on this particular occasion, I happened to be carrying this knife on me at JFK International Airport. As Papa and I were making our way from customs, a security guard approached us, a big, tall built serious dark man. This guy was big and stern. A black man who happened to be a menacing total stranger to me.

He immediately detained us on the grounds that I had not been properly inoculated prior to our departure and could not be allowed to leave the airport to go home until I was first inoculated with a Smallpox Vaccination. We were led into a small private room off the main course which had a patient table with a white paper covering it. The patient table was pretty high off the floor. On another table right near the table was a large clear glass jar. In the jar were on one side broken pieces of glass. One the other side, right next to the broken pieces of glass stood lead sticks, like soldiers, straight up. The security guard told me to roll up my sleeve and proceeded to go to the glass jar and take a piece of the broken glass to start the inoculation procedure. Shit I got scared! Nobody was going to touch me, especially not a total stranger and especially not with a piece of broken glass. He told me he was going to vaccinate me. I jumped up onto the table and pulled the knife on the man. I shouted, "Nobody but my father is going to touch me. It's my father or nobody". The Guard looked at my father who was beside himself beaming with pride and delight at my insistence that he himself only give the vaccination.

My father could hardly contain himself and yet was also worrying about the ramifications of my sudden erratic behavior. He was so appreciative and relieved when the guard turned to him and nodded his head giving my father clearance to give me the vaccination. My father then thanked the guard gratefully and proceeded to give me the Smallpox Vaccination. Sometime in between that moment and the first encounter, my knife was confiscated, and I never got it back. When I asked my father to inquire about the return of my treasured knife, he told me not to push my luck. We were then allowed to gather our luggage and return home. Thank God!

62

THE TEENAGE YEARS

*Jill and Papa sharing a quiet moment
with a family dog, late 1950s*

I was not an easy teenager to put up with. I smoked cigarettes, that was o.k. I also liked smoking pot. That I did on my own, daddy was not involved with that. He informed me that he wanted me to be an actress, I didn't share his enthusiasm. I was just very verbal, very dramatic. He would throw a syringe at me and tell me to become an actress. He said someone should give me one swift kick in the rear end and send me out on stage. I countered by saying whoever kicked me out would get a kick back, and I adamantly refused.

I wrote poetry in masses, Roscoe encouraged that from me. It was everything to me. It came directly from within me, deep within my soul, my unconscious mind. It was a massive part of me. It belonged to me. He also critiqued my work, not just to please my father, he also did it out of kindness for me. When Roscoe reached deep within his heart, soul and wisdom that only he possessed, and related to me and encouraged me to write, we were one on one.

It began with an informal discussion on Edna St. Vincent Millay. It progressed to learning that a lady paid for Mr. Millay to go to college after Ms. Millay published her first poem. The name of the poem was "Renascence", published in the "Lyric Year" magazine. It was suggested to me to get ahold of "The Poets Market" from the library where I could find hundreds of places listed to submit my poems, also Poets and Writer's magazine.

When the amphetamine rolled in and I took some, I felt relieved from loneliness and despair. It made me feel alone again and strong. I was always by myself and alone, but not lonely anymore because I had my poetry, which flowed out of me like an out-of-control river running down into a stream. And lest I be accused of being ungrateful, it was the amphetamine, late at night, which gave me additional energy to continue writing my poetry after my body, my psyche, wanted to continue and my conscious center didn't have the natural stamina to continue. It was a small shot from papa which enabled me to finish my writing. Once I finished, perhaps half an hour or so, I went right to sleep. It was no big deal, one shot intramuscularly. Papa knew exactly how much to give me. That was all the time I needed to complete my poem.

Unfortunately, there was a time when I went out with some unsavory characters. I had to have my boyfriends. I thought of them as wild beaus, great sex, etc., but won't elaborate on that. My father tried to put a stop to that, the unsavory characters, of course I didn't know in advance that they were unsavory. I guess my father figured that out long before I did. Once I tried to sneak out during the day to meet up with a boyfriend during my winter break. It turned out to be disastrous. The date was horrible. I wanted to cut the guy loose. The guy showed up, stood across the street from where I lived and waited until I came out from my building and then approached me. It was embarrassing and the doormen didn't appreciate it. It took a long time for me to realize that my father may have had a point. Luckily it was only that one boy who was bad news. All the other ones luckily were very nice. Most of my boyfriends from Windsor Mountain School were nice.

Jill in kimono gifted by Japanese Consulate General and his wife, early 1960s

It was a complete love fest all the time, at least until my mother died. Then things started to change drastically. Daddy was lost and grief stricken, he had a breakdown and dealt with it singularly. He would say, "My wife has died, what do I have?". He found himself in a dilemma with me, his teenage daughter and turned to Gertrud for help. She told him that only time would heal. When I was home, my father would send his assistants or patients to check on me when he could. When it came time for Christmas vacation and I was packing to leave school, I didn't want to go home and deal with my father who wouldn't let me go out. I just couldn't stand the thought. I went crying to Heinz Bondy, our headmaster who was just like a second father to me. Heinz was so kind, caring and very understanding. He was just wonderful to me. I went to him and told him there was no way I was going home for those two weeks unless he spoke to my father and persuaded him to let me go out with boys while I was at home.

Heinz called my father and spoke to him for at least an hour, long distance all the way in New York City and succeeded in persuading him to give me some freedom upon my return home. I was not rebellious. I just wanted to be able to go out with boys or whichever boyfriend I had at the time. I thought my father was being far too protective and that I was right and knew full well what I was doing. Boy was I wrong.

Upon my arrival home for winter vacation with two and a half weeks ahead of me, which gave a chance for all the students to get to their far away homes and spend quality time with their families, to me that was a long time. Sometimes we traveled to Europe, Belgium or Switzerland, or just took a short trip to the Lilac Farm upstate New York, but other times we stayed in the city and went to see Broadway plays. One winter we went skiing in

Switzerland. I don't remember what winter it was, only that we went courtesy of Phillipe Waldberg, and daddy insisted on buying me brand new skis to go down an intermediate slope which were two "no no's". I took one look down the slope and refused to budge and nearly passed out. That was the end of that. I know most kids would relish the thought; the adventure to ski down a steep slippery slope wearing brand new slippery smooth skis. Well, not me. I was one big scaredy cat.

Getting back to speaking of boyfriends, I got pregnant a while after my mother died, about 6 months after. I really wanted a baby so badly ever since I was a little girl but also had this fear that just because I wanted a baby so badly, just because of that fact, that I wouldn't be able to conceive. I really believed that. Well, I got pregnant. I couldn't believe it. I contacted this psychic patient of my fathers in New York City who confirmed the fact that I was pregnant. I asked him what I should do about it. He agreed with my suggestion that I call this nurse in my father's office. That was a big mistake. Valerie Chung was trying to get into my father's pants and into his life in any way that she could. She had a husband and two young sons at home but that didn't stop her. Besides, my mother had been dead for a while so I guess she figured she could have him. Stupidly, I called her. I think she told me that she would make arrangements and to come home. When I called her, I thought my secret would be safe with her, yeah right.

When I arrived home, my father was awaiting my arrival with his own long black leather belt in his hands. He was preparing to give me my first belt whipping ever. I was scared. Right away my father demanded, "Who was the boy who did this?". Of course I lied. "Where did all this happen?" I lied. Man was I a lousy liar, bad. No, he never hit me. He ended up taking me down to Puerto Rico for an abortion. I was over three months, and I was just 16 years old. To make matters worse we went to a hospital where the doctor didn't give me proper anesthesia. I was fully awake and in extreme pain the whole time. I kept calling out to my father to tell the doctor to give me more pain medication. The whole procedure took 45 minutes, and the doctor told us afterwards that I had twins which made the procedure take longer and made me feel even worse just thinking about it. We didn't ask any further questions because I was so in shock from the news about the twins and drained from the whole situation. Papa and I returned home to N.Y., and I was so upset that Heinz allowed my cousin Tony to be excused from school for a few days to come and visit me at home. He didn't really know what had happened. When he found out I told him he had to keep quiet about the facts. He knew my boyfriend very well and I made him promise not to say a word.

A few days after the saga with my abortion, I was allowed to return to school for my own sanity. Heinz felt I was better off at school than with my father at home, but I couldn't tell anyone what had happened. I felt so sorry for the guy whom I got pregnant with, because I didn't want him to be blamed for my pregnancy or get into trouble with my father, I purposely stayed away from him. I wished afterwards that I'd returned to him and shared all my grief and feelings with him. I felt we both needed it. But we were so young, and I really didn't know what to do, so I went back to school and went crying to Tony for moral support since he knew what had happened but was told by me not to say a word. I was a mess emotionally and needed consoling. Tony was always there for me and was so good with that kind of stuff. He always gave me a shoulder to cry on.

What I'm saying is I didn't handle the pregnancy thing right. From the beginning to the end, I didn't handle it right at all. I also resented, quietly resented the fact that my father never asked me if I wanted to have the baby and keep it. I couldn't. All I wanted, or thought I wanted, was to get married and have children, that was it. And since I never had any sisters or brothers who lived with me, I wanted children even more. Since my father didn't give my mother the option of staying home and raising me, I decided I wanted to be a mother who stayed at home and took care of her children personally. I also decided in my early twenties that I would have two children no matter what. I didn't feel it was fair to have only one child. I personally felt very lonely as an only child and didn't want the same for my children. I had two boys twelve years apart, but I did have two children.

Luckily at Windsor, after the abortion saga I met a nice girl whom I befriended and who became my roommate and best buddy, Donna Francescott. She laughed me to death if that is possible. She possessed a sense of sarcasm like nobody I've ever met and made everything that was stressful seem quite tolerable and eventually became my best friend with whom I am still in touch.

Bruce Landy, David Werner and I, my new friends in a new year at school, became very close. For a while the three of us were inseparable together. Then after a while of a wonderful bonding and great sexual relationship, Bruce and I drifted apart. I felt tremendous kinship with Bruce, sexually as well. He was my second boyfriend, and we were both shy individuals and liked smoking together. Damn we really bonded, sexually it just came naturally. David and I were like brother and big sister. I really loved and adored him like he was my little brother.

All through the years and many additional pregnancies that I was forced to abort, it took me years to be able to understand why my father wouldn't allow me to have these babies. First, I was too immature, hadn't finished high school plus I didn't have a job, wasn't working and had no job training or money of my own. And my boyfriends, all of them, were not sufficiently employed. We were all so young. While I was in high school, I wasn't employed nor was I enthusiastic about approaching daddy for money, even my weekly allowance which I think was $10.00. All I needed was cigarette money, which I sometimes approached patients for.

We moved from 73rd Street to 83rd Street in 1965. I called an old friend of my dad's, Mike Samek, and asked for some info. He told me my father moved from the 72nd Street office because the lease was up. Maybe it was also because my mother died, and the memory was too much so we moved. He said that might have also been a reason. On 83rd Street, he had his office on the ground floor and our apartment was upstairs. The office had rooms in the back, which he used as his laboratory. The apartment upstairs was a smaller two-bedroom apartment. We moved so many times, I just remembered a third apartment but don't remember when we lived there. After 83rd Street in 1968, we moved to 86th Street between 2nd and 3rd Avenue. We had a two-bedroom apartment. It was o.k. It had a yucky terrace which sadly we never used except to park African Violets which my father liked. My father liked that apartment though. Then my father moved his office to East 87th Street between Madison and Park, I don't know why.

*Jill and Papa at Lyndon B. Johnson
campaign event, early 1960s*

I saw my father working so hard when he was in his office on East 83rd Street. He was forced to work, no rest, no time for rest, no matter what anyone said, because his patients, and I could name each one of them, wouldn't let him go home to sleep. These were self-centered speed freaks who bugged him until he gave in and treated them. I felt so sorry for him. They just decided they wanted shots. Arkadi Gerney, a businessman, came twice yearly at the most, but he came in the middle of the night, woke my father up out of a deep sleep. It was unbelievable. And there was nothing I could do about it. I really tried. I found it so depressing to watch my father being so abused by his own patients. After high school I had real trouble approaching my father for money. I felt that If I asked him for money, I was indirectly contributing to his need to work. It's just that I saw it that way. And there were always those patients bugging him for treatment.

In my opinion, for whatever reason (or non-reason), some really needed treatment and others didn't. They were so inconsiderate to him. If they saw he was tired, very tired, even falling asleep in his chair in the office, they never relented. They just kept on prodding him. I fought them, I didn't care. It was always the same people, a handful of them. He couldn't just throw everybody out of his office, he was in too deep to get out. And the fact that he was using himself, he was lucky he didn't go to jail. He couldn't get out from under it all, because the people who were close to him were using, and they pressured him into it. They were his so-called close friends, a click. It wasn't that easy to just say "no". During his freshmen year, from the fall of 1966 through most of 1967, Stephen Vedro would come down on weekends and work in my father's lab to help set up equipment. He saw my father start to deteriorate from the lack of sleep so he would unplug his phone.

I started getting into fights with the patients who were imposing on my father. There were other patients who tried to help me fight the imposters.

My father never said a word. He just aimed to please and didn't want to disappoint any of his patients. The hard thing was getting those vultures away from my father. Alan J. Lerner was not one of them. Mark Shaw was and only recently, very recently I found out that his demands, needs of my father's treatment were legitimate. He was doing secret work for the President and had to work late nights on secret missions. How the hell could I have known that? I was told I was shielded from all that stuff.

Yes, I've been told amphetamines are addictive, I know, but I saw my father being ogled and harassed time and time again. Unfortunately, very few patients were thrown out. And there was one woman who conned her way into my father's office, then his life and then persuaded him to marry her who was the worst one of all. But there were others who were just as bad. The weird thing was, of all his patients whom I ever saw who really needed speed, it was in fact his third wife. I saw her when she was without a shot. I wouldn't have wanted to be within one city block of her when she didn't have a shot. She was that bad. She shuffled in, dragging her legs and feet into the office and into his room, and that was before treatment.

Again, as far as needing money for anything at all, I felt so bad watching my father working all those crazy long hours and running himself ragged that I simply couldn't approach him for any needed cash. At one point, my mother's sister Aunt Carla stepped in and spoke to him and worked something out where she would get money from him and give it to me if I needed it. It worked for a little while.

There were times when I had to go shopping for clothing. The weird thing was as soon as I knew I had to go I'd get symptoms of the flu, aches and pains, bad ones. My father would call me at home and say, "You haff to go shopping", I couldn't. "I just couldn't go" I said. He responded, "Come by, I vill give you an injection" or "I vill give you somezing, zen you'll goh". I told him I couldn't go; I just didn't feel well. He demanded I come over to the office and get a shot. I did. Then I went shopping and bought what I needed. I guess the injection lifted my conscience, or it calmed me down. I guess if it was amphetamine, it did calm me down. That was what amphetamine did for me.

There were occasions when patients would buy clothing for me as a gift and bring them to my father for me. Some of the things I would never have bought myself, but they were so nice I was delighted to receive them and happy to wear them. One patient had just come from Paris and brought me a light blue silk sweater set. It was pretty and soft and most pleasant to wear. Years later someone stole it from my bedroom while I was away on my travels, but at least I had it for a while.

At some point, I don't remember the exact circumstances, my father and I had a discussion and must have come to a decision. We arranged whereby if I went clothes shopping and found something I liked and absolutely couldn't talk myself out of getting, because I liked it so much and just had to have it, then I could buy it, no matter how much it cost. It worked out great. I ended up buying a gorgeous wrap around Mache skirt for $20.00. I still have it and wear it.

So many times, I confronted my father with questions like, "What are you giving to me? An intramuscular injection?", or the time I had throbbing pain in my little toe, which I got whenever it was humid or rained. This was the result of the accident I had when I was five years old, in Point Lookout during the hurricane. I didn't have much faith in my father years ago, his patients did. I was always his greatest skeptic. I suppose that was because he was my father, and I saw him differently from everybody else. I never had much faith in him or his treatments.

However, when I started getting severe migraines around my late teens, 1967 through 1974, I called my father. By the time he came to rescue me, the migraine was so intense that I was unable to think clearly about anything. I got very sick very fast. He gave me an injection in my stomach. Ordinarily I would have totally freaked out and gotten hysterical. This time I was so sick I just lay there submissively. He injected me in my stomach, I felt no pain. The migraine had consumed my entire body, every inch of me. After the injection took effect, within five minutes, I was feeling fine, tears rolling down from my eyes with sighs of relief, now feeling ready to resume my responsibilities, and no doubt feeling like painting the town red.

Anyone who has ever suffered a migraine of such intensity, one which makes you gradually want to give up everything, and makes you feel depressed, unable to function, and then frighteningly ill, will understand just how incredible an experience it is to be relieved of one's misery at a time like that. I was very grateful to Papa. I only wished in retrospect that I had once, just once, taken the initiative to ask him what it was that he put into that injection, what elements he combined to make this cure, and show me how to mix it so that I could have my own vial, thereby not having to impose on him in the future.

Not me. I was not made up of that at all. It never occurred to me to ask him; it never entered my mind. That stuff was way over my head. It was inconceivable for me to consider taking a syringe and putting needles in vials and mixing potions together. Then to inject myself in the stomach, never had the guts. Besides, I would have waited until the very last minute to seek the treatment. By then it could, would have been too late.

Besides the fact, he was very strict about that. He was the doctor. He was the one who had been in practice for forty years and knew damn well what the hell he was doing. No one, especially not I, knew what the hell they were doing. He felt he was the only one qualified to treat his family, patients, and sometimes friends. My mother suffered from migraines. I inherited them from her. She was so afraid of needles and injections. There were many times she wouldn't let my father know she was sick. It was only my mother who was that way.

Being a teenager, besides putting up with all this bullshit was fun too. I got to meet people like Monty Rock III. My father also spent time driving me around the countryside and talking to me.Once, I was in a musical camp, where I don't remember. I only remember getting into the book Marjorie Morningstar. In that camp I was assaulted by a girl and injured. My father drove up, picked me up, drove a stretch on the New York Freeway somewhere and pulled off the road, parked the car on a stretch of grass and taught me how to fend off a choke hold. I still remember some of it although I have had no need to use it, thank Goodness. He also taught me how to curse in foreign languages so that I could curse, and no one could understand what I was saying. To me the great parts mostly outweighed the bad ones.

TRAVELING

Jill in Venice, Italy with Grandpi,
early 1960s

Since I was young, 8 to 10 years old, I traveled often, mostly to Puerto Rico or Germany to see relatives. My father taught me how to pack when I was going on a trip to utilize space. He showed me how to roll my clothes tightly. Did I listen and follow his instructions? Not until years later. There were times I traveled by invitation from a friend of my father's. I traveled alone only twice to visit my brother Tommy at an Army base. That trip was quiet.

Papa almost always took me traveling with him. And he managed to fly wherever I was to join me. I didn't drag my father from the office. It just happened we went to the same places together. Or I went and he arrived shortly afterwards to visit me and the rest of the family.

Traveling was always a hurried and nerve-wracking experience where daddy was concerned. The rules, the rules, the rules, how much luggage one could carry. How much luggage one was permitted to take on board. Apparently, my father took a lot of belongings and took some medical bags as well. He always insisted on carrying a lot of luggage, so we got muscle strain from carrying a lot of bags through the terminal and onto the airplane. He would check in three bags, one more than allowed, and got away with it. For some reason he didn't want to have to pay too much extra for being overweight. He was an excellent packer but often he didn't have time to pack. He would send an assistant up to the apartment to pack things and would leave the office at the last minute, nearly missing the flight and causing us to rush, walking hurriedly to the plane at the very last minute.

It seems that wherever we went; Europe, France, Germany, Belgium, Puerto Rico, there was always someone or some people anxiously awaiting our arrival and awaiting treatment. From the Lamberts, pronounced Lambear, very French bankers in Brussels, Belgium to the President of The El San Juan Hotel in Puerto Rico. Upon our arrival in Puerto Rico a car was waiting to drive us to the hotel. At the hotel, our luggage was taken to our awaiting suites, adjoining, very nice. And a complimentary welcoming large basket of fruit.

Pineapple, pina colada, guava jelly, all sorts of fancy delicious delectables were awaiting us, and cigarettes for me, a whole carton. I dressed for the beach right away. Almost as soon as we arrived at the beach after the cabaña, Antonio Betancourt, a dear sweet man was always showering us with gifts, before and after treatments. Mostly he showered us with gifts upon arrival.

I was totally hooked on cigarettes from when I was 13 to when I was 29 or 30. Antonio knew the brand I smoked were cheaper in Puerto Rico. The carton to me was a great gift. He also gifted us with native desserts and came by to make sure that everything was to our liking. Sometimes Dona Felisa commissioned him to chaperone us. He made fast friends with my father. He absolutely adored my father; he thought my father was hilarious. The brilliance of my father, Antonio could not quite comprehend. He spoke English well with his heavy Spanish accent. There were some things, however, I thought he couldn't understand. I don't know if he was on speed. That was very hard to figure out in his case. He was hyper, hyper as if he drank strong Espresso constantly. So that after he got a treatment, he became very gracious and somewhat more settled down. But he loved to watch my father in action mixing medicines and making injections. He would offer to take us places while we were in Puerto Rico. My father would graciously and gladly accept.

Tony, as we called him, thought my father was a crazy genius, which he was, and he would try to repeat my fathers' jokes. Somehow with his accent at times it was hard to understand. He was so nice though, like a year-round Santa Claus.

We would only see the President of the El San Juan Hotel for about 20 minutes. He would come to my father's room and ask how everything was, await his treatment, receive his treatment, and promise my father and me a most enjoyable stay. And everything we could possibly want during our stay. Plus, an open charge to his gift shop downstairs and an enjoyable stay at the hotel, and he wanted to be sure Tony Betancourt was expected momentarily to take us wherever we wanted to go. And he wanted to assure us that he would have a car and driver ready to take us anywhere necessary if we needed it. He was a very nice man.

After my father was through giving him his lengthy injection, my father would shoot the remainder of contents of the injection, usually $\frac{1}{4}$ cc of blood and vitamins, straight up to the ceiling. That was my father's trademark wherever he went. He did it for the prestige of it all, or the fun I suppose.

Besides, with all my father's demands, and it was in his makeup to demand this, demand that, demand any damn thing as soon as he knew he wanted something, he demanded it instantaneously, I mean it. Or else! Is how he would put it. But that was usually at the office. And at the hotel, the owner would have all his staff cater to my father's needs before my father even had the chance to ask for it, they did that very well.

We loved staying there. I loved staying there. I loved seeing Dona Felisa. She was so sweet, so intelligent, so interesting. She would explain very diligently how she needed to help the people in Puerto Rico. She explained and detailed the problems of her people and how she had decided to care for them and why she had decided to take certain measures to help them. It was all very interesting. She also had her assistant help me and my mother while we were there and other assistants help my father, mostly Tony Betancourt.

I suspected the president of the hotel was less than amused at my father's injecting the ceiling. I presume that right after our stay he had the painters come up to my father's room to remove the spattered blood mess. At all this, one really had to laugh. My father was a riot at times, especially at times like these. He was really a hilarious creature. The president of the hotel enjoyed my father staying there.

There was a time when I got very sick in Germany. I had developed a kidney infection while vacationing in Italy and feared I got it from drinking which my father loathed. So, I feared facing him. He arrived at the hospital to visit me. It turned out I had gotten Nierenbeckenentzündung, a kidney infection from catching a draft aboard a yacht owned by Stavros Niarchos, so my father wasn't mad. He stayed several days while I was in the hospital, then he left for New York.

64

THE ROBOT

My father had this stoolie (no, not a cigar), more like a gopher, but actually a mindless guy whom he'd send on errands. He would program him, and the guy would act upon whatever my father instructed him to do. There was nothing wrong with my father. He never did that with anyone else, just this robot. This guy named "Lou" was hanging around the office. I don't know why. He didn't work so he really didn't need treatment. This guy, after he got a treatment, his eyes would roll, his arms would swing, and his heels would lift as if he was trying to take off.

He was short, like a young boy, the height of a young boy. He had a weird mustache, almost like Salvador Dali, and the appearance of a midget. And to accompany that as if he needed anything else accompanying his weirdness, he had the strangest laugh, which made him sound like he was trying to stifle himself while he was laughing. He was a so called "artist". Whenever he came in for his treatment, his arms were hanging straight down, but he already had a bounce in his walk, but not as pronounced as after his treatment. The strange thing was, he had a monotone voice just like a robot, and I mean just like. He had a marching walk like a tin soldier, but it was as if a rubber ball were under his shoe pushing him up from under his heels yet returning him to the ground, almost instantaneously, again just like a robot.

He was kind of weird but to see his eyes roll after a treatment, well, that was weird. We, people in the office, both staff, patients, and me, nicknamed him "The Robot". He never appeared to have much of a brain. It seemed to always be the treatment from the doctor that activated him, and I don't know why he was given the treatments in the first place. I saw one piece of artwork that he did in his lifetime, one. It was a plexiglass rainbow pyramid, quite nice. But that was all I ever saw.

My father had some weird patients who were brilliant, very functional and weird and were receiving treatments for reasons unknown to me. He was one of them. But his other patients were also working. This one was not. I must add that just because I couldn't see the reasoning behind his receiving treatments from my father does not mean there was no specific reason. It simply means I couldn't see the reasoning behind it. Nor did I give a damn. I was actually too embarrassed to ask my father, or to even consider questioning him. He didn't like anyone second guessing him on anything, ever. I thought maybe this was an experiment in progress, since to the best of my knowledge my father didn't screw around. This, however, seemed to be the one questionable exception.

65

THE WATCH SAGA

Papa had been given this rather lavish and expensive watch by a patient. The man dared Papa on a bet that if he were to quit smoking cold turkey for one straight year, this patient would give Papa a ten-thousand-dollar watch, a gift that Papa could then donate to his Multiple Sclerosis Foundation if he wished. This patient bet him on it because he said so many doctors order their patients to stop this and that, for example, stop smoking and drinking, yet the doctors don't practice what they preach. So, the patient challenged Papa to see if he had the conviction and discipline to follow through and win the bet. Papa did it and received the watch.

Papa now had this rather expensive lovely watch. After several years of showing off the watch to everyone and anyone, Papa put it away. Suddenly he discovered it was missing, it had been stolen. He was devastated and very angry. He went on a mission to find it. He promptly ordered all his staff, close friends and relatives, one by one to come to the apartment at 225 East 73rd Street to be personally grilled, confronted, and accusingly questioned by him. It was face to face brutal accusations.

He ordered an office staff worker to announce when the person had arrived at the apartment, then he instructed him or her to come to his room and close the door. On several occasions I heard him scream rather loudly. I couldn't hear what Papa was saying to them, but the result was the hurt feelings. My cousin Karen got the worst treatment, unfortunately and especially, she came out crying hysterically. I found out only recently that the whole thing upset Karen so badly it caused her to have a breakdown and break out in hives.

It was traumatic and so very hurtful just to watch all this going on as an observer, which I was. It broke my heart and somewhat destroyed all the great admiration and love I felt for my father at that very moment, because he handled this so poorly. I should have stepped in and stood my ground, become a mediator, an instant mediator. I suppose I didn't do it out of fear of my father, or was I just a coward? Perhaps I was afraid of going against Papa.

All these people, friends and relatives alike had so much love and devotion in their hearts for Max. He hurt their feelings so badly, forever. It was all so sad and seemingly so unnecessary. It hurt to hear my father's yelling confrontations and cold-blooded hurtful accusations.

Ten years later, approximately, we learned quite by accident that our maid and cook, Madame Dupont, who had retired years earlier, had stolen the watch and many other items before she left us and retired. What did I learn? I learned through all this that Papa wasn't perfect, that he didn't handle this crisis well at all. He unnecessarily upset a lot of people, important people to me, close friends, close relatives, my favorite relatives. Was the watch a material object worth destroying all those feelings, friendships and close ties? Was it really? Since then, to this day, my family has been holding this situation against me, directly or indirectly. By not inviting me to family functions or Christmas, major stuff. The whole saga was truly shocking.

66

AMBASSADOR ANTONIO MORALES (PAM)

Antonio Morales first came to my father as a so called "hero". This man was the U.S. Ambassador to the Court of St. James, appointed by the Panamanian government, who presumably cast a vote in favor of partition of Palestine a while back, before he met my father. To me this was just a pile of words having little or no meaning whatsoever at all. Ambassador Morales as he was referred to after a brief acquaintance, invited my father and I (my mother had already passed away) to Panama as his guests and to meet his family. Papa and I flew down to Panama shortly after his first visit to papa's office for a consultation and then treatment. He spoke very fast, almost sounding angry, but came off sounding hilarious, like Abbott and Costello. He made a comedienne out of himself with everything he said.

My father was impressed with his title and his accomplishments and wanted to become friends with him. He became a hero by opening the Panama Canal for political reasons, which intrigued my father. They became fast friends. Apparently, his wife had died a short while before, and he wanted to keep his name in the lights, his title, and become famous politically. When my father addressed him or spoke of him to anybody else, me included, he always made it sound so official because of his title. Upon our return, my father called him PAM instead of Ambassador PAM. Papa was very proud to have this man as part of his inner circle.

After returning home from our trip there, Antonio, "Tony" came over to the U.S. for frequent visits and often stayed at our apartment. He was on speed, and voluntarily and aggressively labored on getting hooked early on. Papa and I took a trip abroad at one point. We were gone for over a week. At that time, we lived on East 83rd Street on the 18th floor. My father's office was on the ground floor. No sooner had we returned from our trip and were looking for a parking space, before we could even pull up to the curb, a court paper server approached our car with the doorman and served my father with legal papers. They didn't even wait for us to depart from the car. I can't imagine that they thought we'd try to escape. Enclosed in those papers were statements of complaint. Apparently, Ambassador PAM (as I called him) had been throwing wild all-night parties during his stay at our place. The neighbors complained bitterly and to no avail. He wouldn't respond to them or respect their wishes, so they went to court. Papa was then served with papers and had to immediately phone his lawyer. Papa was told Antonio was no longer welcome to stay unless we were present.

Unfortunately, he still came to visit, or shall I stand corrected and say he stayed since my father hardly saw him at all and was far too busy at the office to even take notice of him, so Tony would show up at the office, and managed to get my father to give him treatment and then very obviously got strung out on speed. And my father, being much too busy working, failed to notice. I noticed; besides, Antonio was crazy anyway. So, his departure from crazy to scary crazy was really frightening, at least to me. As Papa used to say, "The amphetamine brings out what you already have in you" and this man had a lot of craziness, insanity deeply rooted in his genes, his blood. Also, I'm not sure how he got speed. He might have sweet talked Papa with his Panamanian charm into giving him an injection. There were times he put on a manic charade that would have convinced anyone and normally wouldn't fool my father, however if my father was very busy working, he might have given in and given him treatment. I think papa "the doctor" was wrong to give it to him, yes, but Antonio could be very persuasive and possessed this very potent Panamanian charm!

Eventually he developed a dry itchy skin condition from intoxication from the amphetamine and bad nerves. After some time, he began displaying bazaar behavior. He could often be seen spending countless time in my father's bathroom muttering to himself and yelling Spanish phrases at his reflection in the mirror while obsessively scratching the heck out of his scalp. He had lots of hair and lost a lot in the process; his hair fell out like snow was falling. After repeated scratching and mentally unraveling right in my presence, he began fighting with his own image in the mirror. He was scaring me with his bizarre behavior. Thank God I understood nothing. All that was too much for me, it was hard to take all this in. I was only around 16 or 17 years old at the time. I guess he was getting really strung out, hallucinating, and my father was too busy at the office to take notice of his decline. Finally, he left and returned to Panama. Many of us, me especially, were very relieved to see him go. I somehow don't remember that happening to any other patient, Thank God.

67

JIMMY MORALES (SON OF PAM)

— • —

My father and I had a falling out with Antonio Morales when he got strung out on amphetamine. Then suddenly out of the blue he sent his son Jimmy to stay with us, which he did for a while. He was around my age. As soon as I heard he was coming I was less than enthusiastic at the very thought of anyone related to the ambassador coming to stay with us, and at first, I feared he wanted to press charges against my father for what he [Jimmy] thought my father had done to his father. Utter nonsense! However, that was not the case. He was here to go to job interviews. He found a job. He was thankfully nothing like his father. He was down to Earth, very friendly and normal.

That was until he approached me to prostitute myself and had the nerve to insist on being my pimp. Little did I know then that an ex-boyfriend of mine with an unfortunately twisted mind had put him up to it...oy vey. And Jimmy's idea was to pocket most of the bread. I may not have been good with money, but I never would have gone for that. I guess he misunderstood my relationship with my lovers. I had several at the time. And I suppose exercising bad judgment; I told him. It must have been in conversation since I never discussed my lovers. I always loved making love and wouldn't dream of taking money for it. I told him I had sex strictly for pleasure and not for money. I got quite offended at everything he suggested, and I expressed myself clearly to him. Anyway, I saw him only a few times after that. Jimmy was like a playboy, very debonair. No, he didn't do speed, he smoked occasionally, nothing serious.

68

ALAN J. LERNER

He was a creator, a truly eccentric, neurotic musical genius. I really couldn't handle being in his presence, if only for a matter of seconds being around him, I had the feeling I'd go nuts. It was contagious. He was very nervous and pensive, also while creating. His mind was working all the time, he was constantly creating and writing songs, verses and scores for plays. He would knead his fingers out of nervousness, a compulsive nervousness. And the more brilliantly he was creating the more he paced and the more his fingers would knead. He would get very down at times, and it seemed as if he was brooding, but even then, his mind was working. Sometimes after an injection his normal condition was worked up and ready to roll. Again, very nervous. He would start talking very fast. He wore gloves at times to protect his hands.

On the brighter side, he had the most dashing lovely soft rose petal complexion of anyone I have ever seen, and lovely wavy hair with gorgeous curls. When it came time to go out for his openings, no matter how he felt, he looked dashing and clean. I suspect he was wearing face makeup although he naturally had such a fine complexion that it was possible he was au natural. He acted so cool and calm at those times, he appeared in rare form.

I came to realize that this was genius, brilliance and the eccentricities that go along with it. I saw him in action composing on my father's bed while he was awaiting treatment. Before his treatment, he was testing out lyrics, words, rhyming phrases. He was brilliant and he was repeating lyrics, trying verses out, asking my father's opinion and sounding so enthusiastic over what he had written. The treatment never hurt his creativity, quite the contrary. He wrote "Clear Day" while under my father's care and receiving injections. I personally thought "Clear Day" was brilliant. My father's treatments seemed only to improve his creative abilities. He would say his injections would bring out the best in you and would bring out what you already had in you that you may not have been using to the fullest capacity.

Mr. Lerner, despite all his neuroses, was a very creative driven character. At one point Alan and his wife Micheline were splitting up. They had a son together named Michael. Micheline had changed the locks on their townhouse and had locked him out. He came over to our apartment and divulged plans to scale the walls outside his townhouse, to attempt to break in to see his son and get his belongings. He was obviously very upset. The whole saga of his split from Micheline really took its toll on him, not his work so much but on his nerves.

It frightened me to hear that he planned to scale the walls of his townhouse that he shared with his wife and son to gain access to his home. It sounded like a scene out of the Twilight Zone except that it was very real. Mr. Lerner was about to carry this through and was in the throes of planning it and had gotten himself so worked up that he seemed crazed. I was in my father's room and couldn't help overhearing the discussion. He was rambling because he was so stressed out so I couldn't really understand what he was saying. He seemed totally out of control to me only because I really didn't understand what the hell was going on, or what he was so upset about. I couldn't begin to grasp it. At times, I didn't know if he was crazy or just reacting to a very stressful situation. I guess it was both. And he seemed to be on the verge of flipping out because of it.

On another occasion, my parents and I were invited to attend the opening of "Clear Day" in Boston where we met Jean Kennedy Smith who was Alan's date for the evening. Her sister Pat Kennedy Lawford also attended the opening that night with her. I didn't know at the time that Jean Smith was married. She was all over Alan before, during and after the show. It occurred to me how astonished I was when attending the opening. I was invited to a backstage room with papa where Jean Kennedy Smith and Pat Lawford were staying. Both ladies in my opinion, and I was aghast to see, were dressed rather loud and flashy, with no taste in dresses, bright satin gowns, no petticoats. Both wore high heels. Pat was so astonishingly tall, no stockings either.

The talk of the evening was "Jean Kennedy had a crush on Alan J. and was all over him like crazy". I didn't realize until years later that she had in fact been married to Stephen Smith at the time, the father of William Kennedy Smith. I was 15 years old at the time of the opening of "Clear Day", what did I know? I didn't see them together sexually, only arm in arm and cuddling together in their seats right before the show started. Yes, we were introduced to the Kennedy ladies. They weren't the least bit interested in meeting me. The two sisters were gossiping amongst themselves and spoke briefly to my father and other adults present. Then we all proceeded to the theatre to see the opening of "Clear Day" which in my opinion was spectacular.

 I want it known that Alan J. Lerner was receiving my father's injections when he wrote "Clear Day", one of many shows he had written lyrics for which I personally thought was brilliant. He was also given treatments when he wrote "Paint Your Wagon". Granted that didn't do well, but that was the only movie that he did during that time that didn't do well. He also wrote "My Fair Lady" which did smashingly well and "Gigi". I personally loved "GiGi" and "Clear Day". So how on Earth can anyone say that my father's treatments interfered with or hampered Mr. Lerner's' creativity and work? It helped him. Although the talent was his and was present, regardless of my father's treatment, my point is that the treatment helped if anything and certainly didn't hinder his creativity.

Maybe his personal life interfered, maybe! I think Mr. Lerner had difficulty being able to stop working and possibly suffered from that. Once he got going, he wouldn't and couldn't stop. For geniuses, just stopping while the creative juices are flowing is not an option. If he got tired, drained, or exhausted during the creative process that interfered with his work, then he needed to be medicated, immediately, [sofort}, as they say in German]. It is a gift to have the creative juices altogether, period. And then to have them flowing readily is yet another gift. When they continue to flow and the person gets tired, mentally fatigued, that's awful and very frustrating, and to the sufferer, the genius at work, unacceptable. It's like a car that is en route to an important destination and suddenly the driver realizes he has run out of fuel. He must stop for gas. In this case, it was Mr. Lerner who needed to be revitalized. So, he paid a visit to my father for much-needed treatment. He worked constantly and had imposed deadlines, which were not self-imposed, but imposed by producers of the shows he was writing for. Yes, there were times he knew well in advance that he was running late, that deadlines were approaching. At those times he was overwhelmed by everything that was going on in his life and didn't seem able to deal with the issues at hand. So, he had to come for a treatment to be able to put everything in its proper perspective, which was exactly what my father's treatments were known to be able to do, Thank God. And he was then able to work until he was finished. Also, getting pressure from all those around him to hand in completed work before deadlines hampered his progress.

A.J.L. had a full-time secretary, around the clock, who was very devoted to him. Her name was Doris Shapiro. She wrote a book very recently about her life but mostly about her fantasies concerning "The Doctor", my father. She took shorthand for Mr. Lerner, which was vital to his livelihood and sanity, and advised him of his appointments. She was quite amusingly in adoration of herself. She did have a sweet gentle nature. Most of the time because she was tired and stressed out, her face appeared rugged which was reflected by her obviously dark baggy eyes. Yet her adorable smile made up for everything along with her gentle and kind personality. Sometimes when she smiled enthusiastically her nose would wrinkle and when that happened, she looked so cute, she melted your heart. When she spoke, she spoke softly with a concerned caring edge to her tone of voice, which was kind in nature. She was never stern, which I thought was quite nice. If only she hadn't worn that damn lavish fur coat which was at least two sizes too big on her, thick and cheapened her in my eyes.

Her main goal seemed to be staying by Mr. Lerner's side as much as possible, or at least from what I saw. It was obvious through subtle things she implied or simply her determination to avoid taking calls from her husband, whom she hoped would give up on her if she stayed away long enough. It appeared at times as though she was camping out at my father's place with Mr. Lerner just to avoid being a wife and dealing with her husband altogether. I'm getting at something here. She was married, yes, I know. I almost didn't believe she was married because she spent so much time quite happily with Mr. Lerner. However, once in a while her husband would phone and ask for her. She would get all flustered and answer the phone. Once she got off the phone, she became all-flustered and nervous. I don't think she enjoyed her husband too much. It was either that or she was a closet workaholic. When A.J. came to my father's apartment she would accompany him. She would take off her coat and shoes, take out her steno book pen and cigarette and flounce her long full body upon my father's bed and assume a sexy pose. It certainly appeared as though she was doing all this to impress A.J. and because she obviously considered herself rather dashing and voluptuous. She has claimed in her book she had an affair with my father. It certainly appeared as if she was vying for Mr. Lerner's attention, not my father, who was busy mixing medicines for Mr. Lerner and at the same time engrossed in an intellectually stimulating conversation with him. They had plenty to talk about, my father and Mr. Lerner, including Mr. Lerner's' marriage difficulties with Micheline and wanting to see his son. I mean, so what if my father did have an affair with Doris Shapiro? However, I doubt it really did happen. My father was much too deeply involved in his medicines and doctoring to give any attention to her.

My father and I were invited at one time to visit him at his home in Oyster Bay and had the opportunity to meet his other children, starting with his daughter Susan. I immediately realized they didn't inherit his talent or brilliance, that was a strange thing. I never met his son by Micheline, so I wouldn't know about him. They had a lavish house, pretty fancy with plenty of room outside as well as indoors plus ample servant's quarters. Nearby but still on the property Mr. Lerner built a theatre. It was very gemütlich , which is German for comfortable. It had velveteen carpets, and it was built in such a way that one could lie down to watch a movie.

I had the utmost respect for his talent, creativity and musical abilities. I was simply astonished by the limited knowledge and intelligence of his daughter Susan and her lack of tact when dealing with the servants. There came a moment during our visit when Susan had a confrontation with the daughter and other children of the personal chef, the kitchen help. They were sweet little innocent children only 5 or 6 years old. They came running through the kitchen door and proceeded to run through the house. They were just running, playing and Susan abruptly chased them back to the kitchen. She said the help didn't belong in the house, they had their place and had to stay there. I felt so in shock and aghast at her response to them.

 Later that evening she mentioned to me that she had recently gone to a nearby college to register for some classes. She said they asked her if she wanted to matriculate and when she heard that she bolted out of there. She told me she was embarrassed when they asked her that because she didn't know what that word meant, and she couldn't answer them, so she took off. I think my father finally told her what the word meant. And then she said she'd eventually go back and register.

Morgan, her husband, who always dressed as a ship captain with the white pants, canvas boat shoes, the sea captain hat with the braid on the rim and the mostly double-breasted blue blazer jacket, and a pipe in his mouth, certainly gave the unmistakable impression of being gay. I always thought he was gay. Sometimes these men who were raised from wealth gave that impression but really weren't gay. They were raised and taught to enunciate their every word and be so gentlemanly which in most cases made them appear to be more effeminate. He seemed to be very much the perfectionist, all the symptoms of, well a homosexual. He appeared delicate opposed to macho. He was not a husky manly man, spoke too perfectly and exaggerated every syllable and gave the impression of being a snob. In his case I don't know about the homosexual aspect. They did have children. He was polite but a bit stuffy. He spoke with what sounded like a stuffy nose even if it wasn't.

69

JACK AND JILL

Jack was a friend of my cousin Tony for some years, but I was totally oblivious to his existence on Earth until my senior year at Windsor Mountain School. Out of nowhere I fell for him. As a matter of fact, at one point I almost fell for his best buddy Jay Speakman. I was secretly and momentarily torn between the two of them. But that was my secret. I was already unofficially with Jack. He looked like the James Dean type, very good looking (we modeled together once). He had the sexiest smile in the world, the most gorgeous hair style. He didn't do anything to be sexy. He was just so sexy and independent.

Back in New York, a patient and friend of my father, Ben Murphy, had been commissioned to do a photo shoot for a particular hair style. Somehow, he decided to style my hair and enlist me to do the photoshoot. I agreed. It just so happened that I had made prior arrangements with Jack to see him on that day for a date. I told him I had to go on that photoshoot. Jack decided to tag along. He met us somewhere on East River Drive where they had benches near an overpass. Well, they took one look at Jack, who was more gorgeous than I was, ever, and decided to use him.

70

Transition to Adulthood

I sent out applications to at least three colleges. I guess I wasn't too enthusiastic about the prospect of going to college. But I knew I had to go. I also knew that I had to apply to the colleges and get an appointment to visit them. I suppose that my father knew I was going through the motions, and that I seriously lacked major enthusiasm about looking for a college. I was not your typical "A" student. So, he enlisted Howard Spaeth to personally escort me to my college interviews.

First, he drove me by car from school in Lenox to Pittsfield airport, then we flew, just the two of us in his small Cessna plane to my interview at Goddard College. We had hot dogs and soda, which we placed between the seats during our flight, it's amazing nothing spilled. Howie really had balls. He was diving through the clouds. We dove down, we climbed back up. It was so exciting. It didn't even upset my stomach. I just remember the thrill of it all. And to experience such aeronautics. It felt like we were in Great Adventure Amusement Park. There wasn't much air traffic in those days, so diving through clouds was exhilarating and fun, not very dangerous. It was quite an adventure. Papa and I trusted him completely. I'd say we had a wonderful time.

I must say Howie took a situation which could have been very chaotic to me and made it into a fun adventure instead. I felt that was something to boost my morale. My father was so happy when I was happy. He would throw a syringe and laugh heartily and say in his German accent, "Isn't that vonderful?". I applied to Goddard College, Berkley in Massachusetts, Wellsley College and Burlington, in Vermont. No decisions were made about colleges until a while later. I finally decided to take a sabbatical and go to Germany instead to rethink my goals and directions and then returned to enter Boston University.

I never matriculated. I attended Boston University as a part time student. The whole setup at B.U. unfortunately didn't inspire me. I attended Boston University for one year. That was it, it just wasn't for me. The whole experience was rather disappointing. My private life was far more intriguing than my college life was. I wasn't to learn until years later that it was just the college which wasn't right for me. Later I went to U.C.L.A. and did fabulously well. Boston U. wasn't the right atmosphere for me, the courses or the teachers.

I met a guy in my junior year at Windsor Mountain School. He set my motors running. His name was Jack Levi. I was nuts about him. I was sure he felt the same way about me. He would hitchhike on weekends from school in Lenox to be with me in Boston for a visit. Even in the snow, and it snowed a lot back then, especially in Massachusetts. In those days hitchhiking was not a dangerous sport. We spent wonderful weekends together until he graduated.

I soon learned upon visiting my former school one day that Jack had been two timing me with a girl named Jackie. I guess I should have been grateful to have him on the weekends. I was shocked and surprised to say the very least. Jay Speakman, Jacks best friend at school, felt very badly for me that Jack was doing this. Jay mustered up all the strength that he possibly could to tell me what was happening. He said he felt I didn't deserve this. I couldn't seem to leave Jack despite it all. On a weekend trip that Jack took to New York, instead of coming to see me, he met some girl and had a one-night stand. She became pregnant. He called me several months later and told me what had happened and asked me if I knew of a doctor that would perform an abortion for her. I didn't know of any, I laughed it off as bizarre and beyond ridiculous. It was then that I decided not to take Jack seriously anymore, I couldn't. From that time on I appreciated it when I could see him, and when I didn't, I didn't.

I decided to go back to Germany for the summer, Jack graduated from Windsor Mountain School and decided to surprise me and meet me in Germany. I didn't know he was coming. He showed up about two weeks after I got there. When I arrived in Germany this time, I was 19 years old. I stayed with my grandfather and paid visits to my uncle Peter.

My grandfather Louis surrounded himself with young, or shall I say younger people, very intellectually stimulating and artsy folks in their late 20's and thirties. One of them had just become separated from his wife and was left at home with a seven-month-old baby boy. This man, Joachim Wolff was a photographer in Germany. He even had his own dark room in his apartment. His wife ran off with an older man, a European director, and left the child behind until she could get settled in a new home with this man and take the baby along.

 This took a long time. Somehow in the meantime I became romantically entangled with this photographer. I had nothing to do with his child, however, he was strict about that. I was there for him and with him only. The baby was not for me to tend to at all. That seemed o.k. The mother of the baby, Cybille, happened to be very friendly with my grandfather, who somehow found himself surrounded by younger and very beautiful women, she was one of them.

 Indirectly she knew about me, and either tolerated me, or since I was my grandfather's loving granddaughter, she put up and shut up. Or she was so wrapped up in her new life that she put everything else on the back burner, including her baby. These things happen.

 Grandpi was amused by this sudden romance between Joachim and me. He would come over and bring us food and find out how we were doing. He wanted to make sure everyone was in accord with the situation.

 Joachim and I had a mad love affair, maybe for him it was just another affair. But for me it was incredibly great. Then out of the blue, Jack Levi arrived on the scene. Grandpi phoned me and informed me that Jack had shown up at Uncle Peter's bank and was asking for me, he said "Jill, Jack Levi is here, you'd better come over". I panicked!! I went to see him. He had followed me all the way to Germany to be with me. I didn't want to fluff him off. But at that exact moment he seemed like an imposition. It's amazing how time and the passing there of, and the experiences one encounters can change things, make things look different, and so it did. This time, I could not muster up the time nor the patience to deal with Jack. I became somewhat annoyed with the whole situation. I told him I had met someone else, that I was sorry. I wished him well and left the café to go back to my German beau. I abandoned him (foolish me). He even stayed in Munich for a while. He remained in Munich for several months before leaving for Istanbul. We kept in touch, I guess, through my grandfather.

After about two months, Joachim left me. That made me feel sorry I hadn't stuck it out with Jack. I returned to my grandfather. I shouldn't have continued this because my father all the while was in New York (always forbidding me to hook up with a German, especially if he wasn't Jewish) and had left me under my grandfather's watchful eye. My grandfather was usually very strict and verboten, however under these circumstances, he was rather lax. Years later, I spent a lot of time searching for Jack, even enlisting the aid of an astrologer to try to find him. It was my Aunt Yvonne who finally helped me find him. He was living in India for years and still resides there today. We remain in touch and are still friends.

71

ALWAYS AIMING TO PLEASE

— · —

I felt pressured to meet my father's demands and expectations. He was always demanding me to do things, complete tasks, do better, accomplish this, accomplish that, I had to see him and present progress reports. I felt seriously obligated to produce, to give him progress reports. It was all very tense, very deliberate. I didn't want to let him down.

He spent countless hours lecturing me to become someone and make something out of my life. Whether he gave me treatment or not, he constantly reinforced being constructive and productive. All this was when I was in my early 20's. He did state early on that he also wanted me to become a doctor. I tried to begin studying psychology. That lasted only a short while. He used to tell me stories about refugees in Germany, who escaped with next to nothing but the clothing on their backs. They had to struggle to make a living once they arrived in this country with practically no money, and not always knowing if another meal would come, or if they would be able to continue making ends meet. Some of them had every obstacle to overcome in their path.

'Then", my father would continue, "Look where this so and so is today, doing something they never believed in their wildest imagination that they would ever be able to do, being on top of their field, game (my father while speaking, throwing a syringe) and being that successful. Now isn't zat vonderful?". "Now darling", he would say "If he can do it, so can you! When you get sick, very sick, or when you want to have sex, then you go to bed. But for the common cold and most other ailments, I give a treatment, then go to work!".

BILL BALL, ACT, AND THE FBI

*Papa preparing meds with Bill Ball
(left), mid 1960s*

William (Bill) Ball was the actual founder of the American Conservatory Theatre Company, which was funded by The Ford Foundation in Milwaukee, Wisconsin and made its home base in San Francisco in 1967.

Bill was a character all his own. In my opinion he was the most brilliant theatre director (well, I must say he was as brilliant as Franco Zeffirelli). He would sneak into the theatre while a production was in rehearsal and sit way in the back, slouching in his seat, wearing a big wide brimmed straw hat so that nobody could see him. Then he could sit quietly and observe the action in progress unnoticed, and it always worked. His mind was very creative.

He broke women's hearts everywhere he went without even trying and was supposedly gay. He had a unique and strange personality and was very entertaining. He was very subdued and soft spoken, down to a mere whisper yet at times his voice would be pronounced and vocal, to the point of sounding stern. Everything he did was in a subtle and low-key manner. Somehow, in some subtle way, he appeared stoned or having had a few drinks, but he wasn't stoned or intoxicated. It was his calm cool manner that alluded to something that was not.

Paul Shenar and Scott Hylands studied under him in his company, as did Rene Auberjonois, Austin Pendelton, and Carol Mayo Jenkins (from "Fame"). It was rumored at one point that Carol Mayo Jenkins and Bill Ball were supposedly an item. Bill created and ran the American Conservatory Theatre Company and was the one solely responsible for making it what it is today, a thriving success.

I have a story to tell on this one. I liked Bill and took a liking to Paul Shenar (gorgeous). Paul was very handsome and distinguished looking, a debonair young actor who possessed a deep resonant speaking voice and was quite charming. He was ACT's Cary Grant. I wanted to be in their midst, somehow. My father was treating Bill for allergies and became friends with some of the members of the company during that time. At one point I joined summer stock in Connecticut, at The Good Speed Opera House. The fellowship members stayed nearby in a summer style cottage. Rene Auberjonois taught acting classes to the fellowship students, but that was in San Francisco, I was one of them. After Connecticut we moved on to San Francisco. Late one afternoon, shortly after Bill and the company had set up the theatre in San Francisco, he walked into the theatre office, went to the corner of the office and made a phone call. Everyone that was present appeared tense. He suddenly announced that the company was rapidly going bankrupt. He was in a state of panic and appeared strained.

He called some heavy-duty donor on the phone, turned and told the few personnel around him that he had to go away for a few days, and instructed his secretary and the others not to tell anyone what was going on. He said he'd let them know when he returned. He turned to me and asked me if I wanted to go with him. I had no idea where he was going. Of course I did, I said yes immediately. I jumped at the chance to go. He was having allergy problems and had a vial of my father's injection with him. He said he'd have to stop by a pharmacy and get allergy medicine. He was worried that it would make him drowsy, and he wanted me to accompany him on the trip to make sure he stayed awake and keep him company. Another girl my age wanted to come along, but somehow, I don't remember her accompanying us there. He just took me.

We drove like crazy, non-stop almost two days. Only taking a motel room one night so that he could get about 5 hours sleep. We told absolutely no one where we were going or why. I was a little nervous but just being with him doing this was such a thrill, such an exciting adventure that I didn't mind. I had to leave without a change of clothes. He said he'd buy me a leather skirt along the way (in style) which at that time was about $10.00. I never got a skirt. He got allergy pills. He had bad allergy problems and had to get the pills. He took injections to combat the fatigue, which antihistamines always do.

We finally arrived at the lady's house. She and Bill immediately disappeared into private quarters and had a "Pow Wow", lengthy business talks. The resulting accomplishments were successful. She committed to sponsoring him and his theatre company for years to come. The agreement transpired in 1967, and they are based in San Francisco and flourishing today.

The next day, still under secrecy, having had to wear borrowed clothes, and no one at ACT knowing our whereabouts, I was sitting outside the front house of this lady from the Ford Foundation down by the lake. There stood a big tree between the house and the water's edge, much closer to the water. Under the tree but attached to two strong branches by ropes was a swing. I always loved swings, it was great fun and a great escape. I was busy swinging with my thoughts thousands of miles away as always when two men in business suits approached me, asked me if I was Jill Jacobson. "Yes" I replied. They asked me to accompany them to the house, at which time they identified themselves as FBI agents and told me to call my father. I did, right away. Then my father asked to speak to Bill.

It was exciting, scary and quite funny, an adrenalin rush. Apparently, my father couldn't imagine what had happened to us or why I hadn't called to inform him where I was as I usually had. So, he called the FBI to find me. I certainly had some explaining to do. The FBI men left, then Bill and I had a quick lunch and returned to San Francisco with the daughter of the lady whose house we were in, who was also an apprentice in the summer stock program in San Francisco and had to gather her belongings to return with us. We had driven all the way to Milwaukee, Wisconsin, the beer country, and now we had to drive all the way back. That was a true story. I was a guest apprentice at ACT in East Haddam, Connecticut when I was about 16. It lasted about 3 weeks. Then several years later I joined them in San Francisco. That lasted the summer of 67. I trained there as well. I wanted to direct. They wanted me to act full time. I said, "No way".

I must say, despite it all, that Bill accomplished his mission successfully. He was under an enormous amount of pressure to keep his company afloat. Cheers to you, Bill Ball. Someday, when I open a bottle of Champagne, I'll toast to you!

73

BUNGALOW IN TERRACINA

— • —

Grandpa and I were invited by my Uncle Peter to visit him and his family, wife Candida, sons Charles Peter, Louie and Alexander to their rented house in Italy. Grandpa and I accepted the invitation and drove down from Munich. When we arrived, the place was rather small for all five of them and then for the two of us, too much. But then Peter and Candy started fighting and Grandpa and I left. We drove for a little while looking for a motel or for any place to stay. We drove up a cobblestone driveway to a place lined with rows of all white bungalows to the left and right. It was all very fancy. We pulled into a pebble stone driveway and drove up very slowly. There appeared a nice-looking young man about my age. He approached our car barefoot wearing only a bathing suit and asked if he could help us. Grandpa asked him if there were any vacancies. He said there were bungalows available and asked if we were interested.

I took one look at this young man, and turned to Grandpa and said, I want this guy, buy it! (Meaning the bungalow). Grandpa asked where the nearest bank was, and then we went, returned and Grandpa paid cash, and bought the bungalow, which I have since been told was one of the best investments he ever made.

It seemed as if we stayed there at least one month. I really fell for the guy. We dated for quite some time, had a wonderful fling. After we returned to Germany we visited each other frequently. While still in Italy, we went swimming and boating on a yacht together, and love making. This guy reminded me of Mike Myers in that movie Austin Powers. I took even more trips to Germany to visit Grandpa and to see Ali Meisel. Daddy didn't really want me to go to Germany and wasn't enthusiastic that I was taking up with a German especially since he wasn't Jewish, but I did.

Ali and I kept in touch through the years. He hooked up with another lady for many years, of course also German. At one point I returned to Germany with my little baby, first born son Jason, one year old. Ali and I spoke. Somehow, we had a major argument over the phone in a neighbor's apartment in Grandpi's building over Valium, which I had been taking for bad nerves for a while. The argument was very stern between Ali and me since in the meantime, he had become a pharmacist and was convinced he was an authority on all kinds of medicines including Valium which he regarded as highly addictive. He accused my father of dispensing pills irresponsibly to which I blew up and vehemently objected.

After the argument, unbeknownst to me, this lady had decided to pour me a stiff drink. I saw her pouring coca cola and I thought, how nice. I didn't see her pouring the rum apparently. Well, I drank the coke happily and never tasted the rum. I got violently ill from it. Never again did I partake of any rum for the rest of my life. I learned my lesson.

After that time Ali and I kind of lost touch. He had an older German girlfriend and was behaving more like a strict father figure to me than an ex-boyfriend or a friend. And his girlfriend was treating me as if she was my mother. I thought, who needs that?

Years later, this being 1990, having had my second son Matthew and now living in Brooklyn, I received a phone call from Ali who was in New York for a visit and wanted to see me. Well, I got all nervous and flustered. I asked my younger son's father to guard me and protect me from Ali. Ali wanted to take the subway out to Brooklyn and visit me. He did and found me right away. He walked in and right away, sofort (immediately), I wanted to jump into bed with him, right then and there. I hated myself for telling Steve to guard me so closely. I learned one lesson from that. Never prejudge a situation or anybody. Just go with the flow and leave yourself open to whatever the wind blows in. I didn't hear from Ali for years after that. I have only recently been in touch with him, briefly. We are trying to get together sometime around Christmas.

Back to traveling and Germany, I love Germany for many beautiful reasons and would eventually like to rent or buy a place there, even if I only stay there a few months of the year, or even a month. I love the Germans, and I love to hear them speak German. They have nice houses, grass and lakes, and lovely apple trees great for picking right on the premises, how heavenly. Especially the houses where my grandfather bought his own apartment on Katharinen Strasse, the outskirts of Munich. The ladies wearing their traditional costumes and carrying those baskets. It is so beautiful. The only thing I didn't like was the beer or when the men drank it. I always wished I could speak fluent German, and the wish is still there.

Two years later I think, when I was about 20, I went to visit Grandpa in Germany. This was his very first apartment in Munich since moving back from N.Y. to manage his bank. After Granny died, he got the offer to return to Germany. I lived with Joachim at his place for a while until Grandpi and I headed back to Italy. I traveled with Grandpa a lot, including our planned trip to Italy as guests of Franco Zeffirelli to observe the filming of "Romeo and Juliet".

74

FRANCO ZEFFIRELLI

For me, meeting Franco, this brilliant and magnificent director, was truly one of the greatest experiences of my life. Back in the summer of 1967, he opened his villa and hospitality to the entire cast of his "Romeo and Juliet" crew. Just for the dance scene alone, he had several hundred actors clad in elaborate velvet costumes. The sets were elaborate, and the scenes exquisitely put together. How do I know this?

 He told my father he was filming Shakespeare's "Romeo and Juliet" on location in Italy during the summer, and somehow managed to get me invited, along with my grandfather to visit the set to watch the filming. Grandpi and I flew from Germany to Italy for this extravaganza. We didn't stay at his villa. We stayed at a motel nearby. When we arrived on the set, they were getting ready to film the dance scene, which involved several hundred actors dressed in rich velvet costumes who had taken their places on the enormous dance floor, and Franco on a foghorn was instructing them on their moves. Grandpi and I visited the set on several occasions including the night of the famous balcony scene, which I will never forget. It was quite an adventure just to be an observer.

To me it was the scene of scenes, nighttime, late, 10:30 pm right outside the house. There were trees and woods outside Franco's villa. It was very much like in the forest. Franco introduced us to the cast very proudly. Leonard Whiting (Romeo), sixteen years old, dressed in tights and a fancy white blouse, was instructed to climb a tree, run down a path and climb another tree. I laughed because he looked like a monkey. All this was in preparation for the famous balcony scene, which they filmed the next night. I was there the next night also. It just so happened Leonard; skinny and not so tall, in real life was dating Olivia Hussey, who played Juliet, which made the whole climate so much more intriguing. The tree climbing lasted an hour and a half, maybe longer. We were all there until nearly 1:00am.

 It was fascinating to be there watching Director Franco Zeffirelli cast and crew in action. The following night we returned, apparently Olivia Hussey was nervous about doing her next scene. Leonard was sent up to the balcony (inside the house) to cheer her up. She giggled happily and instructed the crew not to tell her when they were filming, but to simply tell her that they were doing another take. They did as she said, and it worked!

 I also met Michael York and developed a mad crush on him. His girlfriend was on the set. She was older than he was. She was there with him all the time. I was too shy to say a word. At some point my father arrived and joined us on the set. Michael and my father made friends, bonded instantly. Michael did not receive treatment. They simply struck up a friendship. After watching the filming of "Romeo and Juliet", I was so impressed with Franco that I decided to keep in touch with him, which I did for quite some time. He was brilliant and so nice. His cast and crew all adored him. I wish I were still in touch with him. He is one of those personalities who left a lasting impression on me. I don't know what treatment he got from my father, and I don't care. He had the wisdom, discipline, energy and vision to carry out whatever project he set out to do. Movies were his medium. He didn't need anything to help him along. He was his own boss! And if he did wish treatment, it would have been his private business. He always acted consistently before and after treatment. He never lost his temper in my presence. After a treatment it was my keen observation, when I was around that he never went through personality changes that most patients receiving amphetamine in their injections experienced. Chances are he was just getting vitamins!

75

JAILBAIT TO HELL

In the fall of 1967, I had just arrived in Hollywood, California to be an apprentice in the theatre, The Oxford Playhouse at Hollywood and Vine, to be assistant director and scene writer for Richard Donner in his little theatre. The theatre was not so little actually.

I managed to land a nice apartment in a nice, large apartment building at the corner within driving distance of the Oxford Theatre, where I also befriended the super's wife with whom I became fast friends. She was French and a darling person. She conducted herself as a well brought up woman and had a high-class style, which was apparent mostly in her personality. She possessed an air of independence and intellectuality which was refreshing to me. I wondered how she managed to land in this place as the super's wife, (sigh) oh well. I was grateful to have this apartment as my hours were late and rather hectic. I worked late nights until midnight some nights.

Yes, I had a car, a rental and I drove well. I had plenty of lessons. Once I got settled, with what little spare time I had, I made several acquaintances in the building. Namely a tenant named Mel. He seemed to be rather off the wall, slightly neurotic and quite in love with himself. He was Jewish and seemed to be steering towards being a mama's boy.

He approached me friendly, too friendly. We began talking. He had invented an astrology game which he was working on towards having it patented. That interested me tremendously. I was very much into astrology, Tarot and now I Ching. He sort of interested me too.

Our friendship grew a bit. I really got into observing him working on his astrology game and watching it evolve. It was interesting. He appeared to be a very sensitive, crazy genius. Perhaps because of all the totally neurotic, psychotic and absurd people I had come across in my life, and through my father, any extreme or severe absurdities he may have possessed or exhibited did not appear to shine through me, at least not then. So for a while, I continued to see him in friendship. I also continued working at my job at The Oxford Theatre.

I was writing scenes at home, improvisational scenes which the actors performed during their evening acting exercises. I forgot to mention I received prior theatrical training at A.C.T., The American Conservatory Theatre Company in San Francisco under the direction of Bill Ball, its director and founder, and a friend of my fathers. Anyway, the acting classes at the Oxford Theatre were held two or three times weekly. They ran for at least three hours straight. I spent a good deal of time at the theatre and a good deal of time writing scenes, improvisational scenes which I enjoyed watching come to life on the stage the nights we were there working. Watching the scenes come to life and watching the actors having such a great time doing the scenes made me feel so great!

There was one skit I wrote about pigeons flying over a bridge having a contest as actors as pigeon characters decided which pigeon could drop a load on a person and cause the most damage. It was just so funny. I made a sketchy dialogue as we went along suggesting the actors say "Hey, let's get him, over here, no, over there. Hey, let's get that one", all in different directions, naturally. We'd see the actors running all over the stage with their arms outstretched like wings, makeshift wings. They did silly funny stuff like that. "Fly lower, aim closer. Yeah, you got him" and laughing all along.

Sometimes we couldn't get through a scene because we were laughing so hysterically from the way the scene was going that we were almost unable to complete the scene. Or shall I say, we were momentarily unable to complete the scene due to uncontrolled hysterical laughter. It was such fun. I didn't really need much of a life outside of the theatre, however, I did get one.

This character Mel asked me out, oy gevalt. He was taking this drug, Seco-synatan, some sort of psychic energizer. At least that was what he told me. He was studying this astrology project of his and everything closely connected with it to help him with his invention, his game. He also used this drug, pill, as a somewhat recreational drug, by amusing himself at the racetrack and attempting to psychically pick the winning horses, and sometimes it worked. He picked the winners and actually won, sometimes. After a few dates I suggested that we have an open relationship where we would date other people, after observing him indiscriminately flirting with other women that had left a sour taste in my mouth. I felt that for him in particular, it was beneficial. He said he was very pleased about it and relieved with my suggestion.

After a few short days, maybe a week, I happened to have met another tenant who lived in the same building, David. This guy I really liked. He was tall, very tall, slim and very cute and had the nicest speaking voice, very soft and gentle. After only a few dates, David invited me to Paris. Wow, I thought. Heck, I'd been all over the world with my parents. Why not Paris? I told him I had my job but of course I'd be delighted to go. I mean I was thrilled at the offer and thrilled at the prospects of going to France. How many guys offer to take a girl to Paris? Wow! He said he'd planned it for the next three weeks. I got so excited! I traveled the world with my mother and father when I was little, and then later with my father when I got older. I'd been to France before, quite a while before this so I thought, why not go?

I naturally assumed he meant Paris, France. I didn't find out until two dates later that he meant Perris, California! Boy was I surprised, and momentarily disappointed. I felt like such a fool. I also wondered where he was coming from, making me feel like such a fool. I thought maybe he was buttering me up, trying to make me feel great at the prospect of him taking me to Paris, France. In hindsight though, I realize I should have asked more questions, and I should have been equally as appreciative that he was offering to take me anywhere whether it be to Paris, France or Perris, California. But I got over it. Anyway, this new guy named David Oliver was working with The Temptations. At that time, I vaguely knew who they were. I knew they happened to be a great singing group. He took me to a jam session with them. On that day they were having acoustic problems, but after they got started, they were great. David was the one with the high voice. He sang the high C. He didn't need a microphone!

He also took me to watch him during basketball practice. I liked that and I liked him too. He was so cute, dark, tall, and nice. He had such a gentle whisper in his voice when he spoke. Our relationship began to grow.

At one point my father came to visit a patient in L.A., Nina and Nicholas Turtanic, and arranged for me to come and visit him at their home. The musical "Hair" was playing in L.A. and another friend of my father's, Gina Harding, was in the play besides the show's stars, Jerry Ragni and Jimmy Rado. Gina was a young talented actress, closer to my age, and a singer in the show in California and Broadway. We became fast friends. She was a patient of my father's and a friend of Roy B. Loftin, a Texas millionaire and all-around sugar daddy based in Los Angeles. What she got from my father; I don't know. But she did have lots of natural energy. She had to; she was in "Hair". She introduced me to my very first brownie, someone had to. That's the way I look at it.

What an incredible experience it was. My father and I were invited to see "Hair" while we were in Los Angeles. I was on the phone with Gina the day before the show. I mentioned to her that we had been invited to the show. She mentioned she was making brownies with hash or grass and asked if I would like one. She told me I'd enjoy the show more if I ate the brownie beforehand. She knew I liked pot and that was close enough. I said, "Sure, thank you!". We met right in the parking lot before the show. She gave me the brownie, and I ate it.

First, my father and I went backstage where I observed in utter surprise Jerry Ragni applying body makeup from his head to his toes in record breaking swiftness. Then my father and I went to take our seats. While the show was in progress, I noticed sounds bouncing off the walls to my left and right. The acoustics were very dramatic. It came on subtly, I said nothing to my father. I didn't dare. I had a feeling that something was going on. There was like a third dimension to the show.

The brownie had something in it. I was in control or so I thought. I could handle it. It was dramatic, different, nothing bad. I understood that it magnified and intensified the sound, the acoustics. Everything was interesting, captivating my attention, and I felt under control. After the show ended, I said good night to my father, gave him a kiss, and got into my car to drive home. Papa left with Nick Turtanic and went back to Nick's family, the StarKist Tuna empire heirs, where he was staying as a guest in Westwood, Los Angeles. I had to drive all the way home alone from where I was, at least a good 35 to 40 minutes from the theatre to my home.

There was one problem, one major problem! I couldn't remember for the life of me which light, red or green meant stop or go if my life depended on it, I couldn't remember, I panicked! I went to a friend's house, a guy who gave me some cocaine to try to pull me out of it. It didn't work at all, forget about it. It was garbage. So, I tried to tell myself red light means "Stop" and green light means "Go". I drove and drove. I was frightened, petrified in a calm stiff kind of way. After a short while paranoia set in. Not fun. Really not fun.

Finally, I managed to make it home. This was a miracle. I reached my street. I couldn't remember how to park my car, I was stoned! I couldn't coordinate my brain to figure out how to park my car. I was scared into a tizzy. I parked as well as I thought I could. I didn't realize or think how or what I was doing. When I finished, I got out of the car and rushed upstairs to my friend David's apartment. I told him what had happened, everything. I told him I didn't know how I'd parked my car since I couldn't think straight. And I really didn't know what to do. I was kind of hysterical. I told him I had eaten this brownie. I was stoned, I couldn't think straight, and I couldn't remember how to park my car. I really didn't know what I did with my car.

He jumped up, now also in a panic. The very moment he jumped up to run and check on my car his pillow flipped over. Under his pillow was a gun, I flipped out, totally. I confronted him and became even more hysterical. What a trip! While I was so busy freaking out, in the midst of all this confusion, I had thrown him my car keys, and he had already run down the stairs to check on my car. So, he was gone. And I was left alone in his apartment facing this gun. What was he doing with a gun stashed under his pillow? Suddenly he returned, completely out of breath from running to check on my car. He was shaking his head in disbelief, "I can't believe it" he kept repeating. "I can't believe it" again he repeated. "What?", I said, "What?!" Again, "What?". He said, still being completely out of breath "You parked perfectly". He kept shaking his head in disbelief. I was so relieved.

Now about the gun. Somehow, I mustered up the strength to ask, I was shaking like a leaf. He took it and flicked it before I could say a word or scream. It was a cigarette lighter. Hey, in that one second, I could have been dead! He looked at me amusingly. He said from the way I described my state of mind when I got to his apartment, he thought for sure I had parked my car in the middle of the street. I parked it perfectly. What a night that was. Here I was all worked up and ready to have it out with him again over "the gun". So the rest of the evening was spent calming down. I never indulged in hash brownies again after that night, ever. But I stayed friends with Gina Harding for a while. I wish I were still in touch with her. To me, considering everything, that was amazing.

My father never knew what had happened. He was too square or smart for that kind of stuff, depending on which way one chooses to look at it; nothing happened actually. After that time, David and I were friendly but from a slight distance for a while. I suppose my antenna went up from seeing that gun while being stoned. It sort of parked an image in my mind. And I guess one could say David was kind of freaked out by me, my hysteria. C'est La Vie!

I hardly saw Mel anymore, maybe only fleeting moments running into him in the building. Suddenly, David and I ran into each other in the hall one evening, he lived across the hall from me. He began speaking to me and asked me to come into his apartment. He wanted me to speak to his friend and part time roommate about the gun. I guess I was still on guard. I had a short chat with his friend and then rekindled my friendship with him. We began having an affair. He was busy with his schedule, which honestly speaking I wasn't aware of because I was so busy doing my thing. We saw each other maybe twice during the week. I drove places and he'd keep me company entertaining me with his incredible voice singing songs like "I'm Gonna Make You Love Me", which was my favorite and his specialty. With the car windows wide open and me driving rather fast (which I was) the wind was blowing hard and loud and in spite of all the background noise I could hear him loud and clear. So, he sang a very nice concert for me.

After some time, this creep Mel must have come around and apparently wanted to see me. I was totally oblivious to the fact. I tried to be friends with him. I vaguely remember offering to assist him again with his astrology game, since

I was very much into astrology and had a lady friend who was an astrologer named Jann Reynolds, whom I visited from time to time. She was very good at her work. I enjoyed my friendship with her as well. Jann had a daughter who was away at school, so she enjoyed my visiting her. I was only a few years older than her daughter.

No-one was prepared for the drama which was about to unfold. No one. First, Mel began bothering this lady I was friends with, the super's wife, because I was friendly with her and spent occasional evenings going out to restaurants with her. Inconsequential as it may have seemed, he had decided to pursue her to get my attention. It didn't work. He showed up one night at the theatre while I was doing a scene. He must have been there for some time. He interrupted a scene by repeating the line the actor had just spoken. Then he began a very sick laugh and started vocalizing Shakespeare. He would interrupt actors in the middle of their sketches. Maybe he was drunk, who knows. He wanted to be the center of attention when he really had no place at the theatre at all. He frightened me. He got so weird all together, so I put him out of my mind.

Time passed. I was driving around a lot and somewhere in there and for some reason, I can't remember when or why, someone told me I could purchase a lid of pot (an ounce) for $15.00, so I did. I think I smoked it once or twice but that was it. I had stashed it in my closet in a moth ball can and had totally forgotten about it. I had plenty of other things on my mind. The grass had to have been there at least a couple of months.

One night after working late, David and I decided to get together. He came over and spent the night with me, we made wonderful great love. Early in the morning, there was a knock at my door. I couldn't imagine who it could be, but I asked, "Who is it?". The response, "The Police!". I asked, "What's it about?", the police responded, they had found my car vandalized in the middle of the street with the tires slashed. A bank statement was on the seat and in the front passenger seat was a bag of grass. They asked me to come down and look at the car. I put on a robe and obliged. I suppose they wanted me to positively I.D. my car, which I did.

When we returned to my apartment, the police pushed me aside after asking me some questions, like who could have done this, why, and where did the grass come from. Also noticing my boyfriend, lover who happened to be black, they searched my apartment. They started searching my closet. Shock and fright began to set in and emerge. There were moments I blanked out in my memory. I watched as they diligently searched my closet. I hoped beyond any ray of hope I could muster in my mind that they wouldn't search as thoroughly as they did. While they searched I had only a moment's time to think, did someone set me up? I was too panicked and paralyzed to pray for absolution, I hoped they wouldn't find anything. They made eye contact with David who was lying in bed and questioned him. Apparently, someone had told them about the grass. The grass in my car had been planted. It was not mine. They searched for ten minutes in my closet and found the grass (someone had told them where to look), I hadn't figured that one out yet. Immediately thereafter they arrested me and my poor friend David.

Once we arrived at the precinct all hell broke loose. I was taken roughly, shoved to the basement by two cops, who as soon as they got me to the padded elevator announced that because I was a "nigger lover" and they had caught me with a black man, they were going to push me around and put me through hell. I told them my father wouldn't mind if I married a negro and that he could sue them for mistreating me. I got personally offended at the police for threatening me for being caught with a black man. It filled me with anger and rage. I knew my father didn't have a prejudiced bone in his body and would back me up 100% and vow to make an issue of it if they pursued me. I don't remember whether they did or not. I was too freaked out. Once out of the elevator the one cop warned me about negroes and then chained me to a long hard bench for at least an hour.

Once I was released from the bench and escorted to my cell, everything got much better. First, I got my one phone call. I had to call my father where he was staying as a guest at the home of Nina Turtanic. She answered the phone, so I had to tell her. When no one came to pick me up that night I started to cry. I thought my father wanted to teach me a lesson and had decided to leave me in jail for a week. I shared a cell with three other girls. They were so nice to me, Thank God. They had magazines to read. They gave them to me and told me, "Read them and everything will be alright". They were really nice to me.

My body must have been traumatized since I was in a panic, much more than my mind realized. After spending the night in jail, the next morning I had breakfast, scrambled eggs and coffee, the best I've ever had in my life. After breakfast, a corrections officer, brute, bull dike, took me personally, not as in friendly but ordered me to accompany her to the shower. I was to shower from my head to my toes which I did obligingly. I was terrified. Also, as a result of everything that had happened, I got my period early out of fright, I am sure. They gave me a Kotex right away, and a belt. Afterwards I went back to my cell. Within a few hours my father arrived with one of the Turtanics. They had come to bail me out. My father was sad. The man accompanying him was mad at me. God forbid I had fallen from Grace. God Forbid, getting into this mess.

My father was simply concerned that I was alright. He always surprised me, always, with the amount of patience he exhibited, compassion, understanding, and the ability he had where he could digest and comprehend, and ingeniously rationalize the most difficult of situations. He was like the United Nations, always trying to find peaceful solutions to any situation. As soon as I was released, I told my father about my mistreatment at the hands of the cops all because they caught me with a black man. My father was furious. I wanted him to bail David out as well. He said, "One at a time". David got out after a few days. He was upset, flustered but didn't complain and wasn't angry at me. He was just glad to get out. My father got me a lawyer, a friend of my half-brother's. My straight square half-brother was furious that our father had opted to use his lawyer [my brothers] for an embarrassing situation like this. How dare he? He dared! I was concerned that my father approve of David. He said he wanted to meet him and wouldn't mind if I married him, black or white if he was nice.

A while after that I had to leave Los Angeles because I got phlebitis. It happened as the result of my taking birth control pills and not going to the doctor for a checkup. It can happen to 1 in 10,000. Naturally it happened to me. The bout with phlebitis caused me to have to get off my feet immediately, and very soon thereafter I was forced to quit my job, leave L.A. and go back home to my father.

THE AFTERMATH: A HARSH NEW REALITY

I don't feel insanely guilty because having the pot was really none of anybody's damn business. It really wasn't! In my relationship with Mel, or non-relationship as it was, I was frankly honest. I told him I wanted to date other men, that I wanted an open relationship. The only problem was he wasn't being honest with me. And damn him. For that I suffered immeasurably with shame, pain, embarrassment, and money penalties. I was forced to pay a court fine of $365.00 and I got three years' probation. That's quite a lot for a twenty-year-old girl.

I do know a check in an envelope was recovered somewhere between where I had been and where I lived at least 10 miles away. Or was it that the check was found near to another friend? The facts are fuzzy now. However, I do know that Robert Fisher, a well-known comedy writer, and my father's friend and patient had written that check to me for something. It had been returned to him several months later by a stranger who indicated in an attached letter where they had found it. This somehow was an indication to me, my father, and Robert Fisher, that Mel S. was behind the whole saga of my car being vandalized and the pot.

 I don't feel guilty for lying to my father about my guilt. I was scared silly. Yes, on second thought I did feel guilty. You're damn right I did! But what else could I do? Papa had me give my entire statement on a tape recorder three separate times. I had to remember the same thing, same story three times. I did it! The only thing I reproach myself for is choosing the wrong male mates with far too much frequency. That was my only real problem. It was unbelievable, just awful!

It scared me, being very naïve about people and the possibility that anyone could be so cruel to someone. That they would go to such lengths to cause so much evil and harm upon another being, to me that's scary. It was more than sick and evil, it was psychotic, and it appeared as though he was stalking me in the most devious manner.

Mel was insanely jealous of me and denied it by stating that he wanted to enjoy going out and dating other ladies, specifically naming names at times and laughing with a sick sort of laugh. He successfully convinced me that he was really a party animal waltzing around the building, his apartment and the super's apartment with his hot bedroom eyes and making gestures. He would seduce any female entering the room by the simple sick perverted look on his face. His eyes danced, laughed and smiled in ways that cannot be described. He seldom walked. He had a way of sashaying across the room. He would sashay and swish, he knew what he was doing. He would do and say anything to impress a female in the room; he got a real kick out of it. He was a big flirt with nothing to back it up. He never could follow it through with consistency. His swagger was somewhat clumsy leading me to suspect that he was a closet homosexual. He would aim at his chosen target; anchor away and then pursue them like a chivalrous knight. Was I supposed to know this was an act? Not quite! I never figured that one out.

Shortly after the arrest, David and I had a date with Papa, we all got together, Papa liked David a lot. He wanted us to wait a while before deciding to get married. After that, David began acting strangely, screwing up in the most unexpected ways. He began sneaking off seeing other women. I must admit, this guy had an appeal which was, to speak of, rather delectable. He had a face as appealing as Sidney Poittier. He was over six feet tall, maybe six two and was slim. His eyes were dark, his look was intense. There was something puzzling about his look, especially when he reacted to me which was, however, not surprising since I was occasionally off the wall in a manner of speaking. Yet when he spoke, he spoke in a soft and gentle voice. He was laid back, relaxed opposed to uptight, and very cool in his reaction to things.

He exuded sexuality in everything he did, especially when he played basketball. Sometimes he even practiced in his apartment throwing the ball and catching it. He never missed. And he made a concerted effort to focus and concentrate and put his all into it. He had a youthful quality about him as he played. He had the funniest face when he shot the ball into the basket. It was fun watching him play. And after being physically exertive, when he sat down, he'd catch his breath and with a youthful fit quality about him, sit back and relax yet retain his firm physique. He was so at ease within his own body and within himself, and didn't need to do anything, just stand there to be sexy. So, I could see why other women would find him rather appealing. And I must say, he was great in bed.

 Getting back to the downfall of David, he left the Temptations without saying a word and took another job. He started robbing people whom he had begun working for. I only knew something was up because he took a harried call from a lady. I didn't hear what she said, only his response. Apparently, he started working for someone, a new boss he was on a business call with and whom he was nervously attempting to stall for time since he had apparently swindled something from her and caused there to be a lot of tension in the air.

This guy changed overnight. Why? I 'll never know. It wasn't drugs. I think it was that I never really knew him in the first place. He was never uptight, not before the arrest or after, just secretly and cleverly devious and never up front or obvious about it. He always seemed to be busy, but not nervously busy, and never explained what he was doing, work wise. And me, being preoccupied with my own busy schedule as I was and being a non-suspecting individual which I always was, and never asking questions about anything, everything seemed to get by me.

I figured the less I let on that I knew, the better off I was as far as he was concerned. Also, I figured I was better off just acting dumb which was not so farfetched for me at all. All my friends used to call me "the dumb blonde" and I wasn't even blonde, but that's another story. So, it appears as if I gave him the opportunity to pull off all this stuff easily. There were times I was afraid, afraid of confrontations, that's why I sometimes felt it was better to act dumb. It is then that one usually has some price to pay, directly or directly. If I had kept myself apprised of the situation, perhaps it would not have gotten so out of hand. Oh god, just to think back and reminisce. It's getting to be too much for me.

I suppose the trauma stemming from the arrest had created confusion, anger, and emotional distress in me, which ultimately had caused me to feel the need to compensate David for all the hell which I felt I had indirectly put him through.

In hindsight, I guess I felt that this was why I even considered rushing into a marriage with him. So, getting back to the leopard changing its spots, the leopard of course being David. I left him again, traumatized, but this time because of actions caused by his abusiveness.

Boy, I got away from him fast. By that time though, I was living elsewhere anyway. I had moved to another apartment in Hollywood right after the arrest situation ended where even though now, I was attempting to elude him, somehow, he managed to locate me and visit me. And on top of that, he brought girls over when I was out. I went for help to finally get him out. I returned with a friend who helped me throw him out. What a disaster that turned out to be. David and I were through, finished!

I guess there were signs along the way. I missed them. I guess to me he was this cute guy whose soft-spoken voice was both calming and soothing, and with his ability to sing so nicely, well, that just melted me, both my heart and my soul. It was my impression that while we were so-called dating, he was with me only. He would go out a lot, but always alone. And he would return, alone.

Now it was the summer of 1969, in grand old New York City, I experienced running into Mel, his home base and mine (how unfortunate for me). I never expected to see him just then. He was apparently on the east coast visiting his parents. Running into him, oft times passing him on the street, hoping he didn't see me, a bizarre encounter, him being strung out on speed, walking with a bloody syringe sticking out of his clean white shirt chest pocket, being unkempt, unshaven and "un-cool" as could be. This weird creature, his head bobbing downward lightly, with this sick smile on his sweaty face, some teeth starting to corrode, or disappear, a cigarette dangling from his lips, with a look on his face like he was a wild animal searching for his prey, someone to rape, someone to violate in some form or another. It didn't have to be male or female. It was some form of companionship he needed. It was utterly amazing that no one complained, or that the police didn't take notice and stop and question him, especially on Lexington Avenue and 86th Street.

He was the epitome of a lost soul, lost in space and one of society's misfits. It began to be apparent that he was in his own world, his own sick cocoon, separate from any facsimile of the sanity of the world, and within his own hell. His eyes red, he looked tired, but his face had sadness written all over it and yet you couldn't avoid the disgust you felt at the sight of him. This man's body took on a language all its own which I never understood. At times I thought he was a screaming homosexual, out of control who was bursting out of the closet. It even seemed as if he carefully orchestrated his look and appearance to get attention and knew it would create a stir. That's so hard to believe, but then again, so was he.

Wind blows calmer, gentler from now on, no more storms or hurricanes on the horizon. Hopefully now I've weathered my share of storms. Now I pray for clear horizons.

77

THE INSANITY

For a while at papas 83rd street office, things got a little out of hand, I think. I must have been around twenty, around 1967. Papa was working long hard hours. He started getting into paintings making them appear to be three dimensional by putting cream lightly over them, then focusing his ultraviolet lights over them and then he'd want to pass a cloth over the painting. He insisted, swore this process made the colors more accentuated and made the picture clearer and three-dimensional.

He kept closing one eye and passing a cloth over and over to improve the visual of the picture. And he would go on and on and say, "Doesn't that look better? More clear? Nicht?!" (Meaning yes, correct?). And looking for some sense of acknowledgment from his patient. I worried that he may not have been getting enough sleep, and that the combination of him possibly over medicating himself, working long hard hours and sleeping so little were maybe causing him to have these visions. This lasted only perhaps one year. I can't honestly say what was going on.

He would confront his patients rather abruptly and demand them to tell him if they saw the improvements. His patients yessed him to death just to make him happy. And it made him smile and laugh with great pride and a look of self-accomplishment on his face. At times he would yell at a patient if they weren't sure they saw any improvement in the painting. He would call them silly fools and get frustrated and turn to another patient. Actually, he insisted that his patients bring their paintings; works of art to him so that he could do this process to their paintings. He was so proud of this discovery. Some of them saw the change, others didn't. I never noticed my father being strung out or spaced out, never. He was always fully in control except when he worked on these paintings. When he spent an inordinate amount of time injecting himself to stay awake. I felt his judgment and sensibility was stretching the limits of time allowed to oneself under normal circumstances, although these were not normal circumstances by any means.

My father spent hours trying to find a vein, often leaving patients in his waiting room until he was able to find one and inject himself. When I was there with him it was frustrating as hell to watch, time wasted, and time consumed, just watching. I was also concerned at times when there would be a waiting room full of patients waiting to see my father. He realized that if he were to keep working, he would need to stop everything, keep everyone waiting and give himself an injection of vitamins, amphetamine and whatever else he felt he needed; not stop, go home and sleep, thereby disappointing his patients.

 The major problem was he was so tired, so over tired he couldn't think or see straight, and it seemed to take forever, forty-five minutes to an hour in my estimation at least for him to successfully find his vein and give himself an injection. And at times it took him longer. Then the patient had to wait even longer. Sometimes one of them would come in and keep him company while he was trying, and they'd talk to him.

 On two occasions I offered to do it for him because I had a good night's sleep, and I could see very well. I thought for sure I could find his vein for him in one minute, just to get it over with. He refused my offer, the reply was an emphatic, resounding "No", and he tried even harder to concentrate so he could do it himself. Following that there was a sigh, not of relief but that of exhaustion and frustration, of not being immediately successful at finding a vein. And that was the end of it. Eventually of course, he found one. Then once the vein was found and the injectable had successfully traveled through his system, he breathed a heavy sigh of relief and mumbled a tune. Germans are notorious for doing that. They mumble, hum tunes, mostly German tunes.

I think deep inside he was insulted that I even offered to help. I watched him and found it terribly upsetting that he was going through all those changes, poking himself needlessly (pardon the pun) over and over again. I mean just the fact that he would consider doing that was terribly disconcerting to me. And I knew that he was having so much trouble because he was so tired and could hardly think or see straight. Yet he had to be there, awake and aware for his patients. They insisted on seeing him, and only him and it had to be right then and there.

One time, drama coach Betty Cashman was his next patient right after he had successfully given himself a treatment. I guess he was momentarily inebriated, "rushing", which is the street term. He gave her a smirk and invited her in. She laughed and turned to me and said, "There's that crazy old guy again, hello doc!", and she gave me a wink. She went along with merriment. I guess she was happy to see him happy.

I was at the end of my ropes from watching the whole saga. I smiled, took no happiness with me and left. My father had one patient after another who insisted on seeing him when they wanted to or felt like it, regardless of whether it was convenient or not for him. Included in that group were Kennedy photographer, Mark Shaw, Arkadi Gerney and numerous others. My father seldom got the sleep he needed. He never complained about being awakened in the middle of the night, mostly by Arkadi Gerney. By day it was usually Mark Shaw. I suppose there were many others of whom I was not aware.

I have learned not to be so skeptical of him anymore. There were times when I thought a discovery of his was nonsense, like the magnet being passed over the knees. But that turned out to be legit, and I felt so bad that I wasn't more supportive of my father in the case of that one. So, I would not dare venture to make any statements or opinions over his work on those paintings. Perhaps he really had something there.

78

DON HUTCHISON

*Don Hutchison (right) and guest, late
1980s*

I met Don Hutchison one night around midnight when I went to my father's office just to check in and say hello. I knew he was getting a haircut from a friend and patient. Papa and I were leaving the next day for Puerto Rico for a vacation. He was in my father's first treatment room. He was at least 12 years older than me and had recently ended a relationship with Hedy Lamarr. We hit it off instantly. I mean instantly. He joked and asked me if I wanted a haircut, I said "yes". I sat down and he gave me this incredible pyramid cut. It was just wonderful, so was he for that matter, funny and cracking jokes a mile a minute. He had this way of making Charlie Chaplin jokes and saying things in a silly way to make one crack up laughing, but he would also laugh a kind of nervous silly laugh. He was joking about being there at midnight when his fangs came out. We really hit it off.

The next day Papa and I left for our trip. Someone took a photo of me with my new complimentary hairdo in Puerto Rico. I was young and skinny and about 22 years old so the haircut he gave me looked great. As soon as we returned from Puerto Rico, I guess about a week or a week and a half later, we hooked up. We had a wild mad affair. He was a great lover.

Besides being a hairdresser and stylist, he was into astrology, Tarot and I-Ching, and a self-taught herbalist. He got into acupuncture with my father and made his own salves, creams, and parsley tea for my father when he got sick with kidney stones. He also worked on movies, playing a body double for Sean Connery and doing stunt work in "The Valachi Papers" as well as extra work on "The Equalizers".

My father had been giving me intramuscular injections so I could function. His unadulterated vitamins that patients requested in their purest form were something my body chemistry couldn't handle, something in the solution was giving me a rash on my face. Don was staying at the Diplomat Hotel at the time and told me to come over. He invented a salve and facial treatment for me that worked. I visited him at his hotel. He did this whole treatment with me.

First, he put witch hazel on my face, then peroxide and God knows what else. The hot towel came last, he made me keep it on my face for at least ten minutes. By the time he was finished, the rash was gone. We also had incredibly great sex. Somehow, I think I enjoyed it more than he did but that didn't matter. I went to see "Master Don" at the Diplomat Hotel twice a week for months where he put together his own concoction of minerals and medicines like witch hazel, creams, and hot towel dermatological treatments. It worked.

He was doing speed a lot, not just from my father. He took pills, not injections. He was getting it in many different forms elsewhere and he started sneaking off to be with men. Speed does that to men. But when I got to be with him it was great. He also taught me the I-Ching which is now like my Bible. My father didn't really know I was seeing him besides the office introduction.

I got together with him again in Central Park years later and at that time he offered to seriously teach me to do the I-Ching myself. He brought a silver chalice so he could teach me how to toss coins in it and then thrust them out onto a flat surface. One must toss them six times and then he had to do the calculating, which for me was good because I was not good at calculating. One must be good at math because as he explained to me, it is all about math when doing the I-Ching properly. It took me such a long time to learn how to do it. I'm still relying on the book to do it to this day. He asked me to do his cards, which I learned how to do years ago one time, and I did. But then I was not clear about two cards and even called one out wrong. He knew what they were better than I did and started telling me what they meant. I guess he didn't want me to know that he already knew how to do it and wanted to see how far along I was in having learned the craft myself.

 He was great with astrology, except when I asked him to do my chart, he told me what he thought I wanted to hear. I think it's better to have a total stranger do the cards than a friend. Our friendship changed track. He took me out to lunch and dinner and all sorts of places and tried all sorts of salves on me. But mostly he did astrology and the I-Ching. Shortly before he died of cancer, he started getting weird and told me stories I believed but eventually found out were total nonsense. We stopped being lovers when I was about twenty-two years old. After that we remained good friends. He became friends with my boyfriends. They were all hopelessly into speed. It made for strange bed fellows. He did people's hair for a long time. He messed my hair up once, that was it. Before he died, he told me he had some wishes and left instructions for me to follow. They were all discombobulated and I am sorry I agreed to do it. He was basically a very kind and concerned man. Helping people was his calling in life, whether it be medicinal or astrological.

79

TAROT AND THE POLICE

At age 15 when I began to study the occult, friends and family asked my father "What gives?". He said, "I believe she can do it". He would give me this look, somehow, I knew that he knew. I suppose I started getting obsessed by it all, which isn't advisable. At times I'd go into trances, getting messages I could not decode. I was treated with amphetamines which enhanced my psychic abilities, marijuana also heightened my psychic awareness.

Twenty years later, now interested in Tarot cards, my older son said I should do readings and charge money. I had a friend who suggested Central Park, where there were other people who also read cards. I packed up a table, cards, and sign, put on a very gypsy outfit and set out for Central Park. I started getting customers. To get their vibes all over the cards, I made them shuffle the deck thoroughly, which consisted of 78 cards. That ensured an accurate reading for both of us. No sooner had my intuitive energies begun to seriously flow, than a cop showed up suddenly. One of Guiliani's new cops. He ordered me to stop doing it or face eviction and arrest. This really upset me! I do the Tarot to give people guidance. There was nothing like concentrating on another plane and suddenly being jolted out of that state by a policeman totally unappreciative of my powers.

My customers were more upset than I was. I was instructed to apply for a permit. I went to the permit office; they demanded a money order for $35 then turned me down. I had only been charging $5 per reading at the time, so I really felt the loss. My friend Don Hutchison told me "Oh, don't let that bother you. Just go back to Central Park, try some other location". I returned a week later with no problems.

I had an interesting exchange with a potential customer. A woman who at first resisted having a reading, and I agreed she should wait until she felt more comfortable about it. When she returned, I read her cards. I did the Celtic cross, numbers 4 and 5, representing recent past events which were in reverse. Ace of Wands, which ordinarily signifies new beginnings, or birth in this instance, meant death. This indicated a recent death. She informed me that she had recently suffered a miscarriage. Luckily the remainder of her reading was favorable. I love happy endings.

I was deep into another reading, totally consumed by the cards and their meaning, oblivious to the cop watching. This one was on a motorcycle. He threatened to close me down and take away my cards, table and precious stones, which I used not for their mineral or occult values, but to keep the cards from flying away.

What now? I decided to go from 59th Street all the way up to 76th Street, right near the museum. There were hills and valleys there. No one would see me on this remote bench except customers, I thought. I found a nice couple; I began giving the girl a reading. She was a student awaiting word for a college scholarship. The Knight of Cups and The Page of Cups showed she would get the grant. I was halfway through, the guy with her got so excited, he said he couldn't wait for his turn. Gosh he was anxious, I had to finish his girlfriend's reading first.

Then I saw the first cop, all the way from 59th Street. Young, tall, this time on his bicycle riding up out of nowhere. "I thought I told you, you can't be doing this stuff here anymore!", he scolded. Then he added "Why don't you just climb up on that bench and start bleaching our hair?". Gee, I never thought I looked that bad! I hadn't the foggiest idea what he meant. Bad enough he was evicting me, he didn't have to trash my appearance. The poor couple I'd been reading for refused to leave. I was exasperated, humiliated beyond words. It's funny, all those phony readers don't get bothered by cops. I charged a paltry $5, did a legit reading and I was the only one stopped.

After the police left, the couple wanted me to sneak into the bushes to continue. "With my luck, hell catch me there and I'll really be in trouble", I said. I gave them my telephone number, but they never called. I now charge

$10 for a reading, no hocus pocus.

80

BILL LEVI

A tenant in my father's building at 305 East 86th street, he and my father soon became friends, and he became a patient who frequently appeared at the East 82nd street office to say "Hello" or for treatments. He invested money in Europe in disposable underwear and then brought it to America and tried to sell it. He also brought some liquid soap in a nice pink bottle that he was trying to sell, intimating that it resembled some sexual body fluid. That was his standard joke about it. He was trying to sell this stuff and make a million bucks off it.

Bill Levi was from Israel. My stepmother, I was told, early on tried to befriend him. She was contemplating making a play for him and his money but then decided to go with my father instead. In later years when my father visited me at my apartment in Hell's Kitchen on West 46th Street, Bill always accompanied him. Once we decided to meet at the Central Park Zoo so I could show my son Jason all the animals and the seals. So, we went there and made a day of it. It was nice. Bill never imposed on my relationship with my father as so many other patients and friends did. I have to give him that much credit.

He would arrive at my father's office on East 82nd street and walk in and just say hello, not just to have a treatment. Other times he'd show up to show off a new investment. But the soap was the funniest thing. He was my father's buddy for the last part of his life until right before he died. He and my father swam together in their basement pool.

81

PAPA VS. MY BOYFRIEND BILL

When I was in my early 20's, about 22 by that time, I met and started dating Bill, the father of my first son. I got close to him until the damned amphetamine took center stage. Then I would try to relate to him. He drifted apart, would always find another direction to turn and leave me stranded once he got high, which seemed to be almost always.

He was battling schizophrenia, psychosis and drug abuse, all of which I was totally unaware of and in between, he managed to hold down a job. How he did it, I don't know. He worked many jobs, and he worked almost all the time. At one point he was very sick and doing very disturbing things at home. My father called Bill's boss, and his boss admitted that he was having some problems with him and acknowledged that he was having second thoughts about keeping him on. Papa told his boss that he was a doctor, and that Bill was having problems outside of his employment and he needed to get Bill to a doctor for help.

Papa stepped in, interceded, called Bills boss and got him fired. So, it turns out the boss fired Bill at my father's urging. Then my father tried, discreetly first then abruptly to get him out of my life and out of our home because my father was a general practitioner, not a licensed psychiatrist or a qualified doctor who deals with mental cases.

That was a difficult ordeal because Bills parents apparently were intent on dumping him on us figuring that my father was a doctor, and Bill would be taken care of by us. My father vehemently objected to having any involvement and resented the attempted imposition. The main issue here is that my father may have used his position and possibly screwed up Bills life even further without considering future developments or other people's feelings.

I feel my father may have been too quick in taking advantage of his physician's title and position to attempt to fix my situation or screw it up. It depends on which way one looks at it. Maybe he did it in what he considered to be my best interest; however, it was not necessarily in Bills best interest. That scared me.

The whole situation had an aftermath of unnecessary negative repercussions. Bill was forced out of his job; he became depressed, confused and extremely frustrated. He was thereafter sent to a mental institution and evaluated for possible treatment. So, he did receive much needed help. The whole situation was so sad, so unbelievably sad.

And yes, if you ask me, you won't because my father was known to be a genius. I hurt terribly. I loved Bill despite all of his faults. And this whole saga really hurt me. And yes, we were all on speed with some of our innermost emotions, feelings somewhat suppressed. But Bill loved me and cared for me tremendously. He also loved speed more. He got it whenever he could. I wanted to have him whenever I could and not the speed.

82

SUSAN, MY FATHER'S GIRLFRIEND

Susan was the one girlfriend of my father that I did get along with. She was petite, thin, five years older than I was and very pretty and cool. We really got along well. While she dated my father, she did too much speed. She became engaged to my father which of course I didn't like because I didn't consider her distinguished or "right" for my father, but she did and then when she mispronounced the word fiancé with a sloppy New York accent opposed to a proper French accent I went bananas. Anyway, Mark Shaw entertained her frequently. I think he introduced her to my father. She was with my father for at least a year and accompanied us on our trip with Congressman Pepper to Israel.

Once she and my father broke up, she ran off with Bruce Gedman, also a friend. I got to know her better and became much friendlier with her. She married Bruce. Bill, my boyfriend, was friends with her. He kind of had a crush on her and I kind of had a crush on Bruce. They were gay and secretly doing things together [Bruce and Bill], but I didn't know that, stupid me.

Anyway, while my father was still alive, he saw Susan occasionally at my apartment in my presence while visiting me. She wanted to see him, and he was coming to see me anyway. Susan was kind and gentle. I think she needed to express her liking in touching terms. I didn't. I liked hanging out with her. She liked speed, but she also liked smoking pot which I did too. She got into a health regimen after getting sick while being in India for several months. She was from a very Jewish family. Bruce was not Jewish. He looked part Irish and part Italian. They were both into drugs, speed. I developed a crush on Bruce which lasted for years. It was finally Susan who told me he was gay. She was straight with me, thank God. I can almost hear her talking to me right now as

I write this. It was her gentle nature that allowed me to be friendly with her. Also, she was a hippy, a Greenwich Village hippy and I really related to that. She had a baby with Bruce that I spent years trying to get her to allow him to see. It didn't work out. But I still have fond memories of her and her kindness towards me.

83

CONGRESSMAN CLAUDE PEPPER

A rather humble, southern gentleman with a very nasal like southern accent which I could not easily distinguish, is how I would immediately describe Congressman Claude Pepper. Only his accent, a very Southern accent, got in the way of my fully understanding his every word. I guess because he served Congress as a representative from Florida for so many years, his colleagues got accustomed to his manner of speaking, as I did with my father and his heavy German accent. C.P. used to give lectures to my father, which I presume were about health reform, something very much on my father's mind and close to Claude Peppers heart.

Claude Pepper was a Harvard Law School graduate. He served in The House of Representatives, Congress, and in the Senate. He was in office for many years, forty I believe. He never really communicated well with me as I was a young girl, about eight years old at the time and considered to be a "little girl". He did, however, tell me what a great doctor my father was. He would say "Your daddy is a brilliant, wonderful doctor. And I'll bet you're mighty proud of him". Then he would turn to my father and nod his head, being such a southern gent. His wife Mildred was his manager, so to speak. She organized functions, dinners, and speaking engagements and gladly ironed his shirts. Something I never could relate to. She said she was the wife of a Senator which she truly was. She ran the show when she spoke, in her slight southern accent I could understand. She was "mother superior" to her husband and everyone else around. That's just the way she was, sweetly though.

The funny thing was, her husband the Congressman spent years slaving away working tediously to desegregate the south, which my family personally was so proud of, while his wife was known to be prejudiced. On one occasion, my parents and I were invited to visit them in Washington and to spend the night in their home as their guests. My father was with the Senator while my mother and I assisted Mildred in preparing dinner. She made hot dogs and hamburgers. Apparently, she forgot the ketchup. My mother and I offered to go out and buy some. She said, "Oh you can't go out there, there are Negroes around the corner and it's not safe", or something to that effect. I went into shock; I got very upset. I was raised with so called "colored people", and they weren't our servants or slaves. They happened to be prominent people who were part of our inner circle of friends. As a matter of fact, they weren't called by anything other than their names. I saw no difference be-tween them and us. Besides, my mother and father always went out of their way to get tanned. It made them look particularly beautiful. So, when I saw people who were already black, I thought, how lucky, they are already there. I used to see Leontyne Price, Katherine Dunham, and Dr. Thelma Williams. They were all black, talented, smart, and rich. The only thing I knew was they were a whole lot smarter than I was or would be. I knew no difference. My father was never prejudiced against anyone. I never knew it existed. I couldn't understand what it was all about. My mother laughed at one point at the absurdity of the situation that Claude Pepper worked so hard for integration while his wife was so clearly prejudiced.

This was thankfully a one-time experience. She was from the south, and I quickly learned that this was how the people from the south were. I learned that they were taught since early childhood to be this way. I learned to keep my distance from her ever since. She was a bit overbearing with her south-ern charm as well, and she came on very strong and demanding. She was a perfectionist. That seemed to work well as far as the Senator, her husband was concerned. Back to the Senator. He constantly debated issues, whether in the pit on the floor of Congress or on the floor of the Senate to which my mother and I, on this occasion, listened [in the hallway on the next floor] since we were privileged to be invited to accompany my father on this particular occasion. We had been sent for by Claude Pepper himself so that my father could give him treatment while he took a short break from his filibustering.

My father had taken the liberty of inviting my mother and me along with him on that trip. The Senator lectured in Washington. He traveled the country lecturing for his causes, for health care for the poor and the needy. He fought so that all Americans would have the right to be guaranteed free or affordable health insurance coverage permanently. He felt this was so important. And to mention that all the while, through all his travels, he sent for my father's treatment, injections, which were delivered by airplane pilots. Personally arranged by my father himself, whom the Senator called, "The kindly doctor". Claude Pepper would send associates, colleagues or trusted friends to the airport having made prior arrangements with the airline and pilot to deliver the package of injectables from my father specifically to Senator Claude Pepper, or his assistant. My father did this whenever the Congressman urgently needed treatment. This happened to my knowledge rather frequently. At that time all this was legal. He fought hard for all his causes but also needed extra energy to carry it out. He never got strung out or stoned, never. I don't believe he would have taken the injections if they had interfered with his goals in any way.

In later years he fought for the rights of the elderly. The government was threatening to take social security money from the elderly. Then Congressman Pepper fought to keep the Social Security benefits safe and untouched, so that in later years when the elderly people needed the healthcare benefits, they would have them. My parents took me on several trips when the Congressman was lecturing around the country.

Long after my dear devoted mother had passed away, the Congressman invited my father and I, and a friend of my fathers to accompany him and a group of distinguished individuals on his "Goodwill Tour" to Israel to inspect the extensive damage incurred from the aftermath of the war of 1967, which took place one year earlier, but the effects were still being felt ever so noticeably. C.P. wanted to inspect the devastation from the war and find out what the people of Israel needed to repair and rebuild their land after the war. Getting back to Congressman Pepper before elaborating on the trip to Israel, I feel it is important to display a timeline of events in which the Congressman was given credit for accomplishing great deeds for his country while being under my father's care.

The Honorable Claude Pepper had filibustered Congress, almost nonstop for two days single handedly, to secure health insurance for all Americans, saved Social Security for senior citizens [at which time my father flew to Washington to treat him], and outlawed mandatory retirement. C.P insured affordable health care for all Americans, including Social Security for senior citizens. This was approximately 1957. He succeeded in persuading the federal government to play a major role in financing research aimed at preventing and curing disease. The last which I attribute to his long-standing friendship and association with my father.

 My father treated the Congressman with injections of vitamins and whatever he felt the Congressman needed, whenever it was warranted. Back in 1946, before I was born, Congressman Pepper's subcommittee issued a report declaring that the poor health documented by the selective service could be prevented in the future through a federal program incorporating aid for hospital, construction, and medical insurance programs. In 1967, C.P. received The Albert and Mary Lasker Foundation Award for being the principal sponsor of bills establishing five institutes of health.

84

GOODWILL TRIP TO ISRAEL, 1968

HISTORY UNFOLDS, A STORY TO REMEMBER

*Jill, Papa, and guest (right) at the
Western Wall in Israel, January 1968*

I have a story to tell, a true story which happened years ago and is unfortunately still very fresh in my memory. Congressman Pepper had invited my father, his girlfriend and I, and a group of others on a peace, fact finding, and recovery mission to Israel in January 1968. This was following the war in Israel. We were also to make a stop in Rome to visit with the Pope.

We visited sites such as The Golan Heights where Claude Pepper spoke to and interviewed people who lived there and survived having their homes destroyed and had nothing left of their belongings but faith and hope for their future. Some of these incidents which I am going to recall were not as clear in my mind as others were. I got stubborn and decided that all the facts of this journey, excursion, needed to be told with as much clarity, and with as many facts and an accurate timeline as were possible.

I was fortunate enough to get the advice and assistance of some colleagues who directed me to people and places who until now were unknown to me, and since have become of phenomenal assistance to me in my pursuit of crucial information about the itinerary of the trip to Israel. I will now endeavor to accurately describe and detail "Congressman Pepper's Good Will Tour to Israel", which took place in January 1968. This was by no means a happy time. It was very educational, however frightening for me. It goes as follows:

We arrived in Israel following a rather lengthy plane ride. Once we arrived at The Sheraton Hotel in Tel Aviv, it appeared that we were greeted, in general, by rather hostile, cold and unpleasant hotel personnel. It could have been the fact that my father's girlfriend, who was five years my senior, petite and skinny, was dressed in a short miniskirt. The Israelis didn't seem to appreciate that. They commanded a strong hold of some of the most fanatic of Arab philosophy and an area being very turbulent throughout the centuries, the situation as it had become as of the time of our visit.

When the war came all the troops that were living there, the shopkeepers and service personnel, fled. One of the stories that was told to us was that while looting was a commonplace thing among victorious troops during a war, for some reason the Syrian troops turned on the villagers and looted Al Quneitra before leaving. The ravages of looting were very evident, and store windows were knocked out, doors were broken in and one could see the many traces of violence in the whole city.

January 20th, 1968

We had the opportunity to speak with some of the people, in particular a woman who had been moved out of her home near Rafid, which was a Syrian town to the south, an area of mineral springs. It seemed that her family had owned a resort in this area, and the Israeli troops had moved her to Al Quneitra as a refugee until they were able to establish legitimate ownership status and promised that they would move her back. However, she was very unhappy with her situation, and we were all amazed at the fine English she spoke and her tremendous vocabulary. Naturally it was quite an experience chatting with her.

From Al Quneitra we continued our journey further north to the city of Masada, and then southward through Kiryat Shmona and then back down to the kibbutz, where we first started our mornings ride. One of the obvious things that we saw was that it was a simple task for the Syrians to continually bombard the various kibbutzim in this area from their strategic positions in the Golan Heights. It was simply looking down into a valley, lobbing artillery shells and mortars at will, and killing Israeli people and damaging their fields and crops.

Then we went to the city of Safed. From there we went to a beautiful section which was the center of Israel's olive production, then down to the city of Acre. It was through this area between Safed and Acre that was characterized and used as a basis of James A. Michener's novel "The Source".

January 22nd, 1968

On a visit to the Weizman Institute of Science in Rehovot, from there, Congressman Pepper paid a visit to Mrs. Ben Gurion. After seeing Mrs. Ben Gurion, we drove back through the desert and on up to Tel Aviv to see Golda Meir. The drive through the desert seemed like it took 45 minutes. We arrived, all hot and dry, sand flying in the air, we were deep in the desert. We were on a non airconditioned school bus. Apparently, Congressman Pepper got his communications mixed up with those in charge of the visit. When we arrived, there was no one there to greet us. C.P. had to get off the bus and he and another passenger had to walk up to a building only to find out that she hadn't expected us. She had left twenty minutes earlier for a two-day trip out of town. We never got to see her. Within ten minutes we had to turn around and drive back into the hot sandy desert.

January 23rd, 1968

*Papa praying at the Western Wall
with a guest (left)*

On January 23rd, we left Tel Aviv for the last time, stopping in Ramle for a visit to the Vocational Institute.

My own notes from the trip, including highlights:

 It was a rather extensive 14-day journey, not all of which I found fascinating. There were some meetings which although politically pertinent, did not mean anything to me. However, if they were of significance towards peacekeeping measures, I shall mention them.

Of particular interest to me at the time was our drive on the school bus, my father and Susan were not in attendance that day. In attendance was a group of about thirty adults and me. We took a drive to a town in despair, ravaged by the war with the town's people giving the appearance of being mummies, their entire bodies all bandaged up from head to foot. From the war, their villages and homes had been destroyed but their spirits were high. I believe the village was on the Gaza Strip.

I felt so sorry for all these people and couldn't begin to relate to their tremendous will and determination to survive after all they had been through, after all they had lost. They knew no other life, no other home. They had no means with which to pick up and leave and start over somewhere else. They had to stay where they were. They were in shock, emotionally. The destruction was so severe, one couldn't even begin to fathom where to begin the helping and healing process. Congressman Pepper interviewed them, spoke to them. Amazingly, they understood him and some even spoke English. Their will to live and stay alive, after all they had been through, and their determination against all odds was simply amazing.

They had to have hope and faith in tomorrow to have the will to survive. That is human nature. I recall a particular village on our trip as having stood out from the rest with unbearable devastation. There was so much destruction in so many areas, but the very worst seemed to be the Golan Heights.

 The city of Al Quneitra was a desolate, deserted ruin of what was once a prosperous city of approximately 15,000 people. It seemed that the Syrian troops, after the battle, turned on the villagers and looted Al Quneitra before leaving town.

 It was on our way to one of these sights where we passed a truck load of soldiers standing guard with rifles positioned, ready to shoot, guarding a truck load of dead soldiers piled high. They were bodies of slain victims, wrapped like mummies from injuries suffered from the war. It was fierce and horrifying for me to see this. And one could see the shoes of the slain victims still on their feet. It was the cold, mean look the soldiers had which frightened me more than anything.

We couldn't see the bodies; they were piled face down, one on top of another. The soldiers looked as if at any moment they were ready to shoot, even us. They looked so cold-blooded. The bodies one could not easily distinguish except for their legs and shoes showing and flopping on the bumpy road. However, the soldiers with their rifles, which could easily have been mistakenly thought to be aimed at us was terrifying.

 During our trip to Israel, unfortunately, I had to be a reluctant witness to my father and his girlfriend, for whatever reason they had chosen to enclose themselves in their hotel suite and inject themselves with God knows what, amphetamine, vitamins, and I don't know what else. It seems they got so messed up they were unable to leave their room to accompany us on our trip that one traumatic day where I did see that truck with all those dead soldiers. It was just me and a bus full of much older people venturing on this harrowing journey, I don't even recall dealing with my father or his girlfriend upon my return to the hotel. Maybe it's for the better that I didn't. I'm sure I went to him shaking and in shock from all that I had seen that day. There was a moment when I wondered why we had come to that point in our lives, and I was forced to recall some of the wonderful things Claude Pepper did as a congressman when I was a young girl.

We visited the Pope under the sponsorship of Congressmen Pepper. There was a procession of monks following the Pope. There were Brazilian students there to see the Pope. I don't know why; I simply made the observation. The Pope came in seated in his Papal chair being carried by six to eight men. It was as though they were carrying him on a tray as a main course. I'm not being factitious, that was how I would describe it as having appeared to me. The Pope waved with both hands to cheering crowds on both sides. While they were carrying him, as he passed near where I was standing, the strangest feeling came over me. It was like eerie vibes, like spiritual lightning had hit me and all around me, it was earth shattering, yet quite peaceful. There was an aura which took over the entire area. It was quite similar to the feeling Richard Chamberlain expressed when he played Father Ralph de Bricassart in The Thorn Birds, when he put on the robe. It was very heavy, yet it was spell binding. Then they arrived at the podium and let him down near his chair to be seated.

There was such a whisp of spiritual breeze flying about the place. It was as though the sky had opened upon his eminence's entrance and all the dead people in heaven were joyously dancing about in the sky. There was a feeling, a movement, not frightening, just magnetic, like a massive vibration. One could pick it up intuitively, I did. Very seldom in my life have I experienced such a sensation as I did that day at the Vatican. It was a very enlightening, emotionally stimulating feeling, very invigorating and spiritual. It wasn't at all frightening. It was like loose energy.

We did not personally come up close to The Pope. We saw him from a distance. I would have been overcome and hesitant to approach him. We later took a tour of the Vatican Museum and The Sistine Chapel which had beautiful ceilings and artwork. It was a sight to see, breathtaking.

85

RUTH, PAPA'S THIRD WIFE

Ruth Jacobson, early 1970s

I guess you could say that Ruth, "Lady R" for ruthless, had great taste in both men and drugs. She was married to the nicest guy in the world, Harry Rubenstein. They came to my father's office for treatment. They owned a grocery store that wasn't doing well on Amsterdam Avenue uptown. After a while she got into speed. She draped herself all over my father until he gave her some. Her husband didn't do anything about it. Finally, he announced he was leaving. Several of us, me included, begged him to take her along. He wouldn't. She stuck around and learned how to help at the office. She also went home with my father and cooked soup for him. My father invited patients up to his apartment and she accompanied him and served them meals, chicken soup and whatever else I wasn't a witness to. She became an unofficial nurse, learned how to give injections and gave them, she shouldn't have but did. She treated patients and at the same time got herself addicted to amphetamine.

 At one point, possibly to be vindictive to me, or playing one of her sadistic manipulative games at my expense for which she was sadly prone to do and took great pleasure in doing so, unfortunately decided that even though she was unattractive and definitely not sexy, would attempt to borrow my boyfriend, Bill. Naturally she did this without my knowledge or permission. She tempted him with her sick mind in overdrive. And naturally while being under the influence of amphetamine with ulterior motives and insane thoughts flowing from her mind, it definitely helped drive her as it were. She presented my boyfriend with a check for $120.00 to get some street speed, which was a hell of a temptation for a speed lover. And this check was for him to take to his speed connection to buy street meth which he did, happily and obligingly. Upon his return to her with the merchandise, she seduced him first with speed and then sex.

I had to laugh just thinking about it, not at the time, but afterwards. I mean really, what a picture. Bill was tall, slim, and very handsome, dashing luscious, very delectable happy–go-lucky and was nicknamed "Prince" because of his gorgeous hair and great good looks. He had a friendly disposition, and for a man, a very graceful stride. And she, Lady R., well, homely comes to mind. She had a heart of gold, that is if she wanted to, otherwise, out came the daggers with which she sparred her victims, one by one. With her, there was no in-between.

Whether I wanted to hear about it or not, I mean their tryst, fling, whatever, the choice was not mine to make. She ordered him to return to me and tell me all about it [as my father would say, a blow-by-blow report], ALL the gory details such as, "she had hairy legs and hadn't showered", but to my knowledge this was her, usually. She instructed him to dangle the keys in my face, literally, the ones which she had given him earlier in the day to gain access to the private room at the office where they had presumably had their tryst as proof that they had been there. She pulled off what in my opinion was unbelievable, which was to have lured my boyfriend away in the first place. Why, might one ask? I suppose because she could. She lured him away, not for a night, but only for a few hours. I don't really want to elaborate further except to say that he was well worth it. She wasn't! I wondered whether it was a challenge for her to conquer him. I believed it was one she determined she had to take on even if it was just for spite. Maybe it was just knowing that she had access to money [my father's] and speed [also my father's], plus his undying support, moral and otherwise, that made her feel secure enough to pull it off. No, not her clothes, the "boyfriend caper". My boyfriend!

 After a few moments, realizing that as sociable, friendly and unbelievably handsome and happy-go-lucky as he was, he apparently surrendered to her charm and the meth, or vice versa. Nevertheless, after a while of digesting all this, plus seeing her that same night dressed in short sleeved see through baby doll pajamas with track marks running up and down her arms, I began to fight with her for reasons which were obvious, and others which I cannot recall. There was a point where I wanted to scratch her eyes out, but I knew that she seldom bathed and the utter disgusting odor from the cigarettes she constantly smoked, and her long dirty fingernails stained with tobacco. Then I threatened to call the police on her because she had ransacked my closet looking for drugs, among other things!

My father thankfully came home at that very moment, came to the door of his room, overheard the commotion, and immediately ordered her into his room and put a stop to the fight. That was the end of it. Except, I already had the knowledge that Bill was very fertile which brings me to my next point. He had impregnated me so many times in all the years we were together, my father put a stop to it and forced me to have abortions many times. If he hadn't, I would have had a tribe, just from this one young man. He was all about having sex and taking speed. On numerous occasions he would also indulge in marijuana. That we both did.

This time it was her who got pregnant by him, not surprisingly. Everything was hush hush, well, sort of. Suddenly, she became very lady like, where she used to look homely, manly and just plainly unattractive. She started dressing like a lady. She began morphing into a pretty looking lady. She let her hair grow much longer and began looking nice. It was so unbelievable. Normally she maintained an unkempt appearance. It was amazing to see the transition. In those three months before she shipped herself off for her abortion, she looked nice.

Then one day, she appeared outside Papa's bedroom door in the hallway with a long red coat on and a suitcase by her side, with her longer straight hair oily and not as clean, looking nicely brushed and said she was going out of town briefly. I was told she was going out of state to have an abortion. She did and returned about three days later. Not another word was said about it. I am sure my father knew. He was either embarrassed or secretly got a charge out of it. Either way, since it was not a topic open for discussion, I never inquired or knew how he felt. I also respected his privacy. Actually, I was frightened to find out because I was appalled by the whole thing. Even though I thought it was a gas that this woman would go to such lengths to land herself such an attractive sexy young man even if just for a tryst, or perhaps she just wanted to sample my boyfriend. She should have tried Baskin Robbins. They had many delectable flavors. But then a speed freak wouldn't be tempted by food, but would instead opt for sex, speed and yes, sweet revenge which was a form of power and evil which she leashed out against of course, me. For what reason, I don't know. Or if there was a reason, I didn't have the smarts to figure that out. Although certain friends and family members told me that she was extremely jealous of me. I couldn't even figure that one out, since we had absolutely nothing in common.

What was my reaction? At first, I was appalled, yes, then I had to laugh, and at the same time I was feeling sorry for Bill for having been duped by her. I had to laugh because I realized that it took Ruth getting pregnant from my boyfriend to become pretty, which was quite a feat. After she returned from somewhere out of state, baby less, her good looks started fading, and that was it.

The thoughts that went through my mind were overwhelming. Could I blame my boyfriend for this? Really, how could I? I knew very well that she was behind everything. It was her calling card. One other time she tried to seduce another boyfriend when I wasn't home. But we were on to her, set her up, and didn't let her get away with it a second time. Amphetamine can make a normally mischievous person turn evil, really!

I often wondered why my father didn't exercise any control over the situation. He had to have been aware of what had happened. I never dared confront him about it. After all, my father, this strict, strong German, Godlike figure, an immensely possessive being, yet always loving kind and gentle, and always so generous with me, and everyone. How could I? I just couldn't!

And would he even acknowledge involvement with this unattractive and unpleasant person who appeared to be a major presence in his life as someone he was involved with, or simply say he felt sorry for her and wanted to help her, which was what he so often said? She did have redeeming qualities, although very few. She had a rare sense of humor, which was fueled by the meth. And she was extremely agreeable to working incredibly long hours. Without treatment however, she was useless, just a rug under your feet waiting to be tripped over. Once she had a treatment from Papa or administered herself, she was there and functional in a nursing capacity, ready to take on patients, give treatments and work the long hours tirelessly.

She took over everything and turned his world upside down so much so that he was helpless to reverse the damage. She misrepresented herself, everything and everyone else and falsified everything to him. He was so busy working, what did he know? According to Katherine Dunham, treating President Kennedy changed my father. It got to him, to his ego. That I didn't see. Some of his friends in his later years were detrimental to him and those around him. They had a negative effect on him.

My father was generous with speed, unfortunately, and delighted in making his patients feel much better. And she was no exception. She got plenty of speed from him. What he didn't give her, she took. Once, she broke into his safe in his bedroom, took out three vials of meth, and rushed to the office where she quickly assembled her buddies. My father, who had just arrived home from making an emergency house call, knew nothing about what had just happened, but was quickly informed by a patient who was at our home awaiting his arrival, and was quickly summoned by my father to rush to the office to retrieve the vials, empty the place out and return back home to the apartment.

A patient who had been summoned to the office by Ruth for a special treatment was already lying on the treatment table awaiting his injection from her when my father's enlisted patient arrived to empty the place out. After that ordeal, for some unimaginable reason, she was returned to my father.

On one occasion while he was in his private Jacuzzi, she took three vats he had sitting on his treatment table in his bedroom. They contained a bad batch of "injectables". She gave herself an injection and had a severely bad reaction. The maid came into the room and found her in dire straits, rushed to get my father out of the bathtub to revive her but the door was locked, and the Jacuzzi was running with the motor blasting, so he didn't hear her pounding on the door. She busted in the door and got him out. He threw on his robe, rushed into the room and managed to stabilize her.

Unfortunately, my relatives adored her. Why, you might ask, or how? Well, she opened a "bed and breakfast" after my father died where she appointed our housekeeper, whom she now had since she got all the money, to cook, clean and serve food. Amphetamine was also on the menu. Sometimes you knew about it and sometimes you didn't.

Several years ago, I spoke to Tommy and told him I felt very violated by Ruth. The reason was my older son Jason had gone to visit her with a friend of his from Brooklyn, they were maybe 17 years old at the time. They went to go swimming downstairs in the pool where my father used to swim laps every day. After swimming they went upstairs, and Ruth served them (a gracious host indeed) a nice meal. Somehow during the meal, she managed to slip them a nice dose of amphetamine. My son was totally unaware of what was happening.

After he left her apartment, instead of returning to Brooklyn, he went sight-seeing with his friend and walked all over Times Square. He came home early in the morning, still awake and said he wasn't tired. He ventured to stay up the whole next day and even had trouble sleeping the next night. I told my son what was going on, he didn't quite understand it. He said he had a drink from a bottle of wine that sat on the dining room table, perhaps that was it. I wanted to take a urine specimen from my son. I didn't have fifteen dollars to send it to the lab for testing. I decided the next time I would get a urine specimen and send it to the lab. The next time, Ruth gave Jason money to eat out, so the plan never hatched.

Instead, I spoke to Tommy and told him what happened, that Jason was slipped amphetamine without his knowledge. Tommy, who is close to Ruth, and I was not aware, called her and told her everything I said. He called me back and told me that maybe she did it to make him feel good. Maybe she thought she was doing something nice for him. He told me to see it that way. Yeah, right, unfreakin' believable, excuse my language. If my mother had been alive, none of this would have happened, none of it.

Right after Tommy's mother died, I called Ruth and asked her if I could go to her building and watch the 4th of July fireworks from her roof. She said, oh no, you can't, they're painting and renovating up there. No one can go up there at all, sorry dear! Stupidly I believed her. At Litzi's funeral, at the gravesite, Tommy made a speech. How he had a wonderful celebratory evening the night his mother passed away. He celebrated her life and her passing by watching the spectacular fireworks display from the roof of my stepmother's building and couldn't think of a nicer way to celebrate her passing on the 4th of July. With that said I knew how she was getting back at me for snitching on her. She was a very good liar and a very quick thinker. Especially when she was on amphetamine. When there's speed, she stays close. That's the way she is.

The story goes on and on. But it is I who have chosen to end it as I don't wish to endure any more of this nor do I feel the reader of this book would want to endure any more of this either. I have decided not to call her my stepmom. Why? It implies coziness and a loving relationship, which there wasn't. So, stepmother will have to do.

86

Papa Indicted

If anyone asked me to recall where I was and what I was doing at the exact time my father's name hit the cover of The New York Times in 1974, I can assure you I remember. I was living at the Central Apartment Hotel on West 86th Street and was sound asleep when I got an early call which woke me up, fast! It was from Otis Cavrell, who was a dear confidante, friend and patient of my father. He said, "Jill, it's all over". I immediately visualized that my father had landed in a helicopter on the White House lawn and crashed. No, thank God that was not it.

Instead, it was Otis repeating to me over and over that he was sad but had to inform me that my father's license to practice medicine was revoked in the State of New York and there was something on the cover of the Sunday New York Times, with a picture of my father and an article. He said I'd have to go out and get it right away.

I threw on my clothes and rushed out to get the paper. There it was right on the cover of the Sunday edition of the New York Times, a large photo of my father with the captions stating: "11 indictments against Dr. Max Jacobson" plus all this stuff about celebrities and amphetamine. I went into shock. I immediately rushed back to my hotel room and called my father. I was still in shock when we spoke. He too was trying to deal with this pandemonium. He hired Louie Nizer, a friend of Alan J. Lerner, to represent him on the charges. I totally freaked out. The newspapers were writing about my father, and the media was attacking him, writing horrible things about him.

This was my father they were talking about, the larger-than-life man, the doctor whose patients kept telling me how brilliant he was, what a genius he was and how he had saved them so many times. No, it hadn't all gone to my head. I had seen him in action treating patients, saving them, helping them. Making people who were on the brink of death or suffering feel better, much better and in some cases get well. This is what I personally saw. He was so sure of himself, so kind, thoughtful and caring, so giving and so generous. He was everything to me as a father, as a doctor and he was everything to most of his patients. For me to read this was totally devastating, traumatizing.

 What happened to me, his daughter? I was so distraught I went into seclusion. I didn't have any relatives to turn to, no one. After a few days I called my boyfriend Bill who came over. After nearly a whole week of being holed up in my hotel room, too emotionally scarred to have the strength to venture out, Bill finally convinced me to go out and have a bite to eat and get some fresh air. "Fine", I said, I agreed.

 Well, we went out. Maybe four blocks from where I was staying at the hotel. We ventured into this crowded restaurant with an enclosed outdoor café attached, pretty spacious, it was fine. Then suddenly out of nowhere, Marian, Bills ex-girlfriend jumped up out of a seat. She was there with her boyfriend and called out, "Jill, I am so sorry about your father". Well, that did it for me. I turned to Bill and told him I was going back to the hotel. I just couldn't take it.

 The next day I went to see Dr. Robert Freymann for treatment because I was so stressed out, I just couldn't handle it anymore. Bob was a New York physician and a former colleague of my father who was also known for treating patients by injecting vitamin shots. He too was known to have numerous celebrity patients. I'd been to see him before for treatments and felt the need to return now. I put on a coat and pulled the collar up to my face so that nobody would recognize me.

 I walked into his office and to my surprise, I found many of my father's patients sitting there, people whom I knew, felt comfortable around and people who were apparently also seeking treatments from Dr. Freymann sitting there in his waiting room. Jerry Ragni and Jimmy Rado were there, I think, plus several others.

I said "Hi" to everyone and went in to see the doctor. I was visibly shaking; I told him what had happened and that I was so upset that I needed treatment. He gave me treatment. I thanked him and left. After a moment I began to wonder what all those people, patients of my father's and members of his "inner circle" were doing there in Dr. Freymann's office and if they had been sneaking behind my father's back to get treatments from Dr. Freymann. Somehow though, that didn't seem to bother me for very long or hold my attention. It would have hurt my feelings and ego to really give it that much thought. I think reality had set in and the treatment from the doctor having somewhat relaxed me made everything feel if only momentarily more digestible.

Getting back to Otis Cavrell who was very nice, caring and fatherly to me for many years, was now the one who had decided to call me and break the news to me. I will always remember him well. Our lives, my father and mine, went into turbulence thereafter. My father, of course, was devastated. I'll never know why, but he expected the Kennedy's to come to his rescue defending him in court and to assist him monetarily. I told him repeatedly they had far too much to lose to come forward and support him in any way whatsoever, especially considering the Chappaquiddick incident and everything else. My father felt they owed it to him to come forward in support of him. He claimed Clint Hill had advised Jackie, even after she had promised my father, not to get involved in any way. She didn't! Chuck Spaulding was appointed by Jackie to orchestrate lots of money for my father's court case and essentially keep Jackie out of it. That promise of money from the Kennedy clan never came to fruition. He ultimately felt very let down by them.

As far as Otis Cavrell was concerned, my mother had visited his building many years past where he produced movies and documentaries, and occasionally filmed food for commercials. Once he filmed a commercial with a big, beautiful turkey sitting on a table. It looked so appealing that I was tempted to take one bite. Some assistant advised me not to. It had been brushed with something to make it look good and that something was poison.

Otis had a brother, Ira, whom I seldom saw. It was Otis I was the most familiar with. He was more a friend than patient and I doubt he was given amphetamine. I will always remember Otis Cavrell as a nice caring and fatherly person. If I had to hear the news from anyone, I am grateful that it was Otis.

I guess you are wondering why I didn't mention at some point what bonding I might have had with my father during all this fiasco, just daddy and me after everything happened, or why I didn't even consider or seem concerned about his sorrows or anxieties.

My answer is simple, Ruth. My father's third wife, the one big mistake I always felt he really made, not the amphetamine. She was there with him in all her glory, all her evil twisted glory guarding him, their palace, his apartment, and all the speed she was maliciously and meticulously guarding. It wasn't all his fault, she was there, and that was enough to keep me away.

87

Media Madness

It behooves me to see just how much the media has hyped, with much inaccuracy, my father's involvement with amphetamines, and yet failed to stress how much good he did for so many people, how beneficial his treatments were for those who legitimately needed them.

The celebrities were under constant pressure professionally to produce for the big movie studios they were under contract with, MGM Grand, etc. And then, from what I heard, they would come home to their families and unravel, unwind. And that was another whole traumatic event. I saw husbands, wives, actors and actresses trying to hold their own, maintain their own individuality trying to keep their egos intact while trying to lead normal lives at home. And yet at the same time, trying to fully be there as a totally sympathetic half, husband or wife, to their mate. It was explosive at times, something which should have happened in the psychiatrist's office.

With all the media exaggerating everything, all the hype behind all those allegations, there are certain facts I am aware of. I know that far from all the patients were on amphetamine. My father was making and mixing his own unadulterated vitamins. He mostly treated his patients with massive doses of vitamins, oral drops and injectables, plus he invented a cream which the patient could rub on their face, and on their necks to be refreshed which smelled very "vitaminy". I have learned that vitamins can have quite the same effect, like a shot of "speed".

If you had gone in for a treatment feeling under the weather or run down, you left the office with all this energy plus feeling like a million dollars. Vitamins alone can have the same effect. Yes, he did use amphetamine on himself and on some of his patients, but not on all his patients, and not all the time. I personally remember several occasions when he turned down patient's requests for amphetamine for whatever reason. And sometimes the reaction from the patient was nasty, or a tantrum was thrown. But he stuck to his guns about it.

What's all the hype about? What's all the fuss about? I don't give a damn who says what! I don't care what anyone says. And the media even fifteen years ago, when this story broke went haywire, blasphemy! The media should go to hell. What about the speed, amphetamine? Well, my dears, let me tell you something. In that era, all those people alive and well, and in their prime, worked their rear ends off for the studios that contracted them. These people were from poor humble beginnings working just to survive. They were straight, square, and by our standards today disciplined, then more than today and very driven to succeed. A shot of vitamins was a total blast off for most of them. And if they were run down and overworked, which many of them were, pure vitamins were perfect.

For those who took amphetamine, it was not against the law in the early 50's through the 70's. The demands on the celebrities and statesmen's schedules were such that it necessitated them taking something to keep going. They worked hectic hours, grueling schedules. Being on a movie set was an all-day event from very early mornings extending to late nights. My father mixed amphetamine in conjunction with massive doses of all kinds of vitamins plus calcium.

Some of his patients were anemic, very run down for various reasons and legitimately needed vitamins. My father also prepared oral drops for his patients, which were much in demand. It was amazing to see how positively they reacted simply from his vitamin injections.

I remember one instance where my father was treating an M.S. patient whose husband had to drive her to the city from Long Island after a hard day's work. My father treated M.S. patients on weekends and on several nights during the week. This patient's husband was very tired and fell asleep at the wheel, almost causing an accident. He had to pull off the road. After hearing this, my father filled a vial with vitamins and amphetamine and told the husband that since he was nice enough to take the time and trouble to bring his wife in to see him to get treatments, he offered him the vial and gave him instructions on how to inject himself intramuscularly, in the hip so that he could safely drive her in to the city and back. It is not easy to inject oneself intramuscularly, so my father had to spend time teaching the man proper procedure. This case was an isolated incident.

My father always told me and his patients, "I will help you to feel better and to lead a constructive and productive life" and he certainly did. He was living proof. Later, much later in his life he got into magnets. I thought he had gone nuts. He would pass magnets by one's head or over the knees. I thought for sure he had gone nuts. I read recently how some doctors in 1998 discovered using magnets to treat stress and spasms.

What kind of bothered me at the time was I was having doubts about my father and what he was doing. Everyone around him was saying that he was a genius and way ahead of his time, everyone. And people came and were advising me as if I hadn't picked up on it. That there was a genius in our midst – that I, his daughter must know, be aware bubbling with pride and regard my father as a total genius. I, dummy me, wasn't so sure.

He was my father, we had agreements and disagreements, plenty of both. It took me until recently, maybe ten years ago to realize that some major issues that I was convinced he was majorly wrong about, in the long run he was right about.

Early on when I was still a little girl I learned never to ask, "Who are you?" and "What do you do?". In addition to that I wasn't nosey, the only thing I think unfortunately my father taught me, was to inquire what religion a person was. Still, I didn't ask. I guess because my father had celebrities around him constantly and I noticed how they appeared like hunted dogs, constantly having to run and hide. I mean they had to rush out of my father's office to be anonymous. Naturally when they arrived, they wanted to be ushered into a treatment room or inside a room to be shielded from the other patients, which they had an absolute right to want. And I noticed how upset they got when people hounded them for autographs. They already had no anonymity, and this was only the late fifties. Once Pat Suzuki visited us at our home in Point

Lookout and she had to rush into our house. People started to gather around our house with everyone of all ages wanting her autograph and wanting to see her. I felt so bad for her and for myself. I had been so accustomed to seeing her all relaxed and leisurely at our apartment in New York, just sitting and chatting. She was always so sweet to me.

And I felt so guilty when I bought a star or some magazine when I was about eleven years old, once, but I felt so bad, because I liked Debbie Reynolds so much, and suddenly, she and Eddie had split. I couldn't see her anymore because my parents were friends with Eddie and didn't want to upset Debbie further by attempting a visit for me to see her and her children which I loved to do. Not because she was a celebrity, but because she was so nice, sweet, and very friendly, so Debbie Reynolds.

So out of missing her and the desire to see her I bought one of these magazines which are horrible. In it I found photos of her hugging her children, having them all dressed up, especially Carrie, and Debbie looking so intense, but most important of all, shown being a good doting mother. Anyway, that was my one big involvement with the invasion of other people's privacy. None of us really know what goes on when these people's privacy is being invaded. The magazine reps call them and set up an appointment to come over. They interrupt the lives and schedules of these stars to spend an hour or more demanding the celebrity to pose, to do all these poses and different things. Then they tell them to bring out their children. I remember Debbie had a nurse for her children and had to arrange for the nurse to feed Carrie lunch in the dining room while Debbie was busy appeasing the photographer. It took over an hour. I had to wait once while they did one layout.

It's amazing to see these stars, celebrities off camera, in private lost in their own allure. They are human beings of our species whose vamped up public persona oft gets mixed up with who they are in private, self-absorbed, yet with a fascinating past and history. Both off the set and on they are distinguished individuals, distinguished in that they 'll succumb to any intolerable conditions unacceptable to most individuals. They work in overheated studios, sound stages, which are themselves unventilated and overheated, without fans, and without air conditioning. Fans blow hair and air conditioners make noise.

Celebrities were being questioned so often, I learned to fiercely respect their privacy. I always hated it when I heard people ask that of anybody. I mean, what the hell business is it of theirs anyway? As long as you weren't a bank robber or a murderer, who the hell cares? And all this stuff is private, personal. What right does anyone have to ask, or even to know? If someone decides to tell you, that's their business entirely. I always felt so sorry for the celebrities and anyone else who worked very hard at a respectable job or endeavoring to establish themselves with a respectable career, when a nosey son of a bitch would approach them and ask, "Well, what do you do?" What right do they have to ask? Are they just shallow? Empty headed? There are apparently many of those around. Nosey bastards I call them. I still go into stores and turn the magazines around so that people won't see the celebrity photos and am tempted to buy the rags for all the lies they put on the covers and try to protect celebrities from our enquiring minds for salacious gossip. I have said my piece, Amen.

88

AMPHETAMINE IN RETROSPECT

In retrospect, I feel very bad about my days taking speed. It took me away from my immediate family, times, years and occasions that can never be replaced. I also managed to lose touch with many friends. That too can never be replaced. And relationships, personal relationships, intense ones with men I really cared for, were side railed, disrupted, and broken due to the usage of amphetamines, their usage and mine. The only difference was that I had ADHD, my boyfriends didn't. What that meant was that I needed to take the medicine to stabilize myself. They took it to get high. And then there were always side effects. The amphetamine destroyed my personal relationships; God knows where they would have gone had we not been on speed.

I approve of amphetamine, yes, under certain circumstances, such as for learning disabilities, for that it is essential. I did have that, and unfortunately, I still do, yet I am no longer taking amphetamine. I would at times If I could get it, which I cannot. I believe it would be crucial for students who need to do their studying. For college students who need to apply for scholarships and need to maintain an A or B plus grade level to get the scholarship. Even for writing this book, I think it would have aided me having amphetamine in small doses. But I didn't. That gives one something to think about.

My taking of drugs later in life was my doing. My father had nothing whatsoever to do with that. The way I see it, my father was not in any way responsible for my drug taking, directly or indirectly. I am stating that, and I wish other people would see that. I know there are people who love to blame others for their actions and misdeeds. Not me, I take full responsibility for my actions. We had connections, my father was not to blame. Whether I took drugs occupationally or recreationally, yes it does matter. It also matters that I was the decision maker, the one who decided to take the drugs, not my father.

89

Cats, Cats, and More Cats

I have loved cats since I was seven years old. We have had cats since I was nine years old. I had cats which I personally took full responsibility for since I was nineteen years old. From as far back as I can remember, and sadly with a bad taste in my mouth and bitter lasting memories, I can recall Papa taking my cats from my apartment. I have no anger towards the person whom he enlisted to carry out the seizure for him. They were only doing what they were told. It was very traumatic for me.

Beginning with red-haired Casey on my 22nd birthday. I was on my way to my boyfriend Bill's apartment in Greenwich Village, it was my birthday that day. Walking down the street from the bus where I had just gotten off, I spotted a little girl, about six years old. An old man was standing near her. They had at least five kittens they were handling. I walked over, "cooed" at the kittens and asked if I could hold one. The little girl just handed it to me and told me I could take it. I took the kitten immediately and thanked her. I couldn't have asked for a better gift, I just loved cats. I always have and always will. The kitten had strange but interesting markings, it was a mixture of black and white evenly proportioned on its face. I took it to Bill's apartment where I was headed. He named her Lucifer. After a year or so she gave me kittens, she had several litters. I kept one kitten from her litter, Spatshy, who used to sit on my shoulder and go on walks with me because he knew me and trusted me.

On my twenty-seventh birthday, Bill got a pass from his hospital in Connecticut where he had been staying for some mental problems to come and visit me for the weekend and celebrate my birthday. We always made beautiful love together, sex was great between us. He never seemed ready to commit to fatherhood. I loved him terribly. So, I decided to give myself a birthday present, a souvenir of our relationship. Also, I had desperately wanted a child since I was a little girl. As time was running out and Bill was there with me, I decided that this was it.

So that weekend on my birthday I got happily pregnant. It was quite simple since I already knew that Bill was extremely fertile. I had gotten pregnant by him in the past. The problem was that my father had found out and forced me to have an abortion. This time I was going to keep it a secret so he couldn't force me to have an abortion. This time I kept my mouth shut. When I was getting big, after about the fifth month, I was invited to visit my father and his wife Ruth uptown for lunch. I went with my big belly. I had no maternity clothes yet. Their big mouth maid told them she saw my big belly. Papa rushed me off to see my Aunt Carla's gynecologist, Dr. Warner Nash.

When Lucifer was pregnant (so was I with baby number one), she had her litter before I had my baby, at least 3 months before. A friend named Ted built an elaborate cat house for her to sleep in and take the kittens to after they were born. Something happened two days before she had her kittens. I was living near my father at the time, on the ground floor in a nice sized studio apartment in the back. I had a huge empty courtyard outside my three large windows.

I would let my cats (two at the time) sit on the windowsill. One from somewhere I don't recall, his name was Teddy Bear, he was Siamese, light gray and Lucifer. Sometimes, rarely though, they would venture out, especially if they spotted a pigeon. On this day, two days before Lucifer delivered her brood, she and Teddy Bear ventured out (after we made this gorgeous cathouse in my apartment) in the courtyard and captured a pigeon and killed it. They brought it into my apartment, into the fancy cathouse Ted had built, and blood had splattered all over. It was a huge mess! My cats brought two blue jays into the apartment before, but I saved them. Out went the pigeon and the beautiful house into the garbage. I was mortified by all this commotion. Then I had to rush out and get a large wide cardboard box for when the kittens arrived.

Lenny (short for Lenora) was a friend of my part time boyfriend at the time, Larry. She was a sweet girl with long braids who looked Swiss, she asked if

I would come over and get her when Lucifer went into labor so she could watch. Lucifer, who was like my daughter, finally went into labor. I went and got Lenora right away. She insisted on stopping at a restaurant and getting a pizza first, big mistake. The pizza was never touched, Lucifer went into labor, one of the greatest moments of my life to be sure!

During the delivery she had pain. She grabbed my arm with her claws, dug in as hard as she had to and pushed, out came six kittens. It was just wonderful. However, once she started eating the afterbirth, Lenny and I lost our appetites completely. That was ok, I was too choked up with emotion from Lucifer having her kittens. I felt like a proud new mom. The kittens were darling, they'd run all over the place. The next few months were spent with me pregnant thinking I was actually giving birth to a kitten. I guess I'd been relating to cats for so long, that's what happened!

Whenever I opened the door to my apartment, one or two of them would run out. The super complained, the landlord complained. My father had a lawyer, an animal lover whom he hired to help me fight the building from eviction. Six kittens tripping me and running all around me all the time. It was really cute, fun and funny. I absolutely loved it.

After a time, I found homes for the kittens, all but one, Spatshy (sounds Russian or Czech), but that's what I named him. I fell madly in love with him. I had Teddy Bear, Lucifer, and Spatshy. I vaguely remember finding a home for Teddy Bear before I had to go to the hospital and have my own baby. Mentally and emotionally, I was not ready and couldn't bear leaving my cats. I arranged with my upstairs neighbor, a dear sweet lady, to feed them and care for them while I was in the hospital. It was feasible and I left the keys with her as well.

I gave birth to baby Jason in June 1974, right on Father's Day at Lenox Hill Hospital. I also reunited with Bill, whom I had avoided like the plague right before I gave birth because my maternal instincts kicked in and I felt I needed to protect my unborn child from his father. He had been trying to find my whereabouts for days and had just managed to locate me. He had gone to the Salvation Army, telling them he needed to wash up and needed clothes so that he could come up to the hospital and see me and his newborn son.

In walked Bill, cleanly dressed, a new shirt and pants, carrying in his hands a beautiful bouquet of flowers and the most beautiful smile I had ever seen in my whole life, which seemed even lovelier than the flowers which he had brought me! He arrived totally unexpectedly, just as I was about to begin nursing and bonding with my new son for the first time. That was so wonderful, and I was so surprised to see him. We were momentarily one happy family.

All my life I've had traumatic experiences, haven't we all? None of them have devastated me more than losing a cat, none, ever. Apparently, my father had this notion that cats should not be present in the house with a newborn infant. Of course, I felt different. They were my babies too. Papa did not have the compassion, nor could he relate to my feelings on this. He didn't have it within him to understand the depth of my love for cats. It was greater than for humans, I believe. As happy as I had just been with my newborn baby and his doting father at my side, the happiness turned to horror, shocking horror. It just so happened that while I was in the hospital, my mean father decided that I could not come home with a newborn baby and cats in the apartment. Or maybe some evil patient swayed my father into the idea of getting rid of my cats. Unfortunately, Papa took the advice of his patients all too often. Well, why on earth not have cats in the apartment, what's wrong with that? So, he sent Haleigh Murdough, his patient and friend, over to the lady's apartment to demand my keys. She had to give them up, I believe she was ordered. Then Haleigh went into my apartment and took my cats to the A.S.P.C.A.

Of course, I knew nothing about this. I had just given birth to my son. The neighbor got my telephone number, or perhaps I telephoned her and gave it to her, and she phoned me in hysterics. Either way, I got the call. At the exact moment she phoned me, I was nursing my newborn baby. She told me that my beloved cats had been catnapped from my apartment. I cried and freaked out; I was momentarily horrified. Bill immediately asked to speak with her and asked where they had been taken and offered to go and fetch them back.

After calling the A.S.P.C.A., they told me what I needed to do. I pleaded with them immediately not to put my cats to sleep or adopt them out. Then I pleaded with them to hold onto them until Bill showed up to retrieve them. They informed me that they would require a note from me stating the situation and my request. I had to prove that I was in the hospital. Then they agreed to release them to Bill with the note from me. He went right to the A.S.P.C.A. and retrieved them. He spent hours finding a hotel that would allow him to bring cats onto its premises. It was now down to Lucifer and Spatshy. He finally found a hotel and stayed there. He also managed to temporarily misplace Lucifer, who had wandered off, and he had to go through all kinds of changes searching through the oddest places looking for her. After a day and a half, he finally found her and only had to wait two more days at the hotel until I came home. In the meantime, I was going nuts with worry about my lost cat.

Upon my arrival home, things were momentarily a bit chaotic. I put my baby in his basinet, Bill arrived within minutes with my cats. I got the cats out of the suitcase and hugged them dotingly. I was so happy to see them again. Bill went to great lengths to assist me in keeping my cats, but to no avail. I left provisions for my cats at home and left the keys with my neighbor to check in on them and feed them. I did absolutely everything. While I was still at home, in labor and in excruciating pain, I squeezed Lucifer's paw. She didn't even complain.

In my next breath, and I am sitting here in tears, crying while I am writing, I can't help it. Papa had hired a nursemaid, Anne Montgomery, his patient and friend but mostly his patient, to help me for the first few weeks that I was home with my new baby. She took one look at the cats and gave me an ultimatum. She told me, I'll give you one hour to get rid of these cats or I'll call your father. I didn't know what to do, my head was spinning. I didn't have a job, no money, I was being supported solely by my father. Bill was not working. I was given a matter of hours to find new living quarters for my cats. I was totally devastated again. I yelled at her, pleaded with her. She said she would get into trouble if she didn't volunteer the information to my father.

My father came for a visit. Very quietly, but firmly, he ordered me to get the cats out of the house and scolded the nursemaid for not following his instructions. It seemed there was no negotiating at all whatsoever. I had momentarily been so happy, so fulfilled, and suddenly in a moment's notice the rug was being pulled right out from under me. I was forced to give up Lucifer and Spatshy. Papa was supporting me, so I guess he had some rights. I hadn't been working and none of my so-called boyfriends were in any position to help me out. Once they were gone, I felt this great emptiness within me. It was awful. Here I was with this newborn baby at home, which I loved and had always wanted. And all I could think of was my cats that were gone. I should have been allowed to keep them. We would have been one happy family.

My father hired Ms. Montgomery to help me with the baby, cooking and cleaning. This was my gift from my father, for the first two weeks. What she didn't teach me, that I should have been taught, was that to get my breasts to produce milk, I needed to have my baby stimulate them by sucking on them. The baby must be allowed extra time and encouraged to suck thereby causing a normal and healthy flow of milk. All this I did not know! After noticing that my baby wasn't getting enough breast milk, she told me to give up nursing and give him formula instead. Regrettably, I stopped nursing after only a week and a half. I felt totally helpless. I was frustrated, it was all so unnecessary and sad.

My father was calling all the shots. I know I could have easily kept my cats. It hit me so hard. I sat crying with tears rolling down my cheeks onto my newborn baby, with him in my lap. I couldn't even enjoy my new baby. All I could think of, every living moment of every day, was how depressed I was at having to give up my beloved cats. When I realized that I wouldn't get my cats back, after several secret cat napping attempts and then being told that the cats were gone for good, all because I had a baby, I resorted to drinking so that my sadness would go away. It got so bad I even left home and went to the corner restaurant bar. Other people drank alcohol to kill their pain, why couldn't I? I went to the bar and ordered a drink. I did that twice, it didn't work. As a matter of fact, it made things worse, much worse. After having a drink, I could no longer rationalize why I had the problem or why I was depressed. The reason why Papa did what he did in the first place, taking my cats. I became even more depressed. I never really got over it.

Finally, around Christmas, I saw an ad in a store window. It seemed like almost a year since my cats had been gone. The ad read "Kittens, need a good home, up for adoption!". I called the people. They offered to bring the kittens over for a visit to see if we would get along. How sweet, I thought. By that time Bill had a job, and we were ready to tell my father that Bill was going to support us, me and the baby. He was officially living with me, and Papa was totally unapproving of it. Especially considering his past, all the violence and drug issues, so Papa stayed away. Bill and I were ridiculously trying to make it as a family. I thought it wise to consult Bill before adopting the kitten. I figured that was the best way to go.

He had a job working at Alexanders Department store, in the toy department. He was bringing home lots of toys. I had to cautiously approach the subject of adopting the kitten. Finally, he conceded that adopting the kitten was a good idea. His job was also going well, he brought home many gifts for the baby. One of them was a cute fire engine. We adopted this darling kitten, but that was short lived.

The only problem I eventually had to deal with was Bill's deteriorating mental health as the weeks went by. His health began steadily failing. Whether being a family and having a normal life or possibly having some uppers in the house could have contributed to his downfall. Either way, he began falling apart.

I adopted the kitten and grew attached to it, as one does. After some months passed, I was taking on too much. Many stressful situations were cropping up, such as Bill's psychosis and becoming schizophrenic out of nowhere. There were weird signs, not necessarily amphetamine induced. He would rummage through my closet and pick out feminine clothing, even though his friend had just bought him masculine blue jean shirts, the kind with snaps at the wrists instead of cufflinks. These were classic, expensive and nice. He would pass those up for my feminine shirts.

I found a baby's knitted hat in the kitchen sink, half drowned in dirty dish water. I was in a total fog as to what that was all about. He was terrifying me by testing his sexuality. It would come on like gangbusters, and he didn't know how to handle it, certainly neither did I. I think for a time he didn't know whether he should be or wanted to be a man or woman. Outside of the home and unknown to me, he was experimenting quite vigorously on his own with members of his own sex. I was busy at home being a mom, trying to cope with my baby's teething problems which were bad.

At the same time, Papa had his medical license revoked. That was traumatic itself. Papa had been in practice for forty years, so all of this was a terrible shock to us. Everything seemed to be happening at once. Bill began exhibiting extremely bizarre behavior. Strangely as it seemed at the time, a friend of Bill's, Vic, unexpectedly arrived from California for Christmas. For me, that was the beginning of the end.

This man came to N.Y. for the holidays and took Bill because they were lovers. He made plans to drop in on us and showered Bill with gifts and all kinds of clothes. Then under suspicious circumstances, lured Bill away to places unreachable. It took me a while to figure things out. I began to vaguely suspect something, but not anywhere near what was really happening. Bill got worse because of this man's visit, even more so than he was.

I had to leave with my six-month-old baby, and unfortunately, I had to abandon my poor cat. I had to do the unthinkable, for me at least! I'll die before I get over this cat business. I took the cat outside in the pouring rain (it wasn't warm either) and abandoned her in the courtyard around the corner where Bill couldn't grab her and hurt her. I don't remember my exact reasoning behind this horrible action, only that I had very limited time to get the kitten out of harm's way. That was the only time my father was not to blame! I don't know how I did that, how? The memory of it all scorches my mind, torches my soul with guilt. And worst of all, it keeps going around and around in my head. The reality of that moment has never been resolved. I had to get her out of there. I'll never forgive myself. I won't rationalize it, that makes things worse.

I hate myself now for this, however I never forgave my father for railroading (the expression he so often used) me into getting rid of my dearest loved ones, my beloved cats. He may very well have done it for the right reasons, in my best interest and my newborn baby's best interest, but the results were devastating to my emotional state of mind and wellbeing. I do have a conscience. I went by the place where I left the cat the next day, she wasn't there. I still worried, enough said!

Next thing, Bill went completely mad. I saw it coming, went into denial and couldn't figure out what the hell was happening. I had to pack up, take my baby and run. A friend temporarily put me up in a hotel. Several months later, I returned to salvage my belongings and left for Germany to spend safe time with my grandfather.

To get back to my cats, when I returned from Germany, maybe three months later with Jason being a year and a half old, I found an apartment and within months had a new kitten, Kitzella. I was on my own now, no father ordering me around, no boyfriend to go nuts, I was a single mom on my own, and boy did I love my new kitten. I had Kitzella for at least 17 years until he got stricken with cancer and had to be put to sleep.

In between that time a friend brought me a box with four or five kittens which had been dumped on his property in Brooklyn. He gave me the pick of the litter. From this I picked one. I had just suffered a miscarriage, so I named the kitten "Baby". I had him for 20 ½ wonderful years with no one interfering or threatening me in any way. He was the most wonderful affectionate cat. He allowed me to carry him around the house in my arms just like a baby. He was my baby even after I had my children, he was still "My baby".

Unfortunately, I had to have him put to sleep a little over one week ago, June 9th, 2005. Not old age, no way. Health problems, kidney failure, back leg weakness from a seizure suffered two years ago [fur zwei jahre]. Sometimes I think in German. And now I am pouring my thoughts here so I must put down what comes out. Someday I hope to hook up with a German man, sometime before I die.

Baby was losing weight rapidly, the cause of which was phenobarbital, medicine needed to be taken daily to prevent further seizures, and then senility was creeping in slowly. His system was shutting down little by little. He could hardly walk, he was staggering. It was heart breaking to see.

His back legs, stiff and weak from the damn seizure which he had suffered, became even worse every time I had to administer the phenobarbital to him, which I felt I was forced to do by the vet who told me not to dare miss even one dosage. But knowing and seeing the effects it had on his balance and well-being made me even more reluctant to give it to him. I also feared the possible consequences of not giving it to him. I was torn between the two. His balance became progressively worse.

Finally, he began falling all over the place and wasn't enjoying his trips to the litter box even though it was close by. He deteriorated rapidly. I think due to the heat, the hot weather descended upon us suddenly. It hit him very hard. He was barely able to make it to and from the bathroom. The pills were making him go to the toilet far too much.

Before he had to be put to sleep, the darling new vet encouraged me to hydrate him at home for his kidney failure twice a week. I was frightened to be doing this, but I felt being a doctor's daughter I was compelled to do it. Alas, I did it and my cat bounced back and was walking fine. However, once the heat arrived, he spiraled downward.

I had him put to sleep only when I had no recourse. I thought I'd be so relieved afterwards. I wasn't. I felt I should have asked someone with more of a thinking capacity than myself what if anything I could have done to make his life any easier, longer, better. He had begun urinating in my room other than the litter box. Then he urinated with his tail sticking out of the litter box opposed to his head sticking out, thus spraying urine all over the floor. I put newspapers all over the place. I wondered afterwards if I could have had the foresight to tape newspaper onto the wall to catch the urine. I wondered and wondered. Should I tape it to the walls, tape it to the floors, etc. Then he got so weak, he decided to camp out in the bathroom on the floor. I guess he figured he was staggering so badly and had such a hard time getting from my bed ten feet away to the litter box, so he just sat down on the bathroom floor and looked up at me with a hopeless glance. That's when I decided it was enough.

I had been in touch with a pet psychic because I had feared he'd have another seizure or die a horrible violent death at home at night. Well, my other fear was dealing with my younger son and his father, who were already upset with me for even considering putting my ailing cat out of his misery earlier. The psychic advised me, not even knowing my situation, to call them and discuss it with them first. I felt they weren't even living with me and didn't see the condition the cat was in. I had to tell them things were getting bad. The cat was weakening and getting senile.

At one point he stood on my bed, I feared he didn't feel he could make it from my bed to his litter box. I feared he'd just pee on my bed. I lifted him up, rushed into the bathroom and plunked him into the litter box. He proceeded to pee immediately. This went on for a day. It was the next day that I had it. However, and there is an afterlife after ending my cat's life; death, trauma, and depression that has taken on a new life here. We had agreed to let the vet make the final decision.

The next evening, June 9th, he was put to sleep. That began my journey of horrifying sadness and guilt, not intense relief as I had first believed, but intense guilt. I kept thinking, brooding, what could I possibly have done to extend his life? Maybe put newspapers all over the place, get off my lazy rear end and cater to him more? The guilt was endless.

Now, more than one week later, I am slowly coming to deal with the realization that it had to come to that. That it had to be that way. And my cousin granted me my wish to bury him on her property on Long Island. Only I had forgotten to bring an article of clothing along with me to wrap him in. I didn't like having to bury him the way I did. I begged my cousin to let me re-bury him. She politely said no! Now I must give up, not let go. It's so hard. Bye Baby.

90

HELL'S KITCHEN

Alexandra Palmer (left) and Jill at
West 46th Street park, late 1990s

After I returned from Germany, Jason and I had to go on welfare with papa having just had his license revoked. I found a place at 425 West 46th Street in Hell's Kitchen and met Alexandra Palmer, the fashion editor for The New York Times who almost immediately invited my son and I to join the West 46th Street block association. I did, gladly and willingly.

Members of the West 46th Street
block association: Watty Strauss
(left) and guest (right). late 1970s

And as much as I wish to say the rest is history, this is a book I am writing, my book, so in these pages I am going to spell it out. My wondrous glorious productive years spent on the executive committee of the West 46th Street block association.

Since my stepmother was uncooperative

and visits to see my father at his home uptown were unwelcome, my father made weekend visits accompanied by Bill Levi, a pal of his to see me and Jason at our place on West 46th Street. I soon developed a kinship with Alexandra Palmer and several other residents there. I still somehow managed to hook up with some unsavory guys, and unfortunately my father still had to bail me out, although not from jail, thank God. For instance, he gave me the money to buy a police bar and lock for my door, so that a beau who threatened to bust down my door could not, and thankfully soon left the neighborhood.

I must mention that while I lived on West 46th Street, I was right next door to St. Clement's Church, where I frequently went and whose beautiful music often filled my apartment. I also had some very nice neighbors, Barbara and Carlos Pineiro, who besides inviting me to their story book wedding, with a horse drawn carriage and tears in everyone's eyes at the beauty of it all, Carlos came to my aid on one occasion when an ex-boyfriend decided to deceive and hurt me. Carlos took it upon himself to step in and defend me. I will be forever grateful for his caring and kindness toward me.

Please excuse me if I dote on Hell's Kitchen in this chapter, a cause which has been close to my heart for many, many years. I spent years living there and consider it "my baby", meaning that there were wonderful years where friendships were created, lifelong friendships, starting with a friend named Carol whose children I am still friends with and who proved to be a true friend. I lived there for twelve years. I raised my first child there, met wonderful accomplished, professional, artistic, creative, and above all kind, generous and giving people who were always eager to care for and share with me and the community. I feel the need to mention some of the people who stood out in the crowd. Namely, Alexandra Palmer whom I already mentioned elsewhere, but she is worth mentioning again and again. Watty Strauss, Elka Fears from the West 47th Street block association and her dear darling husband who made hot dogs for everyone in the neighborhood for every Halloween party.

Then there was Martha Blacklock who was the residing preacher of St. Clements Church which was my next-door neighbor for all those years. One time I stupidly let my seven-year-old son Jason watch "The Day After" on television even after the news warned against it. I thought it was all hype.

I was wrong, my son flipped out. I rushed him to the church where the preacher greeted us, took him inside, sat him down and carefully, quietly, and painstakingly explained to him all about how the background scenery was done in the movie. By the time she was finished he was all settled down, calm and fascinated by her lecture. I believe she missed the whole movie since she had to sit and talk to my son instead.

After Martha left St. Clément's, we were extremely blessed by the new Reverend Barbara Crafton. The nicest, best and most eloquent preacher ever and who remained there even after I left, but I managed to keep in touch with her ever since. St. Clément's also had some great Christmas parties with Bob Perkins as "Santa".

I must not forget to mention Rose DeSantos, "The lady queen" of the block who sat outside in her garden every day and talked lovingly to everyone as they walked by, to and from their daily chores. She was very kind to me. One day she mentioned to me that I shook my finger at her. I was puzzled. Apparently on several occasions I was frustrated at things she had or hadn't done. Things that I had asked her not to do. So, I scolded her by shaking my finger at her. She just smiled and shook her finger back at me.

From my five years at Windsor Mountain School, where we were taught about community responsibility, which was already in my memory bank, once I got situated on West 46th Street I got really involved with the block association. I was invited to become a member of their executive committee. Of course, I accepted. I loved it there. We had a close-knit group of about ten people, and at their monthly meetings, they served great coffee. We worked together on the 9th Avenue Festival. Alex Palmer made me feel so welcome there.

Windsor Mountain School and West 46th Street, I'd say, were the highlights of my life, besides of course my children. When my father died, I was living on West 46th Street. I wasn't perfect, my life wasn't perfect. However, my father was an exceptional dad. I almost got into drugs, sort of. But Alex Palmer got me so involved with the block association that totally straightened me out. And the executive committee members, Chloe, Watty, Tom and Wanda Gibbons, Mary Clark and George Santana, were all tremendous assets. The great part of getting involved with the block association was that we also partnered with the 45th and 47th street block association that had incredible Halloween and Christmas parties for the neighborhood. Our members were a mixture of society from all walks of life, all very well educated and delighted to volunteer their time and energy. It was so wonderful. The volunteers also excelled in decorating and entertaining for parties. We all happily volunteered and had a great time doing so.

We were enlisted by the block association and midtown north precinct with fighting crime in our community and were expected to attend monthly precinct meetings held by Detective John Tumelty. It was mostly to voice our complaints and hopefully to ask what we could do personally to help our community. Within my block, but not for the precinct, I was given the job of arranging the summer festivities for all the poor and underprivileged children from the neighborhood and that was held each week right on our block. It was very successful except that the children, whose parents were hopeless alcoholics or drug addicts, were so deprived. It seemed to me that whenever one did anything nice for the children one got kicked in the face, figuratively speaking.

After a day of supervising one of these events, which took place from 8:30 am to 4:30 pm, I had to go home and smoke a joint just to unravel. Not every time, but most of the time. And the festivities took place mostly once or twice a week, all summer long. I always took my son along. There were good kids who participated in the festivities and there were bad kids too, it was a little of everything.

What I really enjoyed was preparing for parties along with the other members of the block association. We spent many happy times in the kitchen at Hartley House, the community house on West 46th Street preparing dishes to serve at the various parties. Included in that happy group were Wanda and Tom Gibbons who had me roaring with laughter because they were so funny. She was from England and had a cockney accent and he was from the U.S.A. and sort of had a New York accent. They lived right by the playground, and to hear them crack jokes at each other, and at some of us was more than I could bear. She once said he shouldn't laugh so much because his stitches would come out. She meant it. He had just had surgery. Tom and Wanda were also professional ballroom dancers and were winning trophies and medals for their dances all over the city. That was so exciting.

Back to Hartley House and their Christmas party, which was the most lavish I'd seen in years. But then growing up I hadn't seen many lavish Christmas parties since my father was such a religious Jew. At their Christmas parties there was food, main dishes cooked and prepared, and desserts donated from Restaurant Row. There was a "Santa" also, but it was the food which was so good and plentiful.

Jill (center, standing, white hat, dark shirt) at the 9th Avenue Festival booth, late 1970s

For the 9th Ave festival, Chloe served the best coffee and plentiful jokes to keep us all amused for the duration of time we worked at the booth. Chloe had us all in stitches. I helped at the booth for many years, met interesting people, got to sample Mrs. Rubbios butter cake, which was heavenly and got to sample many more, mostly from Restaurant Row. Mostly I just served cake. The festival went on all weekend, it was so much fun.

All this was happening while papa was still alive. Once I introduced my father to Alex Palmer because I thought that maybe he could help her find a boyfriend. His immediate response to me was that he thought she was gay and laughed off helping to find her a boyfriend. That surprised me!

On December 17th, 1979, I was on route to do my laundry, something I've always hated doing, but this was early because I wanted to get to the hospital to see my father who was not expected to live much longer. I was on my way home from the laundromat when I spotted my cousin Lutte coming off the 9th Avenue bus. I asked her what she was doing in my neighborhood. I guess I took a second look at her and realized that something had happened, something had gone terribly wrong. My father had died, and she was coming in person to break the news to me. At least I had five weeks to prepare for his death. Thank God. It was hard enough but five weeks was long enough time for me to go see him and thank him for everything he'd done for me, especially my braces. Then he told me that he would leave me a trust fund if I raised my son as a Jew, sent him to Sunday school at Stephen Wise Free Synagogue, and agreed to have him bar mitzvahed. Only under those conditions would he leave me a trust fund for us. I agreed reluctantly since I wasn't very religious in the first place and Jason was only half Jewish. Boy what a mess. But I agreed.

When I first moved to Hell's Kitchen my father asked me to visit the Actor's Temple on West 47th Street off 9th Ave. He wanted me to take Jason, so I went with Jason who was only about five years old at the time. As we entered the temple, the head Rabbi motioned to Jason to come up to the front. We just happened to walk in during the service. As soon as Jason arrived in the front the Rabbi poured a glass of wine and instructed him, my five-year-old son to drink it. My eyes nearly popped out of my head. I demanded he not drink it, but the Rabbi assured me it was fine. "Let him drink it. It won't hurt him," he said.

When we returned home, I called my father immediately and told him that the temple he referred us to gave Jason a full glass of wine to drink. I was in shock. My father replied, "That's part of the service!". And this coming from a doctor whom all my life, still now to his death, preached and lectured me and everyone, I mean everyone, against drinking and alcohol. And especially for me, no alcohol. So, I couldn't believe his sudden acceptance.

On one visit to see Jason and me on West 46th Street my father brought a gift for Jason. It was the most elaborate, detailed portable doll house I had ever seen. I guess some patient had given it to my father for Jason. As soon as I saw it, I grabbed it, sat on the floor and started playing with it. My father just laughed and said, "I brought it for my grandson you silly, not for you!". I really got into it. It came with a family and all the furniture one could possibly want. Whoever made it, it was amazing. Jason never really got into it. I took over and got into it. It was a three-story house with bedrooms, a living room, library room, and a separate T.V. room, and bathrooms. It was amazing.

During my years in Hell's Kitchen, I also met a wonderful family while babysitting. It was a mother, Eve Kristin and her two adorable twin daughters, Heather and Heidi, who had been taught from a very early age to play the violin and did so frequently to make extra cash for their small family.

Eventually they moved out of the neighborhood, but Heather returned. We ran into each other at the 9th Avenue festival some years ago and picked up where we left off. She has since married a cousin of mine and is now a member of my family.

Also, around that time or perhaps earlier, I engaged in conversations with Rose De-Santos, the queen of West 46th Street, who sat outside in her garden in front of her house with her cup of tea and talked to everyone who passed by. While I talked to her one day, I encountered a nice man who lived nearby and who came each day to feed the neighborhood cats. He was very good-looking and well dressed, a debonair. I asked Rose about him; she told me he was a very nice and kind gentleman. I finally made his acquaintance and found out that he, Bob Dahdah, was a Broadway writer and producer who coincidentally had discovered Bernadette Peters and was responsible for her break on Broadway. I soon became good friends with him and learned a lot about Broadway history from him. I also learned that he had an apartment full of treasures of all kinds. After a while he became my personal "Santa". Every time I asked him for anything, he would oblige me. But then I wasn't so demanding. Like sheet music for instance, I would get a song in my head and want to learn to sing it with the words right in front of me. I asked him for the sheet music, he would get his copy, copy it for me and give it to me. Then there was a book about Alan J. Lerner that I needed to help me with my book, which he gave me to use until my book project is completed. It's funny, at one point he suspected I was asking for the sheet music for someone else, so he told me I had to sing right in front of him when he gave it to me; I obliged.

Now back to West 46th Street, because I felt my father, my mother, my grandparents and Windsor Mountain School, Gertrud and Heinz Bondy, did a great job in raising me, and I felt they gave me the heart, soul and tools to do all the good work that I did in Hell's Kitchen (formerly known as Clinton), and on West 46th Street. I was there from the fall of 1975 through the late summer of 1987. I was forced to leave the neighborhood a year after my second son was born, only because I was unable to find an apartment big enough for my two children. I had gotten involved with the block association soon after I had arrived on West 46th Street and when I left, almost a year after my second son was born, it seemed all the committee members went their separate ways. We all dispersed around the same time. Yes, I've missed them all terribly. I still go back and visit. Reluctantly, I moved in 1987, very reluctantly.

A Correlation: Papa's Inner Circle

My father had some patients who were also dear friends, members of the inner circle. They were all working towards one main goal. Helping people and providing medical coverage to the poor and the needy. Those were Dona Felisa Rincon De Gautier, Mayor of San Juan Puerto Rico, the Honorable Claude Pepper, Democrat Congressman from Florida, Katherine Dunham, Dr. Thelma Williams, and Albert Dekker.

IN THE COURSE OF PREPARATION

Trying to defend my father, his name and his actions, it has been explained to me that my father was not solely responsible for all the misdeeds for which he was accused. Apparently, while he was consumed by his practice, patients, and his own overindulgence in amphetamine, he allowed certain patients to take over his life, his office, and his practice. It was those people who created chaos at his expense such as Mark Shaw, John Roberts, and John McManus. I would name others, but they will remain nameless. However, I must mention this to prove my father's direct innocence even if this proves a questionable indirect guilt.

There are many people who feel I must come forward and tell the truth, state the facts and defend my father. I believe unequivocally they are right. I especially owe it to my father. He was a very doting dad. I don't know officially or exactly what they were being treated for or with.

Someone told me my father was studying and working with biogenic stimulants, placenta to be a good source. Of what, I don't know. Although I am reluctant to bring this information to light, it is for the reader, so I give it. My father used cellular homogenates in his practice. He got it from a Swiss doctor who pioneered it. The amphetamine was supposed to be used as a catalyst to make the process work. His difficulty in getting large amounts of amphetamine made it necessary for him to get it from Panama using the Ambassador to the U.N. 's diplomatic status to bring it in.

I have been told by the same party who informed me about the cellular homogenates that my father explained to this person: the idea is basically that if you inject a solution of healthy cells into the patient of say a liver, they will "encourage" the diseased liver to get better. Of course, to get healthy cells to dissociate so that they can be put into a solution is a difficult process. You can't just grind up a liver or a spleen and inject it into somebody because the cells would be squashed. There was something to do with radioactivity in the process. It is known, common knowledge, that my father always wanted placenta for experimentation. They have cells much like our organ cells. We're learning about this today with stem cell research. Amphetamine was used to push the process along, my father said as a catalyst. Of course, patients feel better right away because of the speed. It got out of hand. This was all a legitimate and revolutionary way of treating diseased organs. My father wasn't just trying to get people high. He had a vision, goal, and a purpose. I suppose I have a lot to learn.

I was told, although I was not there for the discussion, that my father offered my brother a position working with him as partners in my father's office. My brother refused and then moved to California and opened his own practice. For some reason Tommy was against daddy's practice. Tommy was studying to be a cardiologist and became one. He was also against amphetamine, wanted to have nothing to do with it. Tommy got into arguments with my father because he [my father] was so irresponsible with his own life injecting himself with unknown substances. He claimed he did this to himself before he would ever give it to his patient. My father had taken an overdose of some experimental medicine he had devised in his laboratory. Apparently, he suffered an adverse reaction and an accidental overdose on top of it. I was kept in the dark throughout this entire ordeal. Tommy was called to the rescue in emergency and miraculously saved his life. Thank God. When he started his practice in Los Angeles though, I found out that in the beginning he took a few of my father's patients at my father's urgings.

I heard recently on Channel 4 during an interview with Tom Cruise and Matt Lauer where Tom Cruise mentioned that there were people having shock treatment who initially went in to have two shocks and once in the hospital were forced to have nine more. This totally shocked me because when I was in my very early twenties I had shock treatment. I insisted on having it, I couldn't blame my father for that. It was my insistence and mine alone. My father wasn't supporting me in this endeavor. Reluctantly he referred me to his dear friend Abe Kalinowski who at that time was the only doctor doing this procedure. I went to him, Dr. Kalinowski, and insisted on having the shock treatment. He scoffed at my suggestion, but when I insisted repeatedly, he relented and gave in. We agreed I would have two, only two. Once in the hospital after the initial two shock treatments, two days later, two heavy set tall and very masculine women forcibly dragged me into a room and tied me down onto a table without saying one word. Within the next two days, I was forcibly given nine more. After many years, I thought my father was behind it, I don't know why. I kept wondering why he would use his influence to do this. The puzzlement went unanswered since I feared even considering asking my father such a question. It wasn't until I saw the interview with Tom Cruise and Matt Lauer that I found out that this was common practice and that my father had nothing whatsoever to do with it at all. But I found out about this only last year.

93

FAMILY REVELATIONS

Recently, since the Hagens knew that I was doing this book, my cousin Tony approached me and suggested that before I finish, I contact my cousin John Hagen, Lutte's son who had in his possession the unpublished manuscript of his mother's written by her and completed a few years before she died. I was told that it was all about the Hagens in Germany. So fine, I contacted my cousin John Hagen who very agreeably sent me the floppy disk in the mail, "Yeah you can have it, no problem", he said. Well, I got it. I had never gone to the computer at that time. But I put it in and scrolled. I read the whole bloody thing. Why am I now mentioning it you might ask? It wasn't about Germany or the Hagens. Her book, although all with fictitious names, was all about my family; my parents, my grandparents, my Aunt Carla, me and some celebrities. Allegedly, my mother had an affair with a man named Nepo, who had rebuilt our country home after the original one burnt in a fire. She reveled in the fact that my mother and this man really had an intense affair. She had a detailed diary of my mothers' comings and goings with this man.

She claimed that Nepo strong armed her at our apartment on East 73rd at a Seder gathering and then strong armed my mother to leave my father. But then on another page she claimed she was fantasizing about their relationship. Someone years ago, mentioned to me that my father found out my mother was having an affair with this man. In my heart I know that the truth was that Lutte somehow managed to make sure my father found out my mother was seeing this man.

Apparently, this man Nepo nearly destroyed my parents' marriage. I cannot remember him at all, yet I remember my nurse when I was about three years old. Anyway, I guess that is not important even though to me it is. Next Lutte went out of her way to say how my father dedicated his whole life to helping people. She said he did enjoy boasting about all his celebrity patients and telling everyone that he was the son of a kosher butcher and "Look what I've become!". And she did state that Nepo worked as hard as my father and amazingly didn't experience the meltdowns my father did after putting in a full workday.

Lutte really loved my father. In her book she even mentioned her animosity against my mother for not loving my father enough. In my opinion, from what I saw, my mother was totally devoted to my father and even suffered through all the demanding celebrities coming at all hours demanding treatment from my father. Nepo was the one who built our house in Point Lookout and apparently was also cooking and preparing food for us as well.

The affair was so intense my father threatened to divorce my mother if she didn't stop seeing the guy. The guy was manhandling my cousin Lutte to deliver messages to my mother to leave my father and be with him or else. I knew, suspected absolutely nothing ever about any of this. My cousin even stated in her book that my father left my mother and I out in Point Lookout for the summer to stay while he worked in the city and my mother played house with this guy, meaning she was the wife, he the husband and me the baby. My cousin claimed that even I got confused about what the hell was going on.

When I read this, I freaked out, so much so that I called my stepmother and my brother. My brother told me more about the whole situation and that it was true. But he told me to get over it and get on with writing my book. I didn't know what to believe. By the time I found out, everyone was dead already, everyone. There was no one alive to ask. Suddenly, I felt, well, if my parents were incompatible, then what did that make me? Half of one and an uneven half of another? Not a very secure feeling. So, I learned that my parents were not getting along very well. Perhaps my mother had an ego, even if she didn't put it on display and she too needed attention and affection.

Well, if you ask me how my mother and father got along, from my observations, fine. I don't even remember how or where I learned that they were going to get a divorce. Or even what went through my mind when I found out. I knew my mother couldn't handle all the celebrities coming over to our apartment for treatment at all hours of the day and night. It was unnerving to say the least. Katherine Dunham told me recently that once my father started treating President Kennedy, it started going to his head. I guess that put strains on the marriage as well. I didn't even confront either of them about it, the divorce or the reasons. I was always afraid of confrontations. And they never called me into the room to discuss it with me.

I thought that at least my mother wanted a divorce because she couldn't handle the constant intrusion of the celebrities, constant, all hours of the day and night, at home in the city and in Point Lookout. It just never stopped, that's all I knew. I was at Windsor Mountain School, so I had little knowledge of anything that was happening at home, plus my parents came up to visit Heinz and Gertrud Bondy and me rather frequently and seemed together as a couple. In retrospect she didn't appear to be well. She looked run down and tired. I guess I must have figured my father and Gertrud would take care of her. I never asked her how she felt, I never bothered to ask. Damnit.

94

THE DOWNFALL OF DR. MAX JACOBSON

His downward spiral is strangely unclear. He became so consumed with celebrities and with his schedule of making house calls for the President, and with CEO's who called him in the middle of the night from the airport having just returned home from a business trip, namely Arkadi Gerney, that had to have treatment pronto. This interrupted the doctor from his necessary sleep. There were other patients who wanted treatment that he simply couldn't devote enough time to himself, his need for sleep or the proper running of his office. He suffered as a result. He had assistants who were also partaking of speed. Those assistants were only responsible for getting him home when he had to travel by plane and had to bathe and change to go to the airport, but not to make him go home and get sleep. As I have said earlier, "God forbid!".

He was much too kind, too generous to a fault and had the greatest difficulty saying "No" to anybody. He saw patients at all hours of the day and night. He was personally deprived of sleep by those who draped themselves around him bodily, his shoulders, his face, everywhere verbally harassing him with their sob stories and all just for a treatment.

They demanded speed injections from him. If he relented or refused, they draped themselves all over him until he gave in. It was those people who assisted in his demise because when they were on speed they stayed up, kept him up. It was a vicious circle. Either way, my father was very overworked and hardly slept at all.Some of his patients, the ones he indulged with amphetamine, felt obliged to assist him at the office, or wanted to just hang out with him. Mostly it was out of gratitude afterwards that they wanted to help him at the office.

I was also told that Anthony Quinn came to visit him at the office after hours to show my father his paintings. My father had invented this 3D process he did to paintings. I thought he was hallucinating, but Katherine Dunham swore she saw it. Anthony Quinn would show up and spend hours at my father's office with him, indulging my father with paintings on which he happily obliged to try his invention, to work on his 3D process.

Lost in all the comings and goings in his life, mostly his office life, the demands of his patients, namely John McManus and John Roberts helping him out in his office, and I also learned helped him invest some money. Then other patients took advantage of his preoccupation with his inventions, the magnets, and the 3D paintings. There was just too much happening which was making him spiral out of control.

About my father losing his license, because he was treating the President someone came to the office to look at his bookkeeping. Something wasn't in order and people complained. My stepmother told me about this. My father was singled out as a scape goat. There were others. I read Doris Shapiro's book about my father and Alice Ghostley taking her poor dear husband Felice to the hospital. Apparently, he had taken too much speed over a period of days and was hallucinating, saying things that weren't kosher, like that the FBI and CIA were running my father's office, which I am sorry to say I find hilarious. It was obvious to me and everyone else that my father literally called the shots in every way shape and form.

I believe my father called attention to himself unfortunately by boasting to too many people about his treating of President Kennedy. Yes, my father got a warning, I never discussed it with him. I didn't know if he was losing control altogether or being caught up in the moment. Gosh he was so generous with everything always. I was told that some model informed him that there was talk of heat around him, that the feds were hot on his trail. He was knowl-edgeable that something was coming, I believe. He scoffed that off. Now I hear that former President Nixon wanted the doctor to treat him and the doctor turned him down. Bobby Kennedy asked for vials of my father's solution. My father generously submitted 15 vials, which were analyzed by the FBI lab and found to have amphetamine in them. Then he had my father investigated.

The AMA took his license off the wall at his office on East 87th Street in the presence of Beatrice Moore. See, I told you my father inadvertently attracted bitches to him for as long as I can remember. And I remember all their names, unfortunately. No, I won't mention them. He didn't win and he never got his license back. He died four years later.

THE ORIGIN OF DR. FEELGOOD

You know, my father was never called Dr. Feelgood, not by his patients, friends, or family, only by the media and the press. Katherine Dunham told me she was asked about him and she said, "Well, what if he is Dr. Feelgood? What's wrong with that, and him wanting to make people feel good? I don't find anything wrong with that!". I personally had to argue that with her. No one except for Anthony Quinn in his autobiography called my father Dr. Feelgood. He was only repeating what the media had called him. My father was called Max, Dr. Jacobson, Dr. J, Miracle Max, and simply Max. or Doctor. The name Dr. Feelgood should be destroyed.

THE SYNOPSIS OF STARS

ALPHABETIZED BY LAST NAME

Mel Allen

You could hear him the second you walked into the office on East 72nd Street, his voice was one that carried. There was no need for a microphone. He was tall, vocal and clear. He was always in and out of the office in a manner of minutes. He was a very outspoken proud man and very sure of himself. He didn't come often though. He exchanged jokes with "The Doctor" which I could not hear. They were two men talking.

Kaye Ballard

I met her once at my father's office; I don't know if she was on amphetamine. I knew her as an actress who did plenty of work, and only later did I find out she was a patient.

Kurt and Renata Baum

Renata Baum was the wife of Kurt Baum, who performed "Aida" at the Met in the late 50's. He was a pure resonating Baritone and could hit a high C after treatment. He would get an injection, his face would turn red and immediately sing his heart out. He would have a glowing smile on his face. He would always warm up to hit the high notes. He was charming, jolly, handsome, and a ladies' man with beautiful black curly hair.

His wife Renata, well, behind every talented creative and successful man is a gorgeous wife. Renata was quite a spectacle. This lady knew how to apply lipstick and makeup chic. She applied her makeup like an artiste. She had the sexiest, most lavish mouth and lips. She had the cutest most darling sexy smile and laugh I ever heard. She had beautiful blonde hair, always well brushed, splendidly groomed. She radiated both sex, charisma and European magnificence. She wore the most risqué, bustier line dresses, naughty and low cut, almost at the point of being classified as unacceptable. And at times I wondered, did she know she was being sexy, or was it coincidental? She made heads turn and needed not to pull up those breasts to put them on display. They were for sure voluminous breasts, lucky for her. Everyone noticed. And since she was wearing low-cut dresses, we wondered at times, would they perhaps pop out? That never happened. My parents were kind of embarrassed by her generous exhibiting of her cleavage and they laughed at her behind her back. I was a young girl. I thought it was funny and cute too.

When she spoke with her strong Viennese accent, that made her sound even sexier. She had that Jayne Mansfield kind of high-pitched sexy voice. What I really enjoyed was her cute colorful personality. She was perky, sexy and very dramatic, like Marilyn Monroe. Adding her smile to that European magnificence, charismatic pretty picture distinguished her as a killer Bee. Meaning, she could sting with her magnificence and her cologne. She wore the most expensive French cologne. She didn't really need it. Her powder and lipstick had perfume already.

She always acted like a dumb blonde who was just so overwhelmingly forthcoming, giving, friendly and polite. She was so courteous and inviting. An enchantingly personable character. Whether she intended to be sexy or even realized just how sexy she came across as being, I had my firm doubts about that subject.

She would take her poodle on the beach for a long walk wearing fancy high heeled shoes. Very seldom did she wear pants. Whenever she greeted my parents and I, her nose would wrinkle, thrust open her mouth with a smile and say, "Hello Dahling", "Max", "Nina", or "Jill dear, how are you?", and her voice would crack. With lovely affection as a grandma talks baby talk with her infant grandchild. Renata was young, but not so young. She appeared as though she was in her early thirties. She and Kurt made a darling couple. I really miss them. In the early 50's women didn't wear makeup like they wear it today. And she knew she looked beautiful. She enjoyed every minute of it.

Considering she was not a movie star, Renata knew how to put on makeup far better than most stars and their makeup artists today.

Aaron Bell

Aaron was a bassist, pianist and composer who worked with Billie Holiday, making "Lady Sings the Blues" with Lester Young. He joined Dukes band in 1960. He worked briefly with Dizzy Gillespie after working for Duke Ellington and then moved to Broadway where I saw him at the Winter Garden theatre one night after work. He was a patient and friend for quite some time, and he and his gal pal were both partaking of amphetamine in their treatment. Neither of them complained. He was always working and was given vials of vitamin injections to take home. He and his girlfriend Carla adored my father and his treatment. They were patients from the early 60's through the late 60's, at least 10 years.

Archie Bleyer and Janet Ertel – Cadence (Capitol) Records

Archie Bleyer, band leader, and Janet Ertel, husband and wife were patients of my father. Archie came to see my father at his office on East 72nd Street often and always came with her. Sometimes we visited them at their home on Long Island. He worked for Arthur Godfrey in the late 40's, and founded Cadence Records in 1952, which later became Capitol Records. Archie had his own orchestra and two big hits. "Hernando's Hideaway" and "Mr. Sandman", which included Janet. He included her on the album as the female harmonizer. During all this time they were both being treated by my father, and I was a witness to this. Whether they were receiving amphetamine, I don't know. Archie was very sociable but also quiet and an older man when I met him. Neither of them acted differently after their treatments. Also, I never saw either of them working. I saw them when they came to the office to see my father for treatment, and on a few occasions, we were invited to visit them at their home on Long Island so that my father could treat both of them. Mostly my father treated him. On occasion Janet came in to see my father with her daughter Jackie, who later married Phil Everly of "The Everly Brother's".

Ruth Bowen

She was an agent for many stars. While I was at boarding school, I kept in touch with her since I was very friendly with Dinah Washingtons son.

Jacques and Rosemarie Cabaud

She was German and he was French. Both were patients of my father. He was a writer. They were both very straight and square. Neither of them had anything to do with amphetamine, of that I am certain.

Betty Cashman

She was the acting coach to the famous politicians and performers. During the 50's she received four consecutive "Show Business Oscars" for greatest development of New York Talent in the Theatre. She was called "The Actors Doctor". It was her personality that attracted one to her. She had the most charming, witty, driving character, and actor's ammunition for a superb performance. She knew how to get the best out of you, and it was her pleasure to bring it out. She was a very attractive lady as well. She made you want to do your speech exercises, and work hard at them, and the training was fun.

I think she liked me for me, but she also liked me because she adored my father. She didn't need amphetamine, she had the energy, the driving force, and the stamina. She was "The Lady with Stamina". With bright eyes and a "You can't fool me" smile, she was one of a kind.

She and Papa were friends. She was a patient for 35 years from the 50's through the 70's, received treatment monthly for years and was subpoenaed to testify in court on my father's behalf when he was indicted. She told the court she visited papa for treatment every 6 weeks, no more or less. And she said she had no dependency on the amphetamine. She was a good witness, and a good friend to Papa and me.

Carol Channing

She was "Carol", always. We all knew who she was. I didn't see her that often, my father saw her privately. If I was lucky, I was permitted to come in briefly to the treatment room and say hello to her. She greeted me with big wide-open eyes, her full wide smile, and she always spoke with that raspy lisp. I would enter the room to a resounding, "Well Hello!" She always wore her wig, was fully made up and charming. She put on quite a show for me when she greeted me. For some reason her husband was against her seeing my father. I never knew why. It was amazing to know and see her privately and know she was the same way in public. She was a patient since I was a little girl, at least 1954, and remained a patient long after, at least until 1964.

Bob and Mary Cummings

Bob Cummings took many vitamins every day for years. He was totally into vitamins. He took them by mouth and vitamin injections. He was taking them long before they were popular. He traveled on publicity junkets with his wife Mary and his six children. He was famous for his T.V. show "Love That Bob". He was invited to do publicity for Disney Land in Hollywood, California. He invited my parents and me to come along. We were the VIP's and didn't have to wait in any line. We were escorted to all the rides. It was exciting.

I really enjoyed visiting his family at their spacious home. They had a lady who sat by the pool and greeted his children after their afternoon nap. She presented us with Baby Ruth candy bars. That was my first time ever having one; I just loved it, the candy bar and of course the pool. I think the lady who gave us the candy was the kids nanny. Mary was such a devoted mother, extremely devoted to Bob and of course the children.

Yes, Bob Cummings got treatment from my father. He took my father's treatment and his vitamin injections very seriously. He was very dedicated to his health and keeping up a health regimen. My father assisted him in maintaining good health. My father visited Bob frequently and during those visits, I became friendly with several of his kids, Robert Jr. and early on Melinda, who looked like her mother, curly red hair, freckles, and such a darling face.

After quite a few years their marriage crumbled. Mary had called my mother from Los Angeles crying on the phone, pleading with her for help to save her marriage. I guess it didn't work. My mother regretted she couldn't help. Bob and Mary split up. They divorced soon after. I was about eleven years old when they split up.

Years later, I read on the cover of the Enquirer that Bob had remarried a Japanese astrologer. I didn't believe it. I even laughed, knowing the reputation of The Enquirer. A short time later, Bob came for a visit to see my father with his new wife, the Japanese astrologer. Boy was I surprised.

I tend to wonder, especially in Bob Cummings case, what the difference is whether you take eight or nine vitamins at the same time by mouth with a glass of juice or if you take an injection filled with vitamins, once daily. Bob was into either or both. He lived for many years and was always very active and healthy. I am sorry I didn't keep in touch with his children. His son was so handsome and very nice. I wonder what ever happened to him. Bob stayed in touch with my father until he [Bob] died.

Albert Dekker and Jeraldine Saunders

Albert Dekker was a long-time patient and friend of my parents. He became a very conscientious chef and enjoyed cooking for us on special occasions. He had a rather neurotic personality. He was very comical and amused us with his stories. He later introduced us to his steady girlfriend, Geraldine Saunders [founder, producer, and writer of "Love Boat"] who was very straight square and sweet. He wasn't square, he was quite wild.

Agnes DeMille

We met her (my parents and I) through her uncle, Cecil B. DeMille. She was by the side of their swimming pool, and I don't remember where that was. Maybe it was in California. She was involved with dance, and she was organizing her own group. She was becoming well known in her own right.

Charles Dumont

We met him on a trip to Paris, France. He was being produced and promoted by Phillipe Waldberg, a cousin of my mother's and longtime friend of our family. He also became a patient of my fathers for a short while. I knew him well from "Et Maintenant Mon Amour", translated in English means "What Now My Love". My mother and I saw him on occasion when we saw Phillipe, who adored and admired this French singer.

The Everly Brothers: Don and Phil

They were both patients of my father. They would come out to Point Lookout for treatment since they were staying nearby. During the years they were seeing my father, they worked for Cadence Records and produced "Bye-bye Love", "Wake up Little Susie", and "All I Have to Do Is Dream", they were patients from the late 50's through the 60's. Phil Everly was dating Archie and Janet Bleyer's daughter, Jackie. Archie lived on Long Island, so they didn't have far to travel to see my father. Phil Everly and Jackie finally got married. Both Everly Brothers were getting married within just a few years. They were both such nice talented young men.

Strangely, Don had the same speaking voice as Michael Jackson, very soft, high pitched and whispery. It appears that having a high-pitched voice makes for a good singer and doesn't necessarily mean that the person is gay. The Everly brothers were nice, young and very popular. They seldom came to Point Lookout together. Don usually came out with his girlfriend, fiancée or wife. They never sang in my presence. I saw them perform on television and in Central Park.

What stood out in my mind was how whispery a voice they both had. They both had wonderful singing voices. I never really got to know them. I was friendly, however, with Jackie and Archie Bleyer. I saw Jackie occasionally when she came to visit her mom.

Ben Gazzara

Actor Ben Gazzara had a shot of steroids to bring his voice back, but he didn't sleep for two to three days afterwards. He had lost his voice after having to scream and shout lines.

Hermione Gingold

She came for treatment, though rarely. She was well known to me for her role in GiGi in 1958 in which she sang, "I Remember It Well" with Maurice Chevalier. I was 11 years old then and I fully remember that movie. She had a very refined British voice. She was a very interesting lady. She appeared on Broadway in 1953's edition of John Murray Andersons "Almanac". Mr. Anderson was both a friend and patient of my father. Ms. Gingold was also in "Around the World in 80 Days" [1956]. She appeared on Broadway in "Oh Dad Poor Dad, Mamma's Hung You in the Closet and I'm Feeling So Sad" [1963].

I doubt very much that she was on amphetamine. She told me how nice my father was, how smart he was and how clever she heard I was. That was all I remembered. She had a funny speaking voice, inflexion. She was already in her 60's when I met her. I was still a little girl.

Joan Hackett

She was so "Hot"- popular around the time I learned she was a patient. She was about to marry Richard Mulligan when she was a patient. She had cancer and was seeing my father for treatment to help her with it. They got married. The cancer came later. She was on a TV show at that time. She was soft-spoken, sophisticated and attractive.

Sonja Henie

Having great agility, a very cute, fresh healthy-looking face, a Norwegian accent and pretty costumes, Sonja Henie was a sensation on the rink. Ms. Henie was both an ice skater and film actress born in Norway. She won the European Championship Gold Metals in Europe. She was the one who introduced music and dance-based movements into free-skating. She was mostly touring the world figure skating. Following that she came to America to perform on television and in shows. We got to see her perform once from backstage. Her costumes were so beautiful.

She was here mostly in the mid 50's. Her mother was her manager. They traveled to America twice a year. Her mother accompanied her to my father's office each time. We only saw her in the office. I was there in treatment room one, the big treatment room. If I came over to my father's office for a visit and she was there, I would be invited in to say hello. Her mother was always very nervous. Only once when her mother popped her ear upon landing in an airplane did she also come to my father for treatment, she was standing silently but in pain. It was Sonja who seldom received treatment. To the best of my knowledge the ones he gave her didn't interfere with her performances.

Leonard Holzer

Besides being the husband of Baby Jane Holtzer, Leonard was the Donald Trump of the late 60's to the mid 70's., and was separated from his wife, sort of. He was a successful businessman. He owned real estate all over New York. He owned the office in which my father worked on Park Avenue and 87th Street, the same office where my father was working when he was stripped of his license. Leonard was in his mid-30's.

He owned and resided in a sprawling 100 room house on the waterfront in Long Island. At one point, my father tried to match make us, it didn't work. He met my father from time to time to go swimming in the basement pool in our building. Whenever he came, he came unannounced with his young blonde girlfriend. My father would invite them in right away.

In my opinion, Leonard took advantage of that offer. But my father was always cordial and treated him when he came over. He invited us to his Long Island waterfront estate for one holiday during the summer. My boyfriend Bill and I and my cat flew in a small plane. It seemed as if we were flying sideways all along the coastline of Long Island Sound. I went swimming the next day and got swept up by the tide. Bill dove in and rescued me. He saved my life.

I liked Leonard from what I knew of him, which was actually very little. He was maybe only 10 years older than me. He was involved with getting his new young girlfriend situated in a Broadway play. He got treatments and to my knowledge showed no signs of amphetamine usage. So, I really could not make a judgment on that.

Jacqueline Kennedy

The one time I met Jacqueline Kennedy was with my mother. It was under the auspices that it was my parents' anniversary. My parents and I traveled to Hyannis Port. As soon as we arrived, my father disappeared upstairs. I momentarily forgot about him. My mother and I were led to a couch and sat down. A few moments later, in walked Jackie, Caroline, and Victoria Lawford, about three years old. My impression was, my God, she was so shy and spoke with such a wispy voice. I couldn't believe she was much shyer than my mother. I couldn't believe it and there she was. Baby John was upstairs in a crib. I never saw him, only Caroline.

The first impression I got of Jackie was that she was a genuine down-to-Earth mother. After having met Jean Smith and Pat Lawford, I found

Jackie to be a much more normal, down-to-Earth person, and a loving mother. I noticed unfortunately in a moment's shock, while my mother spoke to
her, yellow stained teeth and noticed how many teeth she had crowding her
mouth, her big smile. I couldn't understand it. On all the photos she had
this beautiful wide smile with white teeth. So, I was in absolute shock. I
wondered if the photographer had air brushed her teeth on all the photos. I
couldn't figure it out. I was even too in shock from the sight to say anything.
I couldn't believe it; this was Jackie Kennedy with horribly stained teeth. I
didn't understand.

She and my mother had much to discuss, much in common. Both were
beautiful and both were shy. My mother was the champion horseback rider
in Germany when she was young. She was also an artist and painter, had an
exhibition of her own work in a gallery in New York and loved all art forms and
Theatre, and both my mother and Jackie had exquisite taste in clothing. So,
the two ladies had a lot in common. It seemed as though they spoke for a long
time. After our visit, my father returned, and someone took our photos, not
with Jackie, but with my parents and me together at their house in Hyannis
Port. That was all I remembered.

Buddy LaLonde

Buddy was the Evil Knievel of the 60's. He was a great acrobatic ice skater.
He would wow the crowds speed skating very fast with great force, work his
speed up then jump over 11 pipes or leap over cars. Either way, he did it. We
all watched breathlessly; he was fearless. He did a great job and never had a
spill.

He was also hired by my father to give me ice skating lessons at Wollman
Rink in Central Park. He had other pupils also, so I shared lessons, quite a few
with Liza Minnelli, Lorna Luft and Billy, their little brother. We all met later
at Buddy's daughter's birthday party. Liza and Lorna were also acrobats although a different kind. They were dressed alike at the birthday party, which
was held in a suite at the Plaza Hotel. They wore silk red and white striped
party dresses and still managed to stand on their heads and do cartwheels
which really impressed the hell out of me. Liza and Lorna got along very well
and were extremely close.

Buddy didn't come from New York. He came from down south or the Midwest somewhere. His wife was a dancer at the Roxy. However, she managed to spend lots of time with their daughter.

Hermann Landshoff

"Landshoff", as we called him, was the photographer of all the top models from Vogue to Bazaar Magazine. He freelanced from the mid 40's through the late 60's. He utilized the beach at Point Lookout, where we had our country home as his scenic background for many of his shots. He walked on the beach in the winter scouting locations for most of his good shots. He photographed me a lot in Point Lookout to please my father. He also drove up to Windsor Mountain to photograph Missy McKnight and me posing in the pit in the early stages of construction of the Nina Jacobson Memorial Theatre, which was named in honor of my deceased mother. It was the first official theatre built on the school property. He also photographed me, my cousin Tony and my then dear boyfriend J.R. O'Hearn on one of the Windsor Mountain School buses. It turned out to be a nice picture.

Mr. Landshoff had an adorable wife, Ursula, who accompanied him often on his photography ventures and most often to Point Lookout to visit us. She was also the doting mother of their beloved poodle. They were both very German. Landshoff was really very strict and didn't have much of a sense of humor. However, he did get hired a lot to photograph those models for Harper's Bazaar, Vogue, and Mademoiselle.

If he was taking amphetamine, even he didn't know about it, and I don't believe it improved his mood. He was an older low key German man, and rather stern. That is why I doubt he was getting amphetamine. I have known him since I was about 6 years old. He was around for so many years, and he was consistent and mild mannered. So, if he was on amphetamine, it wasn't apparent.

Julius La Rosa

Julius La Rosa, a well-known singer in the late 50's and early 60's, also a patient although scarcely around, came only to the office and briefly. I met him at my father's office when I was about nine years old. He was waiting to be called in for his treatment. He had a great speaking voice. Sometimes he would vocalize after a treatment, just one measure, not the whole song. He spoke eloquently, like a high class well-spoken Italian gentleman. He always dressed very chic. He would blush with pride, for what reason I don't know. Maybe it was a reaction to the calcium.

He was on the Arthur Godfrey show from 1951 to 1953 as were The McGuire Sisters (also patients) and Marion Marlowe. He was signed by Cadence Records in 1952, which was also the debut of his first recording of the song, "Anywhere I Wander" which reached the top 30 on the charts. He hit it big in 1953 with "Eh Cumpari" and got an award for Best Vocalist of 1953. He had his own T.V. show during the summer of 1955 which lasted 13 weeks. He was a patient of my father's during all this.

He was very friendly, only with my father. He would be in the middle of a conversation with my father and then turn to me for a second, wink at me and smile while still speaking to my father. I don't think I ever shook hands with him when we met. I was only a young girl anyway.

Hedy Lamarr

Ms. Lamarr was a regular visitor to our apartment, having been instructed by Papa to wait for him at home for treatment. She was seeking "The Fountain of Youth" via my father's treatments. Weren't we all in some form or another? She talked about her book. I never fully understood who she was except for the fact that Don Hutchison, whom I met at my father's office, had previously dated her.

She was busy writing a book, or someone was busy writing a book about her. She was very upset about going to court and fighting off accusations of a lesbian relationship and discussed it at length sitting at our dining room table.

She was very self-absorbed, yet all of Hollywood has been known to be guilty of that, so why should I or anyone else have singled her out for that? I was so young. I never learned to appreciate her for who she was, nor had I seen any of her movies. She was before my time. She was very daring, having had several facelifts during the time that I knew her and during the time that she saw my father. No, he didn't do her facelifts.

One of the last times I saw her in Papa's office was shortly before he had his license revoked in '74 or '75. She had just had a facelift. It had been done much too tightly; she looked awful. She couldn't smile, poor thing.

When I was in my early twenties, I inherited her ex-boyfriend, Don Hutchison, who had become my father's haircutter. I remained his (Don Hutchison) friend until he died in 1999. Don and I were lovers first, and then we were friends. She couldn't have been gay, Heddy that is.

Judith Lowry

When I met this amazing woman, she was already in her late 70's. She would sit in my father's office and wait for hours to see him. Once I saw her sleeping while she was waiting to be called in. I was very impressed with her work. She did quite a few movies that I knew of.

I asked her about the Joanne Woodward movie, "The Effects of Gamma Rays on Man in The Moon Marigolds". She told me her granddaughter showed up on the set one day that Joanne Woodward was yelling so loud at her and was concerned about her grandmother's wellbeing. Judith explained to her then, and to me as we spoke that Ms. Woodward yelled over her head or to the left or right of her. Not at her or in her face as we both thought. She claimed that it didn't bother her in the least.

During the time that she was a patient of my fathers, she performed in movies, "Super Dad", "Gamma Rays", which I've already mentioned, "Cold Turkey", "The Anderson Tapes", "The Night They Raided Minsky's", and "Valley of The Dolls".

Ms. Lowry was an energetic and spunky person. I truly doubt, especially considering her age at that time, that she could possibly have been on speed. Vitamins maybe, speed, very doubtful.

Marion Marlowe

She was a friend but mostly a patient for years starting in the early 50's through the late 60's. My parents and I were invited to her home in upstate

New York, a beautiful house with a large swimming pool. She always wore Spanish style long skirts and fancy Spanish blouses. She wore lots of eye makeup all the time. She invited me to see Man of La Mancha when she was appearing as the "perfect Dulcinea". I went backstage to visit her after the show. Her eye shadow was so heavy that I got scared of her. Even when she wasn't performing, she wore makeup, lavish lipstick and large hoop earrings.

I recently found out that in the late forties she was one of several staff members under the instruction of Arthur Godfrey and his talent scouts. Also included were orchestra band leader Archie Bleyer, as were Julius LaRosa and The McGuire sisters. Phyllis was also a patient of my father's, although not friendly with our family.

Nan Martin

A patient for as long as I can remember, I would guess the late 50's. She was a character actress of films and television who found many roles in the late 50's through the late 60's, because at that time there was so many roles being written for parts that she played. "The Man in the Gray Flannel Suit", "Toys in the Attic", "For Love of Ivy", "Goodbye Columbus". These were movies and T.V. shows she was a part of while she was seeing my father. Was she getting amphetamine? I sincerely doubt it.

Roddy McDowall

Roddy and my parents became fast friends. My parents and I came from the east side, he would meet us on Central Park West, upper 70's and we'd park the car and take long walks. Sometimes we'd walk along the park just inside Central Park West. Mostly he would engage in long conversations with my mother. My father spoke of him proudly because he was a patient, friend and famous even then. But from what I could see, he was mostly friendly with my mother. I loved his British accent. He was a very handsome man. He had the look of an intellectual.

Phyllis McGuire

She came to our apartment on East 73rd street for treatment. I met her on one such occasion very briefly. Once she brought her sister Dorothy. That is all I remember.

Joan Morse

She was a patient of Papa's for many years. She even appeared young when she'd grown older. She was a far-out clothing designer and very popular with the disco crowd. Yes, she received treatment from my father. My father was not her exclusive supplier, she found other ways to get uppers. She was photographed in nightclubs and known to have enjoyed cocaine which she did not get from my father. She was a party girl who frequented Studio 54 and Trudy's Tricks. We went clubbing together and she invited me to her showroom to try on clothes. She allowed me to pick something.

One of the things she was known for was creating unconventional color combinations into beautiful modern designs, such as in sweaters. She made them very "In", such as pinks and oranges both in the same sweater. She combined reds and purples beautifully. They were difficult to digest at first, but after a while they were considered beautiful. She started a new trend, Nouveau and Avant-garde. Personality wise, she was fiercely wild and all over the place. She was high a lot, skinny, stern, and dressed chic. I liked her even though she was wild.

Zero Mostel

I met him one memorable time backstage at the theatre where he was performing "A Funny Thing Happened on Broadway". He had a rabbi in his dressing room. Other patients of my father did also except some of them had priests instead. Zero was famous for his performances on Broadway in "A Funny Thing Happened on the Way to the Forum" (1962), "Fiddler on The Roof" (1964) and "The Producers" (1967).

He was very funny in person as well as in private. He and my father bonded like two old chubby Jewish men, so naturally our visit lasted quite a while. But it was enjoyable. He suggested introducing me to his son, Josh, who must have been close to my age. He was a patient and being treated by my father throughout his long Broadway theatre run with much success. He won rave reviews for all his shows.

Patrice Munsel

She was an actress who had her own television series in 1956. She was in "I've Got a Secret" playing a celebrity guest in 1961. She was a patient of my fathers in the late 50's during the time she was doing her show. She appeared on The Dean Martin show twice.

Ben Murphy

Ben was the "IN" hairstylist of the late 50's and 60's, and he knew it. He had a large ego and yes, he was gay, very open but a great stylist. He got treatment from my father and treated himself on his own also. He was very into speed all the time. It was part of his personality. He experimented with a hairstyle and asked me to model it. He did it to please my father, naturally!

I showed up for the shoot with my boyfriend Jack Levi, who had decided to accompany me. The photographer took one look at my boyfriend and decided immediately to include him in the shoot. That he did not do to please my father. Jack was so gorgeous and handsome. The picture came out astonishingly well. As a matter of fact, it turned out to be so great, I kept it as a souvenir of our relationship. I still have it and cherish it. The picture that is.

Patrick O'Neal

Mr. O'Neal was an established actor. My mother had become rather friendly with his wife, and we took long walks along the East River, once while he and other show biz patients were putting together a performance for my father's birthday. Patrick was more friendly with my brother Tommy than with me. He was always stepping into character. One could instantly tell he was an actor by his demeanor and dress. Whenever he was working on a film, he would stop over for treatment. He always came to the office with a script in hand and went right into the treatment room. In and out as the saying goes. And I don't give a damn if he was getting speed.

Leontyne Price

We must have been introduced to her by Franco Zeffirelli, because I remember her coming to the office for treatment before and during rehearsals for "Antony and Cleopatra" at Lincoln Center, which was being directed by

Franco who was also a patient and longtime friend. She was naturally exquisite singing Opera. She was already quite well known before appearing in the show. She came by to see my father frequently.

My father took Ms. Price on a tour of his laboratory, which was very interesting, and she was extremely impressed. At that time, we lived on East 83rd Street off 5th Avenue. My father's office was on the main floor, and his laboratory was in the back. It took up two rooms. My father had a tank of liquid nitrogen, and an electric Eel swimming in a tank. He was experimenting on scientific projects using the Eel, liquid nitrogen and other elements, which were way over my head.

Apparently, Ms. Price was very impressed by my father's kindness towards her. She became smitten with him soon after her personal tour. He tried to keep it hush hush but said she had fallen in love with him and although he thought the world of her, he somehow couldn't fit himself into her life or imagine fitting her into his life. And I guess he fell for her. Unfortunately, he was not willing to give up his career and work for her.

They were both from different worlds. He told me he felt he couldn't give her what she deserved because he was too involved with his work. He had to tell her he was sorry, but he felt it wouldn't work. She went through a very sad period because of it, so did he, he felt very guilty. I know about the saga of Leontyne Price because my father told me about it in confidence.

When she was my father's patient she was on top, the most famous, the biggest name. She had just arrived. I would not believe it for one moment if I learned that she was taking amphetamine. She wouldn't have been able to sing as beautifully as she did if she was on it.

She remained a patient for some time and remained in touch with my father for several years after. She continued coming for treatment while her show was in town.

James Rado [Jimmy] and Jerry Ragni

The producers, writers, and stars of the hit show "Hair". And yes, they were patients of my father. They were among the select few that I would go out of my way to accommodate and get into my father's treatment room on East 83rd Street from outside in the waiting room. That was because I knew for a fact that they had a curtain call. They really had to be out of my father's office by a specific time. They never complained, never said a word. I'd coincidentally show up at the office (we lived upstairs at the time, on the 18th floor). I'd seen them pitching up their tent in my father's waiting room or lying on hiking bags waiting to get in. I'd come in and rush them right in, ahead of everyone and anyone else because I knew they had a curtain call and had to get out. No one ever said a word, not even them.

Jimmy Rado, the blonde, was the low key shy quiet one. Jerry was the outspoken one. My father and I were invited to see the show once. We were invited backstage before the show started. They put on their makeup in ten minutes, that's it. It was incredible. They were always together. What was so amazing about these two was that they never pushed their weight around. They were not divas. They were just the opposite, quite humble and unpretentious. Never, not once did either of them say they were in a hurry and had to get to work. They just sat quietly and waited. And If I ran into them outside of Papas office and away from the theatre, they were down to Earth, very creative, driven, relaxed and cordial.

Lee Remick

Mostly famous for "Days of Wine and Roses" in 1962, she also won acclaim for "No Way to Treat a Lady" in 1968, "Damn Yankees!" in 1967, played in "The Tempest" in 1960 and "Anatomy of a Murder" in 1959. She won an Oscar for "Days of Wine and Roses". She was a patient off and on through all those years.

Bob Richardson

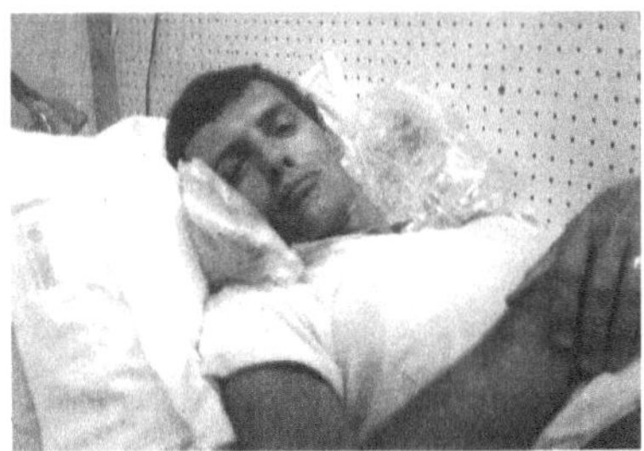

Photographer Bob Richardson during treatment, mid 1960s

Boy was he a character. And I consider that the understatement of the year as the expression goes. Dare I explain what I mean? Yes, I dare. Bob was a fashion photographer for Bazaar and Harper's Bazaar. He was bazaar. He was most known in the late 50's and early 60's. He was a patient mostly and sort of a friend. He was working all the time, where I don't know. He had openings of his works in galleries. If he was exposing sex in the sixties through his photographic work, I knew nothing about it. I was a very young girl when we met him, so I knew nothing of his work. I just saw this neurotic tall and skinny man walking around the office pigeon toed with sunken cheek bones looking gaunt as if he was having a serious Oedipus Rex complex. He was being treated by my father all that time, although for what I don't know. He was heavily into drugs, and I didn't know it. I do know he got drugs from other sources too. He was very obviously on amphetamine, and God knows what else.

After receiving treatment, he would suck in his cheeks, get this serious morbid look on his face, place one foot carefully in front of the other as if he were going to do the Tango, and if I didn't know better, and perhaps I didn't, he appeared to possess all the symptoms of a screaming homosexual. Yet you knew that had to be the farthest from the truth.

He had a wife, Naomi (Norma), who was darling, adorable, so devoted, and seemingly in love with him. They were like sister and brother, always glued to each other. And they also had a child together, a son named Teri. Naomi was so normal, straight and appeared to be so very down to Earth. She looked just like a cute doll. Bob appeared so Dracula like, so oedipal. He mostly appeared very serious and gaunt looking, both before and after treatment. Only on rare occasions did I see him working at his craft, photography. There was one occasion where there was an exhibition of his work in a gallery in London. My parents and I happened to be in England at the time and were invited. We attended the opening of his exhibition and spent time with them.

In New York some years later, Bob offered to photograph me in a photoshoot, I guess to please my father. I was to be dressed all in black, even a black turtleneck sweater. I was also supposed to get a good night's sleep the night before and wake up early the next morning bright-eyed and bushy tailed and go to his place to be photographed. Apparently, he flipped out during the night and threw all his photography equipment out of the window, threatened his wife, and threw her, their child, and their dog out of the house. The shoot was cancelled, forever.

Melinda Rogers

I include her here although she was not a celebrity. She was the one model lady friend of Monty Rock III. She was a very "en vogue" model of the 60's. She had a very intellectual look unlike most models, and she was quite intelligent. She wasn't from New York; she came from the Midwest. Her sister Victoria Webber went to the same boarding school that I did, Windsor Mountain. Victoria and I both adored Monty, but it was Melinda who was dating Monty.

Victoria and I became friends through our mutual admiration for Monty. It was my father who succeeded in introducing us right in his office on East 82nd Street. Both Melinda and Victoria were very hippy-like, and very intellectual looking, yet they looked very different.

Kay Schunk

Kay was the daughter of Dr. Koebner, a general practitioner and survivor of the holocaust. Her father had referred her to my father. She came to my father as a patient then became a friend. She came with her husband and her two young daughters.

Paul Shenar

When Paul entered the room, any room, he just took your breath away. His thick black hair, his deep distinctive resonating voice, his intoxicating charm. He was so good looking, handsome and debonair. Even I had a mad crush on him. It seemed obvious to everyone except me that he was Bill Balls counterpart. He seemed so straight. His thick dark eyebrows, incredible smile and masculine perfect while teeth painted a perfect picture. He could have been a tennis player: he had this rustic look and physicality to him. There are pictures of him posing on the rocks above the water. He was courteous to me, but extremely charming and a gentleman.

He and Bill Ball were patients of my father. They came for a visit when they came to town. While Paul was under treatment from my father, he made many movies and performed in plays for The American Conservatory Theatre Company. He worked on movies and T.V. shows including my favorite, Dynasty, Columbo, Mannix, Gemini Man, Hawaii Five-O, Scare Crow and Mrs. King, The Invisible Man and Wonder Woman.

There were occasions when he invited my parents and me to his performances. I believe he received treatment then. In my opinion, Paul didn't need treatment. It was Bill who suggested he get them. To my knowledge, Bill received treatment from my father quite often. Paul Shenar

seldom saw my father for treatment. My father obliged them out of friendship.

It was nice seeing him with Bill. Paul was one of Bills main actors in ACT and his best pal. They made a great pair. He was also a patient of my father for many years. He never appeared to be high. He always appeared fully in control, so it seems the treatments didn't interfere with his work.

Leonard Sillman

Leonard dressed, moved and appeared at times with the guise of "The Phantom of the Opera" and seemed to be trapped in Frankenstein's body. He looked like a phantom with his complexion, a cool white, his eyeballs bulging, wearing a red and black silk cape, and would throw it over his shoulder dramatically, and thrust it back as a sign of dramatic expression. Included in his wardrobe ensemble was a Catholic Cross which he wore on special occasions around his neck.

Leonard is joined by an impressive group of sparkling actors and was the one master creator responsible for "New Faces" on Broadway. He was the one man famous for taking yet undiscovered, unknown aspiring actors with great talent and putting them into his shows and making them famous. Leonard was putting together his show and considered hiring John Murray Anderson, also a patient and close friend, to direct his play. Mr. Anderson was already directing The Ringling Brother's Barnum and Bailey Circus, which was where I met him as a very little girl. John Murray Anderson apparently was driven back to the theater at some point by an insistent Leonard Sillman and was placed in the show in 1952. It was during that time, a period of approximately three years that Leonard had employed two young men to write songs for a musical of his which flopped, titled "All in Fun". The two men were apparently so lousy that after the flop Leonard left Broadway. At one point, possibly engineered by my father, Leonard saw Alan J. Lerner's "My Fair Lady" and decided to return to Broadway where he continued to produce "New Faces". Mel Brooks [The Producer's] wrote sketches for "New Faces" of 1952 and 1957. The list goes on and on. He must have referred his actors and actresses to my father for treatment. He made Ronnie Graham and Ellen Hanley, plus a slew of other talented unknowns famous.

Ronnie was in Leonard's 1952 production of "New Faces", and met my father soon after, around that time I was five years old. Ronnie claimed he was my father's first patient at his East 72nd Street office. Hermoine Gingold, also in "New Faces", was a patient of my father's. They were all my father's patients.

Sometimes Leonard would arrive at my father's office on his way to an opening of a show adorned in his favorite black cape realizing how dramatic and theatrical he appeared. There were times he would arrive in Priests attire, why I don't know. He would glide in like a warlock, like a mysterious man of eternal secrets; his soft and delicately spoken word was as dramatic and equally as fierce as his entrance. He would announce himself with the flamboyant thrust or twirl of his cape like a ballerina, and announce to the world that, "I have arrived at the Inner sanctum", then give this mischievous smile. That meant that he had arrived at my father's "Inner Office". He had a very serious expression on his face most of the time bordering on scary. On occasion one could catch him with the most sarcastic smirk on his face. After receiving his treatment, he would elaborate on some theater people in a somewhat sarcastic teasing manner. Verbally he would create colorful drawings right out of the air in space so to speak. He was very descriptive in a most dramatic and yet sarcastic manner. I guess I am trying to say he had a unique way of expressing himself. He was a colorfully creative person with a touch of dark humor attached to his many faceted personalities. That was Leonard Sillman.

One night, Leonard became violently ill from eating lobster at a well-known restaurant in Manhattan. He was at death's door, food poisoning from seafood. He called my father who told him to get in a cab and come right over, which he did. My father treated him, and according to Leonard, saved his life. This happened when I was about 9 years old, and I can still remember hearing them talk about it. My father would repeat this happening over the years. Leonard was quietly indebted to him. I personally didn't interact with him.

From my perspective, he was rather eerie with his dark humor. Being a very young girl, I feared coming close. For a child it was rather daunting being around someone of his dark nature, whereas being around Ronnie Graham, Ellen Hanley and Alice Ghostley, all his proteges, were super delightful, entertaining, and perfectly fun.

Marc Sinclaire

He was brilliant and flourished in the early 60's through the early 70's. He was a hairdresser, clothing designer, and personal stylist, both hair and wardrobe. He was a patient of my father. Since we had to attend the opening of Franco Zeffirelli's "Cleopatra" at Lincoln Center with Leontyne Price, as a favor to my father, he came up from the office for an official visit to assist me. First, he asked me to show him the way to my closet. He went through my closet, tore one skirt off a dress, took one black sweater, stitched the black sweater to the light blue skirt thereby making me an instant formal dress for the evening. He also loaned me a wig for the occasion which he attached to my hair.

During the show I forgot I had the wig on my head and pulled it off. Boy was that embarrassing and a relief as well; I mean to get the wig off. He normally worked for famous people, celebrities, high society people.

Andy Williams

Andy came to see my father only twice in New York. He was married to Claudine Longet then. He received treatment from my father while he was working, doing singing engagements and while on tour. He was a patient, not a friend. To my knowledge he wasn't getting amphetamine.

Tennessee Williams

Tennessee Williams was a friend and patient of my father for many years. He was a very complex, neurotic man. He hung around adults, never around kids. It was my intelligence or the lack thereof which prevented me from appreciating this man's genius.

I remember running into him on several occasions at my father's office and when I was in San Francisco training at ACT. He was there for the opening of his play "A Streetcar Named Desire". The students from ACT were asked to see his show pretty much as a homework assignment, but I ran into him a while before the show. Since he knew me anyway from my father, he specifically invited me to attend that early evening performance. I happily agreed. He immediately invited me to a nearby pub for a drink. My father brought me up very well. I turned him down, flat. How dare he, I thought!

Then after sitting through the show, my very first reaction was, damn it!! I only wish I'd accepted that drink! It most probably would have enabled me to relax and enjoy the play that much more. What a fool I felt I was! I didn't see him after the show, but I had such a spell of confusion and a bloody headache, so I went straight home.

He thought the world of my father and swore he did his best work while under my father's care. There were articles written by Mr. Williams in defense of my father, stating how he believed he did his best work while under my father's treatments. I've heard the more talented a person is the more neurotic they are. I couldn't understand him on any level. Then again, I couldn't handle the play either.

97

REBUTTAL

I have read many books about my father. These include authors such as Doris Shapiro and Gene Lee. I find it fascinating and amazing how some of the comments printed are incorrect, speculative and how others are simply so judgmental. Although I suppose I should not be so surprised at some of their passages, I must admit that I am also disappointed with parts of their stories. I think it is important to remember that many of these people, patients and supposed friends of my father, relied on him. I am saddened that many of them turned on him and forgot those times, those in the "middle of the night calls" when they needed him, when he opened his office for them, when he made house calls going to their aid. The following books were written by or about patients and mentioned him to a degree or have written about him rather extensively.

"Been There Done That"

By Eddie Fisher

Copyright 1999

Hardcover

Starting with Eddie Fisher, who failed to tell the truth in so many instances, such as misrepresenting his relationship with my father, by implying that my father was his drug connection and shot giver when in fact they had become good friends. My father had become a father figure, confidant and unofficial psychiatrist to Eddie, and was his and his manager, Milton Blackstone's physician in New York City and traveled to meet them on the road.

Eddie keeps referring to "Max and his drugs". It was Eddie who arrived at the office prior to an engagement requesting treatment. And there is no proof whatsoever that he was given amphetamine on each visit. The way he described my father and his interactions with him doesn't convey the rapport they truly had together. I personally witnessed Eddie receiving treatment from my father. I observed him before and after. I would hardly say he was flying. He became a bit chipper, nothing major. That was on East 72nd street at his office when I was younger in the early 60's.

It was never my father's goal to make anyone super high or flying. He sought to make them feel refreshed. And to the best of my knowledge, he didn't make mistakes or exceptions, ever. I cannot believe that under the circumstances of Eddie Fisher being devastated over the legal separation with Elizabeth that my father would venture to give him a shot to take by himself, however I have read that accusation by other patients. I still don't believe it. My father wanted to be the one administering the injections.

When Eddie needed a place to hide, rest or get away from the paparazzi, especially after returning from the set of Cleopatra when Elizabeth dumped him, my father offered him the town house of friends [of my father] and yes, also patients. In general, Eddie slanted situations making them appear as if the other person initiated the irresponsible act or behavior towards him, opposed to Eddie himself being the initiator who imposed on all these people when he was down and out, and caused them to feel the need to rush to his aid and help him out, unconditionally. He was such a sweet, nice and charming individual, no one would have ever considered turning him down, except Elizabeth of course.

My father did diagnose Elizabeth over the telephone long distance when she was in the hospital fighting for her life in London. Eddie stated that he was shocked. I will quote him directly from his book. **But after five days Elizabeth was still in critical condition, still mostly comatose. So, in desperation I called Max. After I gave him a medical update, he sighed and asked, "Did they check her gamma globulin?" To which Eddie replied, Gamma globulin? Ask me about the arrangement to "Lady in Paris". I had no idea what he was talking about. But incredibly just as I hung up from talking with him, Dr. Carl Goldman came into the room and told**

me, Eddie, we've made a terrible mistake, we forgot to check her Gamma globulin". Eddie claimed the coincidence was chilling. That is a ridiculous statement for Eddie Fisher to make. Eddie Fisher knew unequivocally that that's one of the things my father was most famous for.

He lied to his readers about his love and devotion to his own faith. Everyone around him knew that he was a very religious Jew including my father. That was one of many bonds they had together.

My father did not mix and match at random. At times it appeared that way. But he was studiously concentrating before each injection and knew exactly what he had injected into each vial and took from those vials to fill his syringes. God forbid if he had filled the syringes with medicines from random vials he would have had a lot of sick complaining patients.His vials were all in front of him on three shelves very well lit. He liked it that way. And, if the treatment wasn't adequate, he gave another treatment following that one. But that happened very seldom. It is simply my opinion that my father wouldn't have acted so irresponsibly with any patient, ever.

My father never had dirty fingernails. He took baths regularly, went swimming regularly, and had a collection of nail brushes at the office, but especially at home. And he always had a cotton towel on his lap to catch the drippings. He always wore clean white shirts to the office and changed the dirty shirts during the day. I can't understand why in particular Eddie Fisher and his other detractors would say that about him. It's unbelievable, on one page he's making my father appear as an irresponsible slop. On the next page he's claiming that without my father's injections and caring, he wouldn't have been able to make it. And he's also claiming that he was able to do his work despite everything bad that had happened to him thanks to my father.

Regarding President Kennedy and my father bringing Eddie along on some of his visits to the President, Eddie Fisher was invited to the White House, yes, but that was in 1960. That came by my father to join him on an official house call to treat the President. I tend to wonder whether Eddie may have been jealous of the attention the President was getting from my father since according to Eddie, he was the center of attention in my father's office for the longest time, who knows? My view, from a child's eyes mostly when I was young until my teens, conveys what a dear, sweet, charming man Eddie Fisher truly was opposed to the creep he made himself out to be.

GENE LEES: THE MUSICAL WORLDS OF LERNER and LOEWE

Robson Books

1991

Paperback

University of Nebraska Press

This book portrays my father in a very intriguing light and even portrays him as scary and freakish. Mr. Lee's descriptions of my father, the layout of his office, his descriptions of my fathers' mixing and blending his concoctions in a cauldron like a medieval necromancer, all are dark and exaggerated, and in my opinion deceptive.

I describe the same room he describes and my father before, during and after a treatment which appears colorful, basic and standard. His treatment room, the bottles, vials and oily medicines are definitely very different from those described by Mr. Lee.

Upon entering my father's treatment room, there was a counter with five shelves above it where the many vials sat. Each vial was properly labeled except for the one on the counter in front of my father which he used primarily for mixing the medicines he was preparing to inject. Next to that on the counter were the syringes, disposable and sealed. Everything was orderly and in its proper place. Thanks to my fathers' assistant.

However, my interpretation is different. I saw my father almost every day and saw all the things described in a clearly and completely different per-spective, that of an insider. And by that time, I was old enough to understand what I saw.

Page 215: quotes Miles Kruger "I would hear lurid stories of how patients would go there, and he would stir up cauldrons, medicines. Whatever it was, it seemed cultish and eerie"

The assistant to whom Kruger refers to was Doris Shapiro, whose book extensively documents the visits to Max Jacobson with whom Shapiro states, she eventually went to bed.

There were no cauldrons, there were vats of medicines being made up for suspensions, injectables, vitamins etc. and for oral drops. Whether it appeared cultish or eerie is left to the eyewitness, I saw it as a small laboratory being used to make and store injectables for intravenous and intramuscular injection, and for oral drops.

Patients he would encounter in the office were theatre people, playwright Tennessee Williams, Stash Radziwill, Cecil B. DeMille. Both Doris Shapiro and Miles Kruger claim that the atmosphere was all very cultish.

And it was all as Miles Kruger and Doris Shapiro confirms, all very cultish, with Jacobson selecting potions from his vials, including one marked "Meth" and blending his concoctions like some medieval necromancer, and then slipping the mixture into the arm of his client, on whose face would appear a smile of beatific peace.

I am choosing to respond to the above paragraph. The same book, just another page claims that the doctor took from vials at random to fill the syringes for his patients. In the above paragraph you can read that the vials were clearly marked, one marked "Meth".

Cont. of page:

The doctor at one point confronts Mr. Lerner, "Do you vant to work or don't you?", Jacobson fiercely demanded of Lerner.Lerner's response, "Yes, yes, I want to work". Jacobson made up his mixture and slipped the needle into his vein. The result was that Lerner then went back to work on "Clear Day".

In response to Gene Lees book from the above statement, I would say the treatment was legitimate and worked. Mr. Lerner was able to go right back to work and create. What more do you want?

Page 260: par.2

My father knew about Max Jacobson dispensing Amphetamines. He said that it was typical of middle Eastern refugees to this country to give shots rather than pills, because it would build up their practices. If you give a patient a prescription, he doesn't have to see the doctor for the pills. But if you give him shots, he has to see the doctor every day. My father said, "I think we can get him off that" And I told him, "I hope so". I'm worried about that. I didn't understand then the extent to which Alan was dependent on Max Jacobson.

Page 275:

On December 4th, 1972, The New York Times broke a story on which a team of reporters had been working for some time. The report, noting that many doctors were giving potent shots to patients with enough money to pay for them, singled out Dr. Max Jacobson as the most notorious. The story bylined Boyce Rensberger, gave as a list of his clients Truman Capote, Cecil B. DeMille, Alan J. Lerner, Representative Claude Pepper from Florida, Otto Preminger, Tennessee Williams – and the late John F. Kennedy.

 The first lady, Jacqueline Kennedy, was also named as one of the recipients of the doctor's attentions. Mrs. Kennedy tersely admitted through a spokesman that it was true.

One Man Tango

Anthony Quinn

Harper Collins, Clarebooks

1995

Hardcover

 Mr. Quinn, rather rash and ill-humored, and sounding quite macho on almost every page of his book first claimed my father used monkey placenta in his injections. Not true. It was human placenta. Mr. Quinn states correctly that my father was a miracle worker, almost a caricature of Freud. Yes, there was an air about him of tremendous import. That was created by his patients as a result of his miraculous treatments and cures which are elaborated upon.

Mr. Quinn said his wife Katherine thought of my father as a savant, a worldly scholar, which actually he really was. Mr. Quinn claims he succumbed to Dr. Jacobson's black magic, and I respond, what black magic? Anthony Quinn was run down and overworked just as so many other show business actors have become after rehearsals and before performances. So, he received a treatment from my father that restored his voice and energized him. For all Mr. Quinn knew, he could have been getting massive doses of vitamins and calcium.

Fact, he could not possibly have gotten a warm rush from an injection in his hip, which is called intramuscular. It was only the I.V (intravenous injection) that contained an ampoule of calcium that caused the warm rush.

My father wasn't known to curse or say, "You son of a bitch". I have my own theory as to why, if true, my father supplied Mr. Quinn with needles and vials. However, I am unable to prove or disprove my theories since up to now I couldn't reach Duncan Quinn to get any answers.

Mr. Quinn accused my father of showing up at his house and stealing a "Rodin" sculpture. Never would my father have stolen anything, plus my father, accused of running down the street with the sculpture, couldn't run. He had injected himself with medicine experimentally years ago and had lost the normal use of one of his legs. Therefore, he could not run. Regarding his statement of sleeping aboard a yacht, how Mr. Quinn could sleep for three days straight without even getting up and going to the bathroom puzzles me. It is only his word.

Obviously, I knew my father well, besides Katherine Dunham told me that Mr. Quinn was very attached to my father and would come to his office nights, late, all unkempt and show his paintings to my father and behaved as if he wanted to please him. It always takes two people to keep a relationship going and Mr. Quinn could not have felt threatened by my father. My father always treated him well. My mother and I were also friends with his wife, Katherine and his eldest son, Duncan. And long after Mr. Quinn senior stopped seeing my father, his son Duncan still came for treatment, and Duncan was not hooked.

I am still trying to locate Duncan Quinn to clarify most of these allegations since he was also a patient and continued seeing my father long after his father stopped being a patient. He was seeing my father for other matters but that needs to be officially confirmed.

We visited them at their country home and at their town house in New York. My mother and I were friendly with Katherine. I knew Duncan. He worked with the same theatre company that I did, The American Conservatory Theatre Company in San Francisco. To my knowledge he was not on amphetamine (at least not from my father) and was friendly with my father long after his father stopped coming.

We Danced All Night

Doris Shapiro

Barricade Books

Copyright 1990

Hardcover and paperback

Doris' life was filled with fantasies, hallucinations and imaginations, which she elaborates on in her book. When I read her book, amazingly, I found that she had clarified certain aspects of my life that until then had been a mystery to me such as the facts surrounding my mother's death. I saw the events surrounding the death of my mother unravel right before my eyes.

However, the misinformation pertaining to the aftermath of my mother's death was totally inaccurate. After my mother's death my father immediately offered to marry my aunt if it would please me. It wouldn't have. He took me away, far away out of town for at least a week. This she did not know.

According to Doris, my mother's death as well as Alan J. Lerner's mothers' death were non-events, and my father's office was open and operated, business as usual. In truth, the office was closed for at least a week. I know this because my father decided to take me and get the hell out of town and away from everything and everybody.

I was present much of the time that she and Mr. Lerner were in my father's apartment. To clarify her fantasies with the truth, reality as I saw it and as

I knew it to be. Obviously, I was not aware of the going on behind closed doors, meaning in his romantic life.Although I must say it was quite a known fact that his life and love was medicine, treating patients, and swimming. Regarding everything else, I was there, present. To me she was a dear kind lady always. I learned from reading her book that her intentions were to marry my father even though she was married to a man named Burt, was miserable in her marriage, wanted out of the marriage desperately and was definitely a 24/7 workaholic regardless of her words or actions to the contrary.

I saw her with my father and Mr. Lerner together, busy at work and in another light entirely than purports to in her book. I wish she had become the next Mrs. Jacobson, but truly I don't believe he had her in mind that way.

Rebuttal to Gene Lee/Doris Shapiro

Page 214, Gene Lee's book:

No one [Alan J. Lerner, my father, or Doris Shapiro] but the parties involved would be qualified to make a judgment call on the necessity of these people needing treatment. Whether they warranted a treatment or not, only the doctor and his patients could be the judges of that. And today only Doris Shapiro is alive to give her opinion. The main receptor, Alan J. Lerner, would arguably disagree on the grounds that his need to create greatly outweighed the negatives at hand. The man needed to write for his shows. My father's treatments awakened his creative juices and lengthened his energy level so that he had more time to meet his deadlines and to complete his masterpieces. This was Mr. Lerner's reasoning for requesting and accepting my father's treatments.

Also, by Dr. Jacobson treating Mr. Lerner prior to a rehearsal of his play, Dr. Jacobson enabled Mr. Lerner to be alert and functional. To look, hear and see his show and discover any strengths or weaknesses it had and to change them, if necessary, before opening night.

Page 215: Dr. Jacobsons office at East 83rd Street opened at 5:30 am and often remained open until late hours.

I wish to dispute that. My father seldom got to the office until 11am especially since he stayed up so late and sometimes was even awakened during the night by patients needing treatments, both celebrity and non-celebrity patients. If Doris Shapiro was hooked on the doctor's treatment, it wasn't noticeable. As far as I could see, she was hooked on herself. She thought that she was so beautiful and filled with self-importance at being Alan J. Lerner's secretary.

Yes, she was tall, nicely built and an attractive lady with a seductive voice and a darling sweet smile. She never gave the impression she was hooked on anything. As far as the doctor having the taste for being surrounded by the rich and powerful, and in particular theatre people, what is wrong with that? He also had a strong taste and desire to help people, especially Multiple Sclerosis patients. He devoted one night a week to them, no exceptions. He saw them at home, particularly Laurie, a young girl.

Page 216:

It is true there were celebrities at times, sitting particularly in the doctor's office waiting to be called in, such as Tennessee Williams who has spoken out outstandingly in defense of my father. And yes, the doctor did boast at times of his encounters where he came to the rescue of his patients. Perhaps that was his downfall, or was it human nature? My father came from a very poor and modest family. If it pleased him to boast I can only see the harm in the breaching of confidentiality, telling people he treated the President when it should have been a secret.

Oh, before I dare forget patients such as Doris Shapiro and Miles Kruger. I am sure, I assume, entered my father's treatment room totally buttering him up with compliments telling him how great he was and how much they had heard about him and his travels, encounters, and experiences. I assure you all this dialogue took place, transpired, to cause my father to boast as he did. There was nothing cultish about it. The doctor knew how to treat his patients and which specific medicines and combinations to give them. That made all the difference.

Yes, the doctor selected vitamin solutions from different vials and combined them in a syringe, different combinations for different patients depending on what symptoms each patient had. He filled the syringe accordingly. He knew what he was doing. He had it down to a science and was extremely intuitive. He could place the path to your future in front of you, thereby clarifying matters and enabling the patient to visualize and proceed with their lives. He didn't cast spells on people. Besides medicinal treatment, he offered direction, guidance and advice, those were his most generous assets.

Page 216:*middle of page*

Doris describes very well a momentary rush she and Mr. Lerner experienced when the calcium in the I.V. injection passed through her and Mr. Lerner's bodies. It lasted perhaps three minutes. That was it. It was smooth, warm, and relaxing, but it didn't last long.

There were times Mr. Lerner came to the doctor for treatment so that he could relax. At those times he received another mixture. So, if my father sternly demanded to know whether Mr. Lerner wanted to work, it was so that he would know what to fill the syringe with.

Page 78:

Doris was clearly overworked, suffered from a lack of sleep and was unaware of the time or day it was. It appears she couldn't have known precisely what day it was since she'd gone so long without any sleep. Why didn't she put the brakes on it? My father was fully aware of what he was doing. He very reluctantly gave her a treatment. He felt obliged by Mr. Lerner's presence to offer Mrs. Shapiro treatment. That part was unfortunate. My father was too polite, nice and giving. His patients took such advantage of him. I don't see any harm in my father's wanting to make Mr. Lerner feel better, enabling him to be able to write.

Page 79:

Mrs. Shapiro states that she saw a letter from Dr. Halstead praising Dr. Jacobsons treatment of a patient's cancer which thanks to Dr. Jacobson had disappeared entirely. Dr. Jacobson was so involved with Mr. Lerner that he felt responsible for helping Mr. Lerner and was determined to help him meet his deadline in getting his show completed on time.

Page 79:

Whatever treatment the doctor saw fit to give the President no matter how outlandish it may have sounded was totally appropriate. The doctor knew damn well what he was doing, or Mr. Lerner wouldn't have continued to see him. No one was forcing him. He went of his own accord.

Page 99:

Doris Shapiro's recollection of walking through the doctor's office at 2:00 am, as factual as it may have been, failed to mention that all the patients at the office at that time were there because they had to work within hours of seeing my father. And Bill Ball was working on a script and had a different timetable than 9 to 5 people. The fruit and vegetable man had to be at work when most of us slept preparing for a day's work.

She states that at the same time Anthony Quinn was at the office as well as Eddie Fisher. These people found the doctor indispensable and the doctor couldn't say no.

I can only be saddened to realize at reading all this that it seems no one cared enough to stop the doctor. No one made him go upstairs and get sleep. I find that rather sad and deafening. If Doris Shapiro can stand and reprimand my father for working such crazy hours and treating so many patients, I can ask why she and others did not put their needs to rest and even once attempt to be concerned about their caring physician.

Page 227:

I cannot comment on Mr. Lerner's marriage. I was a young girl back then. I can only question whether Mrs. Lerner actually paid a visit to the doctor or got injections second-hand. The doctor never gave an injection that got a patient high. And as far as I know, she was never my father's patient. In regard to Mr. Lerner's nervous habits, I was told that he suffered nervous disorders and that the more talented he became, the more nervous he was. I had quit smoking once and days later was invited on Mr. Lerner's yacht on a cruise. My father and I accepted the invitation. After spending three hours on the boat, upon docking, I headed for the nearest cigarette machine to buy a pack which I immediately started smoking. He made me that nervous. And no, unequivocally, Mr. Lerner did not receive treatment while we were aboard the boat. He was just a very nervous high-strung man. Most brilliant talented artists are both nervous and neurotic.

Page 240:

If Mr. Lerner was in the doctor's office late at night, that meant that he was lucky enough to find him still in at that time. And was lucky to be able to get an injection so he could continue writing "Clear Day" which was running behind schedule.

Page 242:

Alan Lerner was getting treatments from Dr. Jacobson, yes. Bud Widney was never a patient.

Page 260:

This talk of side effects from the amphetamine from which Mr. Lerner obviously suffered. The doctor deliberately prepared mixtures of vitamins and calcium along with amphetamine. The vitamins and calcium would have counteracted any such side effects in any case. The vitamins give you natural energy and appetite comes later. That's just the vitamins. The calcium made one feel relaxed. The doctor at no time gave Mr. Lerner straight amphetamine.

I don't know anything about the assumed customs of European refugees of the 40's and 50's. So, I cannot pass judgment on that, only to say that anyone knowing the doctor or any of his patients would unequivocally say he was not concerned about the money in any aspect of his practice. He was only concerned about the progress of his patients and their possible cure, which was his ultimate goal.

Page 261:

I accompanied my father to Oregon to the set of "Paint Your Wagon". We were there less than one week. Lee Marvin was also being treated. My father was told to treat him to try and keep him off the booze. My father didn't see Mr. Lerner that often on the set. We were kind of miserable having stayed in a trailer on the set, and it was hot outside. Mr. Lerner was not receiving numerous injections on the set. The location set was on acres of woods, pastures, etc. Mr. Lerner wasn't always around, my father was, he was with me.

Page 272:

If Mr. Lerner chose to stay at the doctor's office after receiving treatment that was very wise of him. He had received treatment so that he could work. If it made him able to work then he probably went to a private room, undisturbed. If he became tired after a while and was in the middle of writing something and went to the doctor for an additional treatment, all that was understandable, although the doctor did go to bed most nights even though Mr. Lerner didn't. I gather my father gave him permission to remain at his office to be able to work.

Needless to say -

Regardless of anything Doris Shapiro has had to say about Mr. Lerner 's creative performance while he was under my father's treatments, I must admit here, that often times I will wake up singing "Hurry It's Lovely Up Here", one of the most beautiful songs I believe were ever written from "Clear Day". I'll be walking down the street, suddenly I'll hear the song and start singing it. It is so encouraging, so beautiful the melody, just perfect and the words a perfect match. That is my opinion of course. Now I was not in love with Mr. Lerner. However, the shows he wrote, the music, the lyrics, "My Fair Lady", "Clear Day" he definitely wrote while under my father's care.

"On A Clear Day" was the name of a song in the show. The show was great, but the songs in the show were really spectacular. So I would beg to differ in response to Mrs. Shapiro's statements that Mr. Lerner was totally out of it and unable to function properly while under the doctor's care.

He may have been stressed out, sleep deprived and pressed for time, but undeniably he produced some of his best work ever at that time. I consider myself a good judge of that, especially since I have an ear for Broadway tunes. Let's not forget "Hear My Voice" from "Clear Day".

I suppose I could go on. I think my father saw the genius in the man, proof of his talent and was determined to help him. My father's firm belief by which he practiced medicine was to help his patients become their most constructive and productive, and that he did. The process of picking and choosing actors to play in the shows that you have written, and putting together these entire productions does not come together easily.

JFK: Hidden Illness Pain and Pills. Robert Dallek

An Unfinished Life

Robert Dallek

Little Brown and Company

Copyright 2003

Hardcover

In his book, Mr. Dallek states what most of the other Kennedy books state, that President Kennedy relied on treatments from my father quite regularly, that Dr. Jacobson had made a reputation of treating celebrity patients with "pep pills" or amphetamine that helped combat fatigue and depression and that this was kept secret.

President Kennedy was being treated by other doctors because he had so many constant and recurring ailments. Dr. Travell treated the President as well.

The strange thing is my father was blamed for everything, and I find it a relief to hear someone finally admit that other doctors were also involved.

That's my point. My father was not the only doctor treating the President and was not only using amphetamine. He was administering Vitamins B-6, B-12, calcium, minerals, and human placenta. All these additional ingredients combined made quite a difference. He never solely administered amphetamine to anyone ever. He prided himself on making a colorful combination and worked hard making vitamins in his own laboratory. I was not aware of my father's treating his patients with "Pep pills". I knew only of the injections.

All Too Human: The Love Story of Jack and Jackie Kennedy

Edward Klein

First Pocket Books

Simon and Schuster

1996

Paperback

Edward Klein described my father as a short, dark-haired man with bright cheeks. He quoted Jackie as saying, "I need pep, that's why I need Max". My father was rather tall, not short, 5'8" maybe. He often had a tan complexion.

Page 289: President Kennedy needed a shot in his back before the Vienna debate because he knew it could go on for hours...

The doctor treated Jackie for migraines and depression. In the book "All Too Human", the author made a constructive and positive statement about the doctor. When Mr. Klein wrote that the doctor stated to the President before administering a treatment to him that, "At least he wouldn't have that as an excuse for not doing well at the Vienna Debate". That statement proves my father was acting responsibly. It was his wish and intention to enable the President to feel better so he could function to his fullest capacity, and what is wrong with that?

Jack Kennedy: The Education of a Statesman

Barbara Leaming

W.W. Norton and Company

2006

Hardcover

As with all the Kennedy biographies, they portray my father in a rather negative light.

According to this book, Chuck Spaulding introduced the President to my father while Kennedy was on the campaign trail. He was complaining of weakness and fatigue which was why Spaulding recommended he see my father.

Jackie, upon meeting my father, apparently described him as hulking and unkempt with

black stained fingernails. What did she expect? When the President summoned the doctor to treat him, my father had to drop everything he was doing, abandon his patients at the office, jump on a plane and make it to the President with no time to change clothes, clean up or shower, plus his fingernails were never black. My father was summoned to treat Mrs. Kennedy because she was complaining of having headaches. When he injected her the headaches went away. Why would anyone seek to criticize my father, when all he did was come when called, treat patients and relieve their pain?

I don't understand where all this unkempt stuff and dirty fingernails come from. It was my father who bought me those cute piggy fingernail brushes when I was a little girl to make sure they were clean. He was clean. He took jacuzzi baths and swam every evening in his basement pool.

The doctor gave the President an injection in his larynx after he'd lost his voice and needed to deliver a very important speech at the U.N.

I don't believe my father's pockets were filled with drug paraphernalia at any time. Betty Spaulding accused my father of energizing everybody after a night of partying. I seriously doubt that.

According to my father's unpublished manuscript and other Kennedy books I've read, my father had his hands full treating the President before he was to make a speech, negotiate with Khrushchev or other officials. The President suffered from numerous health conditions for which he was being treated. He took medicines from other doctors and was seen by Betty Spaulding self-injecting right in plain sight. That had nothing to do with my father.

Grace and Power: The Private World of the Kennedy White House

Sally Bedell Smith

Random House

Copyright 2004

Paperback

I learned from reading this book that Oleg Cassini, who designed most of Jacqueline Kennedy's dresses was one of my father's patients. According to this book President Kennedy sneaked my father into the White House, something my father didn't appreciate.

Page 203: *Dr. Jacobson provided the President with additional strength to cope with stress. Trisha Baldridge regarded the doctor as a slimy person, but she felt the shots had no impact on the Kennedy's. According to T.B. she couldn't notice any difference in their behavior.*

My father was not a slimy person. And I claim, as does Trisha Baldridge, that there was no difference in behavior of a lot of patients before or after treatments. This book goes into detail about arrangements made by the Kennedy's to sneak the doctor into Radziwill's residence in London across the street from Buckingham Palace. My father deeply resented being made to sneak into entrances, side or back doors, both in Washington D.C and in London.

The only pleasant experience was meeting Stash Radziwill in London. Mostly the doctor treated the President in Washington, during his trip in Europe and almost constantly for the pain as mentioned. In his memoir, my father made no mention of administering shots to the "group" which included Stash Radziwill, Chuck Spaulding, the President and Mark Shaw. The doctor acknowledged giving Stash oxygen during the 50-mile stretch.

I was obviously not on this trip. I only know from my father's manuscript and from the ill health of my mother and her untimely death as a result of this trip, that it was exhausting for both my parents and my father went out of his way for the President. I also learned from reading these books that the President was not very grateful to my father who from the onset felt it was his patriotic duty to oblige the President. He was a very loyal, devoted and dedicated physician to everyone. But for the President he rolled out the red carpet. He got plenty of grief and no thanks for all his efforts. The only thing he did get was the genuine friendship of Stash Radziwill. And I have pictures of them, and personal experiences traveling with both of them together.

President Kennedy: Profile of Power

Richard Reeves

Paperback

Copyright 1993

Simon and Schuster

My father was a doctor. What's wrong with administering vitamins, human placenta and [at that time not against the law], amphetamine?

Reeves claimed Kennedy was more promiscuous with doctors and drugs than with women. Well, at least that gets my father off the hook, sort of.

On May 12th, 1961, Kennedy called Dr. Jacobson and asked him to come to Palm Beach to treat Jackie for migraines and depression following the birth of her son.

My father agreed to go. He had an incredible treatment for migraines. He treated her, got rid of her migraine and relieved her symptoms of depression.

Kennedy felt his wife wasn't in any shape to travel with him on his European trip and wanted the doctor to fly to Washington to treat her. Following that, Kennedy asked the doctor to rearrange his schedule to accompany him and Jackie on their trip the next week to Europe.

The President then told the doctor to send him a bill. The doctor replied, "I will come, of course [to Europe]". The doctor would not send a bill to the President, whose country he said helped him escape during the war. Next, the President was secretly taking Demerol, which he got from another source and Jackie reported this to Dr. Jacobson [at least my father wasn't blamed for that].

At some point, during the trip but before the meeting of the President with Khrushchev the doctor was asked by the President to give him [the President] a treatment which he did. Dr. Jacobson waited for him in a vestibule outside until the meeting ended. Apparently, the meeting didn't go very well. Afterwards the President became annoyed with my father.

The President whom it seems was very dependent on my father and my father who graciously extended himself to the President was unkindly treated by the President whom we have all come to love and idolize. To me it is very sad.

These are just some of the books written. There are more Kennedy Books, I haven't mentioned them all. These books paint a portrait of my father in route to visit the President being summoned unexpectedly and with no time to prepare for his departure. Somehow many of the things written have been written in a rather negative light.

I think at times that it would be nice if some of these patients would take responsibility for their addictions, or shall I say desire to indulge themselves as frequently as they wished with amphetamines, rather than presumably blame my father for supplying them or encouraging them to partake in it. He never put a gun to anyone's head demanding that they take it.

I must say resoundingly in all the instances mentioned my father went out of his way to accommodate and please everyone, and yes including the President of The United States of America. I was also aware of a genuine friendship which evolved from my father's constant visits to the President, which was with Stash Radziwill, the dashing Polish Prince, who once was married to Lee Radziwill, Jacqueline Kennedy's sister. In all these instances it intrigues me to see how much my father was needed, relied upon by everyone mentioned, even though I'm not sure I am enthused about the reasons why.

98

INTERVIEW WITH PABLO FRANKEL

Pablo Frankel was the husband of Gertrud Frankel, the receptionist at my father's office for many years. Pablo was also the father of my lifetime friends, Anita and Lola Frankel whom I met at the private Hebrew elementary school, Beth Hayelet when I was 5 years old. In the beginning, their mother Gertrud worked as a volunteer for my father at his office. She worked for my father full-time until the union made her get full payment for her work.

Gertrud was very well liked, so was my mother. Dona Felisa personally sent Gertrud an invitation to visit her in Puerto Rico although they never went to Connecticut. Pablo was there every night; he came to pick up Gertrud from work because she was finished so late. Every Wednesday the doctor went to see President Kennedy, Kennedy's death affected my father terribly. Thursday was M.S. night.

Maxwell Vos was a highly educated Wall Street executive who lived on the east side. He left his wife, his kids and his career. He got hooked on my father.

Max had the M.S. foundation and tested the meds on himself; Valerie Chang was there when he accidentally poisoned himself. Every doctor used amphetamine, not just my father.

Donald Thayer wired the 78th Street office so badly that it sent my father's life downhill. It was a townhouse and the office was downstairs. My father got into trouble because of it.

Lucretia Simmons and Alan J. Lerner were somehow connected. Lucretia managed to get her hands on my father's records.

John Roberts and John McManus, both friends, helped my father. John Roberts was helping my father above reproach. Mark Shaw was a loyal friend.

My father had a mail order business whereby he sent packages of injectables all over the country and all over the world to accommodate his patients worldwide.

Pablo went to see my father for treatment. He said to my father, "Doctor I have a weak back" to which my father replied, "I have a weak brain", it was an inner joke. My father had a soft spot, got so weak at the 83rd street office and lost control, everyone volunteered. He was one of the greatest doctors and diagnosticians. He once said, "I will not play God".

99

INTERVIEW WITH KATHERINE DUNHAM

MAY 2004

*Jill and Katherine Dunham during
interview, May 2004*

Part I

Jill: The important thing is to get truth down, even if they upset me.

K.D.: Your father was a researcher, more than anything, an experimenter. He felt that that was what his patients were for. He actually felt that he had the right facility to experiment amongst the patients who were in need. And there were so many people in need that if he hadn't done what he did, that a lot of people would be dead right now. And a lot of them would be out of their minds or not have created as I did. I would not have had the strength, the stamina or the vision and I think that's what he was looking for in people, vision.

In the back of my mind somewhere, I'll try to find an article, try looking in Vogue Magazine, or one of those I would not have expected to find, an article by your father in which this thing, "Opening the Wells of Vision in People". He said to me that I was a "smart ass girl, not so bright". And I knew I was not scientifically gifted, mathematically, whatever, but he passed right over that. He went right over to the individual, to the person and insisted that the person benefit by and respond to his medication. Now if it failed, I tell you personally I did have quite an experience with Anthony Quinn. Him I remember.

Jill: (*I interrupted her abruptly and told her of Anthony Quinn's book where he accuses my father of stealing a "Rodin" bust from his [Anthony Quinn's] house and running down the street with it.*) My father had injected himself in his knee years ago with Mark Shaw, the experiment went terribly wrong, and he couldn't run, in fact he could hardly walk after that. Anthony Quinn had claimed that my father had repeatedly sent him medication, vials of injectables even after he'd refused it. And stated he wouldn't pay for it and ordered the doctor not to send anymore.

The only conclusion I could come to was that Anthony Quinn must have been drinking heavily and was messing up at the theatre, at work and at home with his wife Katherine, and that she must have called my father pleading with him to send vials so that her husband's temperament could be more manageable. I strongly believe his family was urging, pleading with my father to send medication to him to control his temper. Only Duncan Quinn could clear that up.

K.D.: Anthony Quinn actually moved next door to your father's office to be closer, because he depended on him a great deal, in a friendly way, in a good way, he depended on him. I remember one night he came late because your father would sometimes work late, easily work till midnight. He came very late. I was there. He came rushing in all unkempt with a painting. He was in the early stages of painting. He came rushing in with his painting and there were people sitting, waiting, very old people. People would wait, and I saw his painting. And I thought it was nice but nothing special.

But he was coming, it seems to me, in order to let your father know, as though your father would be his father, he wanted to please him. He wanted to let him know that whatever he was doing was fruitful and creative. He felt proud of himself. But he also gave credit to your father at that time. That was the reason why I was so completely dumbfounded when he turned on your father. Because there was this period where he would say, "Listen, I wouldn't be here if it weren't for you!".

Jill: He said that?

K.D.: It was his attitude. And I was always the one. I didn't talk about it. I kept my appointments and got my injections. He taught me how to inject myself.

Jill: Where did he teach you how to inject yourself?

K.D.: Here in my hip, I.M. [*intramuscularly*] and he would give me a memory, he'd say and this he'd dispense when I was traveling, and he would say, "I have my own blood in this" and I thought, how wonderful. And that's how he felt that I merited the best guy in the world. In the medication that he could get together he needed human blood.

Jill: [*In response to what K.D. said*], I think your friend [Preston] is getting sick [*at the mere mention of blood.*] It's pretty spooky. There's a book by Gene Lee about Alan J. Lerner and Frederick Loewe where he goes to my father's office, visits my father. He described my father's office. He said he was like a witch. Like he had all those people under his spell, and this cauldron, and he was mixing vats of medicine. And when I first read that, I thought, Oh my God! What is this that they are saying about my father?! And then when I read the page further, I said to myself, you know, If I sit back and look at it, like try to observe, I could understand how he could see it that way. But I had to digest it. I had to sit back and really...you know?

K.D.: I never thought of him as mixing, maybe he did. But after he married Ruth, she did the mixing. But he did, he was in need of her, valued her, he was in need of blood.

Jill: I want to make sense of this.

K.D.: He wanted to experiment with DNA.

Jill: I know, but there are so many diseases.

K.D.: But he'd be aware of that. He would have had the blood examined because he used his own.

Jill: And you had no reservations about taking it?

K.D.: No, not at all. Sent back to Ruth, was somewhere and needed some of your fathers' and your father was dead, I think, and I'm not even sure she answered me. What's happened to her?

Jill: She's still alive and well. I don't see her. I haven't seen her in quite a while.

K.D.: I wanted to ask her if there's still a vial around that I could have.

Jill: You'd have to ask her. She wouldn't want me to know if there was any around. I'm the last person she'd want to know because she doesn't trust me. But if she did have something, I'm sure that she...

K.D.: I want to find out if she has something.

Preston: Jill gave you the number.

K.D.: If she does, I need it. People say to me, "Oh at your age" etc. And I think that some people expect me to say that he did some magic meditation, and I don't look at it that way. I think I was among his early experiments. He experimented on me, and he didn't do it for me to live forever. He did it for me to feel better.

Jill: Are you sure you are 94? You know, some women are 90 –92, 94, and they don't look like you at all.

K.D.: Well, I don't know who's with Max Jacobson.

Jill: It's also your state of mind and the work you did all your life.

K.D.: Yeah sure, I don't think about age. I think about how I can get something done. That's my main thing, to get it done. And I'm tired more than I'd like to be. So, I have my medication studied again. I have a psychosomatic condition. I always gravitate that way. See If I've taken something I shouldn't. I'm so tired much of the time. I'd like to sleep right now. Then I don't sleep at night, right?

Anyway, your father, I don't know what, something may have happened. I was brought before the Board of the American Medical Association. I testified, and he was there. And I was surprised to see him in that, I might say, reduced situation, in that he was dressed in a suit and thing I never saw.

And he was there. And for me to be able to give him something and help him out, there weren't that many people sitting on the table. One man, one woman and your father there and I was here, and the one man said. "And what did you think it was he was giving you? Was it something special?". And I said, "Whatever it was...", I answered in terms that made your father look wonderful and I was so proud of myself. And I looked at these wretched people, the old man and the awful people who were trying to trap him and trying to trap me. So I trapped them. And I got a kick out of it. And gave him a look. And I was able to trap them because of his care over the years.

You know, when you take the same medication for 10 to 20 years, so forth, the same medication, and somebody takes care of you and someone interested in making you something, then you know, I knew. And I wasn't going to let him down. I couldn't because I told the truth anyway. But shortly after that, he went into the hospital. He deliberately committed suicide.

Jill: Who?

K.D.: Your father. He didn't just die.

Jill: I thought he just died.

K.D.: No, he didn't just die.

Jill: How do you know this?

K.D.: He took medication. Nobody knew this except me. He didn't tell me, but I knew. I saw him in the hospital. And he died a few days later.

Jill: He had a urinary thing, pancreatic cancer.

K.D.: Whatever he had; he gave it to himself.

Jill: O.k., you see it your way. He treated himself a lot and maybe he just got carried away and just gave himself something.

K.D.: It isn't that. He decided he wasn't gonna let them disgrace him and destroy all of his work in front of his eyes. He'd got the kind of sickness they couldn't trace. He didn't have to die.

I don't want to tell you this, but it stresses me out. You just don't want to listen to this, but the truth of the matter is that he himself, sick one night and two days later was dead.

Jill: He was sick for five weeks, some bladder thing, I remember, because I had five weeks to prepare for his death. He went to New York Hospital. He was there for about a week or so.

K.D.: Well, I didn't think it was that long.

Jill: Yeah, 5 weeks. I was freaked out about my mother's death. And Doris Shapiro wrote. I had, I don't even want to tell you, I had ideas in my head about how my mother had died. She died just when she was going to divorce my father. And all these very bad thoughts went through my head. And Doris Shapiro wrote in her book that my mother wasn't feeling well, that she got some kind of infection or something in the airplane while she was flying with my father, and she was also very run down, and she was complaining that she didn't feel well, and he wanted to make her feel better. That's what he always wanted to do, make people feel better. So he started giving her treatments to make her feel better and she said she still didn't feel well, so she finally said, "Yes, I feel better", so that he would stop giving her treatments, because she hated the injections, but then she got really sick and then she died. And when I read this in her [Doris Shapiro's] book, I could immediately understand my father insisting on giving her a treatment. He would even make people like Alan J. Lerner, and other people wait in another room while he gave her a treatment.

K.D.: He got to where really in a way he thought he was God. That was something to him, little by little, and it upset me very much, he was no longer willing to be just Dr. Jacobson. That's where he began feeling himself as being omnipotent.

Jill: Yeah.

K.D.: So now "Dr. Feelgood", the media, oh I was furious. At one time I said why not, why not feel good, to the media. Why are you so upset about it? Don't you think a doctor has the right to want his patient to feel good? "Dr. Feelgood". Everybody referred to him as "Dr. Feelgood".

Jill: I'm not looking to slander anybody. I was a young girl, like between 7 years old and 16 when I met all these people. They must have been on good behavior; they were really nice to me. Eddie Fisher in his book, that's the only person I'm going to upset in a way, because he was so nice, so charming, such a good Jew and good to the Jewish people, he never cursed. He writes in his book that he cursed, that he didn't really like the Jews...I never heard him curse.

K.D.: Yeah, well, you wouldn't. Eddie Fisher did curse.

The office had to be closed, everybody out when the Kennedy's came over. They had to do that. They'd have to empty out the office when the Kennedy's came in.

Jill: He went to Washington too, my father.

K.D.: That was too much for his ego.

Jill: Did you know that Kennedy wanted my father to give up his practice in New York and move to Washington and stay at the White House and be on call 24 hours a day, and my father said no. He refused to give up his practice and let all his patients down.

Did you introduce Maya Deren to my father?

K.D.: Probably it would have been her accompanying me to his office and waiting in his office, Oh Boy!

Jill: You had to wait in my father's office to see him?

K.D.: You should see his office, eight or ten people waiting.

Jill: He couldn't take you right away?!!

K.D.: What could I do?

Preston [Ms. Dunham's Asst.]: Let me give you the scenario. You would come into his office where everybody would bring something from Zabar's, like juices. They had an area where everybody brought something like breakfast, orange juice. All this was at his office on East 82nd or 83rd Street in his waiting room. While patients waited to see the doctor, they had a feast, they had to eat. Everybody wanted something because they knew they had to wait a long time to see Doctor Max.

K.D.: Your father was on the verge of or had arrived at being able to find another dimension. That was his real thing, and the injections did something, I know because I know my own feeling and I'd say that I still benefited from whatever it was that he made my skin, bones and flesh. That's thirty years I went to him.

Jill: He was using among other things, placenta, things we know about now.

K.D.: There was a magazine like "Vogue" with paintings in it. Before he took me as a patient, he treated me as an equal, practically before treating me just because we liked talking so much. I was a good person to talk to. He said, "Now I want you to look at this" and then he did something, put something over it, not spray, but whatever it was.

Jill: Lysol maybe?

K.D.: Maybe something on his hands. I know that this time I began to notice a difference in it. It began to take on a dimension. It was this two dimension and was whatever it was that he used on it and working on various pieces of work and improved its other dimension. I think, I know he put this in black - something that gave it another dimension to your being.

Jill: I kind of have my own take on this. Couldn't it be that he was hallucinating from not sleeping, a side effect from his medicine?

K.D.: Sure it could have, but I think he was at the gateway to a great discovery. And I think he was so frustrated and hurt. He didn't want to admit that he was hurt, but I knew that he was hurt. One reason he and I got along, I knew things about him that he didn't want people to know, like that he was capable of being hurt. I knew he was hurt, and responded to him, and that's one of the reasons that he gave me the best of his experimentation like this is my own blood, take me. I actually had that relationship.

Jill: You know in this book by Eddie Fisher, he claims that my father gave him from his own blood in a syringe. I almost got sick. I didn't believe it. But somebody told me, yes, it's true.

K.D.: It's possible.

Jill: Eddie Fisher was writing it in his book and it really, really... almost got me sick.

K.D.: But the fact that he used it in composing this 50cc vial is the thing that's important.

Jill: Did you have to refrigerate the vial?

K.D.: (*wants to ask Ruth if she has vials lying around which she could send to K.D. who could really use it. Who, if anything could straighten out her problems now, right now.*)

He kind of makes us see things the way they really are. Mankind, we are not using what we have. It makes you use things that you have and see things really, the way they really are. That's what he was fighting for.

My problem now is my inability to separate real from not real. I have a psychiatrist, doctor now who is trying this pill and that. But I am now thinking if I could only have one injection from Max Jacobson. I can say you're Jill and were here talking, but I can just as easily say I think I am imagining it. It could be real, or I could be imagining it, or it's unreal. He was at the door of that real and unreal. And he was at the door of being able to have you strong enough to have this experience and not let it deter you in your life. That was, I think, this great thing with humans, with people. With some people it was too much, especially with very old people. He had to sometimes quit because that's what paranoia is, unable to decide [inability] real and non-real. And...

Jill: That's paranoia? Not necessarily!

K.D.: Not necessarily, but I think that it's a form of...

Jill: If you are having problems differentiating between what is real and what is not real, I would say senility, but you're anything but senile. If Ruth sent you a vial now, would you trust her enough and take the meds?

K.D.: Well, yeah, it's already sealed I have no reason not to.

Jill: It's not my father, it's Ruth.

K.D.: I have no reason not to.

Jill: Well, maybe she's good with you.

K.D.: She probably already had some stored away.

Jill: Well, she probably wouldn't tell me she'd tell you if she had any.

K.D. and Preston: Already mixed, with your father's blood in it.

Jill: You mean with my father's blood in it?

K.D.: I mean as he used to send them to me.

Jill: With his blood?

K.D.: Yeah!

Jill: What if Ruth would be able to put all the stuff in a vial, everything he used to put into it with the exception of his blood, without his blood.

K.D.: I'd take it without his blood. But I'd prefer to have one that was already made up ready for me. He used to send them all over the world.

Preston: Which year was that he died?

Jill: In 79, he died in 79.

K.D.: How old was he?

Jill: 79, he was born in 1900. Do you know why I think my father got along so well with you?

K.D.: Why is that?

Jill: Because you were so grounded, and you had your own life and your own mind. You were so independent. You had everything going for you. So, if you benefited from his treatments, it really made him feel and look good.

K.D.: I did so much for him. I continually tried to create everything he was trying to make me in that bottle, I did. That's why I needed your father. I had this pain.

Jill: You had pain he was treating you for? [again], He was treating you for pain?

Preston: That's what he was treating her for was the pain.

K.D.: I had arthritis. Psychologically my brain, everything in your body was subject to adjustment. I cannot look at television or even people without penetrating, he got me to the point that's one of the reasons I have in my later years, the type of success that I have. Theatre, and what I'm doing in East St. Louis and so on. I am able to know what you're thinking. I don't mean in terms of thoughts, If I could explain to you. But I am able to know you with no trouble. So, I'd sit back and look, and I look, and I look, and I see them, and they come in and out "light". The feeling is there, the aura. Lately I have been trying to capture "the light" that a person carried in them.

Jill: Wow. I can't see, there's only one person in my life that I saw an aura and that was Yul Brynner. It was unbelievable, he came into the room. We had been invited to his summer home on a lake. He came in wearing a necklace. He had just gotten a treatment. He had on a dark blue turtleneck sweater, there appeared an aura over his head and around his shoulders, like a rainbow. I never saw anything like that before or since.

K.D.: I don't see them that materially or to that extent. There is a dimension; like I say, I can't taste or smell. I don't need to; I am developing, being patient and working on it, a sixth sense. I don't need to taste or smell. I can taste or smell on another level.

Jill: Do you have Ruth's phone number? Because If I call her, she will yell at me and say, "How can you tell Katherine Dunham I have this and that?". I never got along with her very well, everybody else did, everybody else.

K.D.: I can understand that. She was jealous.

Preston: How is Jason? What's happening with Jason?

Jill: How do you know about Jason?

K.D.: Is your son's name.

Jill: Yes, I have two sons, and I brought pictures of both of them. My oldest son was a lifeguard for a while. My father, when my son Jason was three years old, told me to come to the swimming pool in the basement of his building, where he lived. He begged me to throw Jason into the pool, where he immediately caught him and taught him how to swim. But when I took Jason to the beach, he would scream and cry and wouldn't go near the water. He has since grown up and out of that stage and become a lifeguard, then a Physician's Assistant course and now he is a CPR trainer in California. And he is considering expanding his business and bringing it here to New York City in the very near future. If you pass out, he'll resuscitate you, that's what he does.

[I showed K.D. and Preston Jason's picture from several years ago. K.D. wants to know Jason]

K.D.: Jill, did you ever hear about your being adopted?

Jill: What?! No [I laugh].

K.D.: About your being adopted, something, somewhere.

Jill: There's been this long-standing joke about the birth announcement card my parents sent out after I was born. I was told a card arrived from one patient stating "When did you find the time? Meaning that my parents were both so busy working at the office, when could they have found the time to create me. It was a joke! My cousin Eve was adopted.

Why would I? From whom would I have been adopted?

K.D.: I have to tell you what hits me.

Jill: I learned things recently which absolutely blew my mind. I'm working on the book about my father, and my cousin Tony told me to get hold of the manuscript that my cousin Helga Hagen wrote, that I should read it before I finish my book.

(*In response to something K.D. said*) No, Nina Hagen, she's the niece of Helga Hagen. My cousin Tony told me to get a copy of the manuscript that my cousin Lutte wrote, and I got it in a floppy disk form. I have to put it on the computer. I don't know anything about the computer, I got it and it said a whole bunch of stuff in it. It said I'm definitely my parents, my mother's and father's daughter. I am really in touch with my brother. He told me my cousin Eve was adopted. I always thought she was the daughter of my uncle Simon and a woman who came around and was a patient of my father, as I was told since I was six years old. I'll have to find out. I'll have to ask my brother.

K.D.: Well, what I can do to make me feel that Max Jacobson's legacy is still alive is just to keep Erich Fromm, and he had been very close. Max was continuing this molding on a different level, psychoanalyst, biochemical therapist. He was one of the most important people in my life. He knew that Erich Fromm was in my life. That's another reason Papa appreciated me, because me and Erich Fromm were very close. He took some of the things that Erich Fromm had been molding in me.

Max was continuing this molding on a different level. Erich was doing it like a psychoanalyst, not a psychiatrist. And your father was doing it as a Biochemical Therapist. That's what he really was.

Jill: My father – Biochemical Therapist?

How much longer are you going to be in New York?

K.D.: I am looking for a place to live, Jill. I have made up my mind to live to 100. I don't know why I feel I need something. I have things to finish. I've gotten in the habit. I lay in bed and look at my book.

Jill: Your autobiography?

K.D.: I have 400 pages done.

Jill: Did you have it edited, or is it straight 400 pages, 400 pages clear?

K.D.: All I have is pages and I want a book out of all of it. It's time for me to do it. The people, I don't pay for my living here. People pay for it.

Jill: That's wonderful, why not?

K.D.: They're running downhill, running out of money.

Jill: Who's running out of money?

K.D.: People who are in charge of a little group, Julie Belafonte is in charge of a small group of people who brought me here two and a half years ago.

Preston: 3 years ago, 3 1/2 years ago.

K.D.: O.K., if you say it, 3 1/2 - finish my book, and the other day I found them [papers I'd lost], I'm so glad.

Jill: I would say the heck with your bookshelf, work on your book.

K.D.: Of course, any sensible person, but I am not that sensible. I am so...

Jill: Preston should just take your books out of here till you work on your manuscript.

K.D.: Oh no, then I would just never write. Oh, I'm stubborn that way.

Preston: She will do it when she wants to.

K.D.: It will come to me, It's sad. I don't know that I have any moments in the day when I feel well. And, you know, I don't show you everything I feel.

Jill: You look so well!

Preston: I know why you're feeling sad. Believe me, I can't talk about it. Everyone's sad because they left.

K.D.: They're staying with me from Haiti, she's leaving because she got married and she had a baby. The baby is just like mine. I just adored the little girl. The nurses took her. They've gone now to live with the father. She's the love of my life. That hurts!

Jill: So tell them to come back and visit.

Preston: They had a disagreement today. It's not a good day. We knew that she was leaving.

K.D.: Little by little it happened.

Preston: We knew then that she was leaving because she was married, but we didn't know that it was going to be that quick. She didn't give notice that she was leaving. The kid was 5 years old.

K.D.: If you know of anyone who needs a job who would be willing to be a live in companion, be a retired nurse. Someone that's with me all night. Preston can't do it. Preston comes from 4 to 8. I need someone who can stay.

Jill: The lady came with you from Haiti here with her child?

K.D.: She wanted to have the baby here. She was married in Haiti. Her husband couldn't come here for political reasons, Cyril. She couldn't get papers for her husband. And Ms. Taylor [Ruth Anne Taylor] who, here comes Ms. Taylor, who's visiting St. Louis and leaves tomorrow morning.

Preston: I'm going to go down and get your dinner.

K.D.: Alright, O.K.

Jill: Go on the computer to find a nurse. I found Ms. Dunham from going on the computer. Julie Belafonte and Harry Belafonte arranged your stay here?

K.D.: His wife Julie and Harry.

Jill: The reason I am asking is that in Eddie Fisher's book, I think he wrote that Zero Mostel had an adverse reaction to my father's treatment. He sued my father, he hated him.

K.D.: Well, that I didn't even know. The main thing is he just resented him.

Preston: But you see it was a time they were taking methamphetamines. They kept people up.

Jill: I met Harry Belafonte's daughter in high school. Somebody told me I knew the other daughter when I was growing up, but I don't remember that. Adrian was in school with me, and she was friends with my cousin. I remember meeting Shari when she came up to school with me with their mother for weekend visits. According to a friend of mine I knew Shari since she was a little girl, I don't remember that.

K.D.: Julie was in our company; we've been friends for more than 50 years. She was in St. Louis, East St. Louis, in the dance company. The main thing is that they're running out of money to keep me in this apartment. Julie is working on her own project competing with her husband, working, doing projects, lecturing on peace and war. Children are her big thing. She's making a children's movie in Ecuador, and she's having fun doing that. For a while after I got here, I had to gently work behind the scenes to try to keep Julie and Harry together as a married couple. She was with him and then she began branching out on her own. I try and help him and his wife stay together. He wasn't working and I sold some of my life to the library of commerce. But I wanted that money, and I just don't have money. I'm interested in my legacy. I'm interested in what your father knew he should do but didn't do. This, you've got to leave these things where they can be used and useful.

Jill: If you're getting tired, you let me know.

K.D.: I am getting tired.

Jill: O.K. – It's so nice to see you!

K.D.: I'm so glad we got to talking about your father.

Jill: I hope I can get to see you again.

Part II – The Clinic in Haiti

Intro

Marie Christine Dunham Pratt, a dear friend of mine and daughter of Ms. Dunham strongly recommended I contact Ms. Scott, her mother's former assistant and Marie Christines' part time caretaker as a child to get any special information she might have gathered during her visits with Ms. Dunham to my father's office to see him. This is what I learned. That Ms. Dunham was running her own clinic in Haiti and came to see my father for treatments and also for medicines to bring back to Haiti. Without Marie Christine's very helpful assistance I would never have thought to ask about all this crucial information concerning my father and Katherine Dunham helping the needy together.

K.D.: You remember her (Ms. Scott) don't you?

Jill: Yes, I do. I remember riding in limousines with her and Marie Christine, but I don't remember where we were going. I remember what she looks like, her hair and her British accent. Ms. Scott told me that years ago my father gave you medicine to take back to your clinic in Haiti. Did you go directly to my father and ask him for medicines to bring back to Haiti?

K.D.: Oh sure, I would tell him we had serious medical problems there. He would always send medicine back; he would just mail them to me. He was very much interested in the Haitians, and he'd given me a box of stuff to take back and I'd do the injections a lot myself, meaning giving the injections to them myself, and then they'd have nurses. It was a matter of taking care of people who couldn't pay for it themselves. Not only that, they could not have been able to get what he, your father could give them. I know he saved a lot of lives.

Jill: What medicines did he give you to give them?

K.D.: Pretty much what I had. I think that he was very much interested, of course, in examining the possibilities of all of the vitamin B. That was the big thing then, complexes and so forth. He gave me specifically medicines for venereal disease- gonorrhea and syphilis, antibiotics. He was very much interested, I think in the general health, the building up of the body of the Haitian peasants and he felt that if they could use their land correctly for crops...

He'd been there once, to my clinic. He felt that as a people he wanted to build up the Haitians so they could take care of their crops. He felt that as a people, they were so far down that it was hard giving them medicine, general buildup. And a lot depended on their crops. And places in Haiti the crops were wonderful, but in some of the other place's crops were brown, sort of worn out.

Jill: Did my father charge you for this medicine? Or because you were friends, did he just give it to you?

K.D.: He gave it to me. So wonderful of him because I probably couldn't afford it anyway. Not for all the people, anyway.

Jill: Now, did he offer it to you, or did you ask for the medicine?

K.D.: I just told him the situation and said, "Max, we gotta do something about these people, I have to have some medicine", and that's it. We didn't talk about money. I paid him my bills quite regularly. He never asked for any money. He gave me a periodic bill when I made calls to his office. He charged me for medicines, which he mailed to me. Part of it was he did consider me one of his experimental patients and anything that he suggested I would try. I liked to experiment too.

Jill: You had a clinic with licensed, trained nurses?

K.D.: The clinic, "Du Valier", the government did help especially with the Du Valier Clinic. They would send nurses. I had one nurse round the clock. There were three other nurses, special ones for the children. Your father was very much interested in children. I'm sure he had a lot to do with my interest in the health of the children.

Jill: Was It legal for him to be sending you medicines?

K.D.: I don't think there was anything illegal about it.

Jill: Not back then!

K.D.: He was sending samples. I guess he considered them samples.

[*intermission from interview, glass of wine is being served and we toast my father*]

Toast, to Max Jacobson with love —-

Jill: I'm asking this, but it doesn't make sense. Were the mothers with the babies there, were they breast feeding or were they all sick?

K.D.: When the mothers could breast feed, they would. He preferred that.

Jill: My father did?

K.D.: Yes, your father did.

Jill: I know he was getting some amphetamine from Germany, but I don't know how much and under what circumstances. Was he sending amphetamine to you?

K.D.: If so, it was in his concoctions. 50cc's of his special injections and he would put in that what he felt I needed, according to the way I would talk to him.

Jill: Would my father send vials for you and the Haitians?

K.D.: And for the Haitians he would gauge it accordingly.

Jill: So there's a possibility that he sent vitamins and amphetamine for everybody in Haiti?

K.D.: Mmm hmm! Oh yes, mhm hmm.

Jill: Did they keep coming back for it?

K.D.: Well, I had a pretty steady clientele among the Haitian peasants. They were mostly... I didn't treat them.

Jill: Were they skinny?

K.D.: They were sort of drawn, most of them. They just didn't get enough to eat. The problem was that they didn't get enough to eat, not that they were showing the side effects of amphetamine. If they lived out in the country on farms and then it was a little better. They had to grow stuff to sell in order to make it, you know.

Jill: I know my father was very fond of you, and that you brought him stones wrapped in cloth. When he came to see you in Haiti, did he come with my mother?

K.D.: When your father came to see me in Haiti, he came alone without your mother. Your father came to Haiti with a nurse or alone.

Jill: And how long did he stay?

K.D.: Oh, never a week. I'd say maybe 4 or 5 days. I was running the clinic in a section of a building out of the back of my house. I had a converted sitting room, like a converted barn, kids would come. Preston would give cereal to the kids.

Preston: If there was amphetamine that he was sending her [K.D.] that she was giving the Haitians, I think it was the vitamins your father and Ms. Dunham was giving the Haitians. That there might have been amphetamines in the vials my father was sending her. The vials that were made for them, the Haitians wouldn't have had the same formula which hers had.

K.D.: Once he said to me, the ones which he sent me, for my own use, had his blood in them.

Jill: Oh, I think he was just boasting and being cute. I think that's what that was.

K.D.: No, we have the same blood type.

Jill: Wow! Eddie Fisher said in his book, as I mentioned a while ago, that he claimed my father took some blood out of his arm and injected it into Eddie Fishers arm before his performance in Philadelphia. I called a friend when

I read that. The thought repulsed me. My friend who was not a doctor or a nurse said Eddie and my father must have been the same blood type for him to have been able to do that.

I am asking you this because I want to know if my father was acting responsibly or irresponsibly. Because my cousin wrote in her manuscript, even though it had all fictitious names, that my father lived to help people, that he treated patients his whole life. He just wanted to help people, make them feel better.

K.D.: He had two things that dominated him, to help people and to create. His medicine was creative. I wish I could remember. I have two kinds of visions of "Harper's Bazaar", color photographs. He showed me a beautiful picture. He rubbed something on his hands. Your father once said, "We look at things and this is where they seem to us, but it isn't what they are".

Jill: Yes, I remember he would do that with me and some other people in the room where he would say, "Look at this! ", where he'd pass something, a treated cloth over a painting and say, "See that?". I thought he was out of it. He hadn't had any sleep.

And the invention of passing the magnet over the knees. I thought he was really out of it, and thank God I read the newspapers all the time because it was from that, that I read that scientists, doctors recently [as of 1988] discovered that forcing together one negative and one positive magnet and passing them over the knees causes something to happen inside the body, it forces together tissues and ligaments to heal themselves...

What has been damaged by Olympic athletes can be quickly and easily repaired by this procedure. It actually works and my father actually first discovered it. This was what my father was doing. He had this pink brush. He had it all taped up with electrical tape with the positive and negative magnets forced together. And would pass it over the knees. And I thought he wasn't sleeping he's completely nuts, but he wasn't!

K.D.: Oh, he was so far ahead of his time.

Jill: This is one thing this book is going to teach a lot of people, that just because you see somebody doing something that doesn't make sense to you, that looks farfetched does not mean they're nuts. It just means that you don't know about it and maybe you should ask questions about it, and you should learn.

I was his greatest skeptic, I'm not proud of it, but I'm proud in that I can say he was right on the money about this, that and the other. And I questioned him, but now it turns out he was legit about it.

K.D.: Did you, before he died, did you begin to understand him better?

Jill: I don't know except that I went swimming with him quite a bit and I was singing, and I got into this one song, and he loved when I would sing, and Ronny Graham came over to see him about six weeks before he died and we didn't really, we knew he wasn't doing well. We didn't really know he was going to die. So Ronny sat down at the piano and played, and I sang this one song. And Ronny was so fantastic, he did the background, and I did the singing. So my father was just thrilled. The one thing I also got to do was to thank him for everything he ever did for me. Thank God, because I never got to do that with my mother. Thank God I got to thank him for everything he ever did for me my whole life.

K.D.: It's great that you did that.

Jill: I did that. I thanked him for everything, the braces, seven years and nobody believed I had braces. And once I had them taken off because I went to the Hollywood Bowl with Debbie Reynolds. No, we went to take Debbie Reynolds to the Hollywood Bowl, and I refused to be seen at the Hollywood Bowl with braces on my teeth, so my parents took me to an orthodontist and had new braces put on my teeth again. It never occurred to me to ask my father if it cost any money to do all this. He did it with pleasure. I only recently learned how much it costs, how expensive it is to have braces put on, and taken off for that matter. I don't know, he never said a word to me about the cost of the braces, not one word. I got to see him a lot, quite a bit before he died. I didn't think I would be able to.

He forced me, kind of forced me ...I'm leaving you money. I'm leaving you a trust fund under the condition you bring up your son as a Jew. And if you don't, I'm not leaving you any money. Now my oldest son, his father was an

Irish Catholic. My son always looked Irish. Jason always looked Irish, blue green eyes. He'd be running around his Hebrew school and parents would say," Oh, look at that Irish kid running around", he didn't look Jewish. He had blonde hair, now he has dark brown hair. My father made me do it. And when it came time for him to do the bar mitzvah, and somehow in the back of my mind, I thought, three hundred dollars we would pay. And they wanted substantially more money, and I simply didn't have it. And we tried to negotiate and make it cheaper, and then we moved to Brooklyn. And then we were going to do it in Brooklyn and never did it. But my father made me promise to send him to the Hebrew school. He went from kindergarten all the way till he got to the Bar Mitzvah thing and that was it.

I wouldn't have done it. I would not have done it. But he insisted on it. And I was glad I got to thank him for everything he ever did for me. So many kids say, "Oh, I wish I could have told him how much I loved him and thank him for everything", I did all that.

K.D.: He was very deeply involved with human rights, very.

Jill: Leslie Bennett from "Vanity Fair" interviewed me, mentioned that my mother had an affair with Chuck Spaulding, I don't believe it for a second. Do you know about it?

K.D.: No, I don't believe it.

Jill: My mother had no one to turn to if she was having an affair and needed help. Everyone was so loyal to my father. Everyone was so indebted to him, even I was, not because of the injections, but because of the way he was with me.

K.D.: I would just forget what this woman said (laughing it off).

Jill: Yeah, it just doesn't make sense. Getting back to the Haiti thing; so he sent you medicine whenever you needed it, for yourself and for the Haitians, antibiotics and vitamins?

K.D.: I always felt that he had things that he and I didn't discuss. He was after all experimenting, and I believe that he may have put something that would have generally been good for the constitution. They would have no need for amphetamine.

Jill: Did they get I.M or I.V.? Did anyone get oral drops?

K.D.: They got I.M. Children got oral drops, I gave injections, I gave I.M injections. I taught myself only I.M. He sent me the vials.

Jill: Where did you get the syringes?

K.D.: When I had the clinic, the doctors came and brought the syringes. The government of Haiti treated Haitians for T.B. They had their syringes.

Preston: Look Magazine did a whole story on Katherine Dunham and her clinic in Haiti in the 50's.

Jill: Did my father teach you how to inject yourself?

K.D.: He didn't have to teach me; I watched your father injecting me. I learned from that.

Jill: Did the government in Haiti know that my father was helping you with medicine?

K.D.: The government in Haiti may or may not have known that your father was helping me with medicine. The government sent doctors to treat my patients for T.B.

Jill: How did you start this whole thing?

K.D.: It started with my very beginnings in Haiti.

Preston: It was just word of mouth. When she had the clinic, there were volunteer doctors in Haiti. They would test people for Tuberculosis. Go on the internet look up "Look Magazine 1950's." I was there.

100

EXASPERATED

I went into the writing class at The New School with all my defenses up. I felt uptight, worried that this new teacher would somehow not meet my standards of perfection. When she entered the room, with a dramatic air and an intellectual appearance, she excused herself for being slightly late. She introduced herself as our memoir writing instructor and explained that she had to leave her last class early to get to us on time.

She embarked on a Ballet Pas De Deux Excellence. She asked us to write who we were, why we were there, and what we wanted to get out of the class. Her speech and the way in which she conducted herself led me to become so inspired, upbeat and brace that I wrote a page about my father, my A.D.D., and his determination to make me develop to the best of my potential as he practiced with all his patients.

All my defenses melted as she went around the room, asking each student to offer their story. It came time for me to speak. I said, "I'm Jill Jacobson, I am here to write a book about my father, the late Dr. Max Jacobson". I didn't even get the chance to finish my sentence when I was interrupted by an immediate gasp from the teacher. I froze and panicked. She said, "Oh my, Eddie Fisher". She swallowed and paused, "He was the doctor of all the celebrities, and Eddie Fisher!". I suddenly felt a time bomb ticking in my head. I was desperate for help with my memoir. "Yes", I said. "I need help writing this book". She said, "Oh, he was the celebrity doctor, the famous doctor to the stars". I felt powerless yet determined to fight for my rights. I continued, "Yes, but I need help writing this book". She seemed flustered just thinking about my father. I sat there hardly able to breathe. She said, "You don't belong in here". "Why not?", I shot back. I needed help and I felt I had the right to be helped regardless of who my father was. Just because he was smart, did not mean that I was automatically smart. How could anyone assume that? She said, "You are writing a fact-based story. You will be doing research. In this class we are exploring dreams. Nobody has a clear-cut idea of what they are writing. You are advanced in your project. I'm afraid you don't belong here".

 That was the end of it. She told me to try a non-fiction class. I realized she was star struck and couldn't gather herself to teach. Most people are that way. I felt sad. I thought she was so together, so awe inspiring. I walked out frustrated and discouraged. In retrospect, I suppose I came on too strong; dropped a bomb. She was not prepared for what I had to say. It surprised me that she knew instantly who my father was, about Eddie Fisher and all the other high-profile celebrities he'd treated. After trying to digest her response, I realized there would be folks out there who would get "ga ga" over my story, because my father's life revolved around celebrities, prominent figures.

 Due to the Kennedy's, he became somewhat of a celebrity himself, called "The Amphetamine Doctor". It was greatly exaggerated. The state revoked his medical license in 1974. My father died in December 1979, at the age of 79. He was so angry at the New York Times for placing his whole story on the front page. He left instructions with his wife not to send an obituary column to the New York Times or any other paper. His wishes were granted.

101

AWARDS

— • —

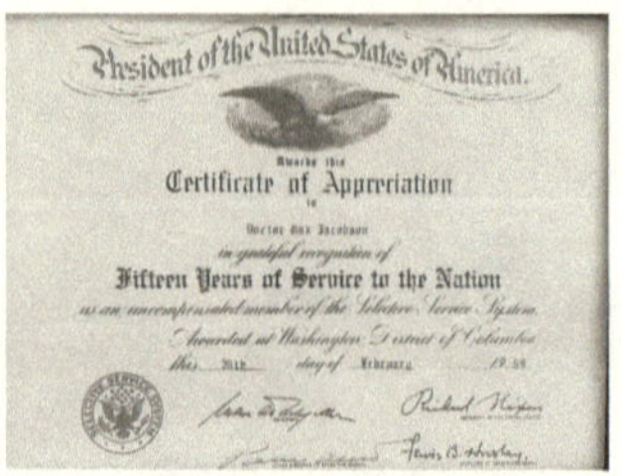

*Dr. Max Jacobson's U.S.
Government Service Medals:
Selective Service, 10-Year,
and 15-Year*

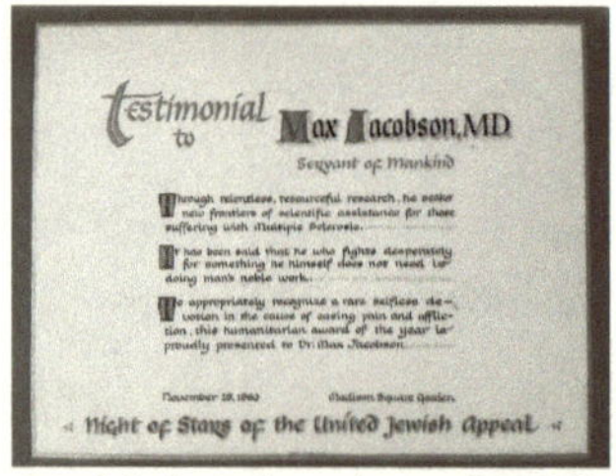

*Multiple Sclerosis testimoni-
al issued by the United Jewish Appeal at the "Night of
Stars" event, November 5th,
1963.*

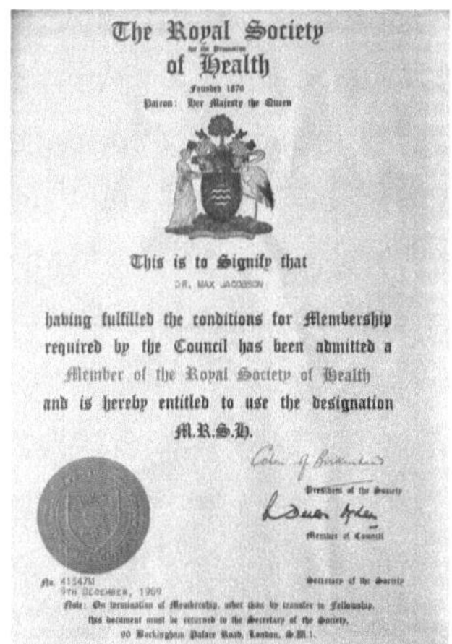

U.K. Royal Society of Health membership designation (Issued December 9th, 1969).

I never really had anyone that I felt I could connect with in my life besides my parents and my grandparents. I felt that everyone had their counterpart, their soulmate. I never had my match. I sort of connected with Larry, Bill, Jason and Matthew. Larry seemed to be "It", yet I knew he wasn't. Bill seemed to be "It", yet later I found out he really wasn't. And somehow in an unconnected sort of way, with celebrities. But I always felt like I was on the outside looking in. Even with my mother when my father was treating patients, I was on the outside looking in. That was the way it had always been. I felt close to my parents, especially to my father, yet in an unspoken way very at one with my mother. I never had to think about that. I was always close to her, leaning against her, holding my hand around her arm. We were always attached - always close. It was with everybody else that I felt somehow disconnected, except for my cousins Karen, Tony, Nina and Jackie, and lifetime friends Anita and Lola.

Yet as I stand here and think, I was never able to relate to anyone, except for Jack Levi, maybe for a while, or J.R. at school, and Bruce Landy. I was able to connect with Heinz and Gertrud Bondy. George and Barbara Gold related to me, took me in like he adopted me as his child. He liked me because I was truthful and honest, he appreciated that in me. She also appreciated my honesty and truthfulness. She helped me in friendship and gave me medicine which I needed to help me focus. Roscoe and Cecily, they took me in like a lost kitten from a litter whose mother had taken off, and I felt accepted by them.

Like the boy in the bubble, I felt isolated, separated from the real world, protected from that other part. Yet when I was little, 5 or 6, I remember bounding into my father's office. Mommy or Grandpi had brought me. And the moment I arrived, I was the main attraction. I was daddy's little girl. I would run up to him so fast and plant a kiss enthusiastically on his cheek. I was such a happy little girl.

I always imagined myself a bit like Bo Derek in the movie "10". I always saw myself sitting on a grassy hilltop with my hair long, thick, wearing an Indian headband with part of my hair braided. I would be sitting there with two sterling silver rings, one on each hand, sitting there with all the tension of the world upon me, smoking a joint. It's that simple!

My father was the main attraction. They all flocked to him by the dozens. They waited sometimes all day just to see him for his treatment. He was the "Big Shot" because he was the main factor. The one who made you feel well. He was so determined to succeed. Failure was not in his vocabulary. He was such a complex soul. He was charismatic and funny to the bone, speed or no speed. His humor, wit and charm were unavoidably a show.

I would see all those patients. I became so bewildered. My parents were so busy, so preoccupied. I would conjure up the courage to ask my mother why this person was acting this way. I don't remember what she said. She probably didn't say anything. Or she would say, "We will discuss that later on". I would ask my father. He would go into a lengthy explanation as to how this person had come from a life of difficulties and was trying to make a better life for themselves, trying to make something out of themselves.

What came to pass thereafter my little brain couldn't digest. Daddy would take them into another room. They would disappear for 15 to 20 minutes. They would reappear; Daddy would have his hair combed shiny. The patient would look better and be holding cotton on their arm. And daddy would say, "Well, now do you feel better?". My father naturally beaming with pride that he had just helped a patient feel better.

He was studiously aware of what he was doing, all the while one could just imagine his mind traveling a thousand miles per second thinking of thoughts you and I would never imagine. He was in touch with other levels, life forces not visible to human perception. Yet one instantly knew he was on to something, and oh he was.

He went through a myriad of experiences and focused on one main path in his life. Each journey bringing him onto the path of another medical venture, awakening, and each time taking from it new experiences and knowledge, knowledge that he would later use towards his own driven cause, desire and determination to improve the health and wellbeing of mankind. That was Dr. Max Jacobson, with his white shirt and tie, often with splatters and colorful splotches displayed on it from the medicine he was preparing for his patients.

Papa holding his grandson Jason (5 years old) shortly before his death, circa 1979

The birth of his grandson Jason in 1974 was the one happy moment he managed to savor just as his license was being revoked. He still managed, however, to be a very loving father and grandfather. When I found out that he had cancer and was given five weeks to live, Jason and I went rushing up to his apartment for a visit. I got permission from Ruth to talk to him alone and thanked him for everything he ever did for me, especially my seven years of braces. I told him how much I loved him. After having a lengthy discussion with him, I decided it was time to immediately unspoil Jason and me and go cold turkey, so to speak. He told me that he had left a will, a trust fund for me and Jason. The stipulation for my part was as long as I raised my son in the Jewish religion, he left me money. Oy Gevalt, I've never been a good Jew. So it happened that weeks after Papa died there was no money at all.

 The estate made it that I had to wait one year before I could get a penny. Thank God I had friends who when I approached them, offered to give and lend me money and whatever else I needed. Those in charge of the estate kept politely telling me to wait just a little while longer for the funds to come. They didn't have the capacity to comprehend just how difficult it was to live on a strict budget being a single parent and not working full time. I could barely make ends meet. I will forever be grateful to those dear people who had the decency to help me out. Carol was one of the main ones, also my half-brother Tommy who owed me nothing and yet came forward and helped us out in needy times.

Unfortunately, I felt the necessity to sneak downtown to the records building to see the original will that my father wrote to see just how accurately and honestly the people who were put in charge were doing what they were supposed to do. Then I learned that my father had entrusted some colleagues to invest some of the funds which were left for me with the instructions that the money would ultimately grow for me. The only problem with that stipulation was that the executor, Sidney W., decided to take liberties that were not his to take. Sidney and certain others close to him borrowed the money and placed it in investments which they claimed lost a lot of money. No one, it seems, was willing to take responsibility for what they did. I was told to go on welfare.

Its surprising nobody went to jail for the misappropriation of funds, although at least two of them should have been penalized. At least after looking downtown in the records, I felt better knowing what had happened and why. In good faith, my father had offered Sidney to partake of the funds as partial payment, and that allowed this conniving man to legally maneuver the money when he did and the way he did. Sidney borrowed the invested money and reinvested it for his own interest without any questions asked. It was all above board. Once he lost the money in failed investments, I and whomever else he borrowed from were out the money. Others whom he borrowed from were a lot better off than I was. They didn't have to apply for welfare as I did.

The sad part of the whole thing was that he was never brought to justice and forced to make amends on those losses. Thereby, I was out money. How much, I don't know. I do know those working with him prospered while working for him. My stepmother being one such lucky soul.

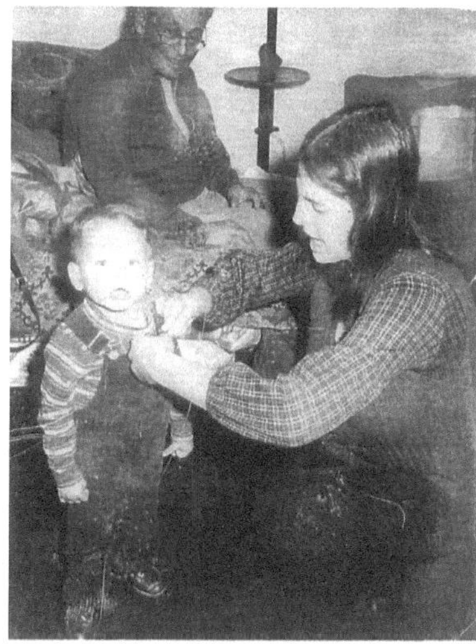

Jill visiting Papa with Jason at his apartment, circa 1979

I had five weeks to prepare emotionally and mentally for my father's death. The day he died I was doing my laundry; I was going to go to the hospital and see him. I was on my way home with the laundry. Lutte was just getting off the bus across the street from me. And I thought, how odd. I approached her and I said, "What are you doing here?". She looked at me and I knew that she was coming to tell me that he had died. I started to cry but I held it in until I got home where Jason and Sandy, a friend, were waiting for me. I burst into tears, but I was all right, and at the funeral I just remembered a lot of people.

As soon as I knew that my father was going to die, Jason and I left his apartment that night five weeks prior, after our discussion. Instead of taking a taxi home to West 46th Street, I insisted on us walking at least 8 to 10 blocks to catch the downtown bus, and then the crosstown bus to Columbus Avenue. I felt I had to do it to get a taste of the hard life of roughing it, the sooner the better. It was wintertime and it was cold. With the snow on the ground, we walked to catch the bus and took it home. The party was over.

THE END